Native Tongue, Stranger Talk

Middle East Studies Beyond Dominant Paradigms
Peter Gran, *Series Editor*

Other titles in Middle East Studies Beyond Dominant Paradigms

Artisan Entrepreneurs in Cairo and Early-Modern Capitalism (1600–1800)
Nelly Hanna

Family and Court: Legal Culture and Modernity in Late Ottoman Palestine
Iris Agmon

The Holy Land in Transit: Colonialism and the Quest for Canaan
Steven Salaita

In Praise of Books: A Cultural History of Cairo's Middle Class, Sixteenth to the Eighteenth Century
Nelly Hanna

Islamic Roots of Capitalism: Egypt, 1760–1840
Peter Gran

The Large Landowning Class and the Peasantry in Egypt, 1837–1952
Raouf Abbas and Assem El-Dessouky; trans.
Amer Mohsen with Mona Zikri; ed. Peter Gran

The New Mamluks: Egyptian Society and Modern Feudalism
Amira El-Azhary Sonbol

Unveiling the Harem: Elite Women and the Paradox of Seclusion in Eighteenth-Century Cairo
Mary Ann Fay

Native Tongue, Stranger Talk

The Arabic and French Literary Landscapes of Lebanon

Michelle Hartman

Syracuse University Press

First Edition 2014
14 15 16 17 18 19 6 5 4 3 2 1

∞ The paper used in this publication meets the minimum requirements of the American National Standard for Information Sciences—Permanence of Paper for Printed Library Materials, ANSI Z39.48-1992.

For a listing of books published and distributed by Syracuse University Press, visit www.SyracuseUniversityPress.syr.edu.

ISBN: 978-0-8156-3356-3 (cloth) 978-0-8156-5269-4 (e-book)

Library of Congress Cataloging-in-Publication Data

Hartman, Michelle.
Native tongue, stranger talk : the Arabic and French literary landscapes of Lebanon / Michelle Hartman.
pages cm. — (Middle East Studies Beyond Dominant Paradigms)
Includes bibliographical references and index.
ISBN 978-0-8156-3356-3 (cloth : alk. paper) — ISBN 978-0-8156-5269-4 (ebook) 1. Arabic literature—Lebanon—History and criticism. 2. Lebanese literature (French)—History and criticism. I. Title.
PJ8078.H37 2014
892.7'0995692—dc23 2014014174

Manufactured in the United States of America

*For Nour, Karim, Suhayl, Layal, Yasmine, Taleen,
and of course Tameem*

Michelle Hartman is Associate Professor of Arabic Literature at the Institute of Islamic Studies, McGill University. She has published widely on literature from the Arab world written in Arabic, English, and French and is the author of *Jesus, Joseph, and Job: Reading Rescriptings of Religious Figures in Lebanese Women's Fiction* (2002). She also works on the politics of Arabic-English translation, publishing in *Feminist Studies* and *Tulsa Studies in Women's Literature*, among other journals. She is herself a literary translator from Arabic to English, primarily Lebanese women's novels, including Alexandra Chreiteh's *Always Coca-Cola* and Iman Humaydan's *Other Lives* and *Wild Mulberries*, which won second place in the Said Ghobash-Banipal Award for best novel translated from Arabic (2009).

Contents

Preface

Capturing the Music of Arabic

> Besides, people have often said, not pejoratively—but for me as a compliment—that "I write Arabic in French." And it is a little bit true, because in the way I construct my sentences, very often you can recognize the rhythm and musicality of the Arabic sentence.
>
> Souvent on a d'ailleurs dit, d'une manière non pas péjorative—mais, pour moi c'est un compliment—que "j'écrivais l'arabe en français." Et c'est un petit peu vrai, parce que dans la construction de ma phrase, très souvent, on retrouve le rythme et la musicalité de la phrase arabe.
>
> —TUÉNI 1986b, 68

When Lebanese poet Nadia Tuéni affirms that she "writes Arabic in French," she makes a claim about the rhythm and musicality of her poetry. The complexity that she claims for her poetic language, on the surface, is about linguistic layering—she speaks on the level of constructing sentences. But Tuéni's claim to write Arabic in French also acknowledges that French is far from a neutral language in the Lebanese context. The act of writing one language in another, no matter how accomplished, is a symbolic act. In this simple claim, Tuéni also expresses cultural pride and makes a political statement—her poetry belongs to Arabic as well as to French. Like so many other writers of colonial languages in locations throughout the world, Nadia Tuéni works to articulate her own reconciliation of languages within her own creative literary idiom.

Native Tongue, Stranger Talk: The Arabic and French Literary Landscapes of Lebanon took shape as an exploration of the kinds of questions posed by Tuéni's statement: Can a work written in a colonial language like French express the everyday realities lived in Arabic in Lebanon? Can this be done in a way that does not simply "spice up" the text and make a French novel seem more exotic? How can a French text speak Arabic? Starting from Nadia Tuéni's claim to write Arabic in French as a point of inquiry, this study rejects the notion that using Arabic within a French-language text should be regarded as "window dressing" or a way to isolate a kind of irreducible "Arabness" within otherwise "French" texts. Lebanese women writers who use French offer a particularly apt corpus from which to address these questions and think about them in multiple contexts.

But though proposing that authors somehow "write Arabic in French" within literary texts is an appealing notion emotionally, politically, and even linguistically, understanding how they achieve this more complex. *Native Tongue, Stranger Talk* was conceived as a way to investigate the complexities of linguistic realities, as they are translated into literature. This study is narrowly focused on a specific group of writings, French-language novels by Lebanese women writers, positioned on the borders between Arabic and French. The argument here is developed using these works as a case study to probe deeply into questions about the politics of language use in literature, particularly within the languages used to implement colonial power. What I am thinking about in the discussions of specific novels in the book is how creative literary languages are produced by using languages that are understood to be different, how words and expressions marked as a particular language (here, Arabic) are incorporated into texts that ostensibly are written in another language (here, French). Following on from Tuéni's statement, I wanted to explore the specific techniques and strategies used to work in more than one language and to think through the different meanings invested in these techniques. Because these are literary texts, I am also interested in knowing if some are more literary or poetic than others and if we can consider some more political.

Because my approach to reading creative texts is concerned with what makes them poetic and political, this study of language in novels is connected to larger social structures. One of my aims in writing *Native Tongue, Stranger Talk* is to directly challenge the false distinction between the Arab/Arabic language and literary "traditions" and the allegedly universal, accessible, or "world" language, French. Using an anticolonial framework,

I situate its argument as a challenge to enlightenment notions of subjectivity and agency. The analyses here propose that bringing together readings of textual politics and poetics, rooted in the study of language, can overturn the fundamental principles of the kind of Hegelian paradigm so long used to understand the Middle East.

I started working with French-language texts from Lebanon because they occupy a position on the borders between Arabic and French, between the Arab world and Europe. Neither quite French enough in the European context, nor exotic enough to be an Other, nor exactly Arabic enough to be considered a serious area of inquiry by scholars of Arabic literature, this body of writing is not easily defined or categorized. As I read further and more broadly in the diverse literary production of texts written in standard French, published in Beirut and Paris, I saw the diversity of ways in which these novels pursued the incorporation of multiple languages within their narratives. Nonetheless, I was actively discouraged from pursuing the study of this body of work, particularly by colleagues and others who shared the popular view that Lebanese women writers of French are marginal to Lebanese/Arab society, not "authentically Arab," politically suspect, or at least not implicated in the politics that matter in the region. It is rare to see novels by Lebanese writers of French considered contributions to Arab culture or literature. Because their works are not written in Arabic and most are members of a small, privileged minority community—and women at that—these writers are often regarded as at best curiosities and at worst "sellouts" within Arab culture more generally.

This discouragement only encouraged me. The more I read, the more that was published, the more interesting both the novels and their use of language became to me. One goal of *Native Tongue, Stranger Talk* is to show how the use of language in these fictional works can be a starting point to investigate crucial issues in Lebanese and Arabic literature and culture as well as a lens into the use of colonial languages in creative literary contexts.

Native Tongue, Strange Talk is written with multiple audiences in mind. As the first full-length study of French-language writing from Lebanon in English, I wrote it partly to show the breadth and depth of this body of works to both literary and nonliterary readers. More important, however,

I use it to investigate crucial questions for many people about colonialism and language, resistance to colonialism through language, and how political views can be asserted through the language/s of literature. The theories and methods used here are combined not only so that the book will speak to people interested in many different elements of the study from different angles, but also because the questions and issues posed by this study are not limited regionally (to Lebanon or the Arab world) or linguistically (to Arabic and French). Therefore, this book provides contexts and historical/political information to make it relevant to regional specialists and students interested in Lebanon and the Arab world, but also to make it accessible to those who are not specialized in the study of the region and are involved in studies of language use in literature or the way in which French operates around the globe.

I have consciously structured *Native Tongue, Stranger Talk* to make it particularly approachable to readers who wish to explore not only the literary texts discussed but also the contexts within which these writers work. This means that it balances its commitment to remaining literarily focused with discussions of linguistic techniques and attention to aesthetics, and to providing contextualization and histories not only of literary trends and movements but also of larger political and historical trends. The specific case study and its details here are also meant to give readers with an interest in literatures from other parts of the globe insight into the ways in which languages are manipulated within literary production in colonial languages. The paradigm of Hegelian universalism that this book challenges relies on dichotomies between languages, cultures, and traditions to claim that "other" literature must be rejuvenated by European traditions. As this is the dominant paradigm through which literary works from the Arab world, and elsewhere outside of white, Euro-North America, are often explained, this reading presents a challenge; French-language writers from Lebanon, who layer Arabic and French together into one poetic language, undermine the very premise of this paradigm.

Native Tongue, Stranger Talk allows works by Arab women writers to be seen as political works of poetic art that can participate in global conversations about war and violence, women's roles in society, class hierarchies, class- and gender-based oppressions, and colonial language/s and education. Locating words marked as Arabic within ostensibly French texts is not done in order to show, recognize, or promote an inherent or constructed "Arabness." Rather, the linguistic, literary analyses here are developed in order to show how textual languages are created to challenge fixed and static ideas of belonging in national and/or linguistic-national terms. These readings therefore investigate the function of literary aesthetics as they are linked to politics in order to challenge culturalist, colonialist knowledge production.

Acknowledgments

This book took its final shape over a long time and through an interrupted process; it was "almost finished" a number of times. Though I wrote it alone, the thoughts and ideas in it are deeply intertwined with work, conversations, and discussions with many people, and I would like to acknowledge that from the outset. Though it is hard to identify this specifically, the work behind this book was collaborative and I thank everyone who has been involved in that thinking.

Several research grants contributed to this project's completion: a "nouveaux chercheurs" grant from the FQRSC, a Standard Research Grant from the SSHRC, and a Fulbright Fellowship to Lebanon and Syria. A new faculty grant from the Faculty of Arts at McGill was helpful in launching the project. I gratefully acknowledge Jo Ann Levesque of McGill University's research office for her help in navigating all of these.

Thanks to everyone at Syracuse University Press who worked hard to make this book finally appear. Mary Selden Evans was enthusiastic and supportive of this work even before we knew it would be published with Syracuse. Series editor Peter Gran was a pleasure to work with, always ready to discuss ideas, and provided me with the most insightful reader's report I have ever had for academic work. The anonymous readers helped to make the book stronger. Deanna McCay is a diligent and attentive editor who I have genuinely enjoyed working with and who helped me finish the book in a stress-free way. Mary Petrusewicz provided thorough and specific editing that I am extremely grateful for.

The book was written while I was working at the Institute of Islamic Studies (IIS), and all of my colleagues there have been generous in supporting my work. I particularly thank Zeitun Manjothi, Adina Sigartau,

Laila Parsons, Robert Wisnovsky, Wael Hallaq, and Khalid Medani. Setrag Manoukian as well as Rula and Malek Abisaab offered invaluable support at different stages, and I thank them for this. Other local colleagues make Montreal a wonderful place to work, thanks in particular to Alia Al-Saji, Wilson Jacob, and Najat Rahman. The McGill Centre for Research and Teaching on Women no longer exists, but when it did it provided me an important intellectual home, and for that I gratefully acknowledge Shree Mulay's guidance and mentorship.

Two IIS librarians went out of their way to help me on this project; both have since retired: my sincere thanks to Salwa Ferahian and Wayne St. Thomas. Research assistants over the years contributed in different ways to this work; I gratefully acknowledge the contributions of Amal Elmasry, Nadia Wardeh, Dia Traoré, and especially Dima Ayoub, with whom I have been discussing these ideas for years. Students in two graduate seminars at the IIS pushed me on many ideas related to the book: thanks to Hana Askren, Dima Ayoub, Jane Leeke, and Line Khatib; and to Florence Béland, Yvette Leboeuf, Asma al-Naser, and Katy Kalemkerian. Pour avoir discuté la traduction du français vers l'anglais, je remercie sincérement, Béatrice Callot, the late Elizabeth Fallaize, and Julia Waters.

There are very old debts accrued in a project that began so long ago. I thank Hana Niklaus, who carried books from Paris to Beirut and back, to Dinah Manisty, who brought me books from Beirut to the UK, and to Nadim Shehadi at the Centre for Lebanese Studies in Oxford, for many connections to French-speaking Lebanon. I appreciate the colleagues who invited me to present this material in its initial stages: Ken Seignurie at the Lebanese American University, Bill Granara at Harvard, and Robin Ostle in Cairo. For help in research on my many trips to Lebanon I would like to acknowledge Mrs. Naamani at the Jafet library at American University of Beirut, Fadia of the Ras Beirut bookshop, and Guita Hourani at Notre Dame University, Lebanon. My AUB colleagues Maher Jarrar and Asad Khairallah have also supported and encouraged me from the beginning; thanks to both of them.

Other colleagues have read and discussed or commented on the project or elements of it with me over the years; thanks to Marilyn Booth, Elise Salem, Nada Saab, Sarah Gualtieri, Stephen Sheehi, Christopher

Stone, and Laila Parsons. For friendship, intellectual stimulation, and some of the best discussions of literature from Lebanon and elsewhere, my sincere gratitude is owed to Iman Humaydan. I gratefully thank Alessandro Olsaretti for reading my work for years; he has always been my most critical and insightful reader and has provided me with material and intellectual support from the beginning of this project.

Colleagues and friends in Lebanon have given me ideas, hospitality, intellectual encouragement, and support over the years. Much of the writing of this book in its different phases occurred in Beirut and it would not have been possible without Omar Farhat, Nada Saab, and Elise Salem.

I owe a very special thanks to Yasmine Nachabe for helping me to finish this book. The final draft was written in her Lebanese American University office, the response to readers in her living room, and most of its revisions were done in the parts of her house without an Internet connection. We drove around taking pictures for the cover of the book and have talked about it for hours. Without her and the rest of the Nachabe-Taan family, who have hosted, supported, encouraged, fed me, and adopted my son, I am not sure how it would have been finished. Merci kteer.

Other friends and colleagues have offered unique combinations of personal, material, and intellectual support over many years; heartfelt thanks to Layla Dasmal, Julia Gualtieri and Maher Barakat, Magnus Bernhardsson, Sarah Gualtieri, and Stephen Sheehi. More recently, as I was trying to complete this book, we lived through intense times in Montréal with the longest student strike in Québec history. To the friends and colleagues who experienced those moments with me, thanks for helping me get where I needed to be to actually publish this book. Un grand merci à Adrienne Hurley, Abby Lippman, the KSRs, and most especially rosalind hampton.

I would like to extend this further to Aziz Choudry, who has genuinely changed the way I look at the world. He opened up spaces that have helped me to think and live differently and helped me get the pages sent off. I thank you.

A wonderful thing and a terrible thing happened when I was finishing this book, the first and second time. In the course of dealing with those two things I accrued debts that cannot be repaid or even expressed properly.

But I wish to acknowledge here that nothing would have been completed without the people who helped me through both: to my mother, father, and sister—there are no words. Further thanks to "Team Tameem," the women whose work caring for my son made it possible for me to work on other things. In Beirut: Samira, Baria, Mona, Farah, Dima Sinno, Randa, and the energetic Caroline of chez Coco. In Montreal: Jordana Vamos, Sarah Mostafa Kamel, Marie Lippeveld, and especially (Mama) Rachel Zellars and Alison Slattery. I would also like to acknowledge the compassionate people in oncology at the JGH in Montreal who have gotten me through my illness, especially Halima Memon, Linda Robitaille, Jennifer Charbonneau, Gladys El Helou, Harvey Sigman, and Gerald Batist.

Finally, a group of friends who were all somehow halfies, "nussies," and bilinguals talked about the issues taken up by this book constantly over the course of many years, across cities, countries, and languages. I am convinced that seeds of this project were sown back then and developed from those conversations. The book is for them—NAA, RM, UMA-D, and LKAD. And it's dedicated to the new generation we are raising, who live between Arabic, French, and English.

Native Tongue, Stranger Talk

Introduction

The Politics of Language and the Languages of Poetics

> What can I say of the fact that I do not use my native tongue and do not have the most important feeling that as a writer I should have—that of direct communication with one's audience? It is like asking what I would have been if I were somebody else. . . . I am both a stranger and a native to the same land, to the same mother tongue
>
> —ADNAN 1986–1987, 17

A Stranger and a Native

Educated in French-language mission schools in Lebanon, Etel Adnan laments that she cannot have "direct communication" with her Arabic-speaking audience as a "stranger and a native to the . . . same mother tongue" (17). Like so many other authors who critique colonial school systems imposed by France throughout the world, Adnan writes about the alienation she experienced being subjected to an education that placed the colonial power at the center and the lived reality of herself and her classmates at the margin. "We were taught the same books as the French kids in Europe. The capital of the world seemed to be Paris, and we learned the names of all kinds of things we never heard nor saw: French rivers, French mountains, the history of blue-eyed people who had built an empire" (16). She recalls children in her school punished for speaking Arabic in class or at recess, emphasizing the emotional difficulty of social ostracization and that the nuns in charge of the classrooms equated Arabic with the notion of sin.[1]

Despite her scathing indictments of the French colonial school system and her lament that she never learned Arabic properly, however, Adnan also calls on Arab authors like herself to take responsibility for their language of expression. She says that she wants to move beyond blaming the colonizers and claim the possibility that Arabic can be learned later in life. But her call also betrays an attitude permeating creative work, scholarship, journalism, and social attitudes about French-speaking Lebanon—in Lebanon, writing French is politically suspect. Underpinning this suspicion is the assumption that writing in French is a "choice" born out of a sense of a Christian nationalist superiority or a false consciousness that betrays an elitist attitude toward ordinary Lebanese. Though of course there are some Lebanese writers who have a choice of their language and even publish creative works in both languages, most authors—like Adnan—are limited in their choice of language by the education they have received.[2] Moreover, there can be many, many reasons for such a choice (or lack of choice).

Another acclaimed author and poet, Nadia Tuéni, adds class concerns to her own pithy formulation of these ideas. "Writing in French means writing in bourgeois, writing in rich, writing in privileged students from privileged schools where one pays . . . dearly . . . for the glory of becoming the by-product of a certain West" [Écrire en français égale écrire en bourgeois, écrire en riche, écrire en élèves privilégiés d'écoles privilégiées

1. She also writes about this in her memoir of growing up in pre-civil-war Lebanon, "Growing Up to be a Woman Writer in Lebanon" (Adnan 1990, 7).

2. One of the authors discussed in this study, Amy Kher (chapter 2), published her journalistic writing in Arabic and many other creative writers do this as well, including the Prix Goncourt-winning Amin Maalouf. Najwa Barakat is one of the few writers who publish creative works in both Arabic and in French. In French, see *Le locataire du pot de fer* (1997). Her Arabic writing is better known; she has published five novels with Dar al-Adab, one of which, *Bus al-awadim* [The Bus of Good People] (1996), won the prize for the best literary creation in 1996 from the Lebanese Cultural Forum in Paris.

où l'on paie . . . cher . . . la gloire de devenir un sous-produit d'un certain Occident] (Tuéni 1986b, 63). For Tuéni, also educated in French in Lebanon, writing in French means privilege pure and simple—the privileges of the elite, private education enjoyed by wealthy, bourgeois Lebanese who express themselves in the French language.[3] Tuéni accurately articulates here what French-language literature represents in Lebanon, culturally and socially. This literary tradition is tied in the public imagination to the ruling classes and a cultural expression that is not part of mainstream Lebanese life.[4] Though not all Lebanese who know French are a part of the most elite echelons of society—and this is increasingly true with widespread emigration and then return from places like France, Sénégal, and Québec—Tuéni's statement underlines two important points about French-language literature in Lebanon. One is that the acquisition of the French language in Lebanon is primarily derived from schooling in French, though there are many French-speaking families in Lebanon today as well. The other is that the demographic distribution of students in French-language medium schools in Lebanon is closely tied not only to gender, religion, and community but also the ability to pay for this education. Therefore, as French-language education in Lebanon relies on access to a private school education, the acquisition of French to the level of fluency is also closely tied to status and class background.[5]

Because the French language is so tied to the elite and exists in Lebanon, as elsewhere in the world, largely as a consequence of an unequal relationship of power that saw France occupy Lebanon under a mandate

3. Tuéni's comment was originally made as part of a speech in October 1975 at the Fondation d'Hautvilliers pour le dialogue des cultures.

4. For current attitudes about foreign languages as prestige languages, particularly French as compared with English and both compared with Arabic, See Shaaban and Ghaith (2002).

5. By class background here I mean not simply people's individual relationships with the means of production, but also their social position in relation to their socioeconomic status and how their family is connected to different types of production and consumption, socially as well as economically, in Lebanese society.

in the early twentieth century, French-language literature is often brushed aside or ignored in the Lebanese context as somehow "not authentically Lebanese," not addressing the concerns of ordinary Lebanese people, or as constituting some sort of false consciousness, alluded to by Adnan and Tuéni. Further, because of these same connotations, it is often assumed that French-language literature from Lebanon is an expression of right-wing Christian nationalist sentiment, nostalgia for the mandate or an elite eulogy to the glory of France.

A closer look at the range and breadth of literary output by Lebanese authors in the French language shows that this could not be further from the truth. French-language literature in Lebanon is diverse, encompassing a range of issues and topics, genres, and ideological inclinations. For every writer who sings the praises of France, there is one who just as vehemently critiques its colonial policies in the Middle East. This study of French-language novels will show just how engaged they can be with the kinds of issues faced by Lebanese people in Lebanon, in particular class conflict, gender hierarchies, and religio-ethnic divisions. *Native Tongue, Stranger Talk* investigates how the Arabic and French languages interanimate each other within nine French-language literary texts by Lebanese women writers.

Despite my claim to read these "Lebanese works" in a "Lebanese context," my purpose here is to develop an analytical framework that goes beyond the national or "local" approaches that remain central to how literary study still operates today. My goal in this work is to focus on a small and limited case study, providing extensive contextualization of the literary works, in order precisely to challenge national/ist approaches to reading. Literary works are written and circulate globally, but even within transnational frameworks like postcolonial literary studies, most investigations remain bounded by the nation in significant ways. Postcolonial literary studies, which is one of the few transnational spaces for investigating literature, remains limited by concerns of language and does not travel well to areas like the Arab world. This is particularly true of works written in Arabic, as it mainly takes up the study of works written in colonial languages from formerly colonized parts of the world and focuses on South Asia.[6] Studies of the novel, in particular, have been and still largely are understood in national—if not nationalistic—terms. At the beginning of the twenty-first century, most literary study indeed constructs texts as fundamentally (and even essentially) belonging to certain countries, cultures, languages, and nations. Literary works that engage more than one country, culture, language, or nation are often depicted as crossing borders, constituting hybrids or mixes of two or more things that somehow do not belong together. Like other fields, literary studies often assume an insidious Hegelian notion of civil society in which the modern reasoning subject "freely" embraces the nation. Even when ostensibly challenging national(ist) frameworks, many works of literary criticism, in the end, essentialize nations and cultures because they cannot transcend the notion that somehow languages are discrete entities—whether pure or mixed.

A literary tradition that falls between recognized categories and resists easy classification can help to probe these issues more deeply. The works investigated here could be considered Lebanese, Arab/ic, French, Francophone, postcolonial, and women's novels, among other things.[7] They are not easily subsumed into either linguistic-national categories like "French" or "Arab/ic"; they fit uneasily into a national category like "Lebanese" or an ostensibly transnational one like "postcolonial," depending on how this is defined. How can we read and write about French-language writers from Lebanon and their novels? Because they exist between labels—between languages, countries, and simple ideological packages—it is particularly difficult to categorize them. This once again challenges the sort of Hege-

6. For a pertinent analysis of this situation, see al-Nowaihi (2000). Waïl Hassan (2002) also takes this up. Muhsin al-Musawi has seriously engaged the postcolonial framework in his studies such as *The Postcolonial Arabic Novel: Debating Ambivalence* (2003), but the postcolonial framework has always existed uneasily with Arabic literature.

7. I would like to assert from the outset that, for ideological reasons, I do not use the term "francophone," except in referring to how others use and engage this label. The following discussion of the littérature-monde manifesto will make abundantly clear the reasons for this.

lian paradigm in which there are firm boundaries between different languages and cultures, one in which an "Arab/Islamic" tradition would be somehow mixed into the putatively universal language of French. Neither fully "French," nor a part of the Arabic literary tradition, these texts exist on the borders of the Arabic and French literary landscapes. They cannot be easily slotted into the kinds of traditionally defined national categories with which we are so familiar today. Works of creative literature thus defying conventional categorizations prod literary studies in new directions. The problematic labels used to categorize literary production pushes critics into uncharted territories, as they come up with new ways to talk about where texts belong.

The task of rethinking literary categories has relevance and urgency beyond specific texts, though certain works are particularly helpful to illuminate these issues. In a global literary marketplace, novels no longer fit into neat national categories, if they ever did. This search for new labels reflects a deeper need as well—the need for a new framework that will allow us better to probe the complexities of literary production not conceived of as either national or merely local. As traditional linguistic boundaries are increasingly and consistently broken down, labels such as "French literature" or "Arabic literature" must shift and change. With increased circulation of literary texts from across the globe, in all its meanings, literary works travel and participate in a number of languages, discourses, fields, and reception environments. Works are marketed, sold, read, and discussed in locations far from their publication; books are circulated in ever expanding ways, through on-line advertising and distribution as well as more traditional means. The tension I am teasing out here is how, by exploring women's texts from Lebanon that use French, we can flesh out some of the possibilities of the expansive category of world literature.

Because of the problematic history of Lebanese particularism in the region and the French language's association with this brand of nationalism as well as affinity with French colonial/mandate control in the region, the anticolonial perspective of this study is somewhat unusual and perhaps unexpected. One of the reasons why I focus the study locally, rather than read for examples these works in relation to other novels produced in French in the region or beyond, is to think through larger questions about how languages are shaped within literature and how in turn literary texts use these languages to advance and promote complex political messages. In *Native Tongue, Stranger Talk,* I challenge the fundamental principles of Hegelian modernity, as they are articulated by a culturalist mode of explaining literary production. The premise of the argument here in fact overturns the notion that there is an authentic "Arabic tradition," manifest in the use of language, that is imposed on or intrudes on the "universal" world language, French. The distinctions between languages in this sense, I will show, are false. One language is not "mixed" with the other, in that there are two completely separate and pure entities that can be defined as different and opposed. In the book, I propose that the texts create new literary languages within and through multiple layerings of Arabics and Frenches. In order to craft new languages and textual worlds, the authors make use of multiple languages, techniques, and approaches. As all of the works investigated here are engaged in the project of crafting textual worlds through language, all of them consistently undermine the dichotomy between Western modernism and Arab-Islamic tradition/civilization.

Literary studies are perhaps not the most common place to undertake this kind of analysis that challenges the dominant paradigm, embodied in Hegel's worldview. I connect this study to such projects, however, in order to underline the ways in which it is entirely consistent to connect an aesthetic literary analysis of language to a deeply political analysis. My discussions of the literary dynamics at play in texts bring out how the use of language in texts can be anticolonial and challenge Enlightenment notions of individual subjectivity and agency. Literary studies therefore can be one of a variety of fields of inquiry that help to challenge the dominant ways in which we think about colonialism, the colonial production of novel, and culturalist modes of understanding the Arab world.

To develop such a framework of analysis I will engage the concept of "world literature," recently the subject of something of a revival in literary studies.[8] As a conceptual framework, the expansiveness and indeterminacy

8. Christopher Prendergast, *Debating World Literature* (2004), gives a good sense of the range of the issues involved. Scholars from the field of comparative literature

of world literature can help us move beyond some of the problems with national and postcolonial frameworks. In order to deepen the analysis of how language works in this overarching framework, I will draw on the insights on language and the novel articulated by Mikhail Bakhtin. The second section below, "Politics, Poetics, and World Literature," takes up the question of the complex relationship between poetics and politics in French-language fiction from Lebanon in a world literature framework, in particular how novelistic languages are crafted in works ostensibly written in one language, French, but permeated by another, Arabic. The third section below, "Exploring Strategies of Language Use," is an overview of the specific ways in which I will understand the term "language mixing" and the kinds of techniques and strategies that the works in this study employ. Finally, this introduction concludes with a discussion of the specific corpus of nine works studied in *Native Tongue, Stranger Talk* and provides a brief chapter outline of the book.

World Literature, Novelization, Polyglossia, and Polyphony

World Literature is an exciting concept, full of possibilities for literary studies. At the same time that it promises to engage texts and ideas on a planetary level, in a time of ever expanding global interchange, it offers the possibility of reading texts in multiple frameworks. The current revival situates itself in relation to Goethe's and Marx and Engels's emphatically articulated, nineteenth-century visions about how it would herald the end

in particular have been engaging this framework to find ways in which to rethink and reshape their studies; see, for example, works by Emily Apter (2005), David Damrosch (2003 and 2006), Wai-Chee Dimock (2006a and 2006b), Haun Saussy (2006), and others. Gayatri Spivak's aptly named *Death of a Discipline* (2003) thinks through possibilities for "planetary" literary studies. Crucial here are works by Mufti (2010) and Lawall (1994) that investigate the reinscription of some of the problems of Eurocentrism in the newly emerging field. In the field of Arabic literature, see Mohamed-Saleh Omri, *Nationalism, Islam, and World Literature* (2006), as well as his special edition of *Comparative Critical Studies* (2007) devoted to world literature.

of limited, national understandings of literary works.[9] Many, if not most, studies that take up a world literature framework employ and/or take distance from these earlier definitions of *weltliteratur*.[10] Different articulations of the concept have ranged from Franco Moretti's grand attempt at a "scientific," if controversial, methodology that advocates "distant reading" to map texts on a world scale (1998), to the Euro-centered argument for a world republic of letters by Pascale Casanova (1999), to Wai-Chee Dimock's proposal for rooting American literature in the world (2006a), to using a translation studies framework to think through the ways in which literature moves in worldwide zones, as proposed by Emily Apter (2005). But part of what gives this conceptual framework its appeal is also one of its weaknesses. So broad as to potentially encompass everything and so vague and indeterminate as to be of questionable usefulness, Haun Saussy (2006), for example, has proposed that the concept can be so vast that it risks meaning nothing. Sarah Lawall's collection (1994) followed by Eileen Julien's later critique (2006), both suggest how the vastness of the concept reproduces global inequalities. Aamer Mufti's (2010) warning echoes this and his arguments about the deeply rooted legacies of orientalism in world literature will be discussed in more detail below.

To build a framework of analysis around the concept of world literature, therefore, certain articulations will be more useful than others. Some of the best-known and most interesting engagements with this concept—Pascale Casanova's provocative and much critiqued *La république mondiale des lettres* (1999), Franco Moretti's evolutionary model with its arguments for distant reading (2000, 2003b, 2004, 2007a, and 2007b), and David Damrosch's tripartite definition (2003)—are especially relevant to this study. These very different conceptualizations of world literature all suggest ways in which to think about literary texts as circulating and

9. See Goethe (1984) and Marx and Engels (1978).

10. To get a sense of how pervasive the citing of Goethe and Marx and Engels are in current scholarship using a world literature framework, see works by Apter (2005), Damrosch (2003), Dimock (2006b), Pettersson (2008), Pizer (2006), Prendergast (2004).

creating movement in multiple spaces in the world. What is problematic in all of them, however, is that they do not manage to take into account the richness and diversities of literary traditions at the so-called peripheries.[11] Aamir Mufti's recent study of orientalism and world literature (2010), for example, points out some of the ways in which these particular articulations of world literature miss out on some of the extremely important power dynamics and interchanges between different parts of the world, in relation to more and less powerful languages, countries, and literary traditions. Mufti critiques how theorists of world literature have largely missed the point about two-way or multiple literary exchanges, especially beyond Europe.

Mufti advances the kinds of questions to be faced when proposing world literature as a problem in twenty-first-century literary studies: What questions we should be asking when studying literature today? How do they relate to world literature? One way in which to begin this process is to focus on how texts circulate and what they engage rather than establishing a canon or criteria for reading certain works that perform in a certain way "as world literature" (Damrosch 2006, 211–20). My focus on language in literary texts does just this—the French language of the works I investigate here is a French invested in the world, a French of multiple genres and registers, and one deeply infused, in multiple ways, by multiple Arabics.

A world literature approach focused on language comes close to answering the kind of call recently made by Mufti in his exploration of

11. For example, Moretti's cursory treatment of the Arabic novel is far from satisfactory, as he himself admits. Many details are glossed over in such a large and broad approach to so many parts of the world. This is clear in his rendition of the Arab world and how he goes about it (Moretti 2000, 60, for example). Moretti's reading draws on major works in the field, like Roger Allen's *The Arabic Novel*, but understands his scholarship rather superficially. There is a deep literature on the rise of the novel and controversies about the extent to which it is and is not an imported European genre. See Allen (2001), which complicates this simplistic picture. For a full-length study, see Sabry Hafez (1993), a thought-provoking study of the controversies around the novel's development in Arabic. There are serious problems with the Eurocentrism of Casanova's approach that have been taken up by many critics.

orientalism and the institutions of world literature. Noting the inherent universality in a project labeled "world," he calls for a world literary inquiry that moves beyond the concept of "diversity" in literary studies and lays an emphasis on the circulation of texts within unequal power exchanges. His formulation calls for "*better* close readings, attentive to the worldliness of language and text at various levels of social reality" (Mufti 2010, 493). Mufti's call is so useful here because he notes the close relationship between languages and powers, particularly in the colonial settings that have affected so much of the world, and links the representative power of orientalism to the development of the novel in this system. In many ways the kind of study I am undertaking here is, as he puts it, a "radically historical understanding of language and the forms of its institution in literature, culture, and society" (493). Mufti brings together a critique of power and its connection to orientalism with a probing of the usefulness of world literature as a framework of understanding literature, revising Casanova's, Moretti's, and Damrosch's versions, but also retaining the question of the circulation and exchange of texts, as I have suggested above.

World Literature is not only a concept bandied about by literary critics. In 2007 a group of forty-four French-language creative writers and poets came together to sign a manifesto titled "Pour une 'littérature-monde' en français" [Toward a world literature in French] and published it in *Le Monde*. This diverse group of writers united behind a common call for a new way of thinking about literature written in French that would transcend the typical labels of "French" and "Francophone." Giving a name to an issue that writers from outside metropolitan France, particularly those from outside of Europe, have faced for decades—the signatories called for an end to "Francophone" as a category of literature. "No one speaks or writes Francophone," as they so simply put it. They hope that the centralizing power of France will be neutralized to show the diversity and multiplicity of literatures written in French in the "world around us all." As they state clearly,

> With the center placed on an equal plane with other centers, we're witnessing the birth of a new constellation, in which language freed from its exclusive pact with the nation, free from every other power hereafter

> but the powers of poetry and the imaginary, will have no other frontiers but those of the spirit. (Simon 2010, 116)

Responses to the manifesto, as to all manifestos, have been mixed. The challenges presented in this document politically undermine the relationship between the French language and the French nation that have been enshrined since the revolution and are thus bound to stir up debate in particular about the conceptualization of nationhood and citizenship in the twenty-first century. Some have critiqued it for what they see as too much focus on "Anglo" literature, simply echoing Salman Rushdie's much earlier, but similar, point in his famous essay "Commonwealth Literature Does Not Exist" (1991).[12] Irrespective of these controversies, this document advances clearly and directly an agenda for French-language literature in the twenty-first century that works well with the approach to world literature developed here. With two authors of Lebanese origin (Amin Maalouf and Wajdi Mouawad) among the original forty-four signatories, this broad concept of "littérature-monde" for French literature is a particularly appropriate conceptual category to think about how the language of literary texts written in French can be placed in dialogue with the languages of other works.

Thinking through the issue of literary language in a large world literature/littérature-monde framework, it becomes all the more pressing to address how languages interanimate one another within literary works, particularly as the labels French, Francophone, Arab, Arabic, Lebanese, and so on all somehow coexist in relationship to one another in these works. In order to investigate what is so interesting about the languages that craft textual worlds, we must look deeply at the multiple and varied levels of language that they use to create these worlds. If literature is, as Roman Jakobson would have it, "organized violence committed on ordinary speech" (Eagelton 1983), then literary texts must use multiple

12. See, for example, David Murphy (2010, 67–75). It has also been criticized for being too broad and general to be meaningful, or too utopian. For a general critique of the manifesto, see Kathryn Kleppinger (2010, 77–84).

techniques to effect this. Picking up on Jakobson, Terry Eagleton has argued that the language used in texts considered "literary" somehow must deviate from the ordinary, everyday, and mundane—even when the language used might in some contexts itself be ordinary, everyday, and mundane.[13]

In the case of the novels discussed here, therefore, the language of the text may be ostensibly French, but it consists of multiple "Frenches" as well as ways of representing Arabic and other languages. Other linguistic distinctions yet are central not only to these texts but also to all novels. There are also formal languages and vulgar languages, the language of "high" literature and that of the marketplace, the language of the home and that of the street. There are languages that represent class, others that are informed by gender and gender identity.[14] It is precisely how all of the different languages of the text work together to create multiple voices and a textual language that is explored here, including identifying moments that present themselves as more and less obvious, but of course far from the only, instances of "mixing"—writing Arabic into the French texts.

Because it emphasizes the crucial role of language mixings for novelistic discourse, Mikhail Bakhtin's theory of language in the novel is central to my argument. For Bakhtin, the novel is the flexible genre par excellence, largely because of how it uses the literal and figurative mixing of languages, which he terms "polyglossia" (Bakhtin 1981, 12). Polyglossia

13. For example, Terry Eagleton's opening to *Literary Theory: An Introduction* (1983) titled "What Is Literature?" sums up literary schools and their varied opinions on literary language and the poetics of language particularly, with an emphasis on the role of ideology in these processes (1–14). See his specific examples on 2. For a full-length study on the issue of difference and language, see Derek Attridge (2004)

14. One of the reasons that Mikhail Bakhtin's conceptualization of language and the novel, particularly language in the novel, are helpful here is that he does not see language as bounded by fixed and discrete language systems. His concept of language is so flexible that recognized languages, Arabic and French, for example, are not identified as stable entities but are always in flux. Far from being one static or fixed system, language, to Bakhtin, is always transforming. When he takes an interest in polyglossia in a novel, for example, he is looking at multiple ways that multiple languages work—not simply the mixing of languages that are usually identified as distinct (1984 and 1993).

is a crucial concept that I will use to read the texts analyzed in this study; like his more famous concept of polyphony, polyglossia has often been understood reductively simply as the mixing of languages. But for Bakhtin, the concept is invested with a deeper social and historical significance. He attributes the origins of the novel in Europe to polyglossia, which he sees as a field both of the exploration of language itself and also of other features of social life through language. Unlike the monoglossia of the epic form, in which language must conform to stricter conventions, the novel is able to challenge these expectations and thrives off of such mixing, for example in parodying and rescripting. In his praise of the novel as an "indeterminate" genre, he also underlines the sliding between vernacular speech and high-flown literary language, as well as the movement between different kinds of languages.[15]

In later writings, Bakhtin explores the mixing of languages and registers of all kinds—generational, gendered, class, status based, and so on—as interruptions of speech genres. When you are reading a novel in which a particular part is narrated through an educated, literate speaking voice, for example, and this is then interrupted by a letter, or the reporting of a television broadcast, or someone speaking in vulgar language, there is a rupture with the speech genre you expect. Speech genres can be used and manipulated in the novel in other ways as well, and this use of language is partly why the novel has such extensive creative possibilities.

The way in which polyglossia operates within the novel, therefore, is both to reflect social life through different languages and also to produce new languages that express a range of different concerns. Polyglossia is the use of many languages together—the languages of generations, times, places, classes, genres, and all other sorts of languages. For Bakhtin, languages are invested in and reflect and produce comments on social

15. It should be recalled here that despite the popular use of the term "polyphony" to mean many voices speaking within a literary text, the use of multiple voices is not what Bakhtin means by polyphony in his definition. Rather, he puts the emphasis on undermining and calling into question the authority of the narrative voice and the equal weight or "truth value" assigned to different voices that are in a dialogical relationship within the text.

phenomena like class and status hierarchies, gender roles, religious differences, and so on. He points out, for example, that languages represent things in literature but languages can also be the object of representation, an idea that I will return to in the analyses below (Bakhtin 1984, 49). I will pick up on this feature of Bakhtin's theory and explore in the readings of individual texts the ways in which language mixings and interruptions work in relation to gender, class, and ethno-religious concerns, in particular the locations in which these come together.

All of these ideas about language are reflected in Bakhtin's often simplified and misunderstood articulation of polyphony; the poetics or stylistics that arises out of polyglossia is its ability to manipulate and use different levels of language and speech unexpectedly and ingeniously. The polyphonic novel is not one in which an author employs multiple languages or even writes a text incorporating multiple voices assigned to multiple characters. In true Bakhtinian polyphony, those voices are permitted to challenge the authorial/narrative voice and ultimately to permeate the text to such a degree that the textual authority of the author/narrator is undermined (Bakhtin 1993, 92).[16] The many languages and voices of the text interact and commingle—multiple voices are put on the same level, expressing alternative or even contrasting viewpoints and different consciousnesses; and all of this happens to such a degree that the notion of authority itself is called into question.

The novel is such a powerful genre to Bakhtin because when using polyglossia to create polyphony it can undermine the authority of the author/narrator. These features of the novel mean that it is not only the site of indeterminacy as the flexible genre par excellence, but also is a force within the literary system that reveals the constraints and limits of this system itself. It may seem odd today, when the novel is so invested in the nation and the reverse, but the Bakhtinian concept of novelization demonstrates that the novel resists being so fixed. It is a genre that collects

16. In his discussion of polyphony, Bakhtin underlines the dialogical relationship between the narrator's voice and other voices leading to their equality (Bakhtin 1984, 251, 255).

scraps and pieces of life, hybrid forms and modes—in particular related to language use—in order to achieve many goals. The Bakhtin scholar Michael Holquist has paraphrased Bakhtin's concept: the novel distils the impulse to insurgency (Bakhtin 1981, 31). This is a class insurgency, a rebellion against strict and tyrannical language systems that would seek to fix words, languages, and meanings. The novel is itself the interanimation of languages used in unusual and surprising ways. Novelization is the process whereby the novel can create this and polyglossia the specific strategy whereby it is achieved.

The interruption of speech genres that in turn creates polyglossia and polyphony is a hallmark of the Bakhtinian view of how the literary language of the novel is a process. Never stable and fixed, languages must always be seen as constantly in motion and changing. Such a conceptualization of language is particularly helpful in theorizing language use in the novels studied here because it allows us to break free from the more limited view that would see Arabic and French as two separate, fixed, and stable language systems having static meanings that then are somehow mixed to create an effect. Moreover, the world literature framework, emphasizing movement and exchange, reinforces this conceptual approach. I will use these Bakhtinian concepts of language in the novel in relation to world literature in order to privilege readings of moments in the texts in which languages marked as different interact and speech genres interrupt one another. These are moments when polyglossia underlines comments on ethnicity, religion, gender, and class-status hierarchies, their intersections in particular.

The world literature framework will then help to interpret the use of language in these literary texts through its notion of exchange and travel. Travel in the world literature framework recalls the third part of Damrosch's tripartite definition of world literature. In this definition he calls world literature works that "travel well in translation" (2003, 281). Elsewhere I have criticized this articulation (Hartman 2011a), showing how it is problematically linked to the contested history and politics of translation into English, especially of languages deemed "difficult" or "controversial," like Arabic. Here, I suggest that the concept of traveling be revised and suggest that translation can conceptually enhance the world literature framework by thinking about textual moments that indicate mixing languages as "translations." Using the concept of translation metaphorically is almost a cliché, but I mean to underline textual moments that operate similarly to how translated texts do. When we talk about texts being circulated and exchanged in the global sense, how they operate as "translations" on different levels—most particularly in terms of language use—can be a point of focus for analysis.

When looked at not just metaphorically but as a textual strategy, translation as a literal and figurative process can also shed light on the use of multiple languages in literary texts. With its particular attention to the relationships of power and the connections between texts and society, translation theory can help to draw out some of the ways in which this works. In his pathbreaking study of the history of translation, *The Translator's Invisibility* (1995), Lawrence Venuti argues that the position and power of the translator to create a new text should be made transparent. In his view, the translator's visibility, in multiple ways, helps to allow the experience of reading a translation to be challenging and not naturalize the text for the reader.[17] This unmasking of the translator's role thus promotes a deeper engagement with the dynamics of literature and how translations move between languages, cultures, and spaces. What is relevant here is the way in which disruptions to the "expected" flow of language can be manipulated to challenge hierarchies of power. The textual strategies used by writers in texts that propose themselves to be French but that "translate" realities lived in the Arabic language can be understood through this lens.

17. *The Translator's Invisibility* demonstrates the ways in which the translator's visibility and invisibility within texts is connected to global inequalities and the need for political action. See especially the chapters "Invisibility" (1–42) and "Call to Action" (307–13). See also arguments by Apter (2005) and Eysteinsson (2006) on the connections between translation and world literature. Scholars and translators of Arabic literature have started to heed this call to action and advocated resistant translation; see Marilyn Booth (2003) and Issa Boullata (2003). See also Booth (2008); Hartman and Barakat (2002); Hartman (2012). On the state of Arabic translation into English more generally, see Roger Allen (2003).

Comparisons between postcolonial writing and translated texts have also helped translation theorists better to articulate what it is about literary works that mark and inscribe difference and some of the concrete ways in which this works. Maria Tymoczko, for example, has pointed out that one of the reasons postcolonial writing has relied on translation as a metaphor is the paucity of ways that we have still today to talk about works that exist between recognized categories and are written in colonial languages by the formerly colonized. Her study, "Postcolonial Writing and Literary Translation," argues that rather than seeing translation as a metaphor, literary translation and postcolonial writing might be better seen as analogues (1999, 17–40). She goes on to show how several postcolonial writers of English use linguistic strategies that are akin to those employed by literary translators. Part of Tymoczko's critical project is to enlarge and expand translation studies as a field and the ways in which literary translation engages language to work as art.

Politics, Poetics, and World Literature

Reading French-Language Texts in Lebanon

Native Tongue, Stranger Talk argues that we should read literary texts written in the French language by Lebanese women authors in a world literature framework emphasizing translation, circulation, and exchange. This runs counter to most previous studies of these works. Traditionally, the study of French-language literature from Lebanon, particularly by women writers, has been very much a local enterprise. It is largely focused inward—at the peculiarities of these works and the local traditions of which they are a part.[18] As fascinating as these texts are in their own right, today the study

18. Most studies of French-language literature from Lebanon are published in French in Lebanon: Aoun-Anhoury (1996); Bustros (1988); Darwiche Jabbour (1992); Hatem (1987); Haddad (1996); Tuéni (1986a and 1986b). Or they are published in France by small publishers: Darwiche Jabbour (2007); Najjar (1993). Or in a series like L'harmattan's "écritures arabes," devoted to Arab topics: Hahn (2010); Sicard (2005); Zein (1998). There are some exceptions, like Ippolito's critical evaluation of Dar an-Nahar's

of such literary works can be as much global as local. The importance of how they engage so many elements of both content and form far exceeds this limited context, as they exemplify and engage larger questions crucial to literary studies at the end of the twenty-first century. Therefore, though this book is a study of French-language literature from Lebanon, it also is not. The small, specific group of writers whose works are studied here are really a case study used in order to think through much larger questions about literary language, the politics of language use, colonial power, and anticolonial resistance in literature. Though these writers share a national affiliation or origin, I read works by this small group of French-language Lebanese writers in order to present a challenge to nationalist and culturalist modes of reading literature from the Arab world.

I opened this chapter with quotations by Etel Adnan and Nadia Tuéni that illustrate how the literary language of a novel is closely associated with its politics. The mixing of languages marked as different from each other and the transactions between languages in colonial and postcolonial contexts, creating the polyglossia of literary texts, occur in the context of direct conquest and domination. This level of analysis is alien to the formulations of Bakhtin and is an extension of his theoretical insights to make them relevant to a context different from the European novel in the nineteenth century. It is crucial to remember that the way in which languages deemed "local" engaged with the "colonial" languages had a political dimension. The ways in which languages are expressed in literature are thus often tied to projects of emancipation and should be viewed in this light.

What is so important, though, is to balance the focus on politics and poetics, never focusing on the emancipatory project alone but also on how the form and artistry of texts realize this larger goal. This is why from within its focus on one specific group of texts, *Native Tongue, Stranger Talk* poses the broader questions: How are the politics of language use

"Collection Patrimoine" (2009). Some French-language works are included in broader studies of Lebanese literature primarily treating works in Arabic, but this has much the same effect. See Salem (2003); Cooke (1996); Accad (1992).

relevant to novels written in colonial languages? How do these texts use poetic technique and form? How are the intersections between politics and poetics relevant to literary works in a world literature framework of circulation and exchange? The world literature framework developed here takes into account the importance of politics not only in the colonial/postcolonial setting but also the inequalities of the local/global setting of the texts. In the context of the works discussed in this book, it is equally important to confront the legacies of orientalism and not to overemphasize politics at the expense of an analysis of the stylistic and formal features of literary works. This framework presents the challenge of seeing these novels as innovative in their own right, of analyzing them beyond the kind of interest in "local knowledge" or folkloric interest that has traditionally dominated their study. This means a balance in the study of politics and poetics.

Though I focus extensively on language use—a formal poetic element of literary texts—my framework emphasizes politics. Broadly defined, of course, politics preoccupies literary study in general, but it is particularly relevant to certain areas of literary study. "Postcolonial," "Francophone," and "Third World" literary studies all rightly focus extensively on politics because of the histories they deal with and their own intellectual trajectories as fields (Jameson 1986). When framed as postcolonial and/or Francophone, literary studies are very much focused on language use, as it is one of the major political issues that ties works written in colonial languages together.[19] *Native Tongue, Stranger Talk*'s explicit focus on language, therefore, places it in direct conversation with the debates crucial to such studies today.

19. Some of the best-known postcolonial critics devote considerable attention to language use, for example, Gayatri Spivak, "Can the Subaltern Speak?" (1988) and "A Literary Representation of the Subaltern: Mahasweta Devi's 'Standayini'" (1986). On Francophone studies specifically, see Françoise Lionnet (1995). Farida Abu Haidar (2000) has worked on North African language use specifically, and Nada Elia (2002) investigates subaltern expression in Assia Djebar's *Fantasia*. In Arabic literature, studies like Caroline Seymour-Jorn's "A New Language" (2002) and *Cultural Criticism in Egyptian Women's Writing* (2011) show similar trends.

While politics is undoubtedly central to literary production, literature from the Arab world has faced the problem of being treated with an exaggerated focus on politics particularly acutely. As Edward Said pointed out in 1990, and Hosam Aboul-Ela confirmed again more than ten years later (2001), few literary studies—particularly in the English language—value the aesthetic features of fiction written by Arab authors. The philological legacy of the field has been reinforced by the dominance of the study of history and politics within Middle Eastern Studies and by pressing political agendas, all but erasing a concern with aesthetics and form from the scholarly agenda. This legacy links literature from the Arab world with other literatures, sharing a post-/neo-colonial context, but also sets it apart (al-Nowaihi 2000, 282–303). *Native Tongue, Stranger Talk*, however, emphasizes the formal contributions of the novels explored in it, without relying on the overly detailed description of texts that stemmed from the legacy of classical philology and have dominated the study of literature from the Arab world for so long, proposing it as indelibly different and other. This book is an attempt to participate in still-controversial discussions about language use, content and form, politics and poetics, while at the same time working to develop the sort of "internally developed theories" advocated by literary scholars of the Middle East.[20]

The very title of this book underlines the multiple meanings of languages in literature and their relevance to the construction of identity. "Native" tongues are meant to be opposed to "foreign" tongues; these phrases have a special resonance in colonial and postcolonial contexts. They beg the questions: Who is native? Who is foreign? The foreigner or stranger is defined in opposition to the "native." We do not say that a

20. Depeeka Bahri's *Native Intelligence* (2003, 13–14) discusses the controversy around content and form in Third World literature in Jameson's disputed classic "Third World Literature in an Era of Multinational Capitalism" (1986). Bahri's reading of Jameson is more generous than Aijaz Ahmad's well-known refutation of Jameson (1992). See also Mara Naaman (2008, 321–42). On the call for internally developed theory, see Klemm and Gruendler (2000, 1–11). My first book takes on this issue through developing a contextualized reading method for intertextuality to study the reworking of three religious figures in contemporary Lebanese women's writing (Hartman 2002).

stranger has a "tongue," however, but rather a way of talking or a "talk." "Stranger talk" is a metaphor used by anthropologists and linguists to describe the language with which members of an in-group may communicate with members of an out-group (Clifford 1991, 102). It is the formal way that people speak to those who they do not know, using different words, expressions, and registers than one might with others. Like raising your voice when talking to people who aren't native speakers of your language, "stranger talk" emphasizes your difference and theirs. It highlights a power relationship between the speakers as well as their relative distance to the native tongue. The added meaning of this expression, though, is that it is not only people who are strangers; language itself can be strange. And some talk is stranger than others—particularly when languages circulate in different contexts. Because of the creative opportunities they present, the encounter of multiple languages is a particularly fertile site for literary production. Thus "native tongue" and "stranger talk" each operate on multiple levels as metaphors for Arabic and French and to signify different kinds of language use within these "recognizable" languages.

The opposition between "native tongue" and "stranger talk" is paralleled in the various ways in which language mixing is used in literary works written in colonial languages. The blending of more than one language into a text written largely in a colonial language, a "dominant" or "big" language such as French, is common. Such works integrate at least one language that might be defined as a "dominated," "local," or "small" language, alongside with and in contrast to the main language of the text. Using Arabic words and expressions in French-language literary texts fits this model. Of course, Arabic is by no means a "small" or "local" language. Global power dynamics in the twentieth and twenty-first centuries, however, deeply inform the Arabic-French relationship, forcing upon them these unequal roles.

Native Tongue, Stranger Talk aims to contribute to this discussion by addressing the relationship between politics and poetics directly. More specifically, it argues that both content and form are crucial components of literary inquiry and that a reading strategy must understand and link them together. I will argue throughout this book that the poetics and politics of literary texts are closely related and must be read together. Just as Arabic and French interanimate each other, I show that criticism can reanimate the relation between form and content—as parallel to aesthetics and politics—in order to assert the value of these literary works, as Bahri has argued (2003, 4). Rejecting both a simplistically articulated rapprochement between politics and poetics and also an insurmountable schism between them, *Native Tongue, Stranger Talk* highlights the need to synthesize these in our approaches to studying the languages of fiction from the Arab world.

I propose that each of the nine novels analyzed below uses representations of the Arabic language—words and expressions identifiable as Arabic or meant to invoke it—within a text ostensibly written in standard, literary French as an aesthetic and formal strategy that has political implications and encodes political messages. This is contrary to most readings of how Arabic words operate in French-language fiction from Lebanon (Haddad 2000, 40; Zein 1998). The mixing of languages in a text primarily written in a colonial language, such as English or French, is more often than not understood by critics as a way to "spice up" a text. The "exotic" language—be it Wolof, Urdu, or Arabic—provides merely a sort of local window dressing, adding color but little else to the text according to such analyses.[21] Reading languages not as fixed entities, but as flexible and changing within novelized texts that themselves participate in global exchange of ideas, allows us to move beyond these more narrow and limited interpretations. The analyses of texts in *Native Tongue, Stranger Talk* counter this tendency, therefore, by developing a detailed and nuanced understanding of how linguistic tensions and ruptures operate in literary works, arguing that they must be interpreted accordingly as inscrib-

21. Bahri gives specific examples of how this has affected the English-language Canadian author of Indian descent Rohinton Mistry as well as the African authors Ngugi wa Thiongo and Chinua Achebe (2003, 120–21). In the context of Lebanon, see for example Haddad's numerous comments on Arabic as "local color" (2000, 40, 58), Michel Chiha's suggestions given to Eveline Bustros (Bustros 1988, lvii–lviii), and Rami Zein's *Dictionnaire* (Zein 1998, 84).

ing both poetic and political messages—messages about gender, religion/community, and class.

Exploring Strategies of Language Use

Theoretical and Practical Considerations

Not all critics understand the use of one language within a text written in another as little more than an exotic and colorful "window dressing" for literary works—*Native Tongue, Stranger Talk* is far from the first critical work to explore the complex intersections of politics, poetics, and language use. Several strands of postcolonial criticism have delved into how language mixing operates within literary texts, especially those that mix a "local" language, like Arabic, within a text written in a colonial language, like French. Most studies rely on fixed and stable ideas of language, however, that are confident in what "mixing" means. These critics most often understand language mixing as a challenge to the hegemony of dominant, colonial languages. While coming to different substantive conclusions, I build on their analyses and insights. In each part of the book I rely on the analysis of techniques developed by scholars of postcolonial language-mixing strategies in order to identify which specific processes are at work and read them within my larger theoretical framework. In particular I build on and revise four main strands of thought. The first is the groundbreaking work by Ashcroft, Griffith, and Tiffin (1989), who identified ways in which the "empire writes back" (to colonial powers) by disrupting language through mixing. The second is the process of "indigenization" identified by Chantal Zabus (2007), in particular her definition of relexification. Abdelkébir Khatibi's "radical bilingualism" (1983a and 1983b) is the third concept I rely on in these analyses, particularly its explication by Samia Mehrez (1991). Finally, I draw on the idea of "foreignizing" translation developed out of translation theory to investigate how some texts are written *as* translations. I incorporate these different concerns within a world literature framework that sees layered language use as an integral part of novelistic discourse.

In their seminal work, Bill Ashcroft, Gareth Griffith, and Helen Tiffin claim that by using another language within official English, the (colonized within the) empire are able to "write back" to the colonizer.[22] By interrupting the logic, grammar, and syntax of the colonial language, creative texts written from postcolonial locations use languages other than English to undermine the colonial power structure symbolically, destabilizing its authority and legitimacy. I believe that it is crucial to engage with the arguments put forward by Ashcroft, Griffith, and Tiffin today because they have articulated a firmly anticolonial position to interpret writing in English from around the globe. More recent work on language and literature has often put to one side the importance of the notion of using languages to "write back" against the empire and colonial languages. It is this concept that I would like to preserve, while arguing to revise some of their articulations.

I agree with Ashcroft, Griffith, and Tiffin that so-called postcolonial literatures are in the process of reviving the novel today. I differ from them, however, in that I do not believe that such interruptions of colonial language by other languages always necessarily challenge colonial discourse, and certainly challenges to colonial discourse do not always undermine colonial power. Indeed, such disruptions may not be counterhegemonic at all, depending on the context of the language mixing and the particular politics of language use in different locations. As I discuss in more detail below, I read multiple language use as a process of Bakhtinian novelization that makes creative use of permutations of many languages, registers, and codes within texts. Moreover, it also suggests that more complex processes are at work, reflecting and producing culture through literary languages.

To explore more precisely how these processes work, I drawn on Chantal Zabus's meticulous study, *The African Palimpsest: Indigenization of Language in the West African Europhone Novel.* Zabus argues that rather

22. As its subtitle indicates, *The Empire Writes Back: Theory and Practice in Postcolonial Literatures* (1989) incorporates theoretical perspectives with taxonomic detail.

than appropriating the colonial language to "write back" to the empire on its own terms, novels from Africa use European languages, adapting them to African concepts and contexts, in a process that she calls "indigenization." This process "refers to the writer's attempt at textualizing linguistic differentiation and at conveying African concepts, thought-patterns, and linguistic features through the ex-colonizer's language" (2007, 3). Zabus believes that writers convey African concepts by using African words in texts written in colonial languages, making the latter—as she puts it—"their own."[23] In particular, I will use her articulation of the concept of "relexification" to explain one of the most frequently employed techniques to write Arabic into French by Lebanese women authors. Zabus uses this linguistic term to show how a direct, unidiomatic translation of an African word or expression into a European language interrupts the text, breaking its flow and raising questions about its meaning while at the same time naturalizing this idea within the new linguistic context (101–3). Despite the usefulness of Zabus's study, my readings below will question some of the premises of the overarching notion of "indigenization," for example the notion of languages and texts belonging to "us" and being "our own."[24]

23. Though there is not room to discuss this issue at any length here, it is crucial to note that Lebanese literature written in French, like other Francophone literatures in Arabic-speaking countries, has one major difference from many African literary traditions because of the long history of a written tradition in Arabic in these locations. Written literature in Arabic in Lebanon develops long before and then alongside French language production, and is in competition with it, particularly during the *nahda* (renaissance) of Arabic letters at the end of the nineteenth century. Adnan points this out in her article from which this Introduction draws its epigraph (1986–1987).

24. Another major issue that cannot be investigated in sufficient detail here is ownership and language, in particular two major questions: What does it mean for a language to be one's "own" and how do we "own" languages? I would suggest that Zabus's notions are based on the premise that certain languages belong to certain groups and not to others. For example, we feel uncomfortable claiming that Swahili is not a writer from Zanzibar's "own" language, whereas we might feel perfectly comfortable assuming that English is not "her own." To take another example, an author who is born and raised in Lebanon—with Lebanese heritage, origins, and citizenship—but educated in French, who speaks French at home, and who had moved to France during the war: Is French

My approach underlines the processes of travel and exchange and seeks to undermine the simple labeling of texts, calling into question that a certain idea, language, or system of thought can be somehow indigenous or pure, untouched by processes of travel and exchange.[25] For example, if we argue that one language changes another, then the two languages must be understood as clearly defined and different entities to begin with. The framework I am suggesting challenges this notion of language as so clearly defined, of the ownership of language, and whether languages themselves should be understood as discrete and static entities. Therefore, while taking into account that languages often have been defined as distinct entities in specific times and places, with efforts to distinguish and codify them as such, the flexibility of language is always underlined here.

One possible solution to some of the problems posed by indigenization is the concept of "radical bilingualism" articulated by Abdelkébir Khatibi (1983a, 1983b, 2008). Radical bilingualism posits that because of their inherent mutability, two languages can work together and be reformulated into something new and creative. Khatibi stresses not only the literary effectiveness of this new radical bilingualism in texts but also its social, political, and cultural potential. Khatibi puts this theory into practice in his celebrated novel *L'amour bilingue*. Mehrez's reading of this work shows Khatibi's approach to bilingualism to be figurative and conceptual rather than literal, in Khatibi's argument for the concept of "bi-langue" rather than "bi-lingue" and this text's constant motion between multiple languages.[26] Khatibi's emphasis on how languages work side by side rather

---

then not this author's "own" language? It makes no sense either to insist that it is, thereby resolutely maintaining that French is a Lebanese language, or that it is not, thus depriving a person of the right to identify with her first and most comfortable language. Without arguing for or against any specific cases here, I would like to emphasize that the question of ownership and exclusive rights to languages cuts both ways. My proposition is that language ownership should be questioned and not assumed.

25. On "traveling theory," see also Said (1983, 226–47); and Clifford (1989, 177–88).

26. The literary text in which Khatibi works through this idea is his much touted *L'amour bilingue* (translated as *Love in Two Languages*). Samia Mehrez's argument about bilingualism in *L'amour bilingue*, including an exposition on Khatibi's theory of radical

than layered on top of one another is particularly relevant here and useful within a framework arguing that languages are not static and immutable "things" that abstractly exist in a pure form that you either master or do not. The high or literary form of a language is itself subject to change. What it lacks in specificity, radical bilingualism gains in flexibility by avoiding the notion of language ownership and being open to free play and intermingling.

Writing *as* translation is another strategy that I identify and develop out of the work of translation theory, particularly the notion of "foreignizing" or resistant translation advocated by the translation studies scholar Lawrence Venuti, among others. Texts written to read *as* translations use strategies analogous to those used to produce resistant or foreignizing translations, in that they also resist the tendency to mask the identity of "foreign-sounding" words and ideas and the ideological stances embedded in them. They draw attention to the different cultures and language systems of texts through their use of unusual expressions. Such writing has the dual effect of challenging the reader with difference and also layering meaning in the very "thickness" of the language itself.[27]

The world literature framework of this study incorporates all of these disparate strategies as they emphasize movement, social processes, and the negotiation of complex positions in their analyses of language mixing in literary texts. Drawing on the insights of these studies, but departing from them in significant ways, my framework is able to provide a more complete view of how language works within novels. Language mixing, polyglossia, and polyphony are all integral to the development of the novel throughout its history, in its many locations. These techniques—the empire writing back, indigenization, radical bilingualism, and writing *as* translation—are approached here as specific instances of novelistic discourses that can help

bilingualism, is found in "Translation and the Postcolonial Experience: The Francophone North African Text" (1992, 120–38).

27. This term is drawn from the anthropological concept of "thick description" and used by a number of theorists in their articulations of translation practice, for example by G.J.V. Prasad (1999, 54); Marilyn Booth (2008, 209) draws on the concept as articulated by Kwame Anthony Appiah in "Thick Translation" (2004, 389–401).

to interpret some of the ways in which multiple languages interanimate one another in French-language fiction from Lebanon.

The Corpus of Works and the Outline of the Book

The Arabic and French literary landscapes are dotted with language layerings that take on multiple shapes and sizes. *Native Tongue, Stranger Talk* focuses on how Arabic words infuse the French language of novels written by Lebanese women writers. The book is divided into three parts and each of these is further divided into four shorter chapters. The first chapter of each part contextualizes the literary fields in which these novels are produced. It gives an overview of pertinent social, political, and historical features of the periods in which the novels are written and published and investigates the specificities of the French-speaking community in Lebanon and its literary production in each period.

The next three chapters in each part then focus on one novel apiece in order to discuss the formal techniques and strategies used within the novels both in aesthetic terms and in relation to their social, cultural, and political messages. The ever-increasing number of French-language novels by Lebanese women authors that use words marked as Arabic into their narrations made narrowing down the corpus of works investigated in detail extremely difficult. Indeed most novels written in French by Lebanese authors use Arabic somehow in their narrations, some more explicitly than others. My main consideration in choosing the specific works for inclusion in the study was neither representation of different religious/communal groups nor ensuring specific dates of publication, though I did endeavor to present a range of works beginning from the mandate period and reaching into the twenty-first century and I have included one author of a Druze background with the rest of the authors of various different Christian backgrounds. Most important, I chose works that specifically deal with questions of gender, religion/confession, and class, especially those that challenge systems of hierarchy and power and seek to overturn them. I also focused on the creative use of languages and the examples of strategic and poetic techniques of layering languages marked as different.

In order to decenter the focus on content, political/national allegory, and sociological and ethnographic elements that dominate studies of literature from the Arab world, I had originally planned to organize *Native Tongue, Stranger Talk* purely based on formal criteria. The hope was that it would be difficult merely to glean ethnographic, social, and cultural "information" about Lebanese women or Lebanese society in a book organized by linguistic criteria and the reader's attention would be firmly focused on the poetic value and literary/linguistic virtuosity of these novels, understanding their social, cultural, and political implications through this. But this organizational strategy laid an even more dangerous trap, further undermining the book's larger goals. An intensive focus on linguistic techniques can make the analyses read like laundry lists, whereby no one novel could be discussed as a work of art integrating several elements and messages together. Comparing specific linguistic techniques in several novels meant that the minutiae of linguistic techniques often masked the valuable larger implications of the strategies themselves.

I decided then to reorganize the book chronologically, offering the reader three large, historically influenced groupings that would put works into the context of their time of writing and publication. This allowed me to place three groups of novels into dialogue with one another but also with other works written in French and Arabic in Lebanon at the same time. Organizing the book in this way made it possible to emphasize in more depth the context in which works were produced and to focus on not only literary developments in each period in Arabic and French, but also some of the more specific contours of the politics of language use in each.

It is important to emphasize that though I have chosen to present the works chronologically in three groups, that the book is neither a linear history of the development of the French-language novel written in Lebanon by women authors nor does it offer a neat trajectory of how French-language novels incorporate words marked as Arabic that develop over time. This book's chronological organization is meant to make the literary texts analyzed more accessible through providing a thorough discussion of their literary and historical/political contexts for those readers who will use the texts for insights into Lebanon, Lebanese history, culture, cultural politics, politics of language use, as well as the larger questions about the creation of literary languages through multiple languages. This cushioning provided to the reader is a conscious choice that speaks both to those who are more historically inclined, providing information about the literary context and politics of language use, for example, and for those literary readers who can benefit from a brief outline of historical and political developments from a regional perspective. A risk to organizing the book in this way is that the opening chapters of each part are necessarily brief and cursory. These chapters cannot be fully elaborated histories, but provide brief narrations and directions for further reading and exploration, including names of other French-language and Arabic-language writers whose works could not be analyzed in detail.

It is also crucial to underline that a chronological organization and an ostensibly national categorizing of literary works (as "Lebanese") does not suggest either that there is a nationalist novelistic project in which novels deemed "Lebanese" somehow develop complex examples of language use over time. I studied a particular group of novels as a case study in order to investigate what they share in terms of literary/linguistic techniques, not to propose some sort of "inherently" Lebanese novel or novelistic project that develops. Moreover, while maintaining this system of chronological grouping of works, I insist on not seeing these works in a linear progression, except insofar as later works can borrow techniques and strategies from earlier ones and can make use of a greater range of intertextual items. Here chronology is emphatically not defined as a mark of progress. In fact, the chronological ordering of the texts challenges the notion that "literary modernity" somehow is a process of secularizing and rationalizing the language of expression, as many Hegelians would have it. Rather, new and unique forms of anticolonial subjectivity are expressed through literary languages. I emphasize how this works differently in different contexts and periods but not that there is an inevitable march toward progress, the later works somehow being more advanced.

The first part, "Gendered Interference," deals with works written and published in the period of the French mandate over Lebanon and its early independence. The first chapter thus outlines the major issues and debates that were raging over the shape that the area that would become Lebanon in 1943 should take. After this brief outline, it gives a broad overview of the writing by women and men in Arabic and French in this period to provide the context against which to read the works analyzed in the following three chapters. All three novels in part 1 are characterized as using Arabic in their French texts as "gendered interference." Different specific techniques to incorporate Arabic words into the French text are used to underline textual moments, particularly in relation to how women can function as autonomous individuals within their religious communities and village societies that uphold religious and patriarchal norms. It also provides a discussion of how the genre of ethnography is appropriated and exploited by Lebanese authors of French in crafting their novels.

The earliest novel here, Amy Kher's *Salma et son village* (Salma and her village), discussed in chapter 2, is an example of a folkloric exploration of the life of a young peasant woman in love with the landlord's son in a remote Christian mountain village. It refers to Arabic words in multiple ways to examine social mores. Similarly, the focus of chapter 3, Eveline Bustros's *Sous la baguette du coudrier* (Under the divining rod), also exposes social customs harmful to women through a story of ill-fated love. Bustros uses more daring language, mixing techniques to craft a subtly challenging French language, than does Kher's novel, which makes for an interesting comparison. Finally, Andrée Chedid's *Le sommeil délivré* (*From Sleep Unbound*) is discussed in chapter 4.[28] Chedid's portrait of the oppression of women in "traditional" society foreshadows later, more direct critiques of patriarchy, but also uses similarly subtle techniques of creating a textual language that gesture to Arabic in diverse ways.

The works in part 2, "Arabic as Feminist Punctuation," also treat issues of gender roles and the position of women, but in the context of the Lebanese civil war. A brief outline of some of the issues and debates central to the war itself and the literature written about it is followed in chapter 5 by a discussion of the explosion of literary works published by

28. None of these novels except Andrée Chedid's *Le sommeil délivré* has been translated into English (Chedid 1983). In order to highlight certain elements of language use in this and other texts, all translations from the French in this book are my own.

Lebanese authors, male and especially female, in Arabic and French in the period. This literary contextualization draws parallels in particular between female authors of Arabic and French and how the war opened up new avenues in literary expression for both. While some of the same, subtler techniques used by the earlier authors are employed by the three writers whose works are discussed in part 2, their more direct and didactic style exposes and explains gendered inequities to their readers.

Vénus Khoury-Ghata's *Le fils empaillé* (The son stuffed with straw) is discussed in chapter 6. This novel parallels the patriarchal control of a domineering father over his family with the colonial control of France over Lebanon. Set during the war, the female narrator contemplates directly and forcefully how the French language and patriarchy oppresses her and her siblings. In chapter 7, I show how Evelyne Accad's *Coquelicot du massacre* (A poppy from the massacre) similarly condemns patriarchal control over women and men in a time of war. Dominique Eddé's *Lettre posthume* (A posthumous letter), explored in chapter 8, works slightly differently, while taking up the same themes of the destruction wrought by the war and the way in which men and women react to it. In this novel, it is the male narrator who reflects on the social inequality between men and women and how language might be able to challenge it. The strategies used for inscribing language in all of these works are bolder and often more daring than those in part 1; I have called them "feminist punctuation." A direct discussion of language, the politics of language use, and the ways in which language can challenge patriarchy are present in all three novels in different ways.

The third and final part, "Writing *as* Translation," looks at how works of the postwar period are increasingly diverse and complex and how their use of language reflects this. It also provides some background to the major issues and debates informing public discourse in Lebanon from the 1990s until today, with a particular focus on how literary works have engaged these. The literary contextualization in this part aims to give a sense of the vast diversity of literary genres, settings, themes, and issues taken up by authors from Lebanon and of Lebanese descent in this period. The works in this part vary in their strategies but have in common their use of extensive experimentation with language, genre, and form.

Leïla Barakat's *Sous les vignes du pays Druze* (Under the vines in Druze country), the subject of chapter 10, makes extensive use of a variety of techniques to incorporate words, expressions, and sentences that are marked in different ways as Arabic into a French text. One of the most linguistically challenging works, from this point of view, Barakat's novel is also the only text by a writer of Druze background and this intersection is discussed in some detail. Chapter 11 focuses on Dominique Eddé's masterpiece, *Pourquoi il fait si sombre?* (Why is it so dark?). Written in a stream-of-consciousness style, without an easily discernable plot, this novel creates a creative textual language all its own that at once can only be defined as standard French, but also makes extensive references to Arabic. Chapter 12 is devoted to another novel by Eddé, *Cerf-Volant* (Kite), which is substantially different in its creation of a novelistic language. Taking up a metacommentary on Arabic as much as on French, this story gently pokes fun at the French-speaking bourgeoisie as it narrates their stories through its commentary on language. While all of these works make use of gendered interference and feminist punctuation as the works discussed in earlier chapters do, their more wide-ranging language mixing is characterized here as "writing *as* translation." I argue here how they all in one way or another manage to create the effect of translation in their works by "writing Arabic in French" (écrire l'arabe en français), as Nadia Tuéni claims to do in the epigraph that opens the preface to this study.

Part One ◆ *Gendered Interference*

1

Gendered Interference

French Expressions of Arabic in the Mandate and Early Independence Novel

Three books ending in death, two dead female protagonists and a third who is paralyzed and taken to prison accused of murder, do not immediately announce themselves as tales of feminist emancipation. The three literary works discussed in part 1 are somewhat pessimistic; they subtly underline the plight of women in patriarchal societies with rigid customs and conventions. They all use what might be termed an "accommodationist strategy" that seeks to find ways to mediate between decrying the social practices that harm women and being accepted as an "authentic" part of their communities.

All three works employ polyglossia to navigate these issues, using language-mixing strategies to interfere with standard French in subtle ways that mirror the indirect commentaries they make on social issues. I draw on the metaphor of "interference," borrowing the concept from linguistics, to emphasize the way in which the interruption of speech genres through language mixing—using words that are meant to represent Arabic within a text that is ostensibly written in French—underlines and highlights messages inscribed within the novels. All of them draw attention to the Arabic language in their explicitly French-language texts and do this in particular to underline issues of gender, ethnicity/religion, and class-status hierarchies—for example, the ways in which society limits and constrains women, and at times men, and how this is different for people of different class backgrounds. In many cases, polyglossia draws attention to locations where these issues come together.

The way in which the Arabic language interferes with the French-language text here is very much a product of the time and place in which they are written and published—during the French mandate over Lebanon and its early independence period. This era was one of social upheaval and change in which the shape of the new Lebanon was being furiously debated. As such, the three novels all participate directly—though in distinctly different ways—in the debates raging at the time of their publication in Lebanon and throughout the Arab world. How women would fit into this setting and how they negotiate what are depicted as Lebanese (and/or Arab) customs and traditions in modern Lebanon are an important part of what these works address. Even Chedid's *Le sommeil délivré,* which is set in Egypt, is in dialogue with broader issues that affect women in Lebanon as much as in Egypt, and indeed across the Arab world.

Though the three works are extremely different in plot, setting, and the languages that they draw on, they all share in common that they were written in standard, literary French at a time of direct French influence and involvement in Lebanon. They all fit into accepted genres of literary production that would be recognizable to a French-reading audience. Moreover, the ethnographic flavor of all three works allows the French reader to approach them from the perspective of curiosity and learning about a "foreign" culture, whether or not this is the intention of the works. Words and expressions clearly coded as Arabic are inscribed within the French language enough to interfere with it but not so much as to radically challenge it. At times these are discussed and translated directly, at times they must be deduced from context, and at times they simply flavor the text. As an indirect strategy of mixing Arabic into French, I have identified "gendered interference" as a way to discuss the effect of the language created within these three novels. The next section of this chapter sketches some of the main kinds of social and political changes that occurred in this period when the modern nation of Lebanon was constructed and born, with a particular focus on the role of the French language and French-speaking community in this process.

Polyglossia in Society

Though French-language literature in Lebanon came into its own and established itself in the era of the French mandate over Lebanon, the turn of the twentieth century witnessed its inception.[1] The authors of these early Francophone novels are for the most part members of the Lebanese elite and educated middle classes who moved in an actively polyglot world. The cultural and literary landscape of Beirut, from the early part of the twentieth century until today at the early part of the twenty-first, has cultivated a lived polyglossia, reflected in literary production.[2] Beirut's position as a port city, which had become an important entrepôt for commerce within the expanding world economy by the early twentieth century, allowed the elites of this region to become a part of a cosmopolitan global elite. This group of people from the region thus were active not only within an expanding world economy, but those involved in literary and artistic creation were also able to participate in literary and cultural worlds that operated well beyond Lebanon's shores. Indeed this was a time in which the reading and writing habits in the region were undergoing major changes, which had begun before the fall of the Ottoman Empire and continued into the beginning of the twentieth century. The rise of a middle class and expanded education in the

1. This challenges and revises the claim by Christiane Makward (Makward and Casenave 1988, 204). Though there were not many novelists, there certainly was an active French literary culture in Lebanon from the turn of the century, and women played a greater part in it, beginning in the time of the mandate, particularly as poets. Other general works on Francophonie recognize this. See Belinda Jack's extremely brief treatment of Lebanon in *Francophone Literatures* (1996, 209–10).

2. This is not to make the exaggerated claims that all of Lebanon is bilingual or multilingual or that most people are able to participate in this actively polyglot culture, as some studies have done (Abou 1961 and 1962; Gueunier 2004). A more recent sociolinguistic study has revised Abou's earlier claims and shown the importance of Arabic in all areas of life (Abou, Kasparian, and Haddad 1996). It is crucial to recall here that the limited social groups for whom this polyglot world is a reality make up much of the literary elite of the country.

Arab world meant that there were more active readers and more writers than ever before.

Lebanon's literary cosmopolitans active in this polyglot world included writers who use Arabic as well as French and even some who produced works in English, though this becomes more important in later periods. The French-speaking community in Lebanon arose and was sustained over time because of the confluence of a number of factors, including the proliferation of French-language schools, the development and favoring of certain social and sectarian groups, and opportunities for people belonging to these groups to advance socially through French language acquisition and mastery. In a sense, the French-language creative writers who emerged out of these social groups can be understood as continuing the legacy of the cultural intermediaries of earlier periods who served as "translators"—literally or figuratively—between regional and European interests during the expansion of the world system (Masters 2001). For the most part they belonged to similar social groups in terms of class-status and ethno-religious backgrounds, though women began to play a more active and prominent role in literary life and other spheres as well.

The prestige of the French language in this context is crucial, but it is also important to note that unlike in some other colonial locations, the "local" language of literary expression is not a low-prestige language. Arabic holds a different kind of prestige in literary terms in Lebanon and among Lebanese authors abroad, particularly in Egypt where they played a key role in the *nahda*. Ethno-religious, class-status, and gender hierarchies all impact language use and the way languages interact and intersect in Lebanon. This was reflected within social polyglossia as well as that represented in literary works. French speakers had certain powers and privileges within mandate Lebanon, particularly insofar as many of them worked with the French to develop the shape of the modern Lebanese nation-state. These elites were mostly of Christian background, able to attend private schools, and dominated the literary as well as the social and economic spheres at the time.

The rise of the enterprising mercantile bourgeoisie with the establishment of the French mandate over Lebanon (1920–1943) had its roots not only in the system of government established during the Ottoman period but also in the expansion of port cities that became ever more important with the greater involvement of European powers in the region. Like Alexandria, Beirut grew and became an increasingly important port on the eastern Mediterranean as Palestinian port cities were increasingly affected by political problems arising from Zionist encroachment and could be less and less used for trade and commerce. The mercantile and cultural exchanges between Egypt and Lebanon in particular are tied to these cities, and the Lebanese community in Egypt played a large role in this process.[3]

Local elites of all backgrounds, but French speakers and Christians in particular, worked closely with mandate authorities in constructing the architecture of not only the government but also its economic system. The free trade, laissez-faire economic system that would characterize Lebanon's rise to regional prominence in banking and services by the 1950s, has been referred to as the "Merchant Republic" (Gates 1988). This system downplayed the importance of agriculture and industry in favour of promoting an open, tertiary-oriented economy. Elsewhere, I have argued (with Alessandro Olsaretti) that Michel Chiha, one of the architects of Lebanon as a merchant republic and as a modern nation-state, very much drew on the imagery of Lebanon as a unique and special place in which people could rely on their ingenuity to thrive, whereas he was in fact constructing a system of economics and government in collusion with other elites that would ultimately favor the success of other bourgeois Lebanese like himself (Hartman and Olsaretti 2003).

The Lebanese urban bourgeoisie who participated in the debates around the shape of modern, independent Lebanon were as involved in cultural activities as they were in economics and politics. Many of the same actors in fact were setting the cultural agenda and promoting institutions like the Cénacle libanais, where literary and artistic projects were discussed equally with economic, political, and social topics of interest to

3. This community was well established by this time, after two major waves of emigration, one after the mountain massacres of 1860 (Fawaz 1994; and Schilcher 1985) and the other after the *safarbarlak* (conscription of young men into the Ottoman army) of 1916 (Schilcher 1996; Thompson 2000; and Gilsenan 1996). See also Rogan's more recent evaluation of the scholarship (2004).

people in mandate Lebanon. Lebanon under the mandate thus was not culturally dominated by France in the way that might characterize other directly ruled colonies subject to its *mission civilisatrice.*

Though French is a prestige language, it is not always admired or looked to as the only "high" language. Therefore, while French-language poetry and other literary output at the time were important, Arabic-language literary production was equally important in Lebanon at this time as it was throughout history. Lebanese authors inside Lebanon and abroad—particularly in Egypt—were some of the most important participants in the *nahda* or cultural renaissance of Arabic letters taking place at the end of the Ottoman Empire, promoting its agendas and goals. Even émigrés from as far away as North America participated in this revival. Having moved to the United States with his mother as a child, Khalil Jibran's Arabic language prose poems and short narrative fiction, for example, would have an impact on the development of narrative and the novel in Arabic, though composed on a different continent.

Arabic thus cannot be characterized only as a "local" or vernacular language with low social prestige, even if its spoken, or colloquial, variety is at times characterized as such. Though French was and largely still remains mostly a language of educated, bourgeois people in Lebanon, the range of ways in which it was used in the Lebanon of the period was more complex than such a basic understanding would allow. It is crucial to recognize, however, that women's literary works, in Arabic as well as French, were produced almost exclusively in such elite settings. Women who wrote in Arabic may not have been part of the same social and familial circles as the women who were writing French-language novels at this time, but they did in general hail from the same class-status background. Because Arabic and French both could be seen as "prestige languages," they produced parallel, and at times interacting, fields of literary production.

Women of similar positions in terms of class-status hierarchies within Lebanese society, both those based in Lebanon and outside it—particularly in Egypt where all three of the women discussed in the following chapters lived and worked for a time—used either one of these languages of literary expression (and at times English, though this becomes more prominent in later periods). Though there was not necessarily one large literary circle or school of women writers who constantly interact, these authors tended to write about similar issues and participate in similar debates, and many crossed linguistic borders, publishing in both languages or in mixed-language locations, particularly when it was not a question of literary texts. Amy Kher was a journalist, for example, who also published in Arabic.

The social changes of the mandate and early independence periods link together the class-status consolidation by the Lebanese bourgeois elite and the new way of conceptualizing and institutionalizing religion and sectarian affiliation. The ethno-religious or confessional-sectarian identities with which we are so familiar in Lebanon today are largely "invented," to use the term of Eric Hobsbawm (Hobsbawm and Ranger 1992), in this period. As Ussama Makdisi (2000) has shown, developing out of the Ottoman Empire's policies of land division previously, the modern sense of sectarian identity in Lebanon not only is created in this period but also lays the groundwork for how this will develop into a full-blown religio-sectarian system of government and social organization.

The Lebanon that took shape during the mandate has been characterized as one developed from a Christian nationalist vision of Lebanon, and this is, in many ways, true. One of the reasons is the disproportionately large role that different Christian political actors, identifying themselves as such and using this affiliation to their advantage, played in working with mandate authorities to form the new Lebanon. Contact and exchange with France was largely undertaken by members of these groups, who define themselves increasingly in religious/sectarian terms, and this worked to their advantage as France gained more and more power in the region.

Before the mandate over Lebanon and during the mandate period as well, there was heated debate over whether or not Lebanon should be created and exist as a separate and independent nation. The Lebanese Christian nationalists who espoused Lebanese particularlism against a larger, regional pan-Syrian or pan-Arab identity also hotly debated what form this independent nation would take.[4] Their particularlist agendas were often

4. Some particularist nationalists, like the editor and founder of the French-language daily *L'Orient*, Emile Eddé, advocated the "Petit Liban" vision of Lebanon in order

tied to an identity rooted in another "invented tradition," the ancient history of Lebanon as Phoenicia and the Phoenician ancestry of the modern Lebanese (Kaufman 2004). This interest manifested itself in some cases in collections of antiquities, a renewed interest in the ancient Phoenician language, and even a literary school—the Phoenician school—whose works promote the ideas and ideals of such an identity.[5] Nonetheless, the boundaries drawn that would encompass the new nation-state of Lebanon incorporated many citizens who were farmers, peasants, and factory workers; not everyone was a merchant trader and heir to the Phoenician nation. The Lebanon that was eventually created built an economic and political system that disenfranchised these groups of people in particular.

Though the national solution that encompassed a more diverse population of people had to accommodate them in some ways, it did this while ensuring that certain groups held sway. The political solution that was found, with independence, was the creation of the unwritten agreement that came to be known as the National Pact (*al-mithaq al-watani*) (al-Khazen 1991). It established a power-sharing relationship between the elites of the country that was articulated in religious-sectarian terms and organized citizenship in the state on these principles. The sectarian system was not simply invented in this period, it had longer roots in the region, but its articulation in this way was something very new and "modern"

to preserve a "Christian Lebanon," much in the way the Zionist movement argued for what would become the State of Israel in historical Palestine. For a call for this vision of Lebanon from the time, see Samné (1919). Others, like Chiha, advocated the "Grand Liban" solution that would encompass a large number of Muslims, including Shi'a from the impoverished South and Biq'a Valley. Like all contested national visions, a huge amount has been written on this topic. For a discussion, see Firro (2003, 115–16). Zamir analyzes this in light of the long battle for the presidency between Eddé and Bishara El Khuri (2000, 114–17). On differing perceptions of these solutions for independent Lebanon, see Kiwan (1988, 124–48) and al-Sulh (1988, 149–65). See also Traboulsi's history of Lebanon (2003).

5. Michel Chiha, Charles Corm, other members of their extended families and others were avid collectors; for an analysis of this in relation to the Lebanese national museum, see Zeitlian Watenpaugh (2004, 185–202).

(Makdisi 2000). It is important to note that whether or not this system of government was organized only to favor Christian Lebanese and shore up their power base, it certainly had this effect. The notoriously problematic census of 1932, conducted under the auspices of the French mandate authorities, was the basis on which parliamentary seats were assigned in a ratio of 6 to 5, Christians to Muslims. The most important roles in government were also divided according to religion: the position of president, in which most state powers were vested, went to a Christian, customarily a Maronite; the prime minister would be a Sunni; and the position with the least power, speaker of the house, would be a Shi'i. Voting and representation was all organized on communal lines, and public infrastructure was kept to a minimum with groups encouraged to "take care of their own" in areas like education and health care.

The placing of educational infrastructure into the hands of religious-sectarian groups together with the already well-established system of schools backed by foreign, mainly Christian, religious missionary groups (Italian, Russian, French, British, and American) meant that private education in Lebanon flourished in this period. Though these schools long pre-date the mountain massacres of 1860, the late nineteenth century saw an increase in French missionary activity in the region with French protection of Christian minorities. Though their missionary activities perhaps did not affect education as violently and coercively as in many of its other colonies, France had a strong policy of promoting French education in Lebanon that took root in the mandate. Many mission schools and French-language schools pre-dated the mandate period, however, the number of these schools increased in this period as French was implemented as an official language alongside Arabic (Shaaban and Ghaith 1999).[6] Moreover, during the mandate period the Jesuits and other powerful religious

6. Shaaban and Ghaith (1999) refer to Bashshur's 1978 study in their discussion of private French language schools before the mandate. They cite the number of "Christian schools" at one hundred and the number of French schools at thirty-six on the eve of the First World War. (They also note twelve English, twenty-two Russian, three Islamic, and five public schools.)

orders in France sent missionaries to Lebanon to open schools (Shaaban and Ghaith 1999, 3–4). Children of all different religions, confessions, and sects attended French-language schools, even mission schools, though Christians, and Catholic Maronites in particular, were by far the predominant group studying in these schools—and the most favored by them. A French education and the benefits that accrued from it disproportionally, though not exclusively, reached the Maronite population of the region.[7]

The larger proportional representation of girls to boys in private mission schools points up how gender intersects with the already complex situation of class-status and religious-sectarian identity and affiliation in the mandate and early independence periods. Muslim girls at times were sent to single-sex mission schools that were thought to be conservative in social values and of high educational and cultural value to girls who would not be expected to function in an Arabic-speaking business world, as their brothers might, for example. Thus, a somewhat higher proportion of girls of all religions were educated in mission schools than boys were, relative to their overall school enrolment.[8]

While middle-class and elite girls often received foreign-language—frequently French-language—education in this period, girls and women

7. Shaaban and Ghaith (1996, 99) cite Matthew and Akrawi's (1949) figures for the year of Lebanese independence (1942–1943) that has French schools enrolling 39, 513 students, who were 34,758 Christian, 2,507 Muslim, 1,544 Jewish, 631 Druze, and 73 "other."

8. Statistics that I analyzed based on published government reports of numbers of students enrolled in public and private schools, broken down by gender, back up this assertion. These were based on the numbers published by the Lebanese government's Educational Centre for Research, in a yearly publication titled *Al-Ahsa' al-tarbawi*. In the years before the war, for example, the number of students in private schools far outnumbered those in public schools (a situation exacerbated by the war, as Shaaban and Ghaith show) and this is proportionally truer for girls. For example, in 1966–1967, 305,101 boys attended school; of these 121,026 attended public schools but 184,075 went to private schools. A smaller number of girls went to school; the total number is 235,238, and of these 152,630 attended private school as opposed to only 82,608 in public school. While more and more students attend school and the numbers of girls in school increases apace, the proportional differences remain relatively stable for the years in which such statistics are collected.

were also increasingly participating in other kinds of social life, including debates about the shape of the new Lebanon. Elizabeth Thompson has used gender as a category of analysis in her history of this period, arguing that it is one of a "crisis of patriarchy" in which women navigated their roles in new ways both with and against the French authorities (2000). Divisions between men's and women's societies and roles were being refashioned in this period and subject to strains much in the same way that religious divisions are. Even as women were increasingly located as repositories of "authentic" national traditions, in many of the articulations of nationalism that were debated in the era they were also upheld as new and modern women who were raising the next generation of citizens. Women of different class backgrounds participated in social life in different ways. Middle-class women were faced with the privilege and challenge of increased education and opportunities and how to balance this with traditionally defined roles. Working women, as Malek Abisaab (2009) has shown in his oral histories of the strikes and other forms of resistance mounted by women workers in the French tobacco monopoly, also had a role to play in shaping the nation through their own actions in this period.

All of these intersecting dynamics—particularly those of class, religion, and gender—played out in the literary sphere. Women were actively engaged in writing and discussing literature in the mandate and the independence periods; elite women held literary salons in their houses and more and more women were educated and therefore also produced and consumed literature. This was once again disproportionately true of women of Christian backgrounds, with their greater access to foreign-language mission schools and ties to France, and also elite women with greater social and financial mobility.

This is reflected in the relatively higher proportion of women who published literary works in French, compared with Arabic. Though women produced works in both languages and more men than women published in both, this relative discrepancy has been attributed to different educational, cultural, and social opportunities (Najjar 1993, 15–16). Though after independence curbs were put on the extent to which the French language could dominate in the Lebanese educational system, particularly the public school system—as private, French-language medium schools continued to flourish—it still had a remarkable impact, particularly in this period. Even with the increase in English-language educational opportunities, the roots of the French-language planted by France in Lebanon continued to deepen.[9]

Polyglossia in Literature

The revival of the Arabic language and literature that was at the heart of the *nahda* in this period also encouraged literary developments in genres other than poetry, especially experimentation with prose fiction, and ever more innovations on the level of the language/s of literary texts. This was a time of increasing literacy not only in Lebanon but also the Arab world, and the production of literary works in Arabic and French increased. The socioeconomic realities of the region at the time of the mandate and into the early independence period are reflected in the kinds of literary works produced and the ways in which language changes within them. From the turn of the twentieth century into this period, new genres, especially prose fiction, were becoming important; linguistic experimentations in Arabic literature were tied to other social changes. As Modern Standard Arabic was being developed in newspapers and journals, literary works written in prose developed this language further—both accentuating the difference from and also the awareness of classical Arabic language and literature. At the same time as short stories and oral narratives were developing into longer forms, including the novel, there was a greater circulation of novels coming to the region from the international circuit. Geographical and historical horizons changed during the nineteenth and early twentieth centuries and this change had an impact on the development of literary

9. Though in 1946 Lebanon amended its constitution to make Arabic the only official language (this law has since been repealed) and English was introduced as a foreign-language option on par with French, the latter remained a high-prestige language spoken by the ruling elite. While Shaaban and Ghaith show the ways in which English slowly made inroads into Lebanon as a second language after Arabic, their studies reconfirm the importance of French, especially in this period (1999, 5–6; and 1996, 95–105); their more recent study of students' attitudes toward languages reconfirms this (2002, 557–74).

works, as more circulation of texts brings about change in content as well as form.

Just as I have suggested that Arabic and French literary production should not be isolated from each other in drawing a portrait of the literary context, neither should women's works be seen as isolated from men's works, though the former is the focus of *Native Tongue, Stranger Talk*. This section outlines a number of men's and women's texts to provide a glimpse into the larger contexts of literary production in Arabic and French in the period at the turn of the century and into the mandate and early independence era.

Though the very earliest works written in French and published in Lebanon did tend to experiment less with language and employed fewer words marked as Arabic in their texts, this is not uniformly true. At times, this is a question of genre. If we compare, for example, Jean Bechara Dagher's narrative poem *Souvenirs d'Orient* (1903) with Tewfick Ackad's plays, such as *Les martyres* (1918) or *Une nuit dans la vallée des rois* (1925), this becomes plain. These works were composed in the first part of the twentieth century before the mandate. Dagher's lyrical verses are characterized by an almost prose-like narrative quality in passages that extol and explain the "East" to his French readers. As might be expected, he integrates almost no trace of Arabic into his writing, sticking instead to a standard French poetic language. On the contrary, Ackad's plays make ample use of polyglossia, representing less how people actually speak—as the plays are of course written in standard French—than it does the very idea of speech and language in order to explore the complexities of language mixing.

In early novelistic production, too, polyglossia is at times employed in a variety of ways and to different extents. One of the best early examples is Chékri Ghanem's novel *Da'ad* (1908), about a virtuous Lebanese woman whose name is reflected in the title. Replete with ethnographic flavor, the story is a call for confessional tolerance and a critique of local corruption. This very early novel can be compared with works like that of Dagher and Ackad, but also differs in its genre and form. This is one of the first works of narrative fiction in French in Lebanon and thus, unlike a poem or play, draws neither on the conventions of those forms nor extensive use of dialogue. Its representation of Lebanese culture through the chaste and lovely character of Da'ad draws on the burgeoning trend in ethnographic representation, including studies and travelogues as well as novels. This character is used to demonstrate a particular image of Lebanon and the Arabic language in order to punctuate and highlight certain elements of culture and tradition.

In the period of the mandate and early independence, poetry maintained its canonical position in French-language Lebanese literature. Poetry had been, and remained, the most important genre. This is true not only in terms of prestige but also in terms of the number of texts that were written and published. It was not until the civil war that the French novel in Lebanon came into its own as an important genre.[10] Not surprisingly, there was much less formal and linguistic experimentation with Arabic in poetry than in the novels that began to emerge at this time.[11] Most of this poetry was conventional French verse.

Thematically, many poets take up "Lebanese" topics and issues, often referring to how one can express in French ideas that are "oriental" or "Eastern." The best-known poetic figures of the thirties, forties, and fifties, men like Michel Chiha, Charles Corm, Héctor Klat, and Élie Tyane, who were known as the "Phoenician school," for example, wrote in a highly standard French literary style with relatively little language mixing and few polyglossic innovations. Indeed Michel Chiha specifically did not approve of using too many "local words" in literary texts written in French, something we know from advice he gave Eveline Bustros on how to improve her novel (Bustros 1988, lviii).[12] Klat's often-cited ode to the French language

10. This can be seen in the amount of criticism on poetry and the number of anthologies dedicated to French language poetry, for example, Aoun Anhoury ([1987] 1996), and the amount of space dedicated to poetry in others, for example, Sahar Khalaf (1974). See also Nicolaides-Salloum (1997, 110–12).

11. This very much meshes with Bakhtin's theory of the polyglossic languages of novelization as opposed to the language of the epic, which was by definition monoglossic (Bakhtin 1981, 3–40).

12. Chiha's advice to Bustros will be discussed in greater depth below in relation to her use of Arabic words and the delayed publication of her novel.

in *Le cèdre et les lys* [The cedar and the lilies] betrays a Francophilia deeply invested in the French language itself and touched with not a small strain of orientalism (Klat 1964).[13] These poets draw not only on the standard French language but also styles, imagery, and themes, with only a few exceptions, like Charles Corm. Corm's best-known tour de force, the long prose poem *La montagne inspirée*, can be seen as somewhat of an exception because of the way it plays with language, form, and genre.[14] This ode to the "sacred" mountains of Lebanon invokes the ancient Phoenician myths of Lebanon directly in its melange of styles and themes. Its importance to the later development of Lebanese literature written in French is noted by many critics, and some have even underlined the way in which it is influenced and permeated by Arabic, despite the classic, literary French and the rhyming alexandrines it employs throughout.[15]

Novels written in this period, however, tell a different story. Many "local" Arabic words, idioms, expressions, and ideas are represented and written into this large range of texts. Some of the discrepancy between the novel and poetry can be explained by the greater tendency of novels from Lebanon to depict and organize themselves around ethnographic representations of culture. Relevant examples of this can be seen in the many well-known novels that Farjallah Haïk produced throughout the 1940s and 1950s. The vast majority of his works make ample use of polyglossia and incorporate Arabic words in a wide variety of ways. His novels are set in mountain villages in Lebanon and describe many of their customs and traditions in minute detail (Zein 1998, 201–3).

13. Originally written in 1934, this poem is often cited as a reason Klat becomes a "national poet" of Lebanon; it was published in 1964.

14. *La montagne inspirée* was originally published in Beirut by Éditions de la revue phénicienne in 1934. The publishing house, founded by Corm himself, published many works by Francophone writers, including the magazine *La revue phénicienne*. This prose poem—along with all of Corm's collected writings—was recently reissued by the same press in 2004 as part of a project to republish all of his collected writings.

15. See, for example, the discussion by Sahar Khalaf (1974, 45–59), who devotes almost 15 pages to discussing it in his anthology that in total is only 150 pages long. See also Aoun-Anhoury (1996, 179).

This ethnographic tendency, which I will discuss further in chapters 2 and 3, is more prominent in French-language literature from Lebanon than it is in Arabic-language literature. The representation of the self and other, the navigation of insider-outsider dynamics, is addressed in just about every work written in French. This is not to say that none of the features that I identify below as making texts engage with the genre of the ethnographic novel are present in Arabic. There are a great many parallels between works published in French and Arabic, although the period before the Second World War saw only the beginnings of the full-blown novel written in Arabic, with early experimentations in the form of long prose poems and short narrative pieces developing in the beginning of the century.

A specific example is Tawfiq Yusuf ʻAwwad's 1939 classic novel, *Al-Raghif*, which tells the story of the famine in the period of the *safarbarlak* of the First World War. While his descriptions differ from those of Bustros and her novel operates in different ways, focusing on different issues, they echo each other as well. Jibran Khalil Jibran's early works in Arabic, the short narratives in particular, are also echoed by many of the French-language authors, especially in theme (Jibran 1906, 1908, 1912). Based in the United States, Jibran wrote scathing critiques of the clergy and hierarchies of the Maronite Catholic Church while advocating the values of literary romanticism. With their emphasis on the individual and his view of women as needing to be freed from oppressive gender roles, Jibran's texts are companions to those written by authors like Kher, Bustros, and Chedid, albeit with a somewhat different focus.

"Gendered Interference"

Specific Language Layering Strategies in the Texts

The vast majority of the copious novelistic production in French from Lebanon actively employs polyglossia and/or the representation of mixed languages, to considerably differing extents and effects. The diversity of types of novels and the ways in which these linguistic strategies are used within them underlines the creative breadth of this literary tradition. There is some correlation between this creativity and how much they engage an "ethnographic pact" with their readers: the more they represent cultural difference, the more heavily they tend to draw on unusual combinations of words, expressions, and languages.[16] My own survey of more than fifty novels written over the past hundred years, for example, reveals a wide range of language mixing, both in specific strategies and in the amount of polyglossia of different kinds worked into the text. Some of these works of course may be drawing on Arabic words as representations of an Other and in order simply to "spice up" their texts to give them an exotic flavor. Most works, however, clearly use these moments in a more profound way, as an integral part of the novelistic experiment. What is important here, the different levels and layers of language—particularly language represented as Arabic or "local language"—are integrated into the French language narration and dialogue of these texts. Bakhtin's theory of language use in novelistic discourse provides us with a way of thinking about all of the techniques used by these authors in a broader framework relating to language and discourse, as well as helps us to use a world literature approach to understand better some of the ways in which language operates within the texts.

In this early period of the novel—the mandate and early independence period—texts tend write a French that could only be described as a standard literary language and use Arabic in ways that are more descriptive, less unusual, and contain more contextualization and cushioning. I have characterized the rather subtle way in which messages about gender roles and women's lives in novels by women of this era operate as "gendered interference": Arabic interferes with the French without overturning it, almost always in ways that comment on gender roles and women's position in society. Moreover the language used in these texts to represent Arabic or in other polyglossic moves is without fail the language of the house or

16. In the following chapters, I develop Philippe Lejeune's notion of an "autobiographical pact" to work through some of the ways in which authors activate the genre of ethnography in their fictional works to both provide information about Lebanese peasant culture and society and to challenge some of the ideas typically inscribed within these kinds of texts.

"bayt," words and expressions that are somehow linked to the domestic sphere, spaces that are usually defined as connected to women.

Among the specific strategies used by all three authors—Kher, Bustros, and Chedid—to create polyglossia, are the use of footnotes, bold typeface, and transliterated Arabic words. These strategies often at first glance seem to work in rather obvious ways to explain or make transparent meanings of words that stand out as "different." As I will argue, however, they often operate within the kind of framework offered by Ashcroft, Griffith, and Tiffin, to "write back" to colonial power. Many of these examples, used in conjunction with other strategies and techniques, therefore function in complex and engaging ways. One of these additional techniques, also employed by all three authors, is the subtle and powerful technique of relexification used to interfere with the language of the text, activating the reader's expectations about speech genres to highlight ideas and messages.[17] Put simply, relexification refers to the literal translation of Arabic expressions into unidiomatic, antiquated, or awkward-sounding French. In relexification, as opposed to translation, the connection to the original language is left as transparent as possible, and the way that the resulting word or phrase sounds in the target language is almost always "awkward." The relexified expression thus sounds unidiomatic and may not even make sense within the new language, but this is the point of the technique; it does not strive for an "accurate" translation, but rather emphasizes its difference within the main language of the text. Messages about gender equality—women's roles in society and a critique of patriarchy—are reinforced by this strategy. This is also a particularly effective way to add a layer of subtle irony to the text.

Layering Arabic words and expressions into the text through relexification allows authors to address a multiplicity of readers in different ways, adding meaning to their texts. It is not only the political meanings that are

17. As discussed in the introduction, I am drawing on Zabus's formulation of "relexification" (2007), but I do not take up her idea of "indigenization" as developed in conjunction with the African novel, as I think this characterization of Lebanese novels is overstated. Her explication of different techniques of relexification in particular, but also other language mixing strategies, is invaluable to the study of mixing Arabic in French.

inscribed and layered in this way. Poetically, the effect of using nonidiomatic expressions that clearly are meant to refer to another language has an immediate effect on the flow of the text. The insider and outsider reader will also be affected by these textual breaks differently, in that the reader who knows Arabic will immediately supply the relexified expression in its many meanings and be able to continue reading smoothly with this in mind. The outsider reader who does not know Arabic, however, will be stalled for a moment at the relexification and forced to understand the meaning from the context and appropriate cushioning, further reflecting on the importance of language in conveying ideas. As Ashcroft, Griffith, and Tiffin, and many after them, have pointed out, layering relexified expressions into the text adds a strangeness to it that is exploited by postcolonial writers (1989, 65–67). Calling attention to the fact that another language coexists with French in these texts, and is engaging with it, underlines the importance of language and the multiplicities of linguistic meaning.

Though I have relied on Zabus's conceptualization and articulation of relexification here as an apt way of interpreting these unidiomatic translations of Arabic expressions, I do not follow her interpretations beyond this. My argument is somewhat different because I show that in these texts languages are not necessarily seen as discrete systems that are inherently different to begin with, and thus one does not "indigenize" the other by being mixed with it. Though I do acknowledge that we all tend to reify languages and understand them as discrete entities to be contrasted with each other—we all have a sense of what an "Arabic" word is as opposed to a "French" word—here I do not understand language as a fixed system. Even the attribution of words to only one lexical system is something that is indeterminate and always changing. In order to challenge a paradigm that would propose languages as fixed, different, or oppositional, my readings suggest that the new languages created within literary texts build a resistance to such oppositions.

I insist on the Bakhtinian framework here to underline my commitment to understanding the languages of the novel as flexible and changing. This approach also allows for a focus on reading polyglossia as a way to navigate the complexities of class-status hierarchies, ethnoreligious issues, and gender issues, particularly in their intersections. The complexities of characters' attitudes toward languages reflect this. In the works discussed in part 1, for example, Kher's and Bustros's novels take an anticolonial stance toward French control of the Middle East. But neither expresses French as a wholly imposed, outside language and Arabic as one that is completely "native" or indigenous. They are able to manipulate a language associated with colonial power in creative ways in order to mount their critiques. My framework, which brings together Bakhtin's insights on language and broader concept of world literature, thus allows for the complex strategies of polyglossia in the novels to be understood on multiple levels.

I will propose that these moments in the text that rupture the literary French use their own incongruence to highlight the importance of an idea: this is "interference." I do not think that moments of difference in these three texts are inscribed as something inherently impossible, or even difficult, to understand. On the contrary, the way in which languages shift and are marked as different in the texts is much more akin to the shift in genres described by Bakhtin as a way to elicit a reaction, foil, and/or predict an expectation. In the Bakhtinian reading, Arabic and French languages are not different than other levels of languages that interrupt speech genres and may also be mixed to literary effect in a novelized text.

As the feminist messages of these works about women's role in society being problematic are clear, the way in which they are inscribed is subtle, much like the strategy of relexification itself. The kinds of feminist messages that these authors promote or the way in which they convey them may not always be those that we expect. The poetics of the novels in this sense mirror their politics. The poetic formal strategy used in both works reinforces the book's politics and message both in the layering of words and expressions marked as Arabic into French narratives but also in how they are used. The kinds of ambivalence that these authors and others have toward the French language, therefore, are read through these novels in their treatment of these issues, but also on a deeper level within the very texture of the language of the works themselves.

2

Jamil and Salma

The "Son of a Family" and a Peasant Girl

> Kadisha is the holy river: standing on the heights, clinging to the slopes, nothing but chapels and monasteries have been carved into the rocks as refuges for the pious. A miracle of labor and faith performed by a race to which Salma, without fully probing the reasons, feels proud to belong.
>
> Kadisha est la rivière sainte: dressés sur les hauteurs, accrochés aux pentes, ce ne sont que chapelles et monastères et les rochers sont creusés de pieuses retraites. Miracle du labeur et de la foi opéré par une race à laquelle Salma, sans en approfondir les raisons, se sent fière d'appartenir.
>
> —KHER 1933, 18[1]

Salma et son village [Salma and her village] presents the green slopes of a northern Lebanese mountain village and its quaint peasant inhabitants to a French-reading audience. The work paints an expansive tableau of this setting, weaving together romantic-emotional and sociopolitical novelistic strands into a story about ill-fated lovers. The plot develops with the life story of the heroine, Salma, an attractive young peasant woman who falls helplessly in love with Jamil, the son of a local notable. Much of the narrative space of *Salma et son village* then treats the story of this mismatched couple, whose union transgresses lines of class, family

1. Though I consistently refer to *Salma et son village*'s original date of publication (1933), I have cited throughout from the 1972 edition parenthetically in the text by page number only.

background, and status within the conservative Christian milieu of the fabled Lebanese mountain region of Bécharrée. This love story gone wrong is implicated in Salma's final illness and her premature demise. She dies ambiguously, of some sort of fever, although a broken heart is indicated as part of her malady.

Like so many other literary works of both poetry and prose published during the French mandate in Lebanon, Amy Kher's *Salma et son village* is steeped in the mythology of the "sacred" Lebanese mountains (Haddad 2000, 33–61). Also like many contemporary French-language novels from Lebanon, it engages a discourse that might be considered "ethnographic." The characterization of Kher's work as ethnographic makes sense—its subtitle, "faces of Lebanon" [Visages du Liban], announces its intention to reveal a certain portrait of Lebanon through the story of its eponymous protagonist. Indeed the narration is explicitly charged with sharing the "customs and traditions" of a northern Lebanese mountain village with Kher's French-language readership.

How to understand novels that are deeply invested in such a project presents the reader with a challenge. Novels deemed "ethnographic" often are dismissed as unimportant or characterized as somehow not quite "novels" in their own right because of their focus on detailed descriptions of "local customs and traditions" and the presumed lack of literary artistry therein.[2] This is particularly true of the "colonial," or in this case the "mandate," novel written in a colonial language, like French, presumably intended for an "outsider" audience. A critic like Ramy Zein responds by claiming that what he calls the "documentary aspect" of Kher's novel does not detract from it because it is well integrated into the text. He defends *Salma et son village* against such criticism, claiming, "We should not commit the injustice of judging Amy Kher's fiction using our modern criteria" [Ne commettons pas l'injustice de juger la fiction d'Amy Kher selon nos critères modernes] (Zein 1998, 265). What I show in this chapter is that we can employ "modern criteria" to understand better how Kher's recasting of the genre of the ethnographic novel is tied to her use of multiple

2. Haddad 2000, 18–19, 38; Jabbour 2002, 12.

genres and languages in the text. By reading the text using such criteria, the language, genre, and even ethnography of the text are shown to be part and parcel of its artistry as a literary work. But this means discarding the suspicion of ethnographic texts in order to probe how she uses this genre to produce a novel that is both complex and creative, participating directly in the most crucial discourses of its time.

One of the ways in which to address such suspicion is to see such novels as establishing an "ethnographic pact" with their readers. I am using the notion of a "pact" that follows Philippe Lejeune's conceptualization of an "autobiographical pact" (Lejeune 1975, 1–30). According to Lejeune, texts use a number of formal and paratextual elements to establish a "social contract" that communicates to the reader ways in which to understand and read it (28–29). This reading of formal, literary features echoes the generic definitions that see literary texts in their social contexts, underlining the kinds of functions these works have in relation to how they define themselves.[3]

Here, I build on Lejeune in order to underline the complex ways in which literary texts establish complicity with their readers, in this case to produce ethnographic rather than autobiographical texts, and novels rather than memoirs. By using the concept of an ethnographic pact being established between the author and the reader, I am proposing that such texts draw on the idea of explaining customs, traditions, and culture that is meant somehow to be "Lebanese" to a purportedly French-language reader. As such, this approach demands that we see these novels as more than mere descriptions of Lebanese customs and traditions or representations of Lebanese culture, but rather than intervention, into a discussion about ethnography, cultural studies, and the study of Lebanon in the mandate period from an insider-outsider perspective.

By activating the shapes and contours of novels produced in colonial settings as "scientific studies" of society, but reworking them in fictional

3. I also borrow from Frederic Jameson's definition of genre: "Genres are essentially literary institutions or social contracts between a writer and a specific public, whose function is to specify the proper use of a cultural artifact" (1981, 106).

forms, French-language authors from Lebanon are able to produce deeper and more resonant social commentaries. The "ethnographic pact" created here, I am suggesting, creatively manipulates the truth value of literature. What makes the concept of the ethnographic pact so interesting in reading these texts is that authors set themselves up in a position that consciously posits them as both insiders and outsiders in relation to what they are describing. The pact established with the reader in these novels therefore underlines what is shared and complicit between them. It does this indirectly. The way in which the process works is not by announcing its intentions but rather by activation these ideas through a manipulation of generic codes.

Amy Kher's *Salma et son village* is a good example of a novel that establishes this sort of ethnographic pact with its readers, as is Eveline Bustros's *Sous la baguette du coudrier,* discussed in the next chapter. Kher in this book is able to assure her French-language reader that she has privileged insider knowledge to be explained in standard French. Mastery of multiple languages and their complexities is deeply intertwined with the insider-outsider position. Language use and in particular the mixing of languages marked as different are not only therefore ways to set up the pact but also a way to challenge and disrupt conventions once this complicity is established. One element therefore that can be read through this is the production of alternative knowledge, the disruption of colonial ethnographies through imitation and challenge at the same time. This in connection to the author's insider-outsider status allows her to write a text that can creatively challenge colonial knowledge production.

In *Salma et son village,* the author-narrator who uses extensive ethnographic representations within the novel can be understood as the equivalent of a native informant. The concept of the "native informant" is derived from anthropological discourse, capturing the position of a person who has privileged access to more than one culture and who is able to explain them to each other. More specifically, she is able to translate or interpret a "local" or regional culture to the metropolitan center, usually in its own language. The power dynamics of the colonial encounter demand, therefore, that the native informant transform herself from a postcolonial object of study by the colonizer to a speaking subject who explains certain objects of study to the same colonizing culture. To some extent, it might be suggested, all novelists who write about "their own" cultures, or cultures of origin, in colonial languages act as native informants for metropolitan audiences.

Participation in the discourse of colonial power—despite or even because of the amount of polyglossia prevalent in such literary texts—has led to much criticism of writers like Kher, who, wittingly or unwittingly, takes on this role of native informant, as the comments by Zein indicate. Authors who are positioned in this way lay themselves open to the charge that they are exposing a certain "local" community to a colonial gaze. They are often seen as promoting their own careers at the expense of their community's pride or dignity by exploiting their "exotic" background in a metropolitan location—Paris, London, or important urban centers in the "provinces" like Beirut, Bombay, Cairo, Dakar, and so on—by telling quaint stories about the peasants "back home." One of the most common techniques used to this end is mixing elements of "local" languages into texts written in the "powerful" European language.

Using polyglossia in this way within texts written in European languages is at times understood as pandering to exoticized European notions about "local" cultures and traditions, or simply spicing up these works by using words that represent such difference. Though some authors may of course do this, polyglossic, ethnographically oriented texts need not necessarily be read in a negative light. Kher's *Salma et son village*, for example, forms an ethnographic pact through her use of didactic footnotes to explain Arabic words and concepts, her translations of common Arabic expressions into French, and her descriptions of different kinds of food. She details religious ceremonies unfamiliar to a French-reading audience by explaining or translating them.

In its ethnographic approach, its plot taking up the tragic story of ill-fated love, and its backdrop of a seemingly idyllic yet troubled village society, *Salma et son village*'s outlook very much engages the concerns and preoccupations of mandate Lebanon in the 1930s, when it was published. The period of the French mandate not only produced novels set in the mountains, with an interest in detailing local customs, but also those taking up timeless tales of love and loss. In this sense, the plot of *Salma et son village* is not unique or particularly original. In developing the love story that was not meant to be between the village girl Salma and the son of a local elite, Jamil, Kher draws on a classic premise that could even be termed "universal." The very universality of this tale allows Kher to delve more deeply into the particular ethnographic details about this village and its people, revealing and explaining customs and traditions in detail to a French-reading audience without the distraction of a complicated and difficult-to-follow narrative arc.

All of this is consistent with regional trends in the novel, in both French- and Arabic-language fiction. Romanticism was all the rage in the Arab world at the time of the work's publication (Ostle 1993, 82–131).[4] The novel echoes contemporary texts that extol the virtues of individualism and the rejection of social convention in a highly idealized mountain setting. The works of the pioneering romantic writer Khalil Jibran (Kahlil Gibran), for example, particularly his short Arabic works like *Nymphs of the Valley*, 1906 (*'Ara'is al-muruj*, 1906), *Broken Wings*, 1998 (*Al-Ajniha al-mutakassira*, 1912), and *Spirits Rebellious*, 1990 (*Al-Arwah al-mutamarrida*, 1908), are perhaps the best-known examples of these same themes. In *Broken Wings*, for example, an ill-fated love story implicates the clergy and church as well as class and gender hierarchies in its failure. Kher's novel similarly emphasizes rural prohibitions on love between local social elites and peasants who work the land, demonstrating how this is frowned on within the traditional village context.[5]

4. Though there is not space to explore this issue in detail here, the connections between trends in French- and Arabic-language fiction in Lebanon is an issue that should be pursued in more detail, particularly because Lebanon's large expatriate community did stay in touch with the homeland and the exchange of information and publications. These overlapping and mutually reinforcing ideas and trends are not insignificant to Lebanese literary production and are more complex than one-way traffic from "Western" ideas being imported into the "East."

5. For a detailed analysis of these issues in the Egyptian novel, see Samah Selim (2004).

Salma et son village operates quite differently as a literary work than Jibran's short, experimental Arabic novels and even other contemporary French-language works, however, in how it uses language to establish an "ethnographic pact" with the reader. Her use of footnotes and translated Arabic words and expressions help to set the tone of a text that serves an "explanatory" purpose to its readership. There is no doubt that the way in which Arabic peppers the French-language narration of this text gives it local spice and flavor. In addition, though, *Salma et son village* also employs other levels of linguistic and generic mixing, including untranslated and relexified Arabic words and expressions, to complement this effect and address additional audiences. These strategies then comment on both the challenges from and to the genre of ethnography.[6]

It is crucial to this French-language novel that the Arabic language is invoked and developed in specific ways that illuminate the ethnographic elements of the story, in particular the effect of certain customs and traditions on women's lives. Arabic interferes with the French text therefore in gendered ways, showing the roles of women and men to be constrained by social customs, but differently for each gender. It is crucial to read how these moments reinforce and also challenge many of the important ideas about changing gender roles and the shape of the nation that circulated in mandate Lebanon. In these ways, *Salma et son village* can be read as more than a simple, universal love story of tragic dimensions or an exposé of village customs and traditions, but also as a novel of the 1930s that reflects and participates in debates and discourses

6. Works like this very much draw on, gesture to, and ultimately challenge the kinds of knowledge being produced by colonial-era travelogues to the region that are more specifically written as ethnographies or ethnographic interventions. The kinds of works being written by Europeans about Lebanon and particularly Christian mountain villages are interlocutors to a work like Kher's. See, for example, Constantin-François de Volney, *Voyage en Égypte et en Syrie* (1787); John Lewis Burckhardt *Travels in Syria and the Holy Land* (1822); Alphonse de Lamartine, *Voyage en Orient* (1875) and *A Pilgrimage to the Holy Land* (1837); Gérard de Nerval, *Voyage en Orient* (1884); and Hester Stanhope *The Memoirs of Lady Hester Stanhope* (1885). For a specific account of the events of 1860, see Comte de Paris Philippe, *Damas et le Liban* (1860).

taking place in mandate Lebanon in the period leading up to its independence in 1943.

The Priest's Wife: Explaining the Christian Other to Other Christians

As an ethnographic portrayal of village life in northern Lebanon, *Salma et son village* is very much focused on its Christian, more specifically, Maronite Catholic, identity. This is continually emphasized in different ways throughout the text, particularly in the balance between how this identity ostensibly should unify the people of the village of Hadchit and the internal divisions that we learn of through the novel's narration. Kher pays careful attention to many local customs and traditions that are linked within the public and private consciousness of her characters to what it means to be a Christian in this region at this time. Aimé Azar's preface to Kher's collected works, for example, sees Kher as painting a portrait of a "simple life" in which the characters belong to what she terms an "ethnic group" [un groupe ethnique] whose family and spiritual ties are equally important. Avoiding the terminology of religion or sect, therefore, in her notes Azar prefers to emphasize the traditional life of the "minoritaires chrétiens d'Orient" [Christian minorities of the East/Orient] (1).

This preface perhaps better reflects the time when Kher's works were republished in the early 1970s than their original publication in the 1930s. Azar's introduction was written when Lebanon was on the brink of a devastating civil war that would largely be thought of as divided on religious/sectarian lines, a time in which the issues facing Lebanon tended to be articulated differently than before its independence. Azar's comments do, however, reflect the fine balance that Kher achieves between portraying the intimate details of one community and at the same time as seeing this community as deeply rooted in a land that it shares with many other groups, defined variously as religious, sectarian, and here as "ethnic." With Lebanon under French mandate and striving for independence, Christian individuals and groups, including some living and working outside of the country—as indeed Kher herself was, in

Egypt—played a vital role in shaping the way in which the new nation would identify itself.[7]

The contours of how Kher outlines a Christian, more specifically, Maronite Catholic, identity in the work then are all the more crucial for understanding how this novel participates in the discourses of its time. This takes on additional layers in the context of the putatively French audience, itself presumed to be Catholic, reading about far-flung religious brethren. Writing an exotic story of difference, while relying on some similarity, is a necessary feature of such a work, describing a different kind of Christian community to the European audience of the early twentieth century, a time of French colonial influence around the world, including in the eastern Mediterranean.

The work's Christian village setting is continually reiterated and emphasized in multiple ways. Within the narration, characters are frequently depicted in prayer or simply invoking God in a variety of circumstances, using "typically Christian" Arabic expressions translated into French, declaiming, for example: "par la vierge" [for the virgin's sake] (18). Kher explains local, Maronite customs to a readership presumed to be familiar with Western Catholicism. From the very first page of the narration, it is established that the Maronite Catholic identity of the characters is a crucial organizing principle of all elements of their lives. The novel opens, for example, with the protagonist, Salma, reflecting on the marriage of the local priest's son to her friend, and contemplating their union. This might seem paradoxical to a reader who does not know that Maronite priests are allowed to marry. Kher places this in a short explanatory paragraph embedded within lines of Salma's dialogue about her friend's good taste in wanting to marry this man who will inherit his

7. Christians outside Lebanon, particularly in Egypt, were crucial to formulating its ideas around independence (Philipp 1985; Fawaz 1983). The historiography of Lebanese independence has at times even focused on the importance of these Christian actors, which is a problematic triumphal narrative. See Hartman and Olsaretti (2003) for a counternarrative based on elite coalitions, as well as Traboulsi's work on Lebanese history (1993, 1997, 2003).

father's position: "In the remote Maronite mountain villages, ecclesiastical law still allows married men to take vows, but it forbids these same men from remarrying if they become widowers" [Dans les villages retirés de la montagne maronite, la loi ecclésiastique permet encore de conférer les ordres à un homme marié, mais elle interdit à ce même homme une nouvelle union en cas de veuvage] (6). This is an indicative strategy used by Kher to explain customs and traditions in subtle and indirect ways.

It is within this short opening scene where Salma is by turns excited and happy for her friend and then somewhat jealous that Kher inscribes her first use of a word marked as Arabic in the French text. Here, she follows up her direct presentation of the fact that priests can be married with a "local saying" that she labels as such and then "translates" into idiomatic French: "Salma smiled while repeating the local saying, 'No wife is more pampered than the priest's wife'" [Salma sourit en se répétant le dicton du cru, "Nulle épouse plus choyée que celle du curé"] (6). Opening the text with this scene that includes a "local saying," which is implicitly translated from Arabic into French, serves several purposes. First, it subtly interferes with the text. An expression in another language, even one that is translated like this and fits into the text seamlessly from a linguistic point of view, draws attention to itself. Here, the expression underlines not only that priests can have wives, but also the preferential treatment received by a priest's wife—a role nonexistent among most Catholics, whose priests do not marry.

In the novel, this early emphasis on the priest and his wife foreshadows the importance of these characters. Not only does the church structure the everyday lives of the characters, but how characters relate to the church, the priest (referred to also as the Khouri, the Arabic word for priest), and priest's wife (the Khouriée) also structures the novel.[8] There are four other examples of expressions, presented as local sayings or proverbs, that

8. Unlike other similar texts, including arguably Bustros's and Chedid's, the clergy here is portrayed positively in a setting of rural harmony only interrupted by Salma's untimely death. As I will discuss in more detail below, the church and clergy are not directly implicated in her demise.

are presented as though translated from Arabic into French in the text (29, 41, 67, 106). Two of these also deal with issues relating to the role of the clergy, or at least men of "traditional" wisdom and experience as opposed to "men of science," and the changes in society that affect them.

The first of these two is spoken by Jamil's father, Rachid. "Bah! Cheikh Rachid intervened, you know the saying my boy: 'Ask a man of experience before a man of science'" [Bah! Mon garçon, intervient Cheikh Rachid, tu connais le dicton: "Consultez un homme d'expérience plutôt qu'un homme de science"] (29). The second such expression sees the priest worrying about marrying off his son to his beloved, because there is talk afloat that the church will force Maronite priests to become celibate like their Catholic brothers in other locations. It is Salma's father, Chafik, who eventually convinces the priest to go ahead with it, arguing that "they cannot change our customs so easily!" (67). The reaction of the village people is documented in another expression, claimed in the text as an Arab proverb: "No one is surprised because, as the Arab proverb says, there are three things that cannot be hidden: pregnancy, love, and a camel's hump. The wedding is set for the last Sunday in October" [Personne ne s'en étonne, car, comme dit le proverbe arabe, il y a trois choses qui ne se peuvent cacher: la grossesse, l'amour et la bosse d'un chameau. Le marriage est fixé au dernier dimanche d'octobre] (67).

The other two examples of "local" proverbs and sayings provide moral guidance in a typically didactic way. The first emphasizes the importance of hard work. "Doesn't the proverb say: 'When your heart is at work, your mind is not on the lookout'" ["Le proverbe ne dit-il pas: 'Quand on a le coeur à l'ouvrage, on n'a pas l'esprit aux aguets'"] (41). The second shows how important it is not to lie. "The woman does not take long to realize her blunder and is quiet thinking about the saying, 'Lies walk on a short leash!'" ["Celle-ci ne tarde d'ailleurs pas à se rendre compte de sa maladresse et se tait en pensant au dicton: 'Que la laisse du mensonge est courte!'"] (106). All of the proverbs depicted here as being translated from Arabic clearly are meant to underline village wisdom and reinforce the quaint, traditional setting of the work. Though such a village would certainly not have camels, for example, the reference to the camel's hump gives an exotic flavor to the French language of the text. These didactic sayings together with those directly related to the clergy sum up the worldview Kher is claiming for Hadchit and its residents.

This technique is similar to, though distinct from, the use of idiomatic French expressions in place of a range of other polite, formulaic Arabic expressions, especially those invoking the name of God and the Virgin Mary, that are plentiful in the text as well. I will not dwell on these in any detail because they function in much the same way—they underline certain ideas and interfere with the "purity" of the French-language narration, providing "local color" and activating ideas about the East meant to be present in the French reader's mind. What is more interesting here is how against this background, Arabic is inscribed in the text in other ways that complement this strategy. This includes Arabic words marked and explained through the use of bold typeface, quotation marks, and footnotes.

The Sunday Taboulée: Marking Ethnography

The way in which Salma reflects on her friend's marriage and future life as a priest's wife is presented to help the novel establish its "ethnographic pact" with the reader from its very opening. It therefore begins by unambiguously conforming to the generic specifications of an ethnographic novel. The events are reported as a description of locals, which both demonstrates an intimate knowledge but also a certain distance. It is particularly relevant here once again to underline how the focus of this novel, like so much "ethnographically oriented" fiction by Lebanese and non-Lebanese authors alike, is on peasants, emphasizing the importance of religion and religious/confessional differences between communities. The Lebanon described in ethnographic fiction is rarely that of the elite or upper classes, the communities in which most Lebanese novelists live and work, but rather is almost always centered on rural folk.

That Kher's novel functions in this way very much makes *Salma et son village* a novel of her times. More so than the later novels discussed in the chapters that follow, it openly and unabashedly presents an exotic Lebanese mountain community to what is presumably a French audience, with the authority of an "insider" but the French language of an "outsider."

Kher records the daily life of this community through the story of Salma, her family, and friends, using a village of only one hundred homes where everyone is more or less related, as a model for the way of life of this region of Lebanon (8).

Descriptions of family relationships and naming are the first local mountain customs explored in detail in this portrait; for example, "Youssefia Tannous is a third cousin of the mother of the young woman, who affectionately and deferentially calls her aunt" [Youssefia Tannous est cousine au troisième degré de la mère de la jeune fille, qui l'appelle tante par affectueuse déférence] (8). It includes numerous everyday concerns: the clothes people wear (60, 71), the food they eat and how they prepare it (68, 81,125), how Salma carries water from the well to her home (7), and so on. More general issues are also described in similar ways, for example religious laws (6), church ceremonies (60), wedding customs (68–76) local saint's cults (45, 135), and people's different opinions about husbands beating their wives (50). The importance of these explanations is reinforced through how the Arabic language is inscribed in the text.

Arabic is invoked in many explanations, in a number of different ways. Like the example above in which an expression is "translated" into French, using footnotes to explain Arabic words also lends Kher a certain authority. Ten footnotes are used over the course of the novel.[9] This is certainly not an excessive number in a text over 250 pages long and it means, on average, that there is one footnote only every twenty-five pages or so. These footnotes, however, do serve both a didactic purpose and to underline the alterity of words marked as Arabic in a French-language novel, in a very different way to the "translated" proverbs and sayings.

One example occurs in a dialogue in the third chapter of the book that begins with the word, "Tfadal," footnoted with the translation "prenez place" [come in] (23). The common Arabic expression "tfadal" once again adds local color to the text and makes it seem more exotic. It is not a word

9. The words footnoted followed by their page number are: khouriée 14, tfadal 23, le dar 34, la sayédée 45, le cherwal 71, tombac 81, la souple habrige 89, il propose de dabker 93, mézés 135, ya benti . . . i . . . ! 166.

familiar to a French reader or one that could be deduced from context except in the most general sense. Moreover, the word "tfadal" is extremely flexible in Arabic and can mean many different things, depending on its context (for example: come in, come here, come over, sit down, go ahead, please take this, and so on). The use of the footnote strongly asserts Kher's insider knowledge of the Arabic language as well as the culture of this village. By using the scholarly apparatus not normally associated with a novel but with academic work, she also draws on the "scientific" discourse of ethnography as the study of culture and people. The footnotes show that there is additional information that must be presented, alongside a narrative "fiction," in order to make sense of the work. They also reinforce that this novel and author have the expertise to do so.

Similarly to footnotes, Kher also makes use of bold typeface to mark the difference of certain words within her text, using this strategy to highlight seven different words eleven times.[10] Words referring to food and drink—taboulée (8, 12, 15), arak (33), and mézés (33)—are particularly frequently represented in bold typeface, as "mézés" was also with use of a footnote above in a different location (135).[11] Further, one footnoted word, "tfadal," also appears in bold type. This striking typeface symbolically represents the difference of words marked as Arabic from the French narration. Like using footnotes, this sets the words apart and shows that they are in need of explanation or at least attention. This polyglossic technique has the effect of presenting Arabic words within the text as different and Other, reinforcing the Otherness of the textual material and providing Kher with another way in which to bolster her ethnographic observations and explanations.

10. The words marked in bold followed by the page numbers are: taboulée 8, 12, 15; norag 19, 23 twice, 27; tfadal 23 twice; arak 33 twice; mézés 33 twice; ouadi 37; palace 48. The use of bold therefore stops less than a third of the way through the text, whereas footnotes are employed right up until almost the end.

11. This is a particularly interesting example because it is explained through cushioning and context earlier in the text several times and not marked at all, but then quite late in the text (135) it is footnoted and explained as an "hors-d'oeuvre qui se servent avec l'apéritif" [hors-d'oeuvre served with an aperitif].

Like the "translated" Arabic sayings and proverbs, these strategies for incorporating Arabic words within the French narration are straightforward and reinforce the work's generic identification as an ethnographic novel. They do not significantly disrupt the text's "Frenchness" and indeed reinforce that Arabic is somehow a different language that intrudes onto the main language of narration. Using footnotes, moreover, highlights this ethnographic work's didactic stance. They show that it is not merely a love story with a focus on one young woman, Salma, thereby claiming a certain authority to explain this region, and its peculiarities, "scientifically." The bold typeface does not activate exactly the same discourse but does reinforce it by showing that certain words, even if they are just the names of food, are different, exotic, and need to be explained. In other words, the textual effect of discussing the "Sunday ***taboulée***" ("la **taboulée** du dimanche," 8, 11, 12), rather than the "Sunday taboulée," is to set apart this dish as something exotic needing explanation, which it gets after its fourth mention: "the tasty ***taboulée*** salad with lemon, where wheat, peppers, tomatoes, and onions mix together, livened up by parsley and mint" ["la ***taboulée*** savoureuse salade au citron où fraternisent blé, poivrons, tomates et oignons relevés de persil et de menthe"] (12–13). The frequent mention of taboulée specifically in the very opening pages of the novel is notable not only for the strategy used to introduce it but also in that this most iconic of Lebanese "emblem foods" is so highlighted.[12] Taboulée here is shown to be not only important, but specifically linked to the Christian customs of this village: in Kher's Hadchit, families rotate the honor of preparing this dish to be served to the priest's family on Sundays.

Ethnographic descriptions, such as the references to taboulée or other foods, customs, and traditions are the ideal vehicle to use the interanimation of languages, much as Bakhtin shows in relation to national projects in the novel. In these cases, languages are displayed as "objects" or specimens, metonymically representing a larger language system and by extension culture and even sets of ideas. This seemingly transparent

12. I have drawn on the notion of "emblem foods" as representing ethnic identity and belonging from Leonard and Saliba (1998, 171–80).

technique of integrating Arabic within a French-language text is a more subtle use of polyglossia than a more direct challenge to colonial language, as in many of the examples of language mixing presented by Ashcroft, Griffith, and Tiffin in *The Empire Writes Back* or the indigenization techniques highlighted by Zabus in *The African Palimpsest*. Most examples of the use of Arabic within Amy Kher's text conform to the rules of standard French, and the challenges that they do pose to it carefully invoke a number of Arabic words and expressions in the guise of "ethnographic" explanations.

One way to understand this is to see the novel as a product of its time and the cultural issues and debates that were circulating at its date of publication. Lebanon was still under French mandate control in 1933 when *Salma et son village* appeared and it was only just beginning to forge a path toward independence. Thus the representation of the local customs and traditions as charming, the quaintness of the northern villages, and the emphasis on the peasants' Christian values all resonate strongly within a discourse at the time that proposed Christian Lebanese as model recipients of France's "civilizing mission."[13] A journalist and active participant in the cultural and social life of the expatriate Lebanese community who had lived for a long time in Egypt, Kher is a paradigmatic example of the generation of women who begin to write about social issues with literary works in both Arabic and French and navigate the kinds of changes occurring in this period.

On the surface, *Salma et son village* depicts Hadchit as an idyllic repository for French and Christian values, albeit one that is colorfully exotic. Its people are hardworking peasants and its lifestyle is untouched by the modern era. It can therefore successfully tap into the kinds of discourses of nation building—particularly those promoted by the Christian

13. One place to see this discourse at work is the poetry and essays of the Phoenician school gathered around Charles Corm, the publisher of its journal *La revue Phénicien*. Najjar identifies four main members of this group—Corm, Michel Chiha, Elie Tyan, and Héctor Klat—as important in formulating ideas about Phoenician Lebanon conforming to certain "universal" values, in tune with this "mission" (Najjar 1993, 25–29). On Phoenicianism, see also Kaufman 2004.

elites who were vying for power in the era. The explicitly ethnographic elements of the novel underline the differences between villagers and the reader, seemingly placing them at opposite ends of a certain spectrum of colonial relations and power. At the same time, these very details allow Kher to inscribe more creatively challenging uses of the Arabic language within this French-language novel. Kher adds to these more transparent techniques, "translating" proverbs and sayings, using footnotes and bold typeface, more subtle linguistic interference that negotiates the complexities of how gender, class, and religion combine to prevent Salma from surviving in the traditional village atmosphere of Hadchit.

Family Sons and Daughters: the Subtle Inscription of Status through Relexification

Just as this idyllic village life is more complex than it seems at first glance, so too is the language of the text. Language is not only used as an object of representation in *Salma et son village,* but Kher also exploits her ambiguous insider-outsider position to make Arabic press up against the standard French of her narration in creative ways, thereby also disrupting the text's outward acceptance of France and French colonial discourse. Kher writes about Hadchit as an insider, a Lebanese woman who knows Maronite Christian village customs and rituals intimately, but also as an accomplished writer of the French language who can produce a novel that is also a polished, "scientific" book about its customs. Moreover, she exploits her ambiguous position to inscribe textual messages about the confluence of religion, community, gender, and class.

Like so many insider-outsider authors, Kher is positioned not only as linguistically distant from the characters in her novel, but also distant in class/status and rural/urban terms. Though her father's family background is linked to the northern mountain region of Lebanon, Kher herself spent most of her life as an expatriate in Cairo. It is her mastery of French and ability to manipulate the language of the text in more creative ways than simply using footnotes and bold text, together with the ambiguity of her insider status, that allow Kher to inscribe such complexity within her novel. Kher's use of language in the novel should also be read in this double context, revealing additional layers of messages to her insider, outsider, and insider-outsider audiences.

The protagonist Salma Farès is the character around whom the novel is organized and through whom the most crucial linguistic experimentations are enacted. A peasant, Salma is poor and must toil in the fields, working the land alongside her aging parents. Eye-catchingly beautiful, Salma is glimpsed in the fields by the meaningfully named Jamil (good-looking/handsome) Francis and they fall in love. As the elite son of local landowners, Jamil has lived and studied in the city, unlike Salma, who is permanently rooted to the land as a peasant laborer. Contrasting in almost every way—their manners, clothes, the spaces that they move in—they are both earnest in their brief flirtation. But Jamil's family background is considerably more prominent than Salma's and everyone around them knows that their union is fated to end badly. All of Salma's travails throughout the rest of novel after meeting Jamil—her illnesses, her failing crops, her engagement, and eventual marriage to the less-appealing Anis—are set against the background of the somewhat innocent and chaste flirtatious meetings that she and Jamil share in the fields in early chapters of the novel.

We learn quickly that despite Salma's dreams, her family and community will put an end to this story. This is pronounced in no uncertain terms to Salma by her father, Chafik, who expressly articulates that Jamil is an inappropriate choice of partner because he is a "fils de famille" [son of a family]. He asks her poignantly, "Listen to me, my child. Suppose that this son of a family comes and asks for your hand in marriage, would you turn him down, huh? . . . that's right! neither would I!" [Écoute-moi, mon enfant. Suppose que ce fils de famille vienne demander ta main, refuserais tu, hein? . . . Eh bien! moi non plus!] (56). Though it is clear from the context that the expression "fils de famille," or son of a family, must mean that he is from an important family, as opposed to Salma, who is not, it is not a familiar or idiomatic expression in standard French.[14] In everyday

14. This is one of the most commonly relexified expressions in Lebanese French-language fiction. I include a discussion of it in chapter 4 in relation to Andrée Chedid's

Arabic, by contrast, the expression "ibn 'aylee" ("ibn 'a'ila" in standard Arabic) is an immediately recognizable, common expression, used to invoke a person's background, particularly class and status background, as it is linked to their membership in a family.

To translate this Arabic expression directly into a "strange sounding" French is a form of relexification, a powerful technique to inscribe one language within another. Relexification is the use of unidiomatic language to render an idea from one language into another, letting its "oddness" in the text, rather than any other external markings, make it stand out. In this context, it is important to note that this use of an Arabic expression is not footnoted or marked, in contrast to most others in this work that consciously draw attention to themselves in this way. It is understood from the context. On the one hand, therefore, it maintains the main language of the narration, French, and the text flows along in this language without any major disruption. On the other hand, however, because the resulting expression is often not idiomatic, it also jars the reader's ear, underlining the importance of this textual moment. In interfering with the main language of narration, I argue, a relexified expression then underlines and highlights the idea encoded within it.

Kher's use of the strategy of relexification in this case is all the more interesting because of her insistence throughout the novel on working with Arabic words by translating them or placing them in bold typeface. While translation and footnoting also highlight the foreignness of certain words within a text, relexification is a subtler poetic strategy. It allows the text to maintain its linguistic flow without calling undue attention to the new expression. Moreover, as a reader you naturalize the expression and continue reading, while pondering what it may mean. It also demands

---

Le sommeil délivré (1952), which identifies the protagonist Samya as a "fille de famille." It also recurs in Dominique Eddé's *Cerf-Volant* (2003), discussed in chapter 12. Though this expression is not unknown in standard French and dates back to the era of Molière, in this context it gives the text an antiquated feeling. Within the anticolonial framework of this book, I am here emphasizing in particular the Arabic expression that is being represented rather than focusing on readings within the French language.

that the reader work out the meaning of an unidiomatic phrase and rely on contextual clues and the cushioning offered in order to understand it. The effect of a relexification as opposed to a translated expression with a footnote therefore is less didactic and more challenging to the reader.

The use of the phrase "fils de famille" in this case is particularly crucial to the novel because the notion encoded within it is central to the construction of not only the plot but also the work's main message—there is an unbridgeable gap between a young man who is the scion of an elite landowning family and a young woman who is the daughter of the peasants who work his land. But the text does not spell this out explicitly for readers who do not know Arabic: they must work with the context provided to understand it. For example, the father's skepticism about the young man's intentions and Salma's impotence to act when faced with his power does make it clear that the expression must refer to status. Salma's father lets us know that not only is Jamil a "fils de famille" but also that Salma is not a "fille de famille," and that this is an essential difference between them. As the direct translation indicates, your social status is determined by the family into which you are born. It cannot be overcome; it cannot be changed or altered.

Therefore, by using the expression "fils de famille," *Salma et son village* accents the importance of class and status divisions within this society. The relexified expression both underlines these ideas and also naturalizes them. Just as the expression stands out and fits in at the same time, the work demonstrates how class and status distinctions are devastating in this case, but also that they form an unquestioned part of the everyday life of the villagers. In this way, the poetic strategies of *Salma et son village* inscribe its political messages on more than one level. It is not only by highlighting class and status differences by using an expression marked as Arabic to inscribe them that makes this language mixing technique so effective. The lack of textual attention given to this relexifed phrase—it is not indicated formally in the text in any way—naturalizes it further within the flow of the French language narration. This is itself a message about how divides in status linked to birth and family position organize the lives of people in the village. The entire novel in many ways is overcoded by both of these ideas. There is no way to narrow the class-status chasm between these two social groups. We know that when Salma Farès dies of a broken heart, it is because she is not a "daughter of a family" [fille de famille] and cannot match the status of Jamil who is, after all, a "son of a family" [fils de famille].

The Subtle Challenges of "Salma" and "Jamil"

Relexification of Arabic expressions is not the only subtle, "naturalizing" linguistic technique that Kher uses in *Salma et son village* to both complement and contrast with the footnoted and boldface Arabic words throughout the novel. The way in which names and titles operate within this work is another level on which to read the inscription of Arabic meaning within the French-language text. In some cases, the use of Arabic titles to refer to certain social positions can be seen as a way of further marking difference. For example, the local priest in this novel is referred to in the abstract both as the "curé" and also as the "Khouri." The priest's wife is always referred to as the "Khouriée" (the feminine form of Khouri).[15] This can be understood as a way of providing both ethnographic detail, the reader learns that Khouri means priest in Arabic, and also "local spice"—referring to a priest as a Khouri makes him sound much more exotic than does "curé." The fact that a Maronite priest can have a wife at all, let alone one named a Khouriée, is itself an exotic difference within the Catholic Church.

In addition to titles, a further way in which the Arabic language is embedded even more subtly within the French text is the meanings of the names of the young lovers. In this case, the meaning cannot be deduced in the same way that it is for the Khouri and Khouriée. Though using Arabic names certainly also gives the work a local flavor, it is not a transparent strategy for the reader who only knows French, nor is it meant to be. Because Kher does not provide any information about these names, any

15. It is interesting that "khouriée" (priest's wife) is the first footnoted word in the novel (14) and that the word "khouri" is never directly footnoted or translated at all; it must be understood—which it is readily—from the context. This of course could be because of the role of the "priest's wife" within Catholicism being unique to the Maronite Catholic Church, as discussed above.

meaning derived from them can be only be deduced from the reader who knows Arabic. I propose that this is one way in which we can understand how Kher's text can be read as having a double audience and plays on the ambiguities of the insider-outsider positions of her readers as well as herself as author-narrator.

The dashing young man Jamil's physical attributes are encoded within his name, which means beautiful or handsome. His surname, Francis, is a word not of Arabic origin, which underlines both his Christian identity and also his status position and "foreignness" among the peasants. In contrast, Salma's last name, Farès, is a common Arabic word meaning "horseman," underscoring her family as proud people of noble character despite their lowly social position. Salma's first name also contrasts with Jamil's, as it means complete, whole, or sound. Rather than comment on her beauty by giving her a feminine version of his name like Jamila or Bahiyya or Qamar, Kher emphasizes this young woman's character over her looks. Moreover, the name Salma implies that she does not need her relationship with Jamil to make her whole; she is not lacking something, society simply is unable to sanction this transgressive relationship. That the two names share surface similarities but conjure up such different connotations when analyzed highlights the paradox of their love—they have certain things in common that make them love each other but there is an unbridgeable gap between them. This deeper level of meaning encoded by language, however, is reserved only for the "insider" reader who knows Arabic. Kher does not translate or allude to these meanings and simply presents these as the characters' names.

These naming techniques can be read alongside relexification as the more subtle ways in which Arabic is inscribed within the French text, going beyond simply providing local spice or color. As the French reader would not be aware of the additional meanings that these interlinguistic moments layer into the novel, they can on some level be read as addressing a Lebanese or Arabic-speaking reader. This is not to exaggerate the role that these moments play within the text or to suggest that the experimentation with Arabic is deeper than it is. However, Kher's novel also should not be merely seen as a "French text" that directly participates in a colonial discourse around peasants in Lebanese villages, solely aimed at an "outsider" French audience that does not know Arabic.

Conclusions

Amy Kher's *Salma et son village* is a novel, often deemed ethnographic, that creates its textual language through inscribing words and expressions marked as Arabic within its French-language narration by using a variety of explicit and subtle strategies. The layers of meaning invoked by these multiple and varied uses of language reveal that an ethnographic novel by a Lebanese author writing in French need not simply be read merely as exposing Lebanon to a European gaze. As I suggest, the position of the author, as well as the reader, is more complex than a simple dichotomy between insider and outsider. The audience for this 1933 novel on one level may well indeed have been located in metropolitan France and would find its depiction of Christian village customs and traditions exotic, charming, and compelling. But as the examples above indicate, the language of this novel also speaks to a Lebanese audience, which does know at least some Arabic. This audience is perhaps equally distanced from such customs and traditions—by urban life in Beirut or simply the changing times. It aims not only for the preservation of positive local customs, traditions, and mores, but also to convey a certain critical message about how these intersect with class and gender, particularly some of the disastrous effects of a rigid social structure.

Reading *Salma et son village* as a novel of its time and place, 1930s Lebanon, brings these issues into sharp relief. The period of the French mandate saw fierce wrangling over the shape of the new Lebanon that would emerge after independence. Many social changes were being undertaken and codified. On the agenda were both a desire to preserve some elements of traditional society and also a push to improve others—such as the role of women. The growing importance of Beirut as a center, particularly among the Christian Francophone elite, might have compelled an author like Kher to record some of the village customs and traditions for posterity. Moreover, the class/status and gender critique is rooted in a notion of individualism and the right of people, especially women, to break free of many social conditions hampering their individual freedom. All of these issues clearly echo the tenants of romanticism, the major literary movement sweeping the Arab world at the time.

When read within these social and literary contexts, Kher's novel can be seen as complementing the kinds of critiques an author like Khalil Jibran made in his Arabic works. Kher stops short of an attack on the church or clergy, which in Khalil Jibran's case led to a great deal of controversy and his condemnation by the Maronite Catholic Church in Lebanon, even though he was based at the time in the United States.[16] Kher does, however, call into question the alleged Christian solidarity shared by members of a community that should theoretically stand by one another. The tragic end of the novel with Salma's untimely death from a fever seriously undermines this solidarity. In a truly Christian society, the novel implies, these divisions would not be so stark and surely would not lead to a good, pious, young woman's death.

In a world literature framework it is thus interesting to read the language created in *Salma et son village*, together with its messages, as a creative intervention into the field of French ethnographic novels at a time when this genre is expanding and circulating between Europe and the Middle East and back again. Using scientific notations—footnotes and bold typeface to explain words, phrases, customs, and traditions—enhances this effect. At the same time, however, it also challenges some of the ideas underpinning the ethnographic project from within the text itself, both poetically and politically. Kher here plays with her role as an insider and an outsider within the text by manipulating language and form. She establishes an ethnographic pact with her readers, sharing a French-language inflected complicity with them, which allows her to assert authority over the text and establish herself as an "expert." Through this, then, Kher is able to challenge some of the kinds of ideas inscribed within such texts

16. On accounts of the apocryphal nature of Jibran's excommunication, see Waterfield (1998, 70) and Bushrui and Jenkins (1998, 15, 88). See also more recent work on Jibran by Hallaq (2008).

in a colonial setting. By using more subtle formal strategies of polyglossia, like relexification and not translating meaning-filled Arabic names, Kher highlights and naturalizes some elements of the words representing Arabic within the flow of French. This parallels the messages that these words encode.

All of these techniques work together to give the novel an exotic flair. In so doing, however, the work then also shows itself to be aimed at a readership of both outsiders and insiders. The very exoticism of the text—to French readers, urban readers, and high-status readers—itself is a commentary on the ethnographic novel. The overlap and intersection of these poetic and political techniques of language mixing convey a strong message about the problematic class hierarchies and gendered constraints faced by peasants in a northern mountain village in Lebanon. The multiple readerships and audiences underline the issue of travel and the potential for circulation of such a text. Because of the ambiguities of the author and her audience, therefore, this is not only conveyed to France and a French-reading audience, but also to a Lebanese elite that is in the process of developing how an independent Lebanon will take shape with the end of the mandate.

3

"May You Bury Me"

Dying for Honor in Sous la baguette du coudrier

Also set in a verdant Christian Lebanese mountain village and recounting a dramatic tale of ill-fated love, Eveline Bustros's *Sous la baguette du coudrier* [Under the divining rod] echoes many features of Amy Kher's *Salma et son village*.[1] On the surface, it too is a straightforwardly ethnographic portrayal of the lives of the villagers, this time set in the Mount Lebanon town of Rachmaya, but in an earlier period, just after the time of the *safarbarlak*—forced conscriptions into the Ottoman army—of the First World War (1916) and the famine that claimed the lives of so many people from this region.[2] Reflecting its setting, this novel's plot is also more dramatic than *Salma et son village*'s. The lovers are not mismatched simply

1. Bustros's collected works, *Romans et écrits divers* (1988, 153–337), were published as the fourth volume in Dar an-Nahar's "Patrimoine" series, supported by the Nadia Tuéni foundation. These publications have made a number of out-of-print works by Francophone writers available and the series is still active.

2. The cultural production of Lebanese history, particularly the period around the famine, is rich. For well-known examples, see Tawfiq Yusuf 'Awwad's best-known novel *Al-Raghif* (1939); the Rahbani film written by Mansur Rahbani, directed by Henri Barakat, starring Fayruz, *Safarbarlak* (1967); the first volume of Rabi' Jabir's *Bayrut Madinat al-'alam* (2006); and the French-language author Alexandre Najjar's recent *Roman de Beyrouth* (2005), though these two latter works take on a wider spread of history. Works written closer to the period and Bustros's time include Charles Corm's *Les miracles de la Madonne aux sept douleurs* (1948) and Georges Corm's short poetic collection *Chez les humbles* (1915). For a discussion of Lebanese literature's engagement with history and politics, see Elise Salem's *Constructing Lebanon: A Century of Literary Narratives* (2003);

because of their divergent social status. The tale's protagonist, Anissa, is a married woman with children who carries on an illicit extramarital affair with a much younger man, her eldest son's best friend. Such a grave social transgression cannot be tolerated in the conservative mountain village of Rachmaya. The novel thus ends tragically for Anissa: her brother avenges the family honor by murdering her in her sleep. The story unfolds within a narrative that pays close attention to the village customs of the period in which it is set. Historical events are woven into the plot of the narration together with similar kinds of ethnographic details about mountain life that Kher's work provides, including the preparation of food, attendance at church and local festivals, social relations between villagers, and so on. Like *Salma et son village, Sous la baguette du coudrier* can be read as an intervention into a number of debates circulating at the time it was written in the 1940s and also the time it was eventually published in the 1950s. Indeed, this novel depicts some of the historical events leading up to the mandate directly and addresses French intervention in the region more explicitly than Kher's novel does. Anissa's love affair and eventual murder are the centrepieces of the plot, however, and the work is a psychological portrait of an unhappy and unsatisfied woman.

Both the way in which Bustros's novel recounts the killing of a woman for family honor and how this is connected to the ethnographic details of the plot are very much products of their time. This is true in a literal sense, as we know that Bustros claimed to have written the novel partly in response to a similar killing that took place in Lebanon in 1921 that was vibrantly reported in the local press, capturing the imagination of people in Beirut (Bustros 1988, 153–54). In addition, however, I propose that this novel, written in the 1940s and not published until 1958, also responds to the specificities of those time periods in the way it negotiates issues of class, gender, and identity through its use of the representation of Arabic within its French-language narration. Like *Salma et son village, Sous la baguette du coudrier* was written in the context of a Lebanon shaping itself

---

and for Fayruz and on Lebanese cultural production, see Christopher Stone's *Popular Culture and Nationalism in Lebanon: The Fairouz and Rahbani Nation* (2007).

under the mandate and preparing for independence. Bustros herself was an active participant in the community of people who were working with the French to achieve the realization of the new nation of Lebanon that was formed in 1943. Her father's family, the Tuénis, her mother's family, the Sursocks, and her husband's, the Bustros', were all part of the educated, Orthodox Christian elite—many of them French speaking—that had an important role not only politically and socially but also literarily in the Lebanon of this period.[3] The milieu in which Eveline Bustros moved, therefore, was one in which many of the decisions about the shape of the nascent Lebanese state were made and in which the major political, cultural, and social issues were discussed and debated.[4]

Too Many "Local" Arabic Words?

If the language of Amy Kher's *Salma et son village* maintains its adherence to standard French at least partly because this was expected by an author writing at the time of the French mandate for a supposedly French reading audience, Bustros's *Sous la baguette du coudrier* should be no different. Though it was published fifteen years after Lebanese independence, it was written during the independence period in the 1940s and in a milieu in which straying from standard, literary French was not uncontroversial. Even a French-language novel with an explicitly

3. The Tuéni family, to this day, controls some of the most important publishing venues in Lebanon, owning the prestigious Dar al-Nahar publishing house and *Al-Nahar* newspaper. Until his death in 2012, Ghassan Tuéni ran both and was one of the most influential figures in this scene throughout the second half of the twentieth century and into the twenty-first. His late wife Nadia Tuéni was a celebrated Lebanese French-language poet at the time of her premature death in 1983. Tuéni's son Gebran—named for his influential grandfather—was one of the prominent political figures assassinated in the period after Rafiq al-Hariri's death in 2005.

4. Bustros was one of the few prominent women actively taking part in these circles. For example, she is one of the few women to participate actively in the "Cénacle libanais" (1946–1962) and even presented a lecture there (in 1956). See the bilingual (Arabic and French) summaries published by the Cénacle as *Les conferences du Cénacle/Muhadarat al-nadwa al-lubnaniyah* (1947–1962).

ethnographic orientation was expected to conform to certain standards of "purity" of the French language. As a recently published letter to Bustros from her friend and mentor, Michel Chiha, reveals, she was well aware that he disapproved of her using too many "local" Arabic words within her novel, particularly when included without translations. Within his generally complimentary letter about the novel—in which he suggests that she submit it for consideration to the Prix Rivarol in 1950—he makes five suggestions for improvement, "in the spirit of literary criticism." His fourth suggestion is crucial here: "There are too many Arabic words, local words, untranslated. You should give their meanings, for example 'sebbeir,' 'hassiré,' etc. . . ." ["Il y a trop de mots arabes, de mots du terroir, non traduits. Il faudrait donner les sens, par exemple: 'sebbeir,' 'hassiré,' etc. . . ."] (Bustros 1988, lviii).[5] We do not know to what extent Bustros heeded this advice. We do know, however, that she did not submit the book for consideration for the prize and indeed delayed its publication for almost a decade and four years after Michel Chiha's death. When it was published in 1958, *Sous la baguette du coudrier* included a poignant dedication to him, "In homage to Michel Chiha" [À Michel Chiha, en hommage] (Bustros 1988, 152).

It is unclear whether or not the published text as we have it today reflects changes Bustros made based on Chiha's criticisms or if she simply chose to ignore them and published the book as it was originally written with the same number of untranslated "local Arabic words." It is clear, however, that she uses a variety of techniques to incorporate a substantial amount of language identifiable as Arabic within the French-language narration; Arabic words and expressions generously pepper the French text. For the most part, the techniques she uses are similar to those that we saw in *Salma et son village*. She transliterates the names of the months of the year that are commonly used in Arabic in Lebanon, Syria, Palestine, and elsewhere, for example, Tammouz [July] (244), Nissan and Ayyâr [April and May] (246), and Aïloul and Techrine [September and October]

5. The reproduction of the letter (lvii–lviii) appears within Jad Hatem's reflections on Bustros's writing (Bustros 1988, liii–lxv).

(304). She also discusses wedding preparations (200), and food preparation (169, 310, among others).

Some of these more directly "ethnographic" details include an obvious translation and/or explanation of the words; others do not. Bustros does not use bold typeface like Kher, but she does make use of footnotes throughout the text. There are a total of thirteen footnotes (160, 250, 251, 264, 265, 267, 283 twice, 284, 290, 297, 300, 314), slightly more than half of which explain Arabic words with a translation into French (250, 251, 264, 265, 267, 283, 284, 290).[6] The others add details about elements of the plot or historical context, giving information to place the story in its own era (160, 267, 265, 297, 300, 314).[7] The second group indicates that it is perhaps addressed not so much only to outsiders by a Lebanese insider in order to explain the place, but rather to a modern audience in order to give information about the Lebanon of the past. Footnotes in this case, then, function similarly to how they do in Kher's novel: they provide different kinds of information to different audiences, asserting a certain "scientific" expertise. In Bustros's text the notes appear somewhat haphazard, leaving open the possibility that they may have been added to the text later. Footnote 6, for example, translates the Arabic word "Abi" as "père" [father], though this word, also in its more common form as an appellation "Abou," appears frequently throughout the hundred or so pages preceding this note (267). Moreover, the word "mother," Emmé, appears consistently throughout the narration and is never translated, the reader simply understands what it means from the context.[8]

6. Interestingly, of the two notes on 283, one provides a footnote "in the reverse," telling the reader that the "le confit de mouton" referred to in the main text is "aourma" (included in quotation marks in the note). This shows that what is being explained and why is not simply a matter of an "insider" revealing an exotic Lebanon to a French "outsider" audience.

7. For example, footnote 13 explains that certain coastal towns were not in this period a part of Lebanon but still belonged to Syria (334).

8. This could perhaps be interpreted meaningfully, as in the case of the noting of Khouriée vs. Khouri in *Salma et son village*. It begs the question, then: Why would Bustros wait for one hundred pages to explain it when the word appears so frequently? I

Leaving Arabic words, like Emmé, to be understood from the context, without footnotes or explicit explanations and simply folded into the text with no special markings, is indeed Bustros's favored strategy of polyglossia, referring to Arabic. Another example recalls Kher's use of the salad often used as an emblematic Lebanese food, taboulée, which she replaces with another iconic food from the region kebbé (169, 310). In a parallel to the role of taboulée in Salma's Hadchit as a "Sunday food," Anissa prepares this food in Rachmaya also on the holy day and it is referred to as "their Sunday kebbé" [leur kebbé du dimanche] (169).

Another strategy that Bustros employs similarly to Kher is Arabic names that are meaning filled. In *Sous la baguette du coudrier* this is perhaps even more relevant, as all of the main characters have names that somehow comment on their character, behaviors, or actions. For example, Adib—the given name of Anissa's husband—means "well mannered," which is certainly true of him. It is emphasized that Anissa's dissatisfaction with her life and marriage has nothing to do with this kindly man, but that the cause of the breakdown in their relationship is simply the age difference between them. Anissa's name itself means "friendly" and also "tame." Through the narration we learn that though on the surface she seems to be both, there is a desire and passion lurking within Anissa that will cause her to be anything but tame. The name of their eldest son, Nehmé, is also laden with meaning. It refers to having a life of ease or luxury, which is certainly the opposite of his life or that of any of the characters in the book. But embedded within the root of this word is also the notion of softness and gentleness, which can be read as an ironic commentary on his inability to commit matricide, despite his deep anger and resentment toward his mother and belief that this is the right action to take. Like *Salma et son*

do not wish to spend too much time speculating on these issues and I did not speculate about Kher's text at all, preferring to analyze the text as it exists today. I make the exception in the case of Bustros partly because there is a good fifteen years of delay from the writing to the publication of the text and also because we know that there was external pressure upon Bustros from at least one source she greatly respected (Michel Chiha) to make such changes.

village, then, *Sous la baguette du coudrier* must be understood as using Arabic in different ways to support both its creative vision and its message, addressing several likely audiences simultaneously.[9]

Even more important, Bustros uses a number of transliterated Arabic words that represent concepts difficult to translate outside of their contexts, providing either translations of the word and concept within the text or enough "cushioning" to make sense of them. Two rather important words in this regard are "tawah," which she translates directly as "vengeur" [avenger] within the text, and "abaday," for which she provides no translation at all (it means something like "local strong man"). These two words become central to the plot of this novel that details local customs and traditions around keeping order in "unofficial" ways in a time when the Lebanese countryside was emerging from the famine it suffered under Ottoman rule and coming to terms with the new laws and ideas being imposed by the French mandate. The gender politics of the novel are wrapped up in how men must conform somehow to the role of tawah or abaday to keep order and control women, at the same time as the female protagonist of the novel is suffering from this oppressive system.

The many, direct uses of Arabic words and expressions bolster Bustros's depiction of the mountain village of Rachmaya, like Kher's Hadchit, as exotic and for the most part as charming. Indeed Bustros uses many more such phrases than Kher does. As Chiha complains in his letter to her, she also many times does leave them unexplained or only minimally cushioned. By including these Arabic words in her novel, moreover, Bustros is open to the same criticisms as Amy Kher and many other writers who "mix local languages" into their texts written in colonial languages. Typically, the critique is that mixing languages merely adds local color to the text, spicing it up for the intrusive gaze of the outsider audience who will then interpret the text's "natives" as exotic and essentially somehow

9. It is also relevant that Kher's original text was published in Paris (though the re-edition appeared in Lebanon), whereas both of Bustros's editions were published in Beirut. This need not be the sole determinant of audience—certainly many Lebanese people read novels published in France and the same is true in the reverse, though to a lesser extent—but it does indicate something about possibly intended audiences and readerships.

Other. As the examples of tawah and abaday suggest, in the case of Bustros's novel, Lebanon can easily be cast as not only exotic but also hopelessly violent.

Indeed, despite the variety of techniques that Bustros uses to incorporate Arabic words, expressions, and ideas into her novel, Chiha is not the only critic who is skeptical about the use of Arabic within *Sous la baguette du coudrier*. A more recent commentary by the critic Katia Haddad echoes Chiha's concern, with a slightly different focus. Stating that she is unsure of the effect of the Arabic words in *Sous la baguette du coudrier*, Haddad affirms that she is nonetheless certain of their goal, "These borrowings from the Arabic undoubtedly, as in the case of Corm, have the goal of adding 'local color.' Their effect is debatable" ["Ces emprunts à l'arabe ont sans doute pour objectif, comme chez Corm, de faire 'couleur locale.' Leur effet est discutable"] (Haddad 2000, 58).[10] Haddad thus adopts the familiar position of so many other critics of literatures written in the dominant language of former colonizers, she somewhat disdainfully sniffs at the fact that Bustros uses Arabic "undoubtedly" to give her text "local color."[11]

Haddad's comments are important, however, in how they connect using mixed language to her more serious complaint about *Sous la baguette du coudrier*—that it is not a true portrayal of the Lebanese

10. Haddad criticizes Charles Corm's use of this strategy, claiming that he also uses "exotic words of Arab or onomatopoeic origin (tric trac, arac), but that are familiar to the Francophone Lebanese speaker, thereby by means of poetry helping to valorize the French language of Lebanon" ["mots exotiques d'origine arabe ou onomatopéiques (tric trac, arac) mais familiers au locuteur francophone libanais, contribuant ainsi à valoriser, par le biais de la poésie, le français du Liban"] (Haddad 2000, 40), though in his case they appear in rhymed alexandrines rather than in a novel. As I will argue, I disagree with Haddad's characterization of Bustros's language, which I propose is significantly different from that of Corm or other poets of his school.

11. Such assertions tell of the dismissive attitudes often detected in studies of both women's writing and postcolonial writing, exemplifying the type of double or even triple bind of women writers from the Third World (Trinh 1989). Experimentation with language is seen as "color," not a technique, strategy, or clever creativity, much in the same ways in which women's writing is understood to represent "experience" rather than a complex creation (Trinh 1989; Russ 1983; and Spivak 1993, 77–96).

mountains during the period of the famine. Haddad is concerned not with the fact that Bustros is writing an ethnographic depiction of this region, or that it exoticizes Lebanon, or that it is aimed at an outsider audience, but that it is not "accurate." In her opinion, the novel is ostensibly meant to denounce archaic mountain customs oppressive to women, but instead is rather indulgent of them (Haddad 2000, 57). She also takes Bustros to task for presenting an idealized portrait of the lush green fecundity of the Lebanese mountains that were actually at the time full of cholera and wracked by famine (57).

The next section argues, contra Haddad, that *Sous la baguette du coudrier* does not cultivate an idealized portrait of the Lebanese mountains in a desperate time or downplay serious crimes against women. Bustros's use of Arabic does not simply add color or spice to her text; she subtly deploys a range of different kinds of Arabic expressions to create a language that interferes with the flow of the standard French narration. Through this disruption, she is able to inscribe messages about women, gender, identity, and how their intersections are expressed when individual desires collide with traditional honor codes. Like Kher, Bustros's messages parallel her formal strategy of inscribing them; she does not excoriate the archaic customs that she condemns, but indirectly critiques how they affect women's lives. Her work neither idealizes the Lebanese village nor ignores crimes against women, and instead does the opposite—but in a subtly subversive, rather than confrontational, manner.

Inscribing Subtle Messages: "May You Bury Me"

In many ways the mother-son relationship between its protagonist Anissa and her eldest son, Nehmé, is the focal point of *Sous la baguette du coudrier.*[12] Anissa, who is also frequently referred to as Oum Nehmé (Nehmé's mother) in the book, is excessively attached to him. Aside from this

12. This is even truer when reading the novel as a psychological exploration. For one such reading drawing on psychoanalytic theory, see Jad Hatem, "Réflexions sur les romans d'Éveline Bustros" (Bustros 1988, liii–lxv).

relationship, she feels isolated and alienated in the life she leads in the Lebanese mountain village of Rachmaya. Though her elderly husband Adib, or Abou Nehmé (Nehmé's father), is portrayed as kindly, Anissa is emotionally suffocating in her situation, particularly after her beloved eldest son leaves the village for the city. She fills the void in her life by starting an affair with his attractive best friend, Sami, who is much younger than she is and whom she has known since he was a child. Such an adulterous affair and the seduction of a young man by an older woman, the mother of his friend at that, cannot go unpunished according to the customs of the village. Nehmé then is plagued by the idea that he must murder his mother to avenge the family's honor.

This is the context against which Anissa and Nehmé's relationship develops in the novel and underpins the importance of how Anissa uses the relexification of the familiar, affectionate Arabic expression "taqburni" in relation to her son.[13] In fact, Anissa refers to her favorite child, saying "puisses-tu m'ensevelir" [may you bury me] six separate times in the novel. There are a number of ways in which this expression is important within the context of *Sous la baguette du coudrier,* which I discuss in order below: first, that this is a relexification and how it is translated from Arabic into French; second, the frequency of its repetition and how it is used in different contexts each time; and finally, the way in which these formal, technical aspects engage the meanings of the phrase to encode a layered message.

"Puisses-tu m'ensevelir" is an odd-sounding way to address a child in French. The meaning of the sentiment is of course that a child would outlive the parents, however, this not a commonly or colloquially used term of endearment in French (or English).[14] When read with Arabic in

13. Here, I have transliterated the expression as it sounds when pronounced with the "qaf" of the village accent and "u" rather than "taqbarni." Of course depending on accent and region the "qaf" may not be pronounced, and there is an appropriate variation for the feminine form. It is the Lebanese colloquial expression that is a shorter form of the standard Arabic, "Yasha' Allah an taqbarani."

14. It would sound slightly less awkward in French to say "puisses-tu m'enterrer," though it is neither an expression that one would commonly use with young children nor a term of address. The verb used to say something similar would always be "enterrer," but

mind, however, it is absolutely clear that the expression being relexified is "taqburni," an extremely common Lebanese Arabic affectionate term of address used by parents for their children.[15] The way in which Bustros has chosen to represent this Arabic expression within the French is interesting here as well. She neither uses the literal translation of the formal Arabic expression "Dieu veuille que vous m'enterriez" nor the more idiomatic in French, "puisses-tu m'enterrer." She invokes the colloquial Arabic by representing the informal expression and leaving out the invocation of God, but at the same time chooses the more formal and considerably less common French word "s'ensevelir" to relate the sense of "taqburni."[16] Therefore, though the relexification does not interrupt the flow of French in the way it would if she just wrote "taqburni" in the text as a transliterated but untranslated Arabic word, it still does stand out doubly within the flow of the French narration. First, it is immediately noticeable as an unidiomatic expression (and hence a relexification), and second, it uses an uncommon French verb. This draws additional attention to the important function of multilayered uses of multiple languages in the text.

Further underlining the importance of this unusual relexification's significance is its frequent repetition. The meaning attached to this expression is augmented each time that it is used, building to a climax in its final appearance when it is invoked in relation to the family's honor. Anissa speaks this phrase aloud four times, the first three of which address Nehmé (Bustros 1988, 169, 254, 255), and the fourth, her younger son, Fadel, when she is preparing to die at the end of the story (316). Two of these examples demonstrate particularly well how the phrase is integrated into the text. At one point in the story, Anissa worries why her son Nehmé is so quiet. "Anissa, noting his preoccupied mood, worried, May you bury me my son! What do you suffer from?" ["Anissa, remarquant son air absorbé,

---

this is neither widespread nor common in all parts of France or in other French-speaking countries.

15. For a discussion of this phrase, see Ghada Alshamma' (1986, 107).

16. See the discussion of the same expression in Eddé's *Lettre posthume* (1989) discussed in chapter 8. Eddé uses a relexification of this same Arabic expression in this more standard way.

s'inquiétait: Puisses-tu m'ensevelir mon fils! De quoi souffres-tu?"] (169). In another instance, Anissa notices that Nehmé is about to go out without getting dressed properly: "My son, may you bury me! Cover up, Anissa said" [Fils, puisses-tu m'ensevelir! Couvre-toi, dit Anissa] (255). The difference between these sentences and how the original Arabic phrase would work in the same context is striking here. "Taqburni" is a short, one-word expression that is exclaimed as an affectionate appellation. The expression as it is relexified by Bustros sounds artificial and stilted in comparison, especially when it is used in speech. The cumbersome sentence blocks the flow of the mother's imprecations to her son about keeping warm and questions about why he is so worried. Each of the first four times that this expression is used increases the tension between mother and son and prefigures the final two instances of its use.

Bustros is able to use the last two examples of this expression to layer additional meaning into the text. The penultimate use is when Anissa reflects on the fact that she says this to refer to her eldest child (254) and the final use is when Nehmé himself contemplates how his mother refers to him in this way (262). Anissa's reflections on her own language use come at a point in the novel when its plot is well advanced. The local village people have begun to suspect her affair with Sami and she is compelled to contemplate the consequences of her actions. When Nehmé returns to the village, however, she is so overcome with joy that she pushes these considerations out of her mind. After washing his laundry, Anissa sits to grind the chickpeas that have replaced coffee in their deprived village since the war, but as she uses her mortar and pestle, "Every couple of strokes she stopped, turned her beaming eyes inside, and gazed at Nehmé submerged in sleep, while murmuring: God bless him, may he bury me. Her son's return filled her heart with joy. She forgot everything but him" [Tous les quelques coups elle s'interrompait, tournait ses yeux rayonnants vers l'intérieur, regardait Nehmé plongé dans le sommeil en murmurant: Allah béni, puisse-t-il m'ensevelir! Le retour de son fils comblait son coeur. Elle oublia tout ce qui n'était pas lui] (254). This second use of the expression on the very same page reinforces that Anissa's motivation for her affair was a displacement of her overweening love for her son to compensate for her loneliness when he departed for the city. This sentence can simply be read as a mother's wish for the best for her child. It is also, however, an ironic foreshadowing of the fate that awaits Anissa, and the struggle Nehmé will soon face when he is chosen as the man who should avenge his family's honor by murdering his mother.

Anissa's musings are reflected in Nehmé's own thought processes just ten pages later as he ponders their community's traditions, in particular the punishment meted out to adulterers. He knows that according to custom, he will be expected to kill his own mother because only blood can cleanse honor, "the oriental honor code brought all of its communities together in an eleventh commandment: '*You will stone the adulterer/without weakness or delays*'" ["le code oriental conciliait toutes ses communautés dans un onzième commandement: '*L'adultère tu lapideras/sans faiblesse, ni atermoiements*'"] (262). In order to commit matricide, Nehmé tries to work himself into a furor, repeating to himself that he never did actually love his mother and blurting out, "May you bury me you say? Ah! I will grant your wish" ["Puisses-tu m'ensevelir dis-tu? Ah! Je t'exaucerai"] (262). The image of his mother awash in blood in the center of their family home excites him at this moment, though he is not able to sustain his frenzied commitment to killing her for long, handing the task over to his maternal uncle Khalil, the local tawah or avenger, who has murdered others during the war.[17]

Finally, this use of the relexified Arabic expression "taqburni" is important because of how it provides an ironic reflection on both its literal and idiomatic meanings. *Sous la baguette de coudrier* uses the formal linguistic device of relexification in order to make both a sarcastic and a feminist comment on antiquated, misogynistic customs and traditions in the Lebanese mountains. A woman like Anissa has no way out of her predicament: she cannot continue to live in her village after committing

17. This situation engages with a number of central anthropological tenets about familial relationships in Arab and Mediterranean societies, explored in the literature on honor and shame. The particular relationships between mothers and sons and sisters and brothers have also received extensive treatment in the anthropological literature (Joseph 1999b, 174–90). An expert in folklore, Hassan El-Shamy has done a study of the brother-sister relationship in Arab culture from a psychological point of view that is cited and critiqued by many scholars including Joseph (El Shamy 1979).

adultery—she knows that she will be murdered by her family—but at the same time she cannot envisage her life outside of their fold. She wants to remain a good mother and wife, but she only is fulfilled as an individual when she engages in her extramarital relationship with Sami. Anissa's wish that her sons will bury her is thus fulfilled—they not only outlive her but are also involved in the process of her murder and the subsequent justification of it by their community.

Bustros therefore is able to use this one woman's story, which seems unique and specific, in order to make a larger statement about gender roles and the kinds of constraints they place on individuals. As such, these words have additional layers of meaning, as they point not only to how women struggle to articulate individual identities but also how this relates to their affiliations within communities. Rachmaya, the poor, beleaguered Christian mountain village featured as the setting of *Sous la baguette du coudrier*, is struggling to survive in the harsh conditions of the famine. Bustros demonstrates through this story that one of the ways in which the community holds together—it has this in common with other villages and communities in Lebanon—is its harsh treatment of women who indulge in sexual relations outside of their legally sanctioned marriages, no matter what those marriages are like. The necessity of killing a woman like Anissa is tolerated and even promoted by the local priest. This man claims that such killing for honor is both a Christian custom and also one linked to a broader "oriental honor code." The idea inscribed within the novel, therefore, is that such outmoded customs that harm women may be justified as being part of one community's traditions, but are in fact something that unifies diverse religious and confessional communities in Lebanon. In this reading, the multiconfessional nature of the country is bolstered by customs and traditions that are excessively harsh toward women.

"Translating" Details

The final scene in the courtroom, when Anissa's brother will be tried for the murder of his sister, demonstrates how Bustros uses ethnographic details about the way in which the crime was executed and received by the community. In this, I propose that Bustros is not only challenging the custom of "honor killing" and probing how French rule has and has not helped Lebanon, but also does this through her simultaneous employment and undermining of the genre of the ethnographic novel in *Sous la baguette du coudrier.* After a detailed courtroom scene, in which the case is argued vigorously by the prosecutor and opposed just as vigorously by the community, including the village priest, the closing scene of the book sees the murderer set free, punished with a slap on the wrist rather than the death penalty demanded by the prosecutor. Further, this ending to a sensational tale reveals a nuanced message about the complex relationship between gender, religious identity, and authority.

An insider-outsider dichotomy is portrayed in ethnographic terms within the depiction of the lawyers in the courtroom who are arguing the case for and against Khalil. These men proclaim a number of pithy statements and proverbs to represent the case they are making before the court. Clichés, set expressions, and "the way that people talk" in Lebanon are invoked directly. These phrases are highlighted within the French-language text by being enclosed in quotation marks, though they all are idiomatic French expressions. The quotation marks do indicate textual difference, however, and suggest that perhaps these are phrases translated from Arabic, much in the way that Kher's use of proverbs works, though the latter are not explicitly marked. This is reinforced by their content, all of which is concerned with how local people live and which customs should reign in the village.

The lawyer representing the murdered woman asks for the death penalty, for example, because the murderer is a coward, announcing that, "He who lives by the sword dies by the sword. It must be so" ["Celui qui sévit par le glaive périra par le glaive. Cela se doit"] (332). This line of reasoning falls flat in the courtroom, prompting the narrator to comment that this lawyer could not possibly be a mountain dweller, "Never would a Lebanese raised in the mountains have described the punishment for adultery as cowardice" ["Jamais un Libanais instruit à la montagne n'eut qualifié de lâcheté la punition d'un adultère"] (331–32). This allows *Sous la baguette du coudrier* to mediate between insiders and outsiders in a complex way—it is not merely French and Lebanese people who do not understand each other; there are conflicts between many different cultures coexisting within Lebanon. Here, for example, mountain and city mores are contrasted. The ambiguities that are teased out by the courtroom scene, in terms of who understands village customs and who does not—particularly how to balance between imposing French values and culture on Lebanese people and also allowing for their autonomy—reveals the difficult and unresolved position of women in this equation.

This is all the more true because the notion that wins out in the end is encoded in exhortations like, "Only the blood of the adulteress can wash away the adultery" ["Le sang adultérin seul peut laver l'adultère"] (322), and "In Lebanon as in the Bible, 'a woman's belt holds the family honor'" ["Au Liban comme dans la Bible 'la ceinture d'une femme détient l'honneur familial'"] (322). These ideas are in the end reinforced by the priest's intervention in the trial when he testifies in favor of Khalil. Moreover, we know that a priest spoke to Fadel, recently devastated by his mother's death at the hands of his uncle, in order to convince the young man that Anissa would have wanted her own death to occur in this way. He hints that she wished for this herself because it was her only way out of the situation. According to the priest, Fadel should understand her actions as a kind of suicide and the best possible solution to the predicament in which she was trapped (329–30).

In this scene, we see on the one hand the surface compassion of the priest, but on the other how Bustros is pointing out the pressure exerted by priests on ordinary people. In the end of the novel, the male characters all close ranks and, with the help of the clergy of the Maronite Church, the village people move beyond this incident; Anissa's murder allows them to feel whole and good as a community once again. The way in which the priests swoop in to control the testimony given in court shows how they actively seek to solidify the patriarchal control over the norms and customs of the village people. Their concern is for the reputation of the village in upholding these conventions and a certain life for village men, without concern for the life of a woman.

The intertwining loyalties of nation, religious community, and gender are particularly underlined by the role of the high-ranking Maronite priest who comes to the trial specifically to give the final testimony in the case against Khalil. This priest pleads for Khalil's release from custody convincingly and emotionally. "My mission, he says, is not to ask for leniency for him but rather to honor our national values. I declare here that Khalil is among the most dedicated of our sons" ["Ma mission, dit-il, n'est pas de solliciter pour lui l'indulgence mais d'honorer nos valeurs nationales. Je déclare ici que Khalil compte parmi les plus zélés de nos fils"] (336). The honor of Lebanon is male honor, connected to defending patriarchal customs and traditions. That a priest defends this notion of honor in court points up the complicity of the church and its clergy within this patriarchal social structure. Anissa's brother's glory, accrued from defending his position as a man as well as the honor of the community, is therefore sanctioned by custom, nation, and church. The murdered woman is quickly forgotten.

Sous la baguette du coudrier should thus be read not merely as an ethnographic novel that reproduces and exposes injustice against women in Lebanon or describes village customs and traditions relating to honor and women in the period of the famine after the First World War. Bustros contextualizes the scenes of the priests at the trial and the brother murdering his sister within the larger novel that is largely a psychological portrait of a lonely, unfulfilled woman. The questioning light she throws on the customs that harm women subtly suggests that this kind of killing must be looked at from multiple angles, in different ways, while gently arguing that women should be able to live lives as whole individuals in their societies. Not a direct confrontation of "backward" or "outmoded" traditions, Bustros nuances the story and makes it complex by representing diverse points of view. The novel is not, however, simply a defence of patriarchy or a justification of French versus Lebanese laws. In this way, the novel can be read as a creative intervention through the lens of colonial mimicry as suggested by Homi Bhabha.[18] Bustros does not merely write a story of a village that "accurately" represents its customs and traditions—indeed Haddad argues that her portrait is not accurate enough (2000, 40).

18. Homi Bhabha's notion of colonial mimicry in fiction holds that postcolonial actors take on roles and actions that are thrust on them by the colonial masters, and that through a seeming mimicry on the surface, in fact subvert them at the same time (Bhabha 1994, 121–31, 132–44).

Rather, through employing the language, scenes, and tropes of the ethnographic village novel about peasants, Bustros's story reveals a subversive depiction of religion, community, identity, and gender. One clear example of this is in how she portrays the problematic relationship between ordinary people and the clergy, particularly women. Her critique of the role of priests in *Sous la baguette du coudrier,* for example, may not go to the lengths of her contemporary, Khalil Jibran, but she paints a more cynical portrait than Amy Kher does in *Salma et son village*. Bustros's work draws on the tropes of the idyllic green mountains and the happy community nestled in its bosom, while quietly bringing to light the cruelty lurking within it.

Challenges to Gender Roles and Norms

A *"Feminist" Novel?*

Sous la baguette du coudrier depicts the unhappiness of its female protagonist and her inability to escape her predicament. In Haddad's estimation, Bustros shows Anissa willingly submitting to her own slaughter and presents the village's customs as quaint and its mountains as lush during the worst period of famine in recent memory (40). Though it would be overstated and perhaps anachronistic to suggest that the work is a feminist novel or advocates women's emancipation from their constraints directly, I would suggest that Anissa's seeming equivocation serves two purposes for Bustros that bring her ethnographic depiction of Lebanese mountain village customs together with a statement about the roles and treatment of women. First, Bustros's message, read together with the specific way she uses language to convey this message, is subtle. The novel, for example, shows the circumstances leading up to Anissa's affair to be difficult and it privileges psychological complexity over simple answers.[19] Just as her use

19. Though I have continually highlighted the psychological, I have not taken this reading as far as Jad Hatem does in his Freudian analysis (Bustros 1988, li–lxv, especially lxii–lxv).

of the relexified expression "puisses-tu m'ensevelir" does not incorporate Arabic in the text in a direct way (as transliterating "taqburni" would have done, for example), the message itself is built up slowly and gradually in order to point out a subtle irony.

Bustros's poetic and political strategies for inscribing subtle messages in the novel, I propose, work in tandem to create the gendered interference with the French language. They mirror each other by hinting at and probing an issue rather than spelling it out explicitly. Relexification as a formal technique, for example, is a strategy used to layer multiple languages into the text that breaks up the flow of the standard French with other French words that sound out of place, but without necessarily drawing attention to the expression in a more direct manner. Though Anissa does die, willingly, at the end of the novel, her demise might be read as a pessimistic take on women's positions and roles; and the novel's message about gender is inscribed within this ending. A text need not be a rallying cry for all women in all situations in order for it to call for change for women living under certain conditions in a particular patriarchal society.

By favoring complexity, Bustros is able to show, for example, that though she is a married woman carrying on a torrid affair, Anissa is not a character to be despised. She does love her children and even her husband. Though she engages in an extramarital relationship, she does not lie, is not sneaky, and does not betray her family. Her feelings for her lover are portrayed sensitively and she feels guilty about them. Her husband is never presented as a cruel man, but he simply is unable to understand her, perhaps partly because of the twenty-year age difference between them. The breakdown of their marriage and Anissa's affair are not caused by one man's cruelty; her husband always treats her well. Rather, the damage is done by the custom of arranged marriages between people of vastly different ages who do not know each other.

Sous la baguette du coudrier therefore is not a story about a man or about men's abuse of women, but rather is the story of one woman's needs and desires, which are shown to be emotional, physical, and sexual. The conflict arises because Anissa's happiness and fulfillment as a person and a woman runs contrary to functioning of the communal system. According to the community, Anissa must die for her family to live with dignity.

The tragic ending of *Sous la baguette du coudrier* thus reinforces a message about the lives of women and how customs must evolve in Lebanese mountain village society. The novel uses language to highlight these traditions—and includes with them descriptions of green mountains and charming anecdotes about the way people live there—and the tale of individual psychological depth is also linked to this. Nothing is portrayed as pure evil: the lovely elements of the countryside exist alongside its oppressive customs, Anissa is a good person but violates community norms, Arabic expressions interanimate the French language of the narration. This work thus challenges the assumptions of the genre with which it engages, arguing that change is needed for women to be able to exist as both individuals and community members.

Further, just as I have shown that Bustros's message about women and gender balances between Arabic and French literally in the use of relexification, *Sous la baguette du coudrier* must also mediate between Arab/Lebanese and French cultures and customs in articulating this message. Though Anissa's love affair with Sami is the main preoccupation of the work, the details of the adulterous relationship and family life more generally unfold against the backdrop of the politics of the era, including French colonial involvement in the region and the appalling conditions in which the poverty-stricken villagers live. In depicting positive aspects of mountain life, Bustros is also showing the beauty of the country and the pride of Lebanese people in their land and lives while under the thumb of the French mandate. Many of the characters are seeking to expel the French and other foreigners from Lebanon. At the same time, this relationship is more ambiguous in the novel, as many characters also show a certain respect for France and French laws. The relationship between the village, its customs, and France grows more complex in the work as it is noted explicitly that the killing of a woman who sullies the honor of her family is considered savage by the French mandate authorities. "The murder of a woman by her brother, committed in the name of family honor, seemed to them surprising and savage. . . . They understood even less how the honor of a family, of a church, and of an entire village could depend on a woman's deviancy" ["Le meurtre d'une femme par son frère, commis au nom de l'honneur familial, leur parut suprenant et sauvage. . . . On comprenait moins encore que l'honneur d'une famille, celui d'un clergé et d'un village entier dépendissent de l'égarement d'une femme"] (325, full discussion on 324–25).

Should Bustros have decided to write a novel as a direct challenge to "honor killings" in Lebanese mountain villages, therefore, it could quite likely have been taken as a pro-French, pro-mandate statement—and not likely to convince her Lebanese readership who had just gained independence; nor would it likely be the message that she would have wanted to send about Lebanon abroad. Like Amy Kher, Bustros's mixing of Arabic in French parallels her message. The French language, like French intervention in Lebanon, has brought some positive things to Lebanon, but also must be undermined and critiqued. Just as standard French cannot express Bustros's ideas sufficiently—as shown in her frequent use of untranslated and translated Arabic words as well as the relexification highlighted here—French customs and traditions should not simply be adopted in Lebanon willy-nilly. But as she shows through the plot of *Sous la baguette du coudrier,* they also should not simply be rejected out of hand. In this case, French laws and attitudes related to men killing women are proven to be better than local customs and traditions. The novel shows that France and the French language must be dealt with in a nuanced way that is neither accommodationist nor rejectionist.

Conclusions

Although the end of *Sous la baguette du coudrier* is tragic, Bustros's relexified reflection on the literal and figurative meanings of "taqburni" highlights the complexity of conflict between women's identities as individuals and as members of their communities in connection to the larger question of French colonial rule in Lebanon. This particular use of polyglossia must thus be read as both a political and poetic strategy through which Bustros layers her subtly feminist message. Though it is not as direct as many novels of the 1950s, for example Andrée Chedid's *Le sommeil délivré* discussed in the next chapter, Eveline Bustros's *Sous la baguette du coudrier* nonetheless is very much a novel of its time. Reflecting on social change and writing texts that make a comment on outmoded customs and traditions is certainly common practice in Arabic as well as French from the period of the *nahda* on. Bustros herself noted that she wrote this novel in response to events that happened in the early 1920s, when Lebanon was controlled by the French mandate, and was shocked by violence that seemed to hearken back to a much earlier era (Bustros 1988, 153). At the same time as showing the violence, she also broaches the pressing contemporary question of how to balance French and local customs, rules, and laws. In this way Bustros's text engages its time period that witnessed a "crisis of patriarchy," as women's roles changed and expanded in some ways but remained the same in others.[20] All of these issues were negotiated in complex ways in daily life, and Bustros's novel picks up on this complexity in her sensitive portrayal of Anissa and her family.

Particularly in drawing on a plot that exploits a sensational story like an honor crime, *Sous la baguette du coudrier* comments on many of the central issues facing postindependence Lebanon. The novel takes place in the past, but not the faraway past, rather a time that is just enough removed to provide some distance yet close enough to ring true to the issues of the present. Similarly to Amy Kher, Bustros establishes an "ethnographic pact" with her readers to comment on customs and traditions directly from an insider-outsider perspective. While showing her intimate knowledge of village customs and traditions, Bustros at the same time affirms a certain complicity with her French-language readership, proving that she indeed "speaks their language." The world literature framework insists that, like *Salma et son village*, this novel should be read as intervening in the debates and discussions around the writing of ethnographies and novels that represent people, in particular the question of self and Other. The ethnographic travelogues written at the time by Europeans, for example, were producing knowledge about the region, its inhabitants, and their ways of life. Like other novelists of this period, Bustros both praises and questions the role of the French and what they have brought to her "sweet Lebanon" [doux Liban] (Bustros 1988, 153). Using the relexification of an

20. Malek Abisaab (2009); Sarah Gualtieri (2009); Akram Khater (2001); and Elizabeth Thompson (2000).

Arabic expression within this ethnographic novel is an effective way of creating a language that can probe the interrelation of issues of gender and community. Though the novel does not offer a solution to how to improve the lives of women or even this one woman—Anissa does after all die violently—Bustros is able to use the language she crafts in her novel to call into question both what a pure and "authentic" identity is for a woman in a Lebanese mountain village community and also the utility of these traditions and the French mandate system of government.

4

Language and Liberation in a Woman's Novel of the 1950s

Andrée Chedid's Le sommeil délivré

If *Sous la baguette du coudrier* and *Salma et son village* are love stories gone wrong, then Andrée Chedid's *Le sommeil délivré* is a love story gone wrong in reverse.[1] Instead of the female protagonist dying of a fever-cum-broken heart like Salma, or being murdered by her brother for her sexual transgression like Anissa, Chedid's Samya takes matters into her own hands and murders her oppressive husband rather than continuing to suffer in silence. She does not die in the end of the story, like so many female protagonists before—and indeed after—her. Samya instead is led away by the local police, clutching the revolver that she has used to murder the man who she feels let her die inside throughout the long years of their loveless marriage. *Le sommeil délivré* in this sense is not a love story at all, but shares with Kher's and Bustros's texts a portrait of a marriage between an ill-suited couple. Fifteen-year-old Samya is whisked away from her convent school by her father and five brothers to be married off to a man thirty years her senior. The rich land manager Boutros is an appealing prospect for these

1. *Le sommeil délivré* was published by Stock in 1952 and reissued by Flammarion in 1976; I am citing from the latter version. It is currently available in "poche" versions. It was translated into English as *From Sleep Unbound* (1983). All translations are mine. Chedid's somewhat unique role as an exemplary Francophone and even "French" writer of prominence in the metropole has been noted by critics (Makward 1988; and Hartman 2000, 54–66).

men to ally themselves with, as their business has failed and they despair of coming up with an appropriate dowry for her. Thus, Samya experiences an unhappy girlhood alone in boarding school only to be transferred to the golden cage of Boutros's home in rural Egypt. Samya never experiences true love like Anissa and Salma, and after remaining a "good girl" for many years, commits the ultimate crime of murder.

Le sommeil délivré can be placed in dialogue with *Sous la baguette du coudrier* and *Salma et son village* in productive ways but also sets itself apart as very much a novel of the 1950s rather than the 1930s or 1940s. The message of the text is an unambiguous embrace of women's liberation from patriarchal hierarchies, without the careful cushioning of Kher's and Bustros's tempered view of the positive elements of village life. This makes *Le sommeil délivré* a novel of its time, participating in conversations beyond the merely local but in relation to the ideas about women circulating around the region and the world. The "classic" early feminist novels of the Arab world, for example, were written and published in the 1950s. One need only to think of Layla Ba'labakki's *Ana ahya* [I am alive] (1958) or Colette Khoury's *Ayyam ma'hu* [Days with him] (1959) to see that women's liberation from patriarchal norms and social constraints becomes a central concern of many novels by Arab women, who begin to produce ever more fictional work in this period.[2] Chedid's *Le sommeil délivré* indeed is a somewhat typically construed coming-of-age story of a woman oppressed by a patriarchal society. Her marriage to the much older Boutros, her

2. Less known is Syrian Salma al-Haffar Kuzbari's *Yawmiyyat Hala* [Hala's diary] (1950). In the early 1960s these works increased exponentially; some of the best-known examples include Emily Nasrallah's *Tuyur Aylul* [September birds] (1962), Amina Said's *Al-Jamiha* (1950) and *Akhir al-tariq*, Layla 'Ussayran's *Lan namut ghadan* [We will not die tomorrow] (1962), and Latifa Zayyat's *Al-Bab al-maftuh* [*The Open Door*] (1960). Ghada Samman's first collection of short stories, *'Aynaka qadari* [Your eyes are my destiny] (1962), appeared in this period as well. For publication details of these works and a more complete bibliography of women's novels (published in this period and beyond), see Joseph Zeidan (1995) and Bouthaina Sha'ban (1999). Sabry Hafez offers a similar typology to Zeidan in which he characterizes the writing of this period as "feminist" (1994, 135—55).

need to conform to his family's ideas of propriety and act according to her "rank," and her later impetus to rebel dramatically against this all strongly echo other texts of the period.

Le sommeil délivré's powerful critique of patriarchy dovetails with the related issue of class and status oppression to nuance its message of women's liberation. This element of the text is also achieved subtly. Samya does not undertake to somehow free the peasants from their bondage as laborers indentured to men like her husband Boutros. Indeed she is much more concerned with her own upper-class loneliness and malaise, not to mention her infertility, to pay close attention to this issue. Chedid is careful to layer insights into the text about ways in which multiple oppressions can work together. The village woman Om el Kher faces different challenges than Samya, though they are both women, because the former is a poor peasant and the latter the daughter and wife of wealthy families. Though there are moments of women's solidarity in the novel, this is not a novel that embraces a simple notion of vertical global sisterhood. Samya's travails are always closely linked to her social status and position.

The characterization of this novel as a tale of female emancipation from oppression and the intersection of this with an analysis of class and status should not obscure its artistry or construction as a novel. This is not just a simple story of oppression and liberation, or a fantastical potboiler told through a "militantly feminist" voice. The sophistication of this work as a novel should come as no surprise to readers familiar with Andrée Chedid, though her reputation was largely built originally as a poet. Chedid is in fact one of the best-known and most critically acclaimed French-language writers of a Lebanese background. Her first novel, *Le sommeil délivré,* was written when Chedid was living in Paris after her long residence in Egypt and the few years living in Lebanon after her marriage. Like her later novels, *Le sommeil délivré* is complex and multivoiced, making ample use of polyglossia. It is not polyphonic, however, in the Bakhtinian sense. Though its many narrative voices do compete and expose different viewpoints, it is clear that the perspective is always that of the beleaguered Samya, with Rachida playing the role of the "evil sister-in-law" who oppresses her. The construction of the narration through several voices, the shifting time periods and flashbacks, as well as a layered use of language becomes a hallmark of Chedid's style throughout her novelistic career. Her use therefore of a similar series of techniques to Kher and Bustros to write Arabic within the French-language narration of the novel—footnotes, names of characters, and crucially, relexification—has a somewhat different effect. Like their novels, Chedid's also uses Arabic subtly to interfere with the French, but in a text that generically does not engage as profoundly with the genre of ethnography and rather stays rooted in the rapidly emerging women's coming-of-age novel.

A Move away from Ethnography: Generic Expression as a Novel

Though some of the same kinds of ethnographic reportage of the other two novels do appear in Chedid's depiction of the Egyptian countryside inhabited by Samya and her husband, *Le sommeil délivré* shifts its portrait away from the lives of the peasants and focuses on reconfiguring the position of elite women, in contrast to village women and in relation to elite men. In this sense Chedid's text does not establish an ethnographic pact in the same way that Kher's and Bustros's texts do. Rather than depict an exoticized mountain peasantry as the Other or provide a congratulatory image of elite culture, this self-critical view into the lives of the well-to-do uses peasant women as a sort of foil to contrast with the life of the bourgeoisie. This is a crucial move by Chedid. Though she does of course in many locations still use details about the setting of the work, including the customs and traditions of the peasants, she does not focus on this extensively nor does she report any of them as inherently interesting in and of themselves. This is significantly different than *Salma et son village* and even *Sous la baguette du coudrier.* Though the latter novel does very much formulate a psychological portrait of Anissa, it is also invested in painting a tableau of the world of the archetypal Lebanese Christian mountain village. The details that would echo the elements of the other two works that I have identified as "ethnographic"—for example Samya's visit to a local healer—support the novel itself, in terms of plot, characterization, and so on, rather than the reverse. Chedid's engagement with genre therefore is firmly located within the world of the novel, particularly the women's coming-of-age novel of the 1950s.

The other striking difference between Chedid's novel and those of Bustros and Kher is that she portrays a completely different milieu: elite Christians settled in Muslim-majority rural Egypt rather than Christian peasants in Lebanese mountain villages where they are the majority population. Herself of a relatively privileged Christian background and raised in Egypt, Chedid's authorial position and voice plays an insider-outsider role similar to that of Kher and Bustros. All three authors indeed share a similar class/status, religious, and "national" background and all three lived for an extended period of their lives in Egypt. It is all the more striking, then, to contrast two works set in "native" villages such as those their families left and one in the location of emigration or exile. Chedid's choice of setting, one presumes, might open her up even more to a charge of exoticizing and romanticizing the lives of peasants, using their miserable lives for local color. Such an argument would hold that Chedid exposes these "local Egyptians" to an external gaze, reinforced by the French-language of her narration—a language holding a similar elite, colonial status in Egypt as it does in Lebanon.[3] Interestingly, though in many ways her texts do present "flatter" images of the peasants and rural life—there is less detail, less careful documentation of the customs of their lives, and so on—Chedid's work is not critiqued for this.

One possible reason may be the relative ease with which *Le sommeil délivré*, like Chedid's other works, have found an audience in France. Unlike works more consciously affiliated with Lebanon—through place of publication or even through their ethnographic portrayal of its villages—Chedid's novels are well received within France and have been embraced there. The exoticism with which the countryside is portrayed could be a reason.[4] Another may be the focus on the elite Christians rather than these

3. The situation is analogous in broad terms, but of course not the same. For background on the French language in Egypt, see Kober (1999). Some anthologies include Egypt and Lebanon together as part of the "Francophone Middle East," for example, Jack (1996). The French language is much less widespread and French colonial engagement was less sustained in Egypt, as the British gained control there early on.

4. It would take another study to explore how works by Lebanese and/or Arab authors are received as "exotic" or not in France. On Chedid's role as "French," see Hartman

Egyptian peasants or the "oriental Christian" peasants of Kher or Bustros. Another contrast between these works is that the Catholicism present in *Le sommeil délivré* is clearly meant to resonate with French readers in France. Samya's Catholic missionary boarding school has nothing "oriental" about it. No details are given that would show it to be Other—the priests are not married, there are no exotic customs and traditions. Aside from the early age at which many of the girls leave the school because they are married off, there are no details indicating a "local" Christianity, neither Maronite nor Coptic. We learn nothing of the communal background of the people connected to the school; class is emphasized instead. This focus is particularly important because it is underlined through the elite status of such a school and the centrality of this school to the entire plot structure of the novel. Samya's loneliness, which then transforms into bitterness, is first engendered within its closed walls. She seeks the love of the priests and nuns and is rebuffed. When she later is rejected and alienated by the snobbish attitude of Rachida and Boutros, the reader is able to draw parallels between the two prisons in which Samya has been incarcerated for her entire young life.

This move away from ethnography allows *Le sommeil délivré* to fit more neatly within the traditional boundaries of the novel and to work with its mixing of genres. Perhaps it is for this reason that Chedid can thus make extensive use of creative narrative techniques including multivocality, shifting time frames, flashbacks, and other literary devices. This creates a powerful novelistic effect when combined with creative uses of language. The comparison with the very different texts of Kher and Bustros is interesting, partly because of the similar ways in which she works to

---

(2000). It is notable that the "J'ai lu" pocket version that I am citing from shows on its cover a distressed looking woman covered in a chador-like ʻabaya gazing up at a shadowy figure that can only be seen from behind, and that behind her walking down a narrow alley is a woman in Egyptian peasant dress carrying a child. One can only assume that the woman portrayed is meant to be Samya, who, based on the novel, one would assume to look and dress more like the Egyptian cinema stars of the 1950s—Western dress and high heels. She certainly would not be shrouded in an ʻabaya or wear a peasant dress, given her background and status.

layer the language of the novel with words and related concepts marked as Arabic. Two rather straightforward examples of this are the use of Arabic names laden with meaning and the use of footnotes to explain Arabic words that are not translated within the text.

The novels discussed in the previous two chapters illustrate how footnotes form an integral part of the way in which a novel can engage the genre of ethnography, both appropriating and challenging parts of its project. Footnotes in those two examples establish a particular kind of authorial voice and "expertise" within the text as an insider, but one who knows what explanations the outsider reader needs. Footnotes set up literary works as having a didactic or "scientific" purpose, and analyzing the footnotes in Chedid's work reveals some of the same multiple audiences identified for the works of Kher and Bustros. But because Chedid's novel does not use ethnography in the same way, her use of footnotes cannot be explained in the same terms, though some of the same ideas and issues obviously do apply here. There are only six footnotes in this relatively long 253-page novel (Chedid 1952, 17, 20, 35, 74, 151, 250).

Though *Le sommeil délivré* only contains six footnotes—five of which explain or translate Arabic words—they can be explored productively in relation to how they function in the text. There are three categories of notes, each of which contains a pair of words. Two of the words do not seem to have a particularly significant hidden meaning, they are the non-Arabic "Primus" (translated as a "petit réchaud" [small portable stove]) (20) and the word "feddan," noted at the bottom of the page as "un feddan = environ 58 acres" [one feddan = around 58 acres] (74). The latter is referred to in relation to Samya's probable dowry. The other two pairs of words are more interesting to the novel's analysis, even if the words themselves do not seem so at first glance. First, two words are noted that refer to titles or positions. One of these is Nazer, which Chedid translates in the note at the bottom of the page as "a trusted man who oversees the cultivation of the land on behalf of its owner" [Homme de confiance qui surveille l'exploitation des terres pour le compte du propriétaire] (17). The other is the ubiquitous Egyptian colloquial title Sit (translated as "la dame," meaning "the lady") (35). It is relevant to this discussion that these two words are titles that refer to Boutros and Samya, respectively. It is also important that both words reflect not only position but also social status. In this regard, it is crucial to note that Boutros gains his position through actually managing the land, whereas Samya's title is honorific and simply reflects her position in the social hierarchy.

The second two words carry fewer embedded meanings but still perform an artistic function in the text. The first is chaouiches (defined as "policiers" [police]) (151); the second is Maamour (defined as "chef de la police" [chief of police]) (250). These two translations are relatively straightforward and clearly are related. The use of the first, I would propose, is the foreshadowing of Samya's fate. The final word, Maamour, appears a mere four pages before the end of the work when Samya is found next to her dead husband, revolver in hand. This word reinforces the rule of law that is present as a feature of the text and could perhaps even be a reflection, in a French-language novel written outside of the Arab world at a time of "modernization" in the Arab world itself, of Chedid's desire to show a counterstereotype of the lawless, savage Middle East. Both Boustros's novel and Chedid's end with a murder, but both also end with the apparatus of the state present in some way—though it does not exactly prevail in *Sous la baguette du coudrier* and the fate of Samya at the end of *Le sommeil délivré* is not known. Chedid's text does emphasize, though, that a "misbehaving" woman in an Arab context would not necessarily just be killed, as Bustros's text might be interpreted as suggesting.

The use not only of footnotes but also meaning-filled names is another commonality in how multiple languages are layered in the three novels. Much like *Salma et son village* and *Sous la baguette du coudrier*, Chedid's novel's main characters reflect or contradict the meanings inherent in their Arabic names, but this is never explained explicitly. It is all the more striking in a novel like *Le sommeil délivré* that is primarily, if not solely, directed at a French-reading audience who is presumed not to know Arabic. Chedid lived in France, published her poetry, this novel, and her subsequent novels there. Unlike the other works, this text has no obvious didactic message for Arab readers as opposed to any others in particular, though part of the goal of these readings is to unsettle the idea that the "Arab" versus the "French" reader is opposed. Nonetheless the names of major figures in the work emphasize not only their personalities and characters but also at times their rank within the social hierarchies—crucial here because of the close attention paid to this issue within the novel. This is most obviously reflected in the name of the work's protagonist, Samya, which means "lofty," reflecting her high-status background and the image she is pressured to uphold by her husband. As will be discussed in greater detail below, it is precisely because Samya cannot cope with the constraints on her that many of the tragedies of the novel occur.

Other names have a less clear-cut meaning or purpose. The name of Samya's sister-in-law, Rachida, means "rational," "intelligent," or "following the right path" (in the religious sense). This can be read as a commentary on Rachida's self-defined role as the woman who runs the house properly and feels that there is a specific path that members of the family should follow according to her reasoning—largely based in status-conscious definitions of proper behavior. The prominent male characters' names are typically (but not exclusively) Arabic names of prominent figures in Christianity; Boutros means Peter. This could reflect again the issue of hierarchy and the oppressiveness of the institution of the church, if not religion itself—a topic Chedid does not take up in detail in this work. Reflecting this, the two lower-class peasant men who are mentioned in *Le sommeil délivré* are named Ali and Hussein, both identifiably and specifically Muslim names with Shiite connotations in Lebanon, though there are few Shi'a in rural Egypt.

The names of the lower-class and peasant women who Samya befriends reflect elements of their personality and character. The servant woman who lives with Samya's family before she is married is called Zariffa. This name is the colloquial rendition of a word in Arabic meaning full of life and energy, and in formal Arabic it connotes elegance and gracefulness. In everyday speech it means "kind," "nice," and "friendly," all qualities that few people surrounding Samya in her early life show to her after the death of her mother when she is only five years old. The other peasant woman who is close to her who comes from the village near her marital home is called Om el Kher, which literally means "mother of goodness." A name at times given to women who have trouble conceiving, this popular nickname reflects the kindness of the woman toward the motherless Samya, particularly as she herself had difficulty conceiving her first child, who later dies as a toddler. The fact that her name has the word "mother" in it and that she indeed plays the role of mother to Samya in some ways is notable, as is the fact that she supports Samya when the latter finds herself infertile. This onomastic play emphasizes the personality traits of the village women, while it emphasizes the protagonist's social position. They therefore are brought together as women but at the same time it is underlined that Samya is a "poor little rich girl."[5]

"Hands Too Delicate to Fight": Samya's Rebellion in *Le sommeil délivré*

Though she is trapped in an oppressive marital relationship, simple submission to her situation does not suit *Le sommeil délivré*'s protagonist. Like Bustros's Anissa, Samya faces the religious burden of a Christian marriage with no possibility of divorce. In her case, however, she is forced to leave her all-girls' school, barely a teenager, to consummate a marital relationship with a man thirty years her senior and live with him in a small Egyptian village. Samya's situation differs from Anissa's crucially in three major ways. First, she is completely cut off from other people—her mother died when she was a girl, her father and brothers see her as a burden to be unloaded in marriage, and she is unable to visit women in the village because her husband finds it inappropriate for a woman of her rank to do so. Second, her marriage has made her well off and far from having to struggle to make ends meet in the starving Lebanese village of Rachmaya; Samya is locked in a golden cage in rural Egypt where she has no financial or material hardships. And last, unlike the kindly Abou Nehmé (Adib), whom Anissa is loath to betray, Samya's husband Boutros is cruel and seems to take pleasure in abusing her.

5. Though her name is not Arabic, Samya's daughter who dies of typhoid as a child is called Mia, meaning "mine" in Italian, reflecting Samya's attachment to her and also that the child really belonged to her rather than her paternal family who rejected her from birth because she was born a girl and not a boy.

As these details indicate, Chedid's novel is designed much more clearly as a feminist tale of a woman's longing for emancipation from her gender-based oppression than either *Sous la baguette du coudrier* or *Salma et son village*. The ambiguity layered into *Sous la baguette du coudrier* that shows the kindness of Anissa's husband, the difficulties faced in simply adopting French laws and customs and its measured mediation between a community's conventions and a woman's fulfillment is not reflected in the more clear-cut marital relationship in *Le sommeil délivré*. Samya has everything she could want materially, but the men in her life treat her as an object and abuse her. Her priest willingly delivers her into the hands of her oppressor (118) and her father refuses to entertain her complaints when her husband beats her (190). The women of her own class-status milieu are no better—the nuns in the convent and her sister-in-law Rachida willingly collude with the men to maintain the patriarchal system. Even the peasant women of the village, who are in some ways her allies, showing her affection and love when she is lonely, abandon her when she seems to be barren. The novel, however, is not written as a manifesto nor is its feminist message as clearly articulated as that of, for example, Evelyne Accad's *Coquelicot du massacre* (1988), discussed in part 2. Though its message is clear, Chedid's novel, like Bustros's, uses careful and subtle layering of an Arabic relexification in the French text to inscribe it in a similarly cautious way. *Le sommeil délivré* also links this kind of gendered interference by the Arabic language in French to a critique of class hierarchies, much as *Sous la baguette du coudrier* addresses the question of French colonial intervention in Lebanon.

Set in Egypt, probably though not explicitly among the exiled Christian Lebanese community there, *Le sommeil délivré* makes much less extensive use of Arabic relexification in the French text than *Sous la baguette du coudrier*. The few words of Arabic, especially the relexification that is the focus here, are all the more striking in a text that uses so few instances of words marked as Arabic to interanimate the French text, further highlighting their inclusion. One consistent location of relexification in *Le sommeil* is the many instances in which Chedid puts colorful, unidiomatic French expressions into the mouths of the local village women. These show that the village women speak differently than do Samya and Boutros at home and presumably represent the Arabic language as it looks "in French." For example, on the two occasions when Samya escapes Boutros's notice and goes into the village to mingle with the local village women, we see that their expressions are full of references to God (Allah), polite expressions of joy and greeting, and are clearly meant to add a certain flavor to the French narration.

The speech of village women reinforces many of the same themes explored by the text more largely, but through the representation of dialogue. For example, when Samya cries because she realizes that her future will be as bleak as she ever might have feared it would be in the convent, her family's servant whom she loves like a substitute mother completely misunderstands her apprehension, and says, "A bride's tears of joy are like honey" [Les larmes de joie d'une fiancée sont comme le miel] (113). The comparison of tears to honey clearly is meant to evoke an Arab context and setting and is an exotic-sounding expression in French. Zariffa mistakes the motivation for Samya's tears and tries to naturalize her sadness into an appropriate cultural reaction to the day of her wedding. This particular example is all the more striking because these are the last words spoken to close the first part of the novel. When readers turn to the next page, the opening of part 2, they are faced with the sentence: "It was our wedding day" [C'était le jour de notre mariage] (117). On the one hand this expression therefore is clearly used to show how peasants speak differently to the elite, focusing the French reader's attention on not only their language but also their class-status difference. Polyglossia here comes into play with a double effect. There is an interruption of language not only with phrases that are meant to represent Arabic in French but also on the level of proverbs and the speech of peasant women that permeates the standard French narration of the text. This has the effect of turning an orientalist gaze on the peasant woman, reflecting the gaze of the wealthy woman on her servant. It demonstrates the class-status gap between these two women as well, because Zariffa misunderstands why Samya is crying and Samya does not display the "culturally correct" reaction to her marriage. As a novel set in Egypt written in French for a French-reading audience by a Lebanese author, this distancing of Samya also allows Chedid to suggest that her French readership should identify with Samya. Chedid uses the relexified Arabic expressions of Zariffa and the other poor women to represent difference in language, she employs a French that sounds "strange and alien" and therefore can be used as a foil against which readers can identify themselves.

When words marked as Arabic are then placed in the mouth of the well-to-do, well-educated Samya, it is an even more important textual moment. The speech genre interruption here again is dialogue that intrudes on the narration. Speech not only interrupts language but also represents a linguistic difference in marking itself as Arabic in French, which itself indicates class dissonance. The social realities produced and commented on through language here is thus a complex process that layers levels of meaning into the text. Indeed the expression that Chedid uses and explains is linked to this very idea of social positions and what is appropriate for people of different social backgrounds or "ranks" (rang), as Boutros puts it. The position of women in society, and how position is tied to class and status, is the central issue of the novel. In telling Samya's story, *Le sommeil délivré* returns again and again to how the personalities and lives of elite young women are stifling—everything is infused with boredom, from their education to their daily lives. Throughout the novel, from the first section in the convent, to her married life with Boutros in the second section, and even in the third section when her beloved daughter Mia is born and dies, Samya is constantly being hurried in her tasks and life, though she has nowhere to go and no ambitions to do anything specific.

Moreover, Samya quickly realizes that her education, for which she suffers during ten years at an oppressive Catholic missionary boarding school, will mean nothing in her life. She understands this first from her father when he hints that she will soon be married off since she has had plenty of education for a girl. When she wonders how much this is, he states that she needs only enough "so that you can write a letter to your old dad to announce the birth of your son, that is enough" [Tant que tu pourras rédiger une lettre à ton vieux père pour lui announcer la naissance d'un garcon, cela suffira] (55). The same point is made to her bluntly by one of the village women who befriends her, Om el Kher, when she learns that Samya can read and write like office employees. "Not to offend you, she replied, but how will it help you?" ["Ce n'est pas pour t'offenser, reprit-elle, mais à quoi cela va-t-il te servir?"] (127). Though Samya admits to herself that this idea worries her as well, she lies to Om el Kher, just as she did to her girlfriends in the convent school, bragging that it allows her to read Boutros's love letters, which of course are nonexistent. Om el Kher's words recur in the text to haunt Samya, and they underline the novel's preoccupation with the education of girls and women.

The inability to use her education only underlines the loneliness and emptiness that characterize Samya's life and eventually lead her to the desperate action of murdering her cruel husband. From the loss of her mother and her complete alienation from her father and brothers because they see her only as an object, to her lack of connection to her husband and his sister, Samya has always felt abandoned. The connection of this feeling to her social background and status is part of Chedid's message that she underlines with her use of a relexified Arabic expression. The intensity of Samya's loneliness is cultivated in the convent. Though she is surrounded by women and girls, she still is very much alone. This is crystallized for Samya in the person of one of the elderly nuns who knits sweaters for the less-fortunate children of the world. She seems to care deeply for these unknown children who might be cold, but Samya feels this nun's lack of care and understanding for her, a real "needy" child who the nun does know.

> I would have liked her to remember me in her prayers. Me, who a shirt protected from the cold, but not from myself. I was a "girl of a family" with hands too fragile to fight. I would have liked to offer her my picture and for her to agree to mix it with those of other children [I would have liked for] her voice to rise up to this silent God for all of us.
>
> J'aurais voulu qu'elle se souvînt de moi dans ses prières. Moi, qu'une chemise protégeait du froid, mais pas de moi même. J'étais une 'fille de famille' aux mains trop fragiles pour se battre. J'aurais voulu lui jeter mon image et qu'elle l'acceptât pour la mêler à celle des autres enfants, et sa voix monterait pour nous toutes jusqu'à ce Dieu muet. (50)

To explain the difference between herself and the other less-fortunate children, Samya uses the relexification of a colloquial Arabic expression, set apart with quotation marks, saying that she is a "fille de famille," in Arabic a "bint 'aylee"—literally in English a "girl/daughter of a family."[6] This passage once again underlines markedly the theme of Samya as a poor little rich girl, one who suffers from loneliness because she is from a certain elite background, but it does also hint at the gendered solidarity with other girls and women that will be proposed as a solution for her.

The expression "bint 'aylee" is frequently used in colloquial Arabic in order to make a statement about identity and belonging.[7] The idea implied in saying that one is a daughter or a son of a family is that you are a part of not just any family but an important or "big" family, which would be a more idiomatic translation of the phrase in order to give its sense. The importance of family to one's belonging to a society and community is underlined in this expression as in a number of other colloquial Arabic expressions, which Chedid makes use of not only in *Le sommeil délivré* but in her other novels as well (Hartman 1998, 199–214; and 2000, 54–66). The importance of identity, gender identity in particular, being tied to a village or community or religion can be seen clearly in *Le sommeil délivré* and *Sous la baguette du coudrier*, but both also emphasize that this is linked first and foremost to one's family. In Bustros's novel this leads to the most dramatic ending possible for Anissa, because as a woman who has transgressed certain norms, she must die for her family. In *Le sommeil délivré* a woman's identity as rooted in family is probed in a different way. Samya is not loved as she would like to be by her family because she

6. As in the case of "taqburni," here I represent the phrase in its colloquial Lebanese Arabic transliterated form. It has fewer variations than the former expression because of the letters involved. The standard Arabic transliteration of the expression is "bint 'a'ila." The same expression using the masculine "ibn" rather than "bint" can be used for a boy, with slightly different connotations. These are rarely heard expressions in French and give the use of the expression an antiquated or quaint feel as well as a "translated" one.

7. This expression appears in many Lebanese Francophone novels similarly relexified or translated, as we saw above in chapter 2. In Amy Kher's *Salma et son village* it emphasizes the difference in social position between the poor Salma and her wealthy beloved (56). In Dominique Eddé's *Cerf-Volant*, discussed in chapter 12, it emphasizes class and the important family of a man who is a doctor and contrasted with a postman (50).

is a girl and therefore also a commodity. Her father and brothers need to marry her off with a small dowry so as to relieve themselves of their financial burden; her husband thinks of her as a vessel for childbearing. Thus, her description of herself as a "fille de famille" smacks of more than a little irony, in that it describes her social background, but also how she is ignored and unloved precisely because of this background, not only by the nuns obsessed by the less fortunate but also by her family.

This relexified expression has deeper implications. It layers meanings into *Le sommeil délivré* in the manner in which it ties together gender and social hierarchies. The major comment that Samya makes in bemoaning her situation is that even though she is materially comfortable she is an unhappy child and this is connected to her social status. She is unable to struggle against her situation, not simply because she is not "cold"—that is to say it is not simply because her material situation has sapped her of motivation—but because she is too delicate to fight. This reads as an ironic statement even in the context of this convent schoolgirl's reflections, but certainly has further ironic implications as the plot of the novel unfolds. The class distinction that is underlined and commented on here is deeply intertwined with gender issues.

Samya's situation is completely determined by her gender. She is sent to the convent because she is a girl, she is deemed a burden because she is a girl, she is ignored by her family because she is a girl, and, what is important, she is deemed delicate because she is a girl. The phrase "daughter of a family" underlines this message distinctly because it is an expression used for both genders but with different implications. A "son of a family" has the same class and family background as a "daughter of a family," but with different expectations. There is no delicacy or fragility implied on the part of a "fils de famille," on the contrary, he is the person who would be meant to step into his patriarchal father's shoes and guide a family. He is not subject to the same social restrictions and customs as a "fille de famille"—maintaining virginity until marriage, appropriate behavior in social settings, and submission to the patriarchal authority of a father, brothers, and later a husband.

This short sentence, "J'étais une 'fille de famille' aux mains trop fragiles pour se battre" [I was a "family girl" with hands too delicate to fight], thus layers its meanings not only in the relexification but also the cushioning that the phrase is given immediately afterward. Unlike Bustros's more linguistically experimental strategy of challenging the reader by using Arabic expressions with minimal cushioning, Chedid chooses a technique with a more direct approach. She combines the unidiomatic relexification of the Arabic phrase with some contextualization, allowing for her comment still to be subtle, but also to suggest an irony more immediately discernable even to the "outsider" reader who does not know Arabic. In this, we can read Chedid's use of Arabic as a somewhat intermediate strategy between the relexifications of Bustros and the later transliteration and translation strategies favored by Evelyne Accad and Dominique Eddé that contextualize words in detail and are highlighted in part 2.

In *Le sommeil délivré* in fact, the context that she gives to "translate" the meaning of "fille de famille" is a location in which she layers her message as well, by indicating to an outsider reader that the phrase means that her hands are "trop fragiles pour se battre" [too delicate to fight]. Of course this would not be a common translation of the meaning of "bint 'aylee" in its usual context in Arabic. Though it might be implied that a girl of a certain status would not stoop to fighting, it is certainly not the first thing that would come to mind in defining this expression. Thus, the idea that Samya's hands in this novel are too delicate to fight is a foreshadowing device in *Le sommeil délivré* much in the same way that the expression "puisses tu m'ensevelir" [may you bury me] foresees the end of *Sous la baguette du coudrier.* Just as Anissa's son does indeed bury her, though he does not kill her, Samya also does fight back against her situation, though not with her bare hands—she murders her husband with a gun for his crimes against her and others. The irony layered into the language of the text by Chedid is that Samya is far from "too delicate to fight," despite her social background and her gender. Even a "family daughter" can fight back given her situation—women can take their futures into their own hands.

The way in which social hierarchy and status shapes Samya's gendered struggles is crucial and is underlined by this expression. It is shown that if she remains in the sheltered world of her upper-class background, she will never be free of the limitations placed on her. The only moments of joy that happen in the text are connected to the support she gets from kind women like Zariffa and Om el Kher and two young girls, her daughter Mia and Ammal, the village girl who takes Mia's place after her death. Samya's main happiness comes from the birth of her daughter and this was only possible because she followed Om el Kher's guidance and sought the expert help of a local female healer who gave her powders to help her become pregnant. One of the primary reasons for her chafing against Boutros is his treatment not only of her but also of the servants and other people in the village. He refuses to eat Om el Kher's bread because he thinks it dirty (157) and he punishes a girl who sings outside their window at night (134–36). He refers to this young girl, who simply is amusing herself outside, as a "fille de chien" [daughter of a dog/bitch]—a clear inversion of Samya's position as a "fille de famille." Samya's reaction to Boutros is the realization that she must somehow escape him. Early in the novel she visualizes running away. But her paralysis after the death of her daughter and confinement to a wheelchair leave her no legs but only her (not so) delicate hands.

These inversions are also paralleled by the spaces that women occupy and their significance. Just as Samya is a "fille de famille" and trapped in her house, the young girl referred to as a "fille de chien" is on the street. The public space is thus defined by socioeconomic status and is occupied by poor women, whereas the home is the location for wealthy women. Thus it is not only gender that determines what space one occupies, but also how this relates to one's social status. The notion of the home as private space occupied by women and the street or village as public space occupied by men are thereby also challenged. Women also occupy public spaces, particularly the peasant women who have more mobility. This is shown when Samya wishes to come to the village with Om El Kher but is unsure. She is reassured when Om El Kher states that in the afternoon, "The village belongs to children, women, and the blind man!" ["Le village appartient aux enfants, aux femmes et à l'aveugle!"] (143). Samya's anxiety about leaving her house is primarily fear of being caught by her husband; his fear is the mixing of the social levels that will shame him and his well-placed family if his wife is known to have been in public. Thus the way that gender and social hierarchy are engaged in the text reveal a spillage between the constrained gendered spaces of the elite woman and the public sphere controlled by village women and occupied by them, their children, and the marginalized blind man.

This engagement of social hierarchy/status and gender in *Le sommeil délivré* is not entirely unproblematic, of course. The gaze of the novel on the rural village women very much exoticizes them and makes them different from its heroine Samya; as shown above, one way in which difference is emphasized is in their frequent use of Arabic and Arabic-sounding expressions. The pain and suffering that the novel focuses on is the plight of an upper-class woman in a golden cage, and no detailed mention is made of the myriad struggles of the poor women who help her. Within this context, however, the novel does show that people should not be understood as inherently different because of their social position and that the barriers between people should be broken down rather than erected, especially when questions of gender are at stake. Moreover, gendered issues are not shown simplistically or as universal, just as women are not one unified category. Village women are not locked up in their houses and necessarily oppressed by their husbands as Samya is, though some have difficult family situations. Alliance building between women of different classes and backgrounds is shown to be something for which to strive through this novel.

The linguistic barriers that are linked to social position mirror this and therefore mixing words marked as Arabic into the French text of the novel is a formal technique echoing the message of the mingling of classes called for by *Le sommeil délivré*. Just as Arabic ranges freely in the French text, elite women should indeed go to the village and mix with local women. To reinforce this idea, Chedid layers irony in the moment of transition between languages, and the translated phrase in this case draws out one implication of the actual expression, but also so much more includes foreshadowing the end. This can be read as a way to help an outsider reader unlock the meaning of the expression. More important perhaps, as in the case of *Sous la baguette du coudrier,* it also can be read as a comment to an "insider" audience about distinctions in class and how crucial it is to question ideas embedded in language. What does it mean to be part of an "important" family? What does the expression "bint 'aylee" really mean? *Le sommeil délivré* points out the flawed logic of the way in which this expression is used and how language betrays it.

Conclusions

The "exotic" setting of Chedid's novel cultivates ideas about the Other, but it does not engage ethnography in the same way that Kher's and Bustros's works do. The use of ethnographic details, together with polyglossia, advances the creative agenda of Chedid's carefully constructed novel of a woman's coming of age. Much like the other two works, moreover, *Le sommeil délivré* engages directly with issues and debates of its time, particularly concerns about gender and women's roles in society and how this interacts with class and status. Like these novels it also uses subtle techniques and strategies to craft a textual language incorporating polyglossia on a number of levels. The most important relexification of *Le sommeil delivré* is even the same as the most important one used in *Salma et son village*, "fille de famille," but with the other gender emphasized. Chedid naturalizes her use of Arabic in these ways, assimilating it to the French text. Through this she toys with the notion of exoticism by using her insider-outsider gaze to exploit various subject positions and subtly comment on them.

Chedid's text is very different from Kher's and Bustros's in other ways, particularly in how the insider-outsider status of the author is asserted in relation to its setting. It is difficult to define *Le sommeil délivré* as "Lebanese" in the same way one can *Salma et son village* and *Sous la baguette du coudrier* because of their own self-definitions. Nonetheless, like these two novels it also participates very much in the debates of its time and even place—Egypt, Lebanon, and the Arab world more generally—while also helping us see the limitations of national categories to understand literature. More specifically, it is engaged in criticizing the oppression of women. As a novel of the 1950s, Chedid's text comments directly and forcefully on the struggles faced by elite women, trapped in the bourgeois, patriarchal conventions that make them "die inside." The murder of Boutros in many ways reverses the murder of Anissa. Though it is not shown to be "right" exactly—Samya is taken away by the police—the reader understands how she was pushed to this point. This feminist message, combined with the novel's larger critique of class and gender hierarchies, therefore reflects the struggles of women in Egypt, Lebanon, the Arab world, and beyond. Classics of feminist fiction in the United States, for example, like Marilyn French's iconic *The Women's Room* (1977), are set in the 1950s, the time when Betty Freidan started researching and writing the *Feminine Mystique* (1963). Indeed Freidan's manifesto that exposed the limitation of the type of life available to white, upper middle-class housewives in suburban United States echoes strongly with *Le sommeil délivré*. Read in this way, Chedid's text prefigures the assertively explicit feminist texts by Lebanese women writers that will flourish during the Lebanese civil war. Three of these are explored in the part 2: Vénus Khoury-Ghata's *Le fils empaillé* (1980), Evelyne Accad's *Coquelicot du massacre* (1988), and Dominique Eddé's *Lettre posthume* (1989).

Part Two ◆ *Arabic as Feminist Punctuation*

5

Arabic as Feminist Punctuation in the Novel of the Lebanese Civil War

The three novels discussed in part 1 allow the Arabic language to interfere with French, inscribing messages about gender, women's roles in society, the French mandate, and the shape of newly independent Lebanon. The Arabic language that is the object of representation is a colloquial Arabic that is either "real" or metaphorical and is often tied to spaces defined traditionally to be those of women—the home or "bayt." This layering of language in the texts draws on multiple genres, including ethnographies, to allow the novels to create their own novelistic discourses. The three novels discussed in part 2 break from these subtler strategies and transparent techniques to encode messages, parallel to the way in which the period in which they are written and published—the Lebanese civil war—makes a break from what came before it. The civil war is usually said to have begun in 1975 and continued for almost twenty years, resulting in upheavals and changes in society. The field of literary production is no exception. Part 2 analyzes how three novels written in the period of the war use words and expressions marked as Arabic in complex ways to punctuate stronger and unequivocal messages—again about women's roles in society, the deleterious effects of patriarchy, and the future shape of Lebanon—though these are supplemented by commentaries on violence: domestic violence, the rise of militias, ordinary people taking up arms, and the effect on society.

In some ways these two groups of literary works from two distinct time periods can be said to witness a sort of "generational shift" in the way in which languages and genres are relayered into them. The later works also build on the kinds of strategies used in the earlier works, unsurprisingly if we look at language as a process rather than a fixed, static entity that is "waiting to be mixed." I do not argue that this is a chronological progression, however, though it is clear that the kinds of strategies of language use mirror features of the times in which they are written. The three novels discussed in part 2 are Vénus Khoury-Ghata's *Le fils empaillé* [The son stuffed with straw], Evelyne Accad's *Coquelicot du massacre* [A poppy from the massacre], and Dominique Eddé's *Lettre posthume* [A posthumous letter].

Written and published in the heat of the Lebanese civil war during the 1980s, these works all deliberately and explicitly engage with their time and place, like the works of the mandate and early independence periods. This means that the feminist messages inscribed in them are arguably more direct and forceful, as the 1980s saw sustained feminist activism throughout the world, including Lebanon and the larger Arab world. This is one reason that the language of the house, home, and family—or "bayt"—gives way to a language use that could more properly be defined as "billingsgate," the everyday and even vulgar language of the streets or marketplace.

Bakhtin identifies billingsgate as one aspect of polyglossia in the novel, as well as in some parodic forms of verse, that marks it apart from poetry, breaks "high" literary discourse with "lowly" vulgar language, and inscribes alternative messages and viewpoints (1993, 181, 188–89). The Bakhtinian argument about this "language from below" will help to elucidate how the vulgar punctuation employed by these texts operates. The texts make use of vulgar Arabic expressions incorporated right into their "high literary" French. These moments of punctuation function as speech genres that drastically interrupt the novels' main narration, mirroring the social breakdown of the war, enriching and further complicating novelistic discourse.

It is not only vulgar or obscene words that are represented in these texts, however. All three works also use representations of Arabic referring to the everyday, colloquial language, differently experimenting with gentler, subtler breaks in speech genres as well as more direct and confrontational negotiations. The first novel discussed, Vénus Khoury-Ghata's *Le fils empaillé* [The son stuffed with straw] (1980), makes a metacommentary on language use, offering an anticolonial critique of French that particularly resonates with the analyses of Ashcroft, Griffith, and Tiffin in *The Empire Writes Back* (1989). Evelyne Accad's *Coquelicot du massacre* [A poppy from the massacre] (1988), uses lengthy, direct explanations of transliterated Arabic words in French, some of which are vulgar. Dominique Eddé's *Lettre posthume* [A posthumous letter] (1989) uses both strategies, somewhat less directly, to reflect on the civil war.

The three works in this part demonstrate another major shift in novels of the civil war compared with those of the mandate and early independence periods in that, though "local" customs and traditions are often detailed, the genre of ethnography fades in importance. None of these works makes a comment on the genre of ethnography in the same way that the novels in the previous part do. Instead, they draw extensively on other genres of expression to accomplish their processes of novelization, including poetry, songs, and letters. The generational change that saw a relaxation of linguistic and generic conventions mirrored the relaxation and outright breakdown of social hierarchies and boundaries.

The "Lebanese Novel"

Despite the death and destruction that it caused, like so many wars, the Lebanese civil war saw an increase in creative writing and the production of some of the finest novels to come out of Lebanon. This is particularly true of writing by women, making the authors studied here especially relevant. For this reason, the claim that the novel comes into its own in this period is even better depicted as Bakhtinian novelization, since it affected not only the novel but also the whole of literary production in a variety of ways.[1]

1. Christopher Stone (2007) makes a complementary argument about Ziad Rahbani's plays from the period of the war as "novelized," and also employs a Bakhtinian framework to look more specifically at his production as well as the plays of his father and mother, Fairouz.

The war had a particularly significant impact on the Arabic-language novel from Lebanon in this period. In an introduction to one of Elias Khoury's best-known works about the war, *Little Mountain* (*Al-Jabal al-saghir*), Edward Said makes the claim that the novel in Lebanon only truly emerges during the war. "Indeed in Lebanon the novel exists largely as a form recording its own impossibility, shading off or breaking into autobiography (as in the remarkable proliferation of Lebanese women's writing), reportage, pastiche, or apparently authorless discourse" (Khoury 1989, xvi). Writing as a critic as well as a novelist, Khoury has himself argued that through formlessness and innovation, the Lebanese novel made a great contribution to the development of the Arabic-language novel at this time and that "the Lebanese novel" came into its own in this period (1990, 7–8). Though Khoury rejects the notion that there is such a thing as the Lebanese war novel, he acknowledges that the war had a major impact on the development of the novel in Lebanon (1993, 138–39). Moreover, both Said and Khoury propose that up until the war, many Lebanese authors contributed to the development of the Arabic novel in general, but nothing distinguished it as particularly "Lebanese." As the genre was dominated by Egyptians and developed primarily within an Egyptian context it remained within this domain and slowly evolved in terms of style, form, language, and so on. With the war in Lebanon came further developments in the novel not only in Lebanon but in a more far-reaching way in Arabic literature as well.

Another interesting feature of these debates and discussions is that often works written in Arabic and French are read together in criticism as part of one "literature of the war," whereas most Arabic literary criticism looks at works written in Arabic and French by Arab authors separately—even when considering thematic issues such as war.[2] Most scholarship that studies literature in Arab contexts assiduously works to keep the texts produced in different languages apart and not to underline their similarities.

2. For the classic attitude of literary scholars of Arabic, see the explicit statement by the editor M. M. Badawi in the introduction to the *Cambridge History of Arabic Literature* (1993, 1–2).

Though elsewhere I have argued for the importance of reading works written in Arabic and French together in some contexts, my argument is not so much about seeing women as writing war in similar ways, but rather about communities of writers taking up certain ideas and engaging them—they may be separated by language but this is not necessarily so (Hartman 2002, 20–25). Seeing a literary field not as marked only by language but also privileging other kinds of explanatory elements to think about texts can be instructive. Crucial differences in literary fields that are influenced by language should not, however, be erased. While I argue that it is important to highlight similarities between Arabic and French literary production, we must also not ignore that French-language texts do circulate differently in the global marketplace. They address and have access to different audiences and thus are subject to a different political reception both inside and outside of the Arab world, yet both fields were affected by ongoing social changes affecting the perception and use of language.

As Said hints, women's writing in the context of the newly evolving Lebanese novel is recognized as having particular features of its own and has been discussed in this way in the scholarship. There is extensive criticism of the Lebanese women's war novel, in Arabic, French, and English. Indeed in English-language criticism there is a large body of work focusing on men, women, issues of gender, and writing war.[3] One of the main arguments that dominates this criticism focuses on how women resist war in their fiction in various ways such as writing of its "dailiness," as Miriam Cooke argues in *War's Other Voices: Women Writers on the Lebanese Civil War* (1996). Evelyne Accad goes even further in her contrasting analysis of novels by women and men in *Sexuality and War: Literary Masks of the Middle East* (1992) to posit that writings by women resist war whereas those by men promote it. This type of criticism holds that women write about the war in fundamentally different ways than men do. So powerful is this critical work that a countercriticism arose: some of which argues

3. See criticism by Evelyne Accad (1992), Samira Aghacy (2009), Bayumi and Yared (2000), Miriam Cooke (1996), Lamia Shehadeh (1999), and Anastasia Valassopoulos (2003), among others.

that women's writing about the war should not be separated from men's to promote feminist ideologies (Salem Manganaro 1995, 163–73), others trace the orientalism that subtly underpins the criticism (Valassopoulos 2003, 183–99). This lively critical debate distinguishes the study of Lebanese women's writing from many other subfields of Arabic literary study in the English language, which is a relatively underdeveloped field, scattered between issues and topics.

Social Polyglossia and the Lebanese Civil War

The series of wars that devastated Lebanon for more than fifteen years profoundly impacted every aspect of Lebanese society, from literary production to all other parts of social and cultural life.[4] French-language fiction written by Lebanese women increased during the war, as did literature written in all genres and other languages, especially Arabic. In the 1980s most of the writers still hailed from well-to-do families; their backgrounds are slightly more varied—not all authors are from the ranks of the sociopolitical and literary elite. Of course writing in French means that these authors are still French educated, and French education was largely accessible only to privileged classes, but with the traumatic events of the war came a breakdown of norms and conventions, which at times opened up new possibilities. The war was a period in which boundaries of conventional hierarchies were broken down as social chaos ensued and new hierarchies emerged. Religious/sectarian or ethnic boundaries were reinforced, as the motivations behind the fighting were often articulated in terms of identity and group belonging. In the face of extreme threat, class

4. Perhaps partly because so many of the issues that caused and were created during the war remain unresolved, histories of the war remain incomplete and many of the works written are contested and ideologically driven. Even when biased to one side or perspective, however, many of the works are very helpful in making sense of a complex situation. See Ahmad Beydoun (1993); Georges Corm (2003); Samir Khalaf (2002); Kamal Salibi (1990); Fawaz Traboulsi (2007). Also helpful is the journalist Robert Fisk's *Pity the Nation* (1990) and the film made by satellite television station al-Jazeera, *Harb Lubnan* (The Lebanon War).

distinctions at times were blurred, though members of elite groups often were able to escape the war through travel and emigration. As frequently happens in crisis situations, limitations to women's roles were sometimes relaxed and some women found social mobility and movement in the public sphere a possibility despite the constraints of the war itself.

Because the Lebanese civil war was a diffuse war or series of wars, it affected all of society, though it targeted different groups at different times and many civilians were drawn into it as combatants and/or victims. The war played itself out in religious/sectarian-confessional terms. This is often presented as a paradox—how could a country that represented coexistence as the "crossroads of civilizations" descend into such fratricidal hatred? It makes more sense, however, to see the larger sociopolitical and economic contexts of this modern nation-state founded on the basis of a shaky confessional coexistence; powerful elites used confessional coexistence, but the separation of various groups, to prop up their "merchant republic."

The unstable cooperation between religious/sectarian groups solidified in the early independence period through informal deals such as the National Pact (*al-mithaq al-watani*), forged between the power-brokering elites of the large religious groups, gave way to increasing tensions that culminated in war. The particular arrangement of the National Pact, for example, meant that a six-to-five ratio of Christian to Muslim MPs would serve at any one time in Parliament, with a Sunni Muslim prime minister and a Maronite Christian president in whom most of the power would be vested. The vastly underrepresented and growing Shi'a community was to become increasingly important demographically and increasingly disenfranchised politically and economically. The basis of civic participation in the state from its inception was through each citizen's membership in one of the seventeen officially recognized religious/sectarian groups, as defined by the heritage of the family through the father. Thus if the father was a Sunni, a Greek Orthodox, or a Druze, the children were as well. This information was printed on one's identity card and one was a citizen of the state through this affiliation first and foremost. The so-called identity-card murders in the war refer to people who were killed by members of a different religious group after showing their ID cards with the "wrong" information registered on it.

Many Lebanese people—both those who participated in the fighting and those who did not—resisted these categories. It is important to note that while the fascist Phalangist (*kata'ib*) militia was "Christian," for example, not all Christians held rightwing political views. The same is true in the reverse: the allied, leftist parties based in West Beirut, identified as "Muslim," did not mean that all Muslims were left leaning or that no Christians belonged to them. As the battle lines were drawn, militias and other fighting groups drew on such ethno-religious/sectarian affiliations for their support. But many of the most important battles in the war were fought as members of one group were pitted against another, all the more since at times they were uneasily connected to a larger political or ideological stance, at other times less so.

These divisions were compounded by the way in which non-Lebanese actors participated in the war. External involvement at times has been emphasized to the point of all but absolving the Lebanese from responsibility for the war, an issue dealt with in the discussions below. It is of course an exaggeration. It is crucial to recognize, however, that many local, regional, and international players had interests in the war for a variety of reasons and played out a number of other issues through the war. The issue of Palestine was central to the war narratives of how the war began in 1975, for example; all the stories somehow are linked to a conflict between "Maronites" and "Palestinians." The main allied leftist front linked itself explicitly to the liberation of Palestine from Israeli occupation; many rightwing Christian groups advocated the expulsion of Palestinian refugees from what they claimed should be purely "Lebanese" soil. Some of these groups were allied with Israel and some of the notorious massacres of Palestinian civilian refugees were carried out by Christian proxy militias of Israel, at Sabra and Shatila as well as Tell al-Za'atar—locations mentioned or alluded to in the novels discussed below. Further, the brutal Israeli invasion and occupation of Lebanon, including Beirut in 1982, is one of the most violent and deadly episodes of the war and spurred a great deal of literary production. Some of the most moving and poignant literary expressions of the war were produced in its traumatic aftermath. Not only Palestine and Israel had stakes in this war; Syria and Iran also were involved in different ways at different points. Syria had a long-standing investment in Lebanon and remains directly involved in its political life today. Russia and the United States also played direct and indirect roles in the war, particularly as Cold War politics were being engaged through its actors. Regional hegemony and the balance of powers in the region, construed by various parties differently at different times, all influenced this involvement.

If the political and social orders were profoundly shaken by the ravages of the civil war in Lebanon, the field of education—and therefore the situation of the French language—was no exception. In a period when many institutions of the state simply ceased to exist, some of the locations most dedicated to interconfessional unity that promoted Arabic, like the Lebanese University and the public schools, lost prestige and had difficulty functioning (Shaaban and Ghaith 1999, 7). To fill in this gap, private schools flourished once again, and despite the increase in English-medium schools and universities and in English-language instruction in French schools, the French language maintained its prestige as the language of culture and was cultivated by the elite, and increasingly others, as opportunities arose (Shaaban and Ghaith 1999, 7; 1996, 102–3). The war underlined the importance of foreign-language education for social mobility, particularly outside of Lebanon, and this further entrenched a commitment to foreign-language private schools in Lebanese society.

Furthermore, the war gave rise to new large waves of emigration; two of the popular destinations included France and Québec (primarily Montréal). Relatively open immigration policies at different points during the war encouraged Lebanese people to immigrate to Canada, for example, and though some Lebanese chose Toronto and Ottawa, large numbers settled in the French-speaking province. With emigration to French-speaking locations and more widespread education in those locations and in Lebanon, despite the war more and more people learned French. No longer was French learned and spoken by only a very particular Christian elite. The results will be seen even more in later literary production, however, as the 1980s were really only the beginning of these changes. The details about Lebanese society during the war contextualize some of the profound changes that resulted from it. It can be difficult to navigate through the fraught question of religion/sect/confession in a war that is largely articulated in these terms, but in the writings of authors who themselves are secular and do not point to these as the kinds of identities with which they wish to be affiliated. But within the context of a war being fought in these terms, to reject such affiliations as to not mention them at all, is itself a political statement.

The vast majority of French-language writers in Lebanon were still Christian by background in the 1980s, though in this period more people of different backgrounds start to publish in French. We see in most of the texts a flattening of members of other groups: Muslims appear frequently, particularly to show interreligious harmony as an antidote to war, but are almost always described only in the most general terms. Many authors are keen to show Christian characters with "Muslim friends" or "Muslim neighbors," but rarely are these characters given centrally important roles. The Druze are referred to primarily as coexisting peacefully with Christians in the mountain villages of the past and the Shi'a are all but nonexistent. This will change later, as I discuss in part 3, but not in the French-language fictional production of 1980s Lebanon.

Class and status divisions were affected by the war and the hardening of ethno-religious and sectarian identities. On the one hand, war can be an equalizer of people—under falling bombs it makes little difference if you are from an "important family" or not. On the other hand, it can make all the difference. People with elite backgrounds were shielded in many cases from the worst horrors of the war. Throughout much of the war, wealthier sections of heavily Christian East Beirut were insulated from the worst of the fighting, for example, the 1982 Israeli invasion and occupation that targeted West Beirut.

Francophone Lebanese, almost by definition, had greater access to institutions that allowed them often to escape the war if they wanted to—foreign education, relatives abroad, dual citizenship, language skills to emigrate or at least work abroad, connections to people and places outside the country. This is not to say that French-speaking Lebanese, or Christians in general, were immune to the destruction wrought by the war, but as the biographies of the authors discussed here indicate, many lived outside Lebanon for long periods of time and even wrote the majority of their works in France or elsewhere. This can at times lead to an even greater alienation than was discussed in part 1, where French-language authors felt their ambiguous insider-outsider roles strongly. Writing in French and having such access took on its own meanings in a country in which most people were trapped in the ongoing violence and struggled to survive.

Gender adds another dimension to the ambiguous position that many French-language writers from Lebanon experienced during the war. Women writers experience the insider-outsider role particularly acutely, especially in circumstances when ethno-religious/sectarian identities go through periods of retrenchment and women are expected to uphold community "traditions." The increased mobility of people during the war and the breakdown of many conventions threw this expectation into sharper relief for many women. These issues are expressed in literary terms within the explosion of writing by women from Lebanon; the number of women producing creative works and poetry grew exponentially in the 1980s. It is not only French-language literature that expanded; Arabic literary works written by women also increased exponentially in the war years. An important group of writings in English by women (as well as some by men) also began to flourish in this period.

The war accentuated trends that were already taking place in the period leading up to it; feminism in Lebanon and the Arab world—as in so much of the rest of the world—became more important from the 1960s onward. Women were increasingly educated to higher levels, the expansion of university education benefitted both women and men, and people increasingly read and wrote. This affected all other areas of social life as well. As in other periods of trauma and war, such as the *safarbarlak* and First World War more generally, women took on new social roles. Women trained and fought in militias during the war, as well as actively organized and participated in antiwar demonstrations and movements.[5]

5. More scholarly work, especially literary criticism, has focused on women as actively engaged against the war than as fighters or participants in the war. See Accad (1992) and Cooke (1996) for two prominent examples. The collection edited by Lamia Rustum Shehadeh (1999) addresses this by including studies of women fighters as well as a series of other contributions showing the diversity of women's experiences and expressions during the war.

Similarly, women participated increasingly in all forms of literary production; a number of Lebanese women writers of Arabic and French became increasingly known internationally as well as within Lebanon.

Polyglossia in Literature

To give just a sense of the range of works by Lebanese women authors being produced in French in the late 1970s and 1980s, more than one hundred novels were published, along with the continued production of poetry. Some of the best-known works written in this period—both poetry and prose—were penned by poets. Poetry should therefore not be seen in opposition to prose, as in a Bakhtinian version of novelization that contrasts the epic and the novel, but rather as part of similar novelization processes, with many works by the same authors treating many of the same questions and issues through language.[6] For example, after distinguishing herself in the 1960s as a major French-language poet in Lebanon, Nadia Tuéni wrote some of her most powerful works during the war, *Liban: Vignt poèmes pour un amour* [Lebanon: Twenty poems for one love] (1979) and *Archives sentimentales d'une guerre au Liban* [Sentimental archives of a war in Lebanon] (1982). Nadia Tuéni died prematurely of cancer during the war and *La terre arrêtée* [The earth stopped] (1984) was published posthumously. Like Bustros's works, Tuéni's complete collected writings were issued by the Dar an-Nahar "patrimoine" series, in two volumes—one of poetry and one of essays and other brief prose writings (1986a and 1986b).

Another poet of Tuéni's generation, Etel Adnan, wrote her acclaimed novel *Sitt Marie Rose* (1977) about the war based on a true story of a Christian woman murdered while working with deaf-mute children in a Muslim part of Beirut. It has often been referred to as both an antiwar novel

6. Like prose fiction and theater (as Stone 2007 has argued), poetry was also subject to a process of novelization and the use of polyglossia in this period. While undoubtedly maintaining its prestige and importance, poetry was also changing during the war and increasingly experimenting with language.

and an ethnographic exposé of people's lives in wartime Beirut.[7] She also published her haunting prose poem *Apocalypse arabe* (1980) as well as numerous other collections of poetry written in English; she continues to write and paint to this day, producing some of the most acclaimed creative work by a Lebanese woman artist (Majaj and Amireh 2002). Claire Gebeyli emerges as another important French-language poet in this period with *La mise à jour* (1982) and *Dialogue avec le feu* (1985), both dealing directly with the devastation of the war. Gebeyli only began writing prose in the postwar period when she produced a novel.

Other novels penned in this period were also written by poet-novelists. The best known of these is Andrée Chedid, who published several novels in this period, two that deal with the war directly: *La maison sans racines* (1985) and *L'enfant multiple* (1989). Both of these works are powerful statements against war that promote a harmonious, multiconfessional view of Lebanese society. *La maison sans racines* is particularly pertinent to the discussion here, as its plot intersects with many of the themes and issues of the 1980s novel by Lebanese women writers discussed in the chapters below: one Muslim and one Christian woman work together to organize a peace march at which an innocent young girl watching is murdered. Discussed in detail in chapter six, Vénus Khoury-Ghata is another poet-novelist whose prose works come into their own during the civil war.

All of these writers had careers as successfully published poets by the 1970s, when the war broke out. The war itself, though, gave rise to a number of new writers, and by its end a younger generation began to write. Evelyne Accad began to publish novels in the 1970s. The now well-established Dominique Eddé wrote *Lettre posthume* [A posthumous letter] (1989) at the very end of the war and did not publish another novel until after a ten-year gap. Hailing from the city of Tripoli, Ezza Agha Malak is one of the rare French-language writers from a Muslim background. She published her first collection of poetry, *Migrations*, in 1985, followed by

7. This novel was translated into English by Georgina Kleege using the same title (1982), and Adnan did her own translation of her prose poem *Apocalypse arabe* as *Arab Apocalypse* (1989).

others in the early 1990s. She produced fiction only in the mid-1990s, with *La mallette* [The suitcase].[8]

New male voices also wrote the war from a variety of angles and perspectives, countering simplistic notions of their literary works as merely violent and engaged in reproducing a glorified war. Ramy Zein penned a novel about the war that was introduced by the Lebanese president Charles Hélou, *Le chant des ruines* (1986), before going on to publish his invaluable reference work, *Dictionnaire de la littérature libanaise de langue française* (1998). *La honte de survivant* [The survivor's shame] (1989) was published by Alexandre Najjar in the same year as an acclaimed collection of poetry *À quoi rêvent les statues?* [What do statues dream about?] (1989), which uses some of the same material within it as is used in the novel. Najjar is a major figure in French-language Lebanese literature, as he produces poetry and novels as well as criticism and a critical anthology. He has also continued writing; some of his most interesting works were published after the war.

Another writer who happens also to be an ordained priest, Mansour Labaky, published a sort of trilogy of novels condemning the war that orphaned children, who are the protagonists: *Kfar Sama* (1983–1985), *L'enfant du Liban* [The child of Lebanon] (1986), and *Mon vagabond de la lune* [My wanderer of the moon] (1988). Labaky's works criticize the war and are strongly didactic "message novels" in which the story is subordinated to the ideas that he wishes to get across. Nonetheless *L'enfant du Liban* and *Mon vagabond de la lune* have both won numerous literary prizes in France and Lebanon. Toward the end of the war, he published two more works, *Deux maisons pour rien* [Two houses for nothing] (1991) and a short story collection *Mon pays au passé simple* [My country in the past tense] (1992), the latter of which draws on some of the idealized imagery of Lebanon seen in earlier works. Similarly, Sélim Nassib wrote two novels about the war that in their details of violence could be described as anti- rather than pro-war statements: *Fou de Beyrouth* [Mad in Beirut]

8. Malak and her writings are the subject of several collections of essays (Baritaud 1995; Hahn 2010; and Sicard 2005).

(1992) and *L'homme assis* [The sitting man] (1992). Like the women writers discussed here, these male authors build on the work of the established French-language authors who published before the war, but the generational overlap is not quite as strong as among women writers. Moreover, not as many men established themselves as poets before going on to write important novels like an Adnan, a Chedid, or a Khoury-Ghata.

Because of the vast output of writing in Arabic during the war by men and women writers, it is difficult here to present a detailed picture of the literary production. To give some sense of the context, however, it is possible to say that similar issues and themes were taken up by Arabic-language and French-language texts during the war. The changes in narrative style, tone, language, and other literary devices identified by Said, Khoury, and others as hallmarks of Arabic writing in Lebanon during the war leading to shifts in the genre are not shared by French-language authors, however. Three of the most important writers of the war in Arabic are Rashid al-Da'if, Elias Khoury, and Hanan al-Shaykh, all of whom changed the face of the Arabic novel.[9] Khoury's *Little Mountain* (*Al-Jabal al-saghir*) and *White Masks* (*Wujuh bayda'*), for example, experiment with voice, form, time shifts, and multiple narrations in ways that shook up the traditions of Arabic novelistic writing.[10] Rashid al-Da'if's experimentations with narrative voice and tone in works like *Ghaflat al-turab* (1991) and *Passage to Dusk* (*Fusha mustahdafa bayna al-nu'as wa al-nawm*, 2001) similarly reflect the disruptions of the war and have an impact on later novels in the Lebanese context and beyond. No less important are works by Hanan al-Shaykh, who uses innovative techniques and experiments with language extensively within her Arabic texts, particularly in the use of colloquial and formal Arabic. *The*

9. I have named only three of the most prominent writers during the Lebanese civil war; there are many, many others. The 1980s saw a host of novels published by men and women writers, though it is crucial to note that women's contributions increased exponentially and led to a great interest in them as can be seen in the criticism. For a discussion of the civil-war novel in the context of literary narratives from Lebanon, see Salem Manganaro (2003).

10. Elias Khoury has written and published a number of other novels that also experiment similarly (1977; 1981; 1989/2009; 2007; 2010).

Story of Zahra (*Hikayat Zahra*, 1980) has been acclaimed as one of the most complex and challenging novels about the war.[11]

The French-language novel changes during the civil war, much as the Arabic novel does, though it does not transform the genre of the French-language novel as dramatically as Arabic-language Lebanese novels do. Certainly, though, the way in which language is used in the works of the 1980s, and how this use engages with complex types of novelization, marks a formal break from the earlier works of the previous period. But if the works of the mandate and early independence period engaged the issues of their time, particularly in working with the genre of ethnography in different ways, the novels of the civil-war period engage the ways in which society begins to disintegrate, and this is reflected in the language and style. Ethnography is not totally abandoned—a work like Dominique Eddé's *Lettre posthume*, discussed in chapter 8, picks up on some of its main tropes and techniques. This novel changes the focus, though, in defining itself through the epistolary rather than the ethnographic genre. This is a feature of novelization particularly relevant in a world literature framework. Not only do works engage with different kinds of genres and languages to produce new novelistic discourses, but they also target and engage different audiences. Such novels are then, for example, more liable to circulate within the market for works about war outside of Lebanon as much as within it. Moreover, the explicitly feminist stance of a text like Evelyne Accad's *Coquelicot du massacre*, discussed in chapter 7, puts it in dialogue with other possible audiences.

Many of the stories told in and about this period of course are exclusively focused on the war; moreover, many works offer direct feminist critiques of violence, masculinity, and patriarchy in this context. The French language and references of the text often reflect these social disruptions and we see the increased use of indirect speech, less formal narrative styles, slang, and even obscenity. In all of these ways we can see ties with the changes in the Arabic novel mentioned above, though it must

11. Like the other two, Hanan al-Shaykh's many novels pick up on these war-related themes.

be emphasized that, like French-language novels, Arabic-language novels written in Lebanon by women at this time are diverse and cannot be reduced to simple categorizations.[12]

Feminist Reactions to the War: Arabic as Punctuation

Each of the three works discussed in part 2 is different in its own process of novelization, which to Bakhtin is not linear but recursive. Khoury-Ghata's novel is narrated by the daughter of a family that suffers greatly at the hands of an abusive patriarchal father, she tells their story against the backdrop of a slowly disintegrating Lebanon. Lebanon has already disintegrated in Evelyne Accad's *Coquelicot du massacre*, which employs a frame story of hope for the future told through the voices of feminist characters, who share a hope that through their collective action and antiwar activism they can claim it back from the forces destroying it. Dominique Eddé's *Lettre posthume*, as its title betrays, is an epistolary novel in which a Lebanese priest tells stories about the war to a friend in France. Though so different, all three texts make extensive use of polyglossia, especially representations of Arabic. At times, they draw on the same techniques and strategies that we saw in the earlier novels, at other times they depart from them. The extensive explanations and cushioning that they use in relation to mixing speech genres, especially in referring to Arabic, are present in all of the works and are used to punctuate their French-language narrations with feminist messages; this is what I refer to as the "feminist punctuation" of the text.

The first novel discussed in the next chapter is also the earliest, Vénus Khoury-Ghata's *Le fils empaillé* (1980). Making extensive use of what she calls "franbanais" [French-anese], Khoury-Ghata's novel tells the story of the breakdown of a family in 1950s Lebanon, though the civil war lingers

12. Emily Nasrallah's war novel largely set in Canada, *Flight against Time* (*Al-Iqla' 'aks al-zaman*, 1984), can be contrasted, for example, to her classic *Tuyur Aylul* (1962) [September birds]. The war novel is more sentimental and idealized—even when referring to Lebanon—and the 1960s novel makes a more challenging political, feminist statement.

in its background. The subsequent two chapters discuss Evelyne Accad's *Coquelicot du massacre* (1988) and Dominique Eddé's *Lettre posthume* (1989), both of which explicitly draw on the language of the marketplace to write within the setting of the war being waged in and over Lebanon. Arabic words, and vulgar Arabic curses in particular, are employed to punctuate these texts, not through the technique of relexification, but rather through a more "direct" strategy of language mixing. Both novels transliterate Arabic words into Latin letters and then explain them in some detail, providing a translation, context, and critique. Eddé makes some use of relexification as well, and all of the texts use techniques such as employing meaning-filled Arabic names for important characters. At times these names are not translated or explained, as in the works in part 1, at others they are explained extensively.

As a technique, the transliteration, translation, and explanation of a word marked as foreign, vulgar, or otherwise, can seem to be almost the opposite of a subtle relexification, which must be identified and its meaning somehow "unlocked" depending on the level of contextualization and cushioning. It also works counter to the relexification process in that it does not naturalize the borrowings from Arabic into the French text as a subtle strategy of indigenization, radical bilingualism, or otherwise. Rather than hinting at a range of meanings, this technique isolates a particular word or phrase, draws attention to it, and directly discusses the details of its meanings. Like relexification, this strategy may use a surprising shift in speech genre to interrupt or punctuate the narration, but the shifts tend to be more direct and immediately striking to the reader than relexifications, even those that are well-cushioned. When explained like this, the strategy at first glance might seem the least interesting poetically or formally.[13] Moreover, it can appear to be so clear-cut and obvious politically that it is didactic. In some instances this may be true. The interference with

13. Zabus, for example, sees this as a less creative strategy. She equates more cushioning and more translation with less creativity in her discussions of relexification (Zabus 2007, 7).

French in these examples is clearer than in relexifications; these textual interventions are all but labeled as such and beg to be noticed. The reader is not challenged to discover a deeper message or ironic moment because the author states her message clearly in the translation of these words and phrases. Or does she?

Some critics have privileged the subtler methods of inscribing difference through language as more creative and challenging to the structures of the colonial language. Chantal Zabus, the theorist of relexification, has shown how these instances of language mixing and blending can mount significant critiques from within language. More direct uses of language mixing need not be seen as somehow less creative, challenging, or "poetic," however, especially when seen in light of the novelizing process as Bakhtin has identified it, drawing on a range of types of interruptions of speech genres. The kinds of direct confrontations with the colonial language, French, by words clearly identified as Arabic seem on the surface to be statements of rejection, often a feminist rejection of patriarchal norms and ideas tied to colonialism. But on the other hand, these "translated" sections where Arabic words are explained in detail also represent an accommodation within the text—aren't texts that explain these complexities to French readers welcoming these readers into the texts after all?

A further way of reading these kinds of interruptions or feminist punctuation is to see transliterated and explained Arabic words within the French text as exhibiting "language variance" as it is defined by Ashcroft, Griffith, and Tiffin (1989, 54). Here, language difference is used as a metonym for cultural difference. I would expand on this definition by proposing that transliterated Arabic words be seen as a metonym for Arabic as a language system as well as a culture exhibiting "difference." This echoes Bakhtin's idea that languages can be objects of representation just as much as they can represent ideas. Authors draw on the words that are transliterated to represent ideas that they wish to convey through translation—literal or metaphorical. They are then discussed in great detail, even up to a paragraph worth of description, rather than being given a literal translation. The explicitness that is implied by such long explanations belies the "difference" of the words that are being invoked, simply because of the space used discussing it. This also begs the question of the function of such explanations and if they should be read "literally" in creative texts or rather as part of a creative process of using and exploring language by redefining words and concepts not only to French readers who do not know Arabic but also to French readers who do.

The following chapters demonstrate how the detailed exploration of allegedly "direct" translations of vulgar, transliterated Arabic words and phrases in two civil-war novels—Accad's and Eddé's—is no less interesting than relexification in how it ties together politics and poetics. In fact, the inscription of feminist messages about gender, as well as the connection between gender and language in Lebanese society, is often encoded in such explanations that on the surface seem to be simply didactic commentaries. Reading these textual moments in detail reveals the creative power of language. Language is used to express the depth of political and poetic links that intertwine to advance messages for social change. This technique is another method of mixing and blending genres as well as creating a new language of novelistic expression.

One reason for this is the role of vulgarity of expression itself, similar to the billingsgate defined by Bakhtin in his study of Rabelais. Though these novels that treat the civil war would not be characterized as "carnivalesque" in the sense that it is used by Bakhtin in his treatment of Rabelais, they do make use of the languages of the marketplace in ways that reverse and challenge normative behavior during a period of breakdown of social norms. The kind of move from more polite "gendered interference" to what I have characterized as "feminist punctuation" is exemplified by the use of more shocking language. This is less true in *Le fils empaillé* by Khoury-Ghata than in Accad's *Coquelicot du massacre* or Eddé's *Lettre posthume,* as the former does not use vulgarity. But all of the works use an extensive amount of speech, dialogue, and other kinds of mixing of high and low languages, the languages of the street and public square, compared with the earlier works. The Arabic of quaint village peasants used to highlight customs and traditions and the polite set expressions that represent patterns of speech have been replaced by the urban idiom of war. This means that more internalized and individualized languages—often of women and "outside," including vulgar words of the marketplace—come to the fore. Though everyone is being displaced and moved between locations, often wrenched from their homes because of the fighting, we see how women gain increased access and movement within the public sphere, enabling them to make different kinds of direct commentaries, offering us this "feminist punctuation."

6

Like Soap Bubbles on Our Tongue

French, Arabic, and "Franbanais" in Vénus Khoury-Ghata's Le fils empaillé

> There is therefore a geography of words whose meaning changes when they are pronounced somewhere other than in their country of origin.
>
> Il y a donc une géographie des mots dont la signification change dès qu'ils sont prononcés ailleurs que dans leur pays d'origine.
>
> —KHOURY-GHATA 1980, 113

The fictional embodiment of how patriarchal oppression is enacted through language in the family setting is nowhere better expressed than through the character of the father in Vénus Khoury-Ghata's *Le fils empaillé* [The son stuffed with straw] (1980).[1] This domineering and abusive man is shown to be a cruel tyrant throughout the novel, exposing the damage that patriarchy does to his son Frédéric, the boy's three sisters, and their mother. Language is tied to power explicitly and implicitly throughout this work, where the father exercises not only corporal punishment but also dominates the children's psyches and means of expression. Colonialism, patriarchal control over the family, and the

1. Vénus Khoury-Ghata is one of the most prolific and best-known Lebanese French-language poets who is also an acclaimed novelist, with a reputation second only to Andrée Chedid. She wrote a number of important novels during the civil war, many dealing with it directly (1984, 1986, 1988), and just after the war ended (1992a, 1992b). She continues writing about Lebanon and war but also other topics in the postwar period: *La maestra* (1996b), for example (mentioned in chapter 9), is one of her most acclaimed works.

violence these two mete out against their subjects are invoked in a scene in which the father beats his son mercilessly for a stain—in the shape of the "map of France"—he has left on his sheet by masturbating. It is here that the narrator contemplates how words—her specific examples are "vermine, écraser, anéantir" (vermin, crush, and annihilate)—take on different meanings when used by a colonial power, or by a father who is its local representative.

The narrator is one of the daughters, Diane, who looks back at her family and their struggles in the 1950s from a vantage point almost thirty years later. While clearly drawing on some specific details from the author's childhood, the family in *Le fils empaillé* is also used as a metaphor for society at large and even Lebanon as a postcolonial nation-state.[2] The obvious parallel between the father as the local representative of French power and the rest of the family as colonized subjects runs throughout the work; colonial violence is exemplified in his beatings of his son. Khoury-Ghata uses this family's story to comment on a series of issues including the shape of modern Lebanon, the lingering problems caused by French colonial power in the region, the snobbery of the Maronite community, gender roles and the oppression of women, and religious/sectarian divisions between people.

Language is one of the main fields in which familial, and thus also social and national, struggles are played out in *Le fils empaillé*. Khoury-Ghata deploys a variety of strategies to demonstrate the close relationship between language and patriarchal articulations of power, hierarchy, and domination. The identity formation of all of the characters is intimately linked to different uses of language. Khoury-Ghata's text sustains a running metacommentary on language that reinforces ideas about how colonial power and language are linked and explores the fraught relations

2. Other critics, like Katia Haddad, have pointed out the parallels between this novel and Khoury-Ghata's own family (2000, 157), as has Khoury-Ghata herself (1996a, 8), and one of her English translators (Carollo 2006, 124–25). In relation to this, it could be mentioned here that she published another novel that reworked many of these same details almost twenty years later, *La maison au bord des larmes* (1998b), her only novel to date that has been translated into English as *A House at the Edge of Tears* (1998a).

between Arabic and French. This strategy was not used by any of the authors discussed in previous chapters, but is also a prominent feature of all of the novels of Dominique Eddé. Both Eddé and Khoury-Ghata critique the French language, show its connection to power and authority, and demonstrate the problems with this through the direct commentary on these issues in French in the narrator's own voice. In *Le fils empaillé*, this direct commentary on the French and Arabic (or "Lebanese") languages stands out both because Khoury-Ghata simultaneously uses relexified Arabic/Lebanese expressions and also because she claims that her novels write a kind of "franbanais" (a neologism combining the words "français" [French] and "libanais" [Lebanese]). Spoken Lebanese Arabic is a "mother tongue" here that is combined with French in order to subvert its patriarchal oppressiveness from within the colonial language. For Khoury-Ghata this is a crucial political intervention. Unlike the three novels discussed thus far, *Le fils empaillé* explicitly defines French as a "semi-colonial" language more in line with Etel Adnan's comments about French alienating her (cited in the Introduction). She directly critiques the French language in this way, as well as the snobbery of many people who insist on its use in Lebanon.

It is productive therefore to read Khoury-Ghata's project alongside other French-language writers who have similarly claimed to inscribe a mother tongue within their works while using and critiquing French at the same time. Assia Djebar's meditations on French as a "step-mother" tongue, for example, show her reluctance fully to embrace it while yet finding a certain liberation from the constraints of classical Arabic in using it as her language of literary expression. Djebar has moved from literary expression and used film to capture her mother tongue, much as Etel Adnan claims to "paint in Arabic" (Alcalay 1994, 311). Abdelkébir Khatibi's experiment with "radical bilingualism" is another way to understand the impetus to alter the shape of French from within it by letting Arabic and French coexist side by side (1983a and 1983b; Mehrez 1992, 120–38). Exposing the myth of the supposed bond between "Francophone writers" and Arab writers of the French language at that, the contexts of Lebanese and North African writing in French are different enough that Khoury-Ghata's language use has not been critically received similarly to that of Djebar, Khatibi, or others. In a world literature framework these might be useful points of comparison, as would English-language and other texts that critique and exploit the symbolism and power of multiple languages within them. Reading her work in relation to criticism coming from within the Lebanese context and in relation to works by her Lebanese colleagues writing in French reveals how language operates in her works in particular ways.

Vénus Khoury-Ghata is one of the Lebanese novelists the most daring in speaking about her use of the Arabic language within her French texts: "My dialogues are Arabic written in French. I have integrated the Arabic language into the French language: the form of the sentence is French but the content is Arabic" [Mes dialogues sont de l'arabe écrit en français. J'ai intégré la langue arabe dans la langue française: la forme de la phrase est française mais le contenu est arabe] (1996a 8). Her explicit challenge to French betrays a confidence in relation to language use that we do not see in the novels discussed in previous chapters and that echoes the poet Nadia Tuéni's claim to write Arabic in French that is used as an epigraph to the preface to *Native Tongue, Stranger Talk.*[3] It is not only Khoury-Ghata's own confidence and assertions about her use of this experimental language that have made it noticed. Critics have also taken up the question of her language use directly: "Additionally, the style of her novels is characterized by grafting Arabic onto the French, especially onto the dialogues. According to the writer herself this linguistic contribution is in addition to a 'depaysement,' another way of living, unknown superstitions, which enrich French literature" [En outre, le style de ses romans se caractérise par une greffe de l'arabe sur le français, en particulier les dialogues. À cet apport linguistique, s'ajoute, selon l'écrivain elle-même, un 'depaysement', une autre manière de vivre, des superstitions inconnues qui enrichissent la littérature française] (Nicolaides-Salloum 1997, 111). Such use of language is not always cast in a positive light, however. Katia

3. This counters the proposition by Makward (1998) that "Francophone" women writers in the 1980s had not yet found a voice within which to critique and play with the French language, because of a lack of experience and confidence.

Haddad, for example, goes so far as to question why Khoury-Ghata would write in the colonizer's language at all if she feels so conflicted by its use (2000, 162).[4] This kind of scorn for experimentation with and challenges to French is characteristic of criticism coming from inside Lebanon about Lebanese writers.[5]

Khoury-Ghata's direct approach to the question of language makes a break with the works discussed in part 1. *Le fils empaillé* also serves as a bridge between them and the other two novels discussed in this part because it is set in the 1950s, though narrated from the perspective of a person living in the 1970s-1980s. The question of the timeframe of the novel's setting and narration is crucial because the 1950s, depicted and nostalgized so frequently as Lebanon's "golden years," is viewed through a lens affected by the events of the Lebanese civil war, reflecting its publication date (1980). The narrator of the novel recounts events through a child's voice and perspective, but this is infused by "adult" reflections on feminism, sectarianism, the shape of the state, and other crucial issues. The civil war is only alluded to directly in a brief passage in the epilogue (Khoury-Ghata 1980 221), but the novel is full of implicit commentaries on it through its depiction of confessional tolerance, coexistence, and the evils of sectarianism. More implicitly, the disintegration of the state is paralleled in the breakdown of this family; colonial policies of the French mandate and patriarchal social structures are equally at fault in social failures.

Le fils empaillé creates a complex running commentary on language through its specific discussion of the French language, its critique of French

4. The critique seems somewhat disingenuous in a book on Francophone writing of the eastern Mediterranean, where it is clear that, because of their education in colonial school systems, most writers do not have a true *choice* as to their language of expression.

5. The vast body of writing, criticism, and scholarship on similar kinds of work being done by North African—and other—writers of French is thus largely ignored. There is also no scholarship that sees linguistic experiments of a writer like Khoury-Ghata in conjunction with writers experimenting with English; a world literature framework would connect the circulation and dialogues between these works.

colonial policies and the subsequent use of French by the Maronite elite, and descriptions of how the children in the family use several languages. The novel further supports its own metacommentary on language by also employing a significant number of polyglossic strategies to interrupt speech genres. Though it does use gendered interference like *Salma et son village, Sous la baguette du coudrier,* and *Le sommeil délivré*—for example, playing with names filled with meaning and employing a number of crucial relexifications of Arabic words—it inscribes Arabic more forcefully into its French narration. This confrontational use of Arabic in its metacommentary and also to infuse the French language with references to it points to the more explicit ways in which language is addressed in a novel published in 1980 civil-war Lebanon. The subtler uses of gendered interference have developed and been incorporated into feminist punctuation.

A Metacommentary on Colonial Language

One of the same, subtler strategies of earlier works that Khoury-Ghata employs functions in a slightly different way. Like the works of Kher, Bustros, and Chedid, *Le fils empaillé* includes characters with meaning-filled Arabic names. Rather than leaving these names unexplained—as Salma, Jamil, Anissa, and Samya are—the meanings of the names are often explained in detail. Madame Zakié is one such character. Moreover, the main characters of this novel have French or "Western" names and those meanings are also exploited within the text. The narrator Diane, for example, alludes directly to her onomastic identity when she claims to be not the hunter but the hunted (Khoury-Ghata 1980 13). Naming her for a Greek goddess underlines not simply a use of foreign names for the sake of showing alterity, but also to demonstrate cultural affiliations and estrangement from both Arabic traditions and the Euro-centered Francophilia of this woman's father.

If Khoury-Ghata's use of polyglossia is explicit, her novelizing techniques are less so and operate differently than those of Amy Kher, Eveline Bustros, and Andrée Chedid. These three novels all borrow from the genre of ethnography and its idioms, whereas Khoury-Ghata draws on a different range of discourses and the languages associated with them. So while Kher and Bustros each concentrate on one distinct Lebanese Christian mountain village and Chedid on the Egyptian countryside from the very opening of their novels, it is difficult to discern where *Le fils empaillé* is set. The clues as to where this novel takes place are only revealed as the work unfolds. At first only details that indicate the novel is set in a former French colony are revealed. For about half of the work, it is difficult to piece together information much more specific than this. Then the reader learns that the mother of the family is from the village of Qadisha, in the north of Lebanon, near the village depicted by Kher in *Salma et son village.*

Shrouding the setting of the work in mystery reinforces the importance of French and what it means as a colonial language. Parallel to the practices of "la mission civilisatrice" that would seek to homogenize "natives" into Frenchwomen and Frenchmen, the characters in this novel are first and foremost shown to be (post)colonial subjects of France. Only after we know this do we learn about the specificities of their experiences in Lebanon. Khoury-Ghata exposes the power of language by allowing her clues about the setting to become apparent through discussions of it. The languages that the children in the family speak at home are a central focus of the novel, establishing the parallel between these children as objects of colonial, patriarchal rule at home and in the country. French is imposed on them, just as it was imposed on their country. "We speak nothing but French, the only language allowed by the head of the family who has never gotten over France's departure (from our country)" [On ne parle que le français, seule langue admise par le chef de famille qui ne s'est jamais consolé du depart de la France] (26). The narrative voice in this section is particularly ironic when she comments about her father's relationship to France that he has been "an orphan for forty-some years, our father" [un orphelin de quarante et quelques années, notre père] (26). The child draws on the image of France as the mother of the oppressive patriarch. "His gentle mother, France, abandoned him among the barbarians who do not speak her sweet language, or who speak it, and this is even more dramatic, with an accent which stripped it of all of its sweetness" [Sa tendre mère, la France, l'a abandonné parmi les barbares qui ne parlent pas sa douce langue, ou qui la parlent, et c'est plus dramatique, avec un accent qui lui enlève toute sa douceur] (26).[6]

This ironic commentary is itself a reaction to her father's own repeated complaint, "I should have shot myself in the head the day that Weygand went home" [J'aurais dû me tirer une balle dans la tête, le jour où Weygand est rentré chez lui] (26). As these lines show, the father's extreme loyalty and Francophilia is identified only against the "barbarians" (barbares) in his own country. That country is not explicitly identified: it could be just about any former colony of France. The only specific detail given is the date of French withdrawal, and even this is given as a vague "forty-some years earlier." The reader must match this to the date of publication of the novel in 1980 and guess the location. Lebanon is as plausible a country as another.

On this very same page, however, there is another clue about the location of the novel given when the narrator tells us that, despite the father's tyrannical insistence on no language but French being spoken in the house, the children also speak a language that they call "franbanais." "But we also speak 'franbanais' when the words of our mother tongue make soap bubbles on the surface of the language/tongue of the protector and quasi-colonizer country" [Mais on parle aussi le "franbanais" lorsque les mots de la langue maternelle font des bulles de savon à la surface de la langue du pays protecteur et vaguement colonisateur] (1988, 26). The children prefer this language through which they can express French and Arabic, though they all speak excellent French. The imposition of French is unnatural to these children; they find their father's insistence on this language's purity and the need to speak it in a particular way to be unbearable.

This level of metacommentary, complete with a number of ironic asides by the narrator, uses the discussion of language as a negotiation of social and political issues in *Le fils empaillé*. The much-hated father of

6. This is the same passage that Katia Haddad includes as the representative sample of writing by Vénus Khoury-Ghata in her anthology *La littérature francophone du machrek* (2000, 161–62). She cites it positively in relation to complexities of language use in Lebanon and issues around it, including Arabic and French being referred to as the "mother" and "father" tongues of French-speaking Arabs.

the novel, whose vicious beatings are the cause of his son's madness and the rest of the family's misery, is symbolically represented through the French language. His control over his children and wife is likened to the colonial power of France over Lebanon. French is identified explicitly as a language imposed on Lebanon that represents colonial oppression; this is then mirrored by how the patriarch tries to micromanage his family's use of language. Franbanais, the banned language of the children of the household, "a language born of the need to express one's self in Arabic and French at the same time" [langue née du besoin de s'exprimer en arabe est en français à la fois] (27), is the children's "indigenous resistance" to domination by the powerful patriarch and the systems. Language thus both oppresses and liberates, and as such Khoury-Ghata challenges colonial power and violence through language. Her metacommentary is accompanied by other polyglossic techniques that boost her feminist battle against patriarchal domination, constricted roles for women, and colonialism.

What Is Franbanais?

Franbanais is one solution proposed in *Le fils empaillé* to the problem of French. The children's claim to speak this language is echoed by Khoury-Ghata herself in her use of the neologism in interviews where she claims proudly that she infuses her creative texts, especially in dialogue sections, with Arabic. Like Nadia Tuéni's similar claim, Khoury-Ghata's is more difficult to untangle within the literary language of her works than in their atmosphere and attitude. The main language of Khoury-Ghata's novels is identifiable as standard, literary French. But just because a novel does not radically disrupt linguistic conventions does not mean that it does not employ sophisticated techniques for crafting a creative and original textual language, or that it only uses languages as "window dressings."[7]

7. Even a text that is experimenting with these ideas explicitly and is held up as an icon of radical experimentation, like *L'amour bilingue* by Abdelkébir al-Khatibi, does not produce a language recognizable as "not standard French" (Mehrez 1992). A similar strategy is at play in the English-language writings by the Egyptian-British Ahdaf Soueif (Hassan 2006, 753–68).

Le fils empaillé uses its "franbanais" as feminist punctuation to underline ideas and messages consistent with its time and place, and to comment on family violence, patriarchy, and ultimately the war.

It is the combination of discussing franbanais and also using it, as well as other instances of language tension, that propels *Le fils empaillé* and allows more experimental formal linguistic devices to join together as a challenge to patriarchy and colonialism. Perhaps it is partly the harsh criticism that faces Lebanese authors who choose to write in colonial languages but challenge them at the same time that push French-language novels from Lebanon to make their stance on language clear.[8] The kinds of moves that Khoury-Ghata makes in *Le fils empaillé* by commenting on language even as she writes the novel, shifts the way in which we can understanding the crafting of language in this and other French-language novels from Lebanon. The political stance of franbanais is clearly anticolonial and antipatriarchal rather than somehow being an expression of Francophilia rejecting Arabic on the one hand, or the uneducated French of people who are not sufficiently invested in "proper" speech on the other. By allowing children to control how this language emerges in the text, it develops from a genuine need for self-expression.

Franbanais is not only mentioned in the abstract, however, and examples of "franbanismes" (expressions used only by French-speaking people in Lebanon) reinforce the political claims of the novel, consistent with the concept of feminist punctuation. The narrator's tone is ironic when discussing the "home language" of herself and her siblings, joking that perhaps someday it will be as important as Greek or Latin and studied at the Sorbonne. As ridiculous as she presents this to be, she then offers a humorous discussion of a French diplomat-cum-orientalist who walks around with a little notebook in which he records all of the "franbanismes" he hears in order to study the language (27). This discussion allows

8. It is interesting that Haddad raises this important question though she does not really delve into it at any length. She ponders why Khoury-Ghata would choose to use French as her language of creation if she has such a harsh evaluation of French as the language of the colonizer (2000, 162).

Khoury-Ghata to convey a number of expressions that in their transcription operate similarly to relexifications, except that they are discussed explicitly as such. Although they are common expressions in French as it is spoken in Lebanon, one typically would not hear these words spoken in France.

The diplomat-orientalist's commentary on these expressions connects his voice to that of the narrator-author. Similarly to Amy Kher, Eveline Bustros, and even Andrée Chedid, the explanations of expressions through a voice of authority and expertise allows her both to connect to the French-speaking reader and also to display her insider-outsider status. Her underlining of her own status and expertise is thrown into even sharper relief because it is she who gazes on the diplomat-orientalist who collects the expressions—even as he is gazing on those who speak them—recording them all in his little notebook.

One of the passages in which franbanais is commented on in the novel is a part of the narrator's running commentary on the French language. She describes the people who use this language as "indigenous" Lebanese, again reflecting an outsider tone, though spoken by an insider-outsider narrator. Though she is deriding her father throughout the entire section for his exaggerated attachment to the French language and France, it is somewhat unclear how much she means to poke fun at Lebanese people for using these expressions. She states,

> The respectable French person should betray no surprise on his face at the indigenous person's habits and customs when the latter invites him to "let himself be seen," meaning "come more often." Or when he reproaches him for "whitening his face on his back" ("taking all the credit"), or when he advises him to "show how big his shoulders are," or in other words, to go away.
>
> Nulle surprise ne doit se lire sur le visage du Français respectueux des us et des coutumes de l'autochtone quand ce dernier l'invite "à se faire voir", comprendre "revenir plus souvent". Ou quand il lui reproche de "Blanchir son visage sur son dos", ("tirer la couverture à soi") ou lorsqu'il lui conseulle de "montrer la largeur de ses épaules", en d'autres termes de s'en aller. (27)

These three common expressions, relexified here together with translations into standard, idiomatic French, are similar to many of those relexified by Kher, Bustros, and Chedid in that they are polite expressions to do with social niceties.[9] What I have called "relexifications," Khoury-Ghata identifies as "franbanais" when they are actually used in people's speech. It is interesting that in this passage she reports this speech and represents Arabic within French in terms of what it would sound like to a French person if spoken, but does not inscribe them into the text as spoken words, for example as dialogue.

This step back from an integration of franbanais into the dialogue of the novel, for example, instead incorporates it into an extended metacommentary on language and is typical of the feminist punctuation that I have identified in the novels of this period and that we will see echoed in the texts discussed in the next two chapters. In the earlier examples of Kher, Bustros, and Chedid, I identify the use of such relexifications as gendered interference. In all of those texts, the characters are living in Arabic-speaking environments and are meant to be speaking Arabic in their lives as represented by the novel. Words marked as Arabic permeate and interfere with the French-language narration of these texts to remind the reader of this, among other reasons. Khoury-Ghata's text contrasts with this because the characters are meant to be speaking in French and they use actual relexified expressions, which her own commentary shows are not standard French. These expressions punctuate the text and remind the reader that French is not always the same: these characters use a different French. By discussing franbanais, Khoury-Ghata is thus claiming that people use these expressions in their everyday life and that the French that they create through language mixing is peculiar to Lebanon. Anyone familiar with French-speaking Lebanon who has heard the mixing of French and Arabic knows that the use of Arabic and French mixing can be even more deeply

9. They refer to the common colloquial Arabic expressions "khaleena n-shoofak" (let himself be seen), "bassin snaano 'ala dahar ghayro" (whitening his face on his back), and "farjeenee 'ard kitfaak" (show how big shoulders are). My transliterations here are meant to reproduce the sounds of the colloquial language.

embedded in the language. The adding of the dual ending "ayn" to make something two, for example, transforms the greeting "bonjour" into "bonjourayn" on the streets of Ashrafiyyeh and elsewhere in Lebanon today.

Another important feature of Khoury-Ghata's commentary is her use of the word "autochthone" (indigenous person). It is relevant here that she shows the Lebanese to be not so different from other colonized people throughout the Third World, as indigenous people fighting against their colonizers. This is thus a double challenge to French because the "indigenous people," as they are referred to here, make this language their own—their native tongue is neither Arabic nor French as these languages are commonly understood and they do not need to use "stranger talk" with the French because the language they use is perfectly understandable, if differently punctuated. It is important to note that this political message has a particular resonance at the time this novel was written and published, at the end of the 1970s. Moreover, in Lebanon, ideological battles over the identity of Lebanon and the Lebanese are part of what is being fought over in the civil war. The irony in her narrative voice helps to layer her political message to both "insider" and "outsider" readers, especially in the double context of language use.

The Figure of the Orientalist

The specific examples of "franbanismes" are relevant to Khoury-Ghata's purpose and so is how she introduces them. The figure she uses to insert these expressions into the text is an orientalist ambassador from France to Lebanon who devotes himself to the study of franbanais. He offers a certain authority to this language by demonstrating that an outsider, a "scientific expert," is interested in it—thereby showing its importance outside the relatively few people who speak it. The outsider gaze at the phenomenon not only exoticizes it but also legitimizes it as a language. What complicates this further is that many of its speakers feel that they are speaking "French" rather than a different or new language; this is Khoury-Ghata's own sly commentary on the snobbery of many French-speaking Lebanese.

The orientalist figure signifies a shift from the stance of the earlier novels by making its engagement with orientalism more explicit. Rather than rework travelogues or ethnographies written by orientalists of the nineteenth century, for example, it includes a modern version of such a figure right in the text itself. Therefore the subversion from within the text to comment on the outsider's gaze—as I argued in the case of Kher and Bustros—is direct and specific. Khoury-Ghata states openly that this man is studying the Lebanese and catalogues the specific things he is interested in. In another shift, she shows not only that the orientalist studies their "authentic, native" speech and quaint local village customs and traditions but also that the French language spoken by these Lebanese, who feel it is "superior," is also gazed on and deemed exotic by orientalists. By reclaiming franbanais itself as a quaint tradition, Khoury-Ghata thereby poses a challenge to those Christian Maronites whom she has identified as looking down on "other natives" and makes them the object of study. This "insider" commentary contains an irony that is reprised in her representation of certain expressions but also in her commentary on the "outsider" figure of the ambassador himself. She finds him as exotic as he finds her community. She is a mediator between cultures, much as he is, but her authorial voice allows her to present this situation in a way that brings the colonial relationships to the fore in a powerful critique.

Race and *Métissage*: Lebanese Engagements with Africa

Le fils empaillé reveals its specificity in a Lebanese context slowly. With few indicators of its Arab or Lebanese origin and its harsh critique of colonialism and colonial policy—particularly to do with language—it consistently evokes a larger French-speaking context, placing it in dialogue with many works throughout the world. These features of the text makes the way in which it engages the politics of race and the African continent all the more problematic. Though the colonial policies and politics in the parts of Africa colonized by France were similar and even harsher in many cases, the divides deemed "racial" expose a fault line in the possibilities for solidarity between the kinds of analysis inscribed within *Le fils empaillé* and analogous texts from locations like West Africa.

Africa is depicted throughout this text as Other. This is particularly clear in the character of the mother, who defines herself against Africa and continually denigrates people in Africa. It is somewhat difficult to discern at times whether or not the narrator's commentary on this othering of Africa is indeed ironic, as so many of her other remarks are, or if this is naturalized and the narrator-author relies implicitly on Africa as a symbol of an absolute Other. The main examples of othering come when the speech of the mother is depicted. Unlike her children, the mother does not know French and speaks only a pidgin French, which she refers to using the derogatory term "petit nègre" (27) born of the condescending attitudes of colonizing French toward local populations who speak a nonstandard French. This is followed up by the narrator's comment that the mother has never been to Africa and does not like Africans particularly; she calls them "eaters of missionaries." The narrator's references to cannibalism and to Africans as savages are meant to show the mother as ignorant and are followed up by her comments about other locations that she sees in similarly stereotyped ways.

Textually the effect is to make the mother seem banally ignorant rather than condemning her. In this way, Khoury-Ghata's text reflects the attitudes of a certain privileged class, assimilating and naturalizing them. Such assimilation can be contrasted with a parallel kind of prejudice, a different version of racism, which is depicted in the father's disparaging of Muslims. In the text, Christians looking down on Muslims is shown clearly and directly to be wrong. The mother's condescending views about Africans, however, are portrayed as silly and innocuous. In some ways this contradicts the politics of the novel more generally, which mount an anticolonial critique that one might suppose would include solidarity with Africans, many of whom also were subjected to French colonial rule. For example, the Lebanese are shown in the role of "indigenous people" exploited by the white colonizer, France.

> In this miscegenation between two languages, France, as it should, plays the role of the white seducer, and our country that of the knocked-up indigenous woman, in order to make words that are neither too white nor too black and that wail with the same soul in French as in Arabic. Such miscegenation not only affects the composition of sentences but also their spirit.

> Dans ce métissage entre deux langues, la France, comme il se doit, tient le rôle du Blanc séducteur et notre pays, celui de l'indigène engrossée dans le but de faire des mots ni trop blancs, ni trop noirs et qui vagissent avec la même âme en français qu'en arabe. Ce métissage ne touche pas uniquement la composition de la phrase, mais son esprit également. (27)

The terminology used here that identifies Lebanese people as the indigenous people opposed to the white colonizer clearly invokes Africa and affiliates the Lebanese with the Africans. As such, this passage can be read as a challenge to Lebanese, particularly the elite, Francophone Christian Lebanese people whom Khoury-Ghata parodies so often in this work, and who identify as white.

But these kinds of contradictions easily coexist and Khoury-Ghata's text is certainly not the only one to manifest them. An avowed anticolonial, Third World solidarity stance within the Arab world does not mean that every Arab person is an antiracist or knows how to put that theoretical position into practice in diverse situations. Moreover, when looked at in the context of representations of Africa, Africans, and African Americans by Arab writers, this sort of ambivalent position is shown to be relatively common.[10] Racial "difference" and the way in which Arabs do and do not identify with Africans can be contextualized within the larger, problematic history of these representations that belie these conflicting attitudes.

Khoury-Ghata's intention in using this example seems to be another way of depicting the beloved mother of this family as ignorant but innocent. She opposes herself to Africans and looks down on them though she "speaks like them," but Khoury-Ghata does not take her to task for this any more than she does for her inability to protect her son from the vicious beatings of his father. It seems that in both cases, paralleled within the text, Khoury-Ghata is arguing that we should focus on an anticolonial politics and not on the victims who then revictimize. Though the mother

10. On the image of Africans and African Americans in Arabic literature, particularly the larger context given in the footnote references, see Hartman (2005, 397–420).

is complicit in the son's abuse and evinces racist attitudes toward Africans, it is the father on whom the focus of critique must be trained.

Madame Zakié: Authenticity and Islam

Le fils empaillé is less concerned with mounting a critique of Maronite Christian Lebanese snobbery towards people outside Lebanon, as in its trivialization of the mother's disparaging views of Africa, and focuses more on their superior attitudes toward people inside Lebanon, particularly Muslims. Here, the Muslim character Madame Zakié is used by Khoury-Ghata as a symbol through which she inscribes this critique. Madame Zakié is one of the few Muslim characters incorporated in the creative fictional works written by Lebanese women writers of French who is depicted in any depth or detail. In *Le fils empaillé* it is clear that she is a symbolic figure who plays the specific role of an "authentic" native insider, as opposed to the more "in-between" status of the French-speaking Christian characters. In this novel, this is meant to be positive—Madame Zakié is used as a contrast to elitist Maronites. This is not unproblematic in the sense that we could draw a parallel with the charming or "exotic" peasants of Andrée Chedid's *Le sommeil délivré* who speak French "with an accent" and serve as a contrast to the bourgeois values of the oppressive Boutros and his family. They are depicted in a positive light, but one that is somewhat condescending and casts them as Others.

Indeed, in some locations Madame Zakié is shown to be different because she wears a djellaba and covers her face (37).[11] Madame Zakié is a more complex figure, however, because she is well integrated into the same community as a member of it. Though she outwardly displays symbols of her difference, this is only due to her religion, and it is never shown

11. Though she is usually depicted in a positive way, in this early section in which her covering is described there is also a somewhat ridiculous example given of how she once exposes her backside to the father of the protagonist's family in order to cover her face when he spies her hanging her laundry (37). This is presumably meant to expose how Muslims can carry their "customs" too far, just as Christians do with snobbery. Nonetheless it does not fit in well with the other depictions of Madame Zakié.

to exemplify a class-status division between people in the same way that it is in Chedid's novel, for example. Differences are inscribed playfully. For example, her family lives in the flat above that of the narrator's family and the shoes that she "bought in Damascus"—another nod to her "Muslimness"—click on the floor in a way that disturbs the narrator's already irritable father (36).

Language is used both directly and indirectly to emphasize how Madame Zakié relates to her community, for example, her "superiority" is inscribed in various ways by using polyglossic techniques. To begin with, her name—one of the few Arabic names in *Le fils empaillé*—is infused with meaning. Zakié is the colloquial rendition of an Arabic word meaning "intelligent" (*dhakiya*). In many ways, Madame Zakié is more intelligent than other characters, in that we do not see her acting in the silly and superficial ways that so many other people do. Though the narrator casts an ironic eye on her at times and the elitist father and sister put her down, she rises above this treatment with a sense of humor. Some of her concrete actions also reinforce her abilities; for example, we know that she is a sort of local healer who women go to for help in various situations including illness (37).

As one of the few Muslim characters to appear in French-language literature from Lebanon, Madame Zakié stands out because she is drawn in detail. Though much is made of her as a character, however, she is not given much of an individual personality and functions primarily symbolically. Like Chedid's even flatter and less detailed Om el Kher and Zariffa, Madame Zakié counters stereotypes but at the same time activates them. This is once again indicative of the engagement of Khoury-Ghata's novel with its time. The focus on religion and confession locates *Le fils empaillé* as a novel commenting on the war in Lebanon despite its setting in the 1950s.

Madame Zakié is one of the primary symbols that promote the anti-sectarian message of harmony detectable not far beneath the surface of this novel. When she comes to live in this primarily Maronite community, for example, we see that a number of people question what she is doing there (35) and are suspicious of her, some believing that she is a "spy for the mufti" (37). It is even suggested by several neighbors that she and her family were sent to live among them by the government to see if Christians and Muslims could live together peacefully (38). A number of specific examples are given to show how Madame Zakié integrates into this community: she goes to Mass every Sunday because this is what everyone in town does, and like them she prepares and eats light meals on Friday (35). We also know, however, that she does not have a Christmas tree, is sure to observe the customs and traditions of Ramadan, cooks special foods during that month, and that her sons are all circumcised. Therefore though there is not a perfect understanding between all of the people in the community—witness the snide remarks of the narrator's father, for example—there is no intercommunal strife and they do live together in the sort of confessional harmony that can only be read as a statement against divisions within Lebanese society by religion, sects, and confession, and how these are manifest by the civil war raging at the time of the novel's publication.

All of these details are concretized through uses of language, particularly insofar as Khoury-Ghata critiques the Maronite Christians as being too blindly Francophile in contrast to the Arab and Arabic "authenticity" of Madame Zakié. In a typical use of metacommentary on language, the narrator poses the direct question, "Is Madame Zakié the only genuine article among all these Christians who ape France and the French, calling their children 'poussins' and their partners 'chéri'?" [Madame Zakié, est-elle le seul produit authentique parmi ces chrétiennes qui singent la France et les Français, appellant leurs enfants 'poussins', leurs conjoints 'chéris'?] (39). Khoury-Ghata explicitly calls Madame Zakié a "genuine article," as opposed to her Christian neighbors. Rather than pointing out the problems of their love for France by using a political, social, or economic critique, she puts forward an amusing example of the language that they use to refer to their loved ones.

The implicit commentary that Khoury-Ghata is making about French power and control in the region, and even its links to the war raging for five years when this book was published, therefore is indirect. She gently mocks Christian Francophiles by pointing out how they use French affectionate terms with their children and partners. This direct commentary on language use obliquely recalls the relexification used by Anissa to refer to her sons to recall the Arabic expression "taqburni" (may you bury me). Anissa's use of Arabic in French is reflected in the way that Madame Zakié refers differently to her children and husband than to others in her neighborhood. "Madame Zakié's [children] respond spontaneously to the sweet words, 'my heart's grass' and her husband finds it completely natural to be the 'poppy of her eyes'" [Ceux [les enfants] de Madame Zakié répondent spontanément à la douce qualification 'herbe de mon coeur' et son mari trouve tout naturel d'être le 'coquelicot de ses prunelles'] (39). These expressions are easily understood from context and cushioning, as it is clear that they are meant to reflect a parallel to "poussin" and "chéri." But they are also obviously inscribed as representing Arabic expressions in their awkward, literal translations here.

In invoking relexified Arabic expressions Khoury-Ghata makes a number of comments. First, there is the direct contrast between the use of Arabic and French expressions to reflect the Maronites' love of the West as opposed to the authentic "Arabness" embodied by the Muslim Madame Zakié and her family. Moreover, she plays with the expressions that she uses to further underline difference. The translations of common affectionate appellations make them sound even more exotic. "Herbe de mon coeur" (my heart's grass) directly translates as "hashishat qalbi," meaning something like my essence or my true love. The second example, "coquelicot de mes prunelles" (poppy of my eyes), translates into the common expression "bu'bu' al-ayn" (and might also refer to the less-common "khashkhash al-'ayn"), which more idiomatically in English means "the apple of my eye." This is another version of an expression whereby in Arabic you call your beloved, your children or others close to you, your eye or eyes ('ayni/'ayooni).

This kind of contrast is exemplified not only in the person of Madame Zakié but also in Muslims in general. The example of the different schools frequented by Muslim and Christian children further accents these issues and also indicates that Madame Zakié and her family are not lone Muslims existing in the world populated by the Christian characters of *Le fils empaillé*. In a passage about the different schools, we see that the Muslim children are said to attend a "madrassa" (40). In 1980—long before it started to be commonly used in French or English with the negative connotations that it acquired in the early twenty-first century—this word needed explanation. In Khoury-Ghata's novel it clearly refers to the schools attended by Muslim children within a Lebanon of the 1950s in which almost all children attended schools funded and supported by their own religious-confessional group. Not all of these schools were "religious"; rather, because the state was based on a sectarian system of government, largely leaving infrastructure in the hands of the institutions controlled by different groups, schools were supported by and affiliated to different religions. Khoury-Ghata clearly wishes to show the differences in these educational systems when she points out that Muslim children become well versed in the Arabic poetic and storytelling traditions, learning about things like the heroic figure Antar and the exploits of Abi-Zaid-Al-Hilali. She states that Muslims come home from their "madrassa" with "shining eyes" full of images of gazelles, whereas the Christian children come home with "dead eyes," like dials of watches fixed by the Cartesian system (40).

Though these metaphors may seem a little heavy-handed, they do indicate that it is not religion per se that is being reinforced as the difference between people. She shows how children educated in different ways, in different systems, are taught to recognize different heroes with contrasting imagery. Muslim and Christian children are raised with different points of reference. It is crucial I think that she does not show children being indoctrinated in their madrassa with the teachings of the Prophet Muhammad, or learning about the Passion of Christ in their école. Her emphasis on the loaded communitarian values learned by young people in school is more powerful both because it reflects the lived situation of Lebanon and because of the symbolic nature of religious-confessional affiliation and belonging in the war. Khoury-Ghata is infusing the Muslim schools with a positive value—albeit stereotyped: emotional and obsessed with ancient heroism. By contrast she shows the Christian schools to be so overly focused on science, the details of the battle of Waterloo and the precise direction of the flow of the Rhone River, that the children have "dead eyes." Despite this somewhat tired use of clichéd images of Christians and Muslims, Khoury-Ghata is able to make a strong statement about the war and changes needed in Lebanese society in order to counteract its sectarian strife.

This representation of Arabic, complete with a commentary on how it is more authentic than French, is supported by other similar, but less direct, uses of language by Madame Zakié. For example, she is also shown to be more authentically "local" (or Lebanese, though this term is never used in the novel) because she is able to take an ironic distance from not only the French language but also the French mandate power. In an amusing aside, the narrator comments that Madame Zakié is more authentic than the other neighbors because she is the first one to realize that they do not need the French mandate for her chicken to lay eggs (40). This commentary works on a number of levels. The ironic comment made about the mandate or semi-colonial power is contrasted not only to Christian Francophiles in general, but also to the father of the family specifically. Additionally, we see a common language enter the text, even more strongly than in the use of affectionate terms for children and partners. Chickens will lay eggs in Lebanon whether or not the French are in charge. This kind of statement conjures up authentic, native "folk wisdom" consistent with Madame Zakié's role as a healer of women. In this way, multiple levels of discourse and speech genres coexist within *Le fils empaillé* and function to layer polyglossia into a text written in a standard, literary French that is seemingly completely controlled by the narrator herself.

Conclusions: *Le fils empaillé*

Khoury-Ghata uses a variety of techniques to challenge the power that the father has over his family and the French language has over Lebanon, as represented through exploring how a monologic French-language narration is in control of the novel. Through her metacommentary on language, the advocacy of franbanais as an alternative, and a variety of other techniques including relexification, Khoury-Ghata destabilizes this monologic control to some degree. Though the French language of the text incorporates polyglossia to combat the monoglossic power of standard literary French, this is not a polyphonic novel in Bakhtinian terms. The narrator is still in control of the text. A range of voices infiltrate the narration and speak within it, but the ironic tone of Diane's narrative voice and the distance it takes from the other characters, the scenes and ideas that it describes, mean that a more daring novelistic experimentation does not emerge here.

The "generational shift" in language, though, is extremely pertinent to the novelization process in *Le fils empaillé* and is significantly different to that of the three novels discussed in part 1. Here we see a move from an ethnographic style of writing, detailed descriptions of rural villages, to an exposé of the urban landscape of Beirut. This occurs first in the childhood of the characters in the 1950s and then during the war. It is a shift from the outsider-insider who exposes one community to another to the insider-insider who lays bare all of the inner workings of her own family. The outsiders described—like Madame Zakié—are shown to be a part of this same community, and therefore though the characters all have different relationships to one another, the novel is unmistakably about Khoury-Ghata's "own" people, her own language, and her own community.

Language is the main location of this exploration. The discussion and examples of "franbanais" exemplify this rather than put a quaint language on display in conjunction with traditional customs. Khoury-Ghata shows that her community's "local," native tongue is one closely affiliated with France, but at the same time marked as Arabic/Lebanese. The mediating role of such an "in-between language" is in itself a metacommentary on the way in which multiple languages are used side by side in a "radical bilingualism" as advocated by Khatibi. The languages of the home in this case have moved outside of only the home space; we see the mixing of languages as a community phenomenon though many of the kinds of expressions used still are tied to home-based activities. The shift to a more explicit discussion of language changes the subtle gendered interference to what I have characterized as feminist punctuation. This becomes more and more pronounced in the other two novels discussed in part 2, Evelyne Accad's *Coquelicot du massacre* and Dominique Eddé's *Lettre posthume*, which each take the use of feminist punctuation and public language to a more pronounced and dramatic level.

7

Lebanon Is Tomorrow's Sun

Feminist Nationalism in Coquelicot du massacre

> Lebanon is pluralism, accepting difference within tolerance. Lebanon is tomorrow's sun.
>
> Le Liban, c'est le pluralisme, l'acceptation des différences, dans la tolérance. Le Liban, c'est le soleil de demain.
>
> —ACCAD 1988, 154

Salma dies of a broken heart in *Salma et son village, Sous la baguette du coudrier* demands Anissa's murder, *Le sommeil délivré* leaves Samya paralyzed, and in *Le fils empaillé* an entire family is destroyed by a father who terrorizes them, culminating with his mad son's presumed murder by sniper fire in the Lebanese civil war. Like so many other French-language novels by Lebanese women authors, Evelyne Accad's *Coquelicot du massacre* [A poppy from the massacre] is in many ways also pessimistic. Firmly situated in Beirut of the 1980s, largely among Lebanese university students and professors, this novel treats issues from militarism and factionalism, to drug addiction and patriarchal oppression, to the sectarian violence that is tearing Lebanese society apart. This novel is also distinguished by moments of optimism that pierce through its epilogue, bringing its feminist message to light. Through this epilogue, *Coquelicot du massacre*'s unnamed narrator does give some indication of how Lebanon might begin to escape the logic of war. In this feminist vein, the novel attempts to provide a positive definition for what Lebanon can and should be—a multiconfessional and pluralistic space not only for Lebanese but also for Palestinians, for women as well as men.

Its openly feminist message is perhaps not surprising given that its author, Evelyne Accad, is not only a novelist, poet, and singer, but also a feminist literary scholar and critic of women's literature. Accad's pro-woman agenda is right on the surface of all of her works.[1] It is somewhat odd that her sustained literary engagement with the topic of the Lebanese civil war is her only work that has not appeared in English, considering the number of works about the war that have been translated, including her own.[2] *Coquelicot du massacre* echoes the rest of Accad's oeuvre in that it is a story of women and their lives in a society that is falling apart. Following *Le fils empaillé*, which illustrates the shift from "inside" to "outside" language, from remaining within the space home or "bayt" to using a more open, public space linguistically and literarily, *Coquelicot* is firmly located "outside." In contrast to Khoury-Ghata's novel, and even tracing further back to Amy Kher's, Eveline Bustros's, and Andrée Chedid's texts, Accad's novel makes effective and striking use of direct and vulgar Arabic words to interrupt its narration. The most "didactic" of all of the novels discussed in this book, it also uses language marked as Arabic directly in contrast to the subtler techniques in the earlier works; *Coquelicot* exemplifies this transformation in later works, including the postwar novels.

Accad's directness and even vulgarity must be read through the lens of the Lebanese civil war, particularly because it was published in 1988, thirteen years after the war began. It is not only through its treatment of the war itself and the attendant breakdown of society, but also in the

1. Accad's first novel, *L'Excisée* (1982), is the story of an interfaith relationship between a Christian woman and a Muslim man that is faced with many difficulties. Her third novel, *Blessures des mots* (1993), is about a Lebanese American woman who travels to Tunisia to work with Tunisian feminists organizing a conference called "Quel feminisme pour le maghreb?" The novels are translated into English (1989, 1996).

2. Accad is a well-received writer whose works have frequently been translated from French into English and who is the subject of a book-length series of essays written about her (Toman 2007)—one of very few Arab women writers in any language to have achieved such acclaim (others include Etel Adnan and Nawal El Saadawi). In addition to creative works, Accad has written several books and numerous articles on feminism, the Lebanese civil war, and Lebanese fiction (1992). Her breast cancer memoir is titled *Voyages en cancer* (2000) and is self-translated into English (2001).

themes that are inscribed through this setting that Accad's novel expresses its time. The issue of sectarianism within Lebanese society and also how it affects Palestinians in Lebanon and the Palestinian cause is treated extensively in the novel. The somewhat idealized (though contested) harmony between Christians and Muslims, exemplified by Madame Zakié in *Le fils empaillé*, is replaced in *Coquelicot du massacre* by an epilogue that sees a group of men and women sitting, smoking, eating, drinking, and debating the war in heated disagreement about what confessional harmony means in war-wrecked Lebanon.

The unnamed woman who interrupts this conversation comments on the patriarchal, masculinist assumptions on which the men's analysis of the war is based. This unnamed woman frames this carefully constructed literary text—her story is related in several opening sections to *Coquelicot du massacre* and she then recurs as a character in its epilogue. Like Khoury-Ghata's Diane, this unnamed woman may appear as some sort of reflection of the author herself, as some of her biographical details echo Evelyne Accad's life: she is a Lebanese woman academic who has left Lebanon to teach in the United States but is compelled to return during the war.[3] After these brief sections, the novel soon leaves this woman to interweave the stories of a number of other young women and men—Nour, Najmeh, Raja, Hayat, and Adnan—who are living through the civil war. Each of these characters occupies a different position within Lebanese society and is coping with the war in a different way. All of them share a similar background, as they are educated and even connected to the university, including Hayat the feminist professor and Najmé her student.

The feminism espoused by Accad in *Coquelicot du massacre* is rooted in the 1980s and adds to the chorus of voices at this time that question the exclusion of Third World women of color from the feminist movement. She questions women's solidarities, showing that not all women are the same: women deal with different issues and must face things at times by

3. This may or may not be directly relevant to the analysis here, but it is notable that Accad inscribes characters who in some way reflect her own biography even more explicitly in her later novel-journal *Blessure de mots* [*Wounding Words*] (Harb 2005, 77).

using different strategies. Indeed not all women will want the same thing at the same time. While she demonstrates this diversity among women—even in the local context of the generational, class, and other differences between the women in the war in Lebanon—she clearly also does value and advocate some sort of global sisterhood among women as a worthwhile goal to aspire to, in some ways recalling Andrée Chedid's earlier, similar messages in *Le sommeil délivré*.

Accad uses vulgar Arabic words as punctuation in *Coquelicot du massacre*, accenting its messages about women. At the same time that this text unabashedly advocates a feminist message, it is underpinned by a subtle nationalism that permeates the novel. Her countervision to war-torn Lebanon activates idealized and romanticized visions of Lebanon that inadvertently reinforce stereotypes about it, as they are themselves rooted in a patriarchal version of the nation-state. Nationalist sentiments about prewar Lebanon tinge the narration and seem somewhat ironic in a work that is so avowedly feminist, as they themselves are deeply rooted in a patriarchal vision of the Lebanese nation. Of course Accad's idealized prewar Lebanon does not emphasize patriarchy or paternalism, but rather presents a utopian feminist version of postpatriarchy. This chapter will also raise the questions: Should we read this as optimism? As feminist idealism? And how are these visions related to Lebanese nationalist exceptionalism?

The Symbolic Power of Names: Continuities and Contrasts

The names of Accad's main characters reflect the way in which she uses words marked as Arabic more generally. She not only chooses Arabic names full of meaning for her characters but also explains what these Arabic words mean in French. Accad thus layers meaning into these names both implicitly and explicitly. Even not naming the female character who frames the text itself reinforces the kinds of ideas that Accad is conveying through her narration. Names like Nour (light), Raja (hope), Najmeh (star), and Hayat (life) are filled with positive symbolism in the context of a civil war. Each of these major characters in the narration, enclosed between the bookends of the frame story, embodies a certain idealism.

The most important of these examples is the first-named character in the novel, Nour. Toward the end of the novel, the meanings of Nour's name are implicitly reinforced through a meditation on how religion can resist rather than promote war. In this scene Nour has managed, after much difficulty and hardship, to cross the Green Line to the "other side" of Beirut with her son Raja. When she arrives she finds out that Father Boulos, one of the people who she had hoped to see, has just been murdered while paying a condolence call. Nour is awakened the next morning from her slumber in the bomb shelter to the sounds of people chanting for Father Boulos, and she looks at the walls around her that are covered in writing. She realizes that the walls are covered in religious writing from the holy books of the three major monotheistic religions and that their messages are identical:

> The Torah says: "The Lord is your eternal light." The psalms add: "the Lord is my light and my salvation, what should I be afraid of?" The New Testament responds: "He called you far from the darkness into His marvellous light." And the Qur'an concludes: "God is the light of the heavens and earth. . . . God leads those whom He wants toward His light."
>
> La Torah dit: "Le Seigneur est ta lumière éternelle". Les psaumes ajoutent: "Le Seigneur est ma lumière et mon salut, de qui aurais-je peur?". L'Évangile répond: "Il vous a appelés loin des ténèbres, dans Sa lumière merveilleuse". Et le Coran conclut: "Dieu est la lumière des cieux et de la terre. . . . Dieu conduit à Sa lumière celui qu'Il veut." (141; ellipses in the original)

Here we see the reference to light—a clear allusion to her name—bonding the three major monotheistic religious groups of Lebanon: Christianity, Islam, and Judaism. This is a clearly antisectarian, antiwar message and linked to the possibilities inscribed within this main character's name.

Nour is not the only character with a name filled with meaning; it is clear that her son Raja is also named symbolically. His name is discussed early on in the text, when Nour and Raja are first embarking on their perilous journey across the demarcation line. The child asks his mother why they are the only people crossing that day, and she answers, "Because we are hope, like your name, a symbol of rebirth" (Parce que nous sommes l'espérance, comme ton nom, symbole de renaissance) (64). It is meaningful in the context of this novel that this young boy being brought up by his feminist mother during a war should be called "hope." There are several scenes where it is mentioned implicitly and explicitly that Nour is attempting to raise this child against the dominant social norms that would turn him into a fighter. An early scene in the novel, for example, shows Nour interrupting a game of make-believe where a group of boys are "playing war" (28). Some of the men in the room chastise her for spoiling the children's game, saying that she will turn her son into a "wimp" (femmelette) and that they will never win the war with this attitude. Others—both men and women—support her.

Nour's son is not the only character with the name Raja. In a scene so laden with symbolic meaning that it is even somewhat overdrawn, Nour and Raja get help crossing the demarcation line back to "their side" of Beirut. These are the final pages of the novel before its very important epilogue, and they sum up the stories of the characters, especially the narration of Nour and Raja. After a terrifying confrontation with militiamen who wanted to kill them, another armed man steps in to help them. Nour is fascinated by him and they start talking. As they talk, she learns that he has changed his name from Jihad to Raja because he felt he needed a new name that better fit his "soul." "I found this name too aggressive, badly suited to the state of my soul. I then adopted the name Raja" [J'ai trouvé cette appellation trop aggressive, convenant mal à mon état d'âme. J'ai alors adopté celle de Raja] (145). Nour interjects that this is also her son's name and adds, "What a beautiful, hopeful name!" [Quel beau nom d'espoir!] (145). He goes on to talk about his metamorphosis and how he is working to reconstruct the country. The front according to Jihad/Raja should not be the demarcation line but the border with Israel.

The following two pages then advance the plot quickly. Jihad/Raja finishes his discussion of his name change and how he "saw the light" of hope and change for Lebanon. After this allusion to Nour's name, he helps the mother and son cross the line at the Bridge of Death, and as they are safely on the other side, they see him fall, bloody and lifeless, in a hail of bullets. The words "light" and "hope"—*lumière* and *espoir/*

espérance—translations of the names of Nour and Raja, recur numerous times on these final pages. They are inscribed there not only as a contrast to the scene itself, which sees one of the characters representing hope dying after having met Nour and "seeing the light," but also as hope for the future. However bleak certain scenes of *Coquelicot du massacre* may be, there is no doubt that Accad's novel holds out hope for a better future for Lebanon.

Though the names of characters throughout the novel are meaningful—light, hope, star, life—there is also meaning in the unnamed character who frames the entire work. She is a powerful woman who comments frankly and directly on a number of issues in Lebanese society, most important of course, the war, and offers a direct critique of patriarchal norms and values. Some of her commentaries clearly echo the kinds of issues that other women in the book face. I will discuss her major intervention within the epilogue in some detail because the kinds of analyses that this woman offers are crucial to the novel and it is meaningful that they are placed in her mouth. Some of the same kinds of commentaries, for example, could have been offered by Najmeh, a university student studying feminism, or indeed put into the mouth of Hayat, her teacher. Any of the main female characters in *Coquelicot du massacre* could have provided these analyses without the device of the frame story and the unnamed woman. Including this framing character, however, advances Accad's message by suggesting that it is not one or more specific, individual women who can and should stand up for women's rights in their own society against war, militarism, and patriarchy. Rather, this character stands for all of the women in the novel and is meant to represent Lebanese women in general. She is the Lebanese everywoman who cares about the future of her country and links this not only to the rights and duties of individual Lebanese people but specifically to people who have been most damaged by its situation—women and Palestinians.

Beyond Tabboulé: Food to Represent the Nation

Accad's use of Arabic to name her characters therefore is similar to that of the novelists discussed in part 1, though she is more explicit than they are and more consistent in her style of mixing languages. The same kind of parallel can be drawn in how *Coquelicot du massacre* refers to the names of Arabic foods, the strategic placement of these foods within the text, and the ways in which food and cooking advance certain messages about the expectations around women's roles in society. It is relevant that within a novel that uses Arabic words and expressions sparingly, and makes no use of relexification in favor of direct transliterations of words that are then explained, there are copious references to foods with their names given in Arabic. In fact, there are more foods mentioned in this novel than in any other discussed in *Native Tongue, Stranger Talk.*

This is relevant in specific cases when the foods are used symbolically to advance a specific message; at the end of this chapter I discuss how hommos and arak stand in for a certain vision of Lebanese nationalism (83). In other cases the foods seem to be adding "local color" or perhaps a positive respite from the details of the war, such as when Nour's son Raja is calmly eating "arouss mrabba" just before they set out to cross the Green Line. Accad glosses this food within the text as "Arabic bread covered in jam and rolled up into a long sandwich" (du pain arabe tartiné de confiture, roulé en forme de petit pain allongé) (46). The huge number of food references, I would suggest, are less provided to add "spice" to the novel or to provide ethnographic details, as we saw in the novels of the first section, than to provide a not-so-subtle commentary about women's preparation of food as a way to preserve culture.[4] In many instances, for example, women are shown preparing food when men are having "serious" political discussions. One of these is when Nour is listening to the men talking about the war at the home where she is forced to shelter for the night on her way to cross the demarcation line. She decides not to intervene in the men's discussion about the war though she feels that their analyses are superficial and should be deepened. In this specific

4. On food as women's cultural production, see the introduction to Kadi 1994; and Hartman 2007, 170–203. On what Arabic food represents in exile, see Bardenstein 2002, 353–87; and an Arab American novel taking up this issue is Diana Abu Jaber's *Crescent* (2003).

example, she likens her inability to enter the conversation to her difficulties crossing the Green Line:

> This men's world is forbidden to her, just as it is forbidden to cross the city. Why does she lack the courage to speak up, to force a way through the wall dividing the sexes, her and the men, even though she has decided to cross the city?
>
> Ce monde des hommes lui est interdit, comme il est défendu de traverser la ville. Pourquoi n'a-t-elle pas le courage de prendre la parole, de se frayer un passage à travers le mur sexuel dressé entre elle et les hommes, alors qu'elle a décidé de franchir la ville? (27)

Women do not simply wish to enter men's conversations and worlds that are forbidden to them for no reason; rather, they wish to press men on important points like what it is that pushes them to war. She even raises the question as to why she feels brave enough to cross the city—putting her and her child in peril—but finds herself lacking the courage to push the men in this situation to further their analyses and to challenge their limited and limiting views that lead to violence and war. She finds it easier to risk her own life and that of her son than to leave the kitchen, literally and metaphorically, after all of these reflections. The very next line simply states that she finished chopping the onions (27).

What is so interesting is that this is not an isolated example. Here, Nour is helping her hostess to prepare mujaddara. In the opening scenes, there is a party in Chicago where the American hostess prepares and serves drinks, desserts, and a veal dish that is toasted by her French husband, while he holds forth on culture and civilization. The scene of the epilogue is set in the evening; the unnamed narrator is hosting a group of Lebanese and non-Lebanese women and men at her house, serving them food and drink. The conversation—even some of its most heated moments—is peppered with references to the food being served. Indeed the American man who is offering highly problematic opinions is also being plied with all of the delicacies that the narrator has prepared. She serves him, for example, asking, "You like the tabboulé, the Lebanese national salad. Would you also like koubbé, a Lebanese dish par excellence, and some majadra, manaïches, mahshi koussa, and mahshi malfouf?" [Tu aimes le tabboulé, salade nationale libaiase. Veux-tu aussi du koubbé, plat libanais par excellence, et du majadra, des manaïches, du mahshi koussa, et du mahshi malfouf?] (150).[5] His positive answer to this question is echoed by the Lebanese people present, who also find the mezzes delicious and well prepared. The foods mentioned recall many of those mentioned in the novels discussed in part 1. Here we see tabboulé, the emblematic "Christian Lebanese" food of Amy Kher's Hadchit, operating somewhat differently, as a symbolic Lebanese national dish presented to an American outsider.

The preparation and serving of food is relevant to this scene in a number of ways. It helps to set up the polite and proper way that the evening's entertainment is conducted, despite the controversial subjects being discussed and the direction that the conversation will take. Moreover, it further reflects the earlier scene in which Nour does not enter the men's conversation, when she is also engaged in food preparation. The unnamed woman stands by listening to and reporting on the men's debates. The conversation heats up when the American man makes the observation that the Palestinians in Lebanon are espousing an ethnocentrism similar to that of the Phalangists whom all of the people in their left-leaning circle despise. After he proclaims this rather self-righteously, his Lebanese counterpart agrees and interjects, "Yes, exactly. . . . They are Palestinian Phalangists! After ten years of struggling for their cause, I have the right to say this. And I will even say on top of that: Kiss Oukhtoum!" [Oui, exactement. . . . Ce sont des Phalangistes palestiniens! Après dix ans de lutte pour leur cause, j'ai le droit de dire ça. Et je dirais même plus: Kiss Oukhtoum!] (151; ellipses in the original).

It is this final expression, "Kiss Oukhtoum," and the ideas that it is meant to punctuate, that push the unnamed Lebanese woman to participate in the conversation, despite her fear of being teased or even ridiculed. She feels she can no longer hold her tongue and gathers her courage to speak

5. Accad here inverts the common syntax of these foods, "mahshi koussa" and "mahshi malfouf" instead of "koussa mahshi" and "malfouf mahshi" (stuffed squash and stuffed cabbage). She does not do this with any other foods in the novel.

up. Her response demonstrates not only an emotional response to a sexist expression, but also analyzes some of its underlying psychological roots and impact. She invokes the Freudian unconscious, noting that our language is formed by it and therefore impacts on our sexuality, before saying,

> Sexuality is a taboo subject in our society. But to get at the root of our problems, we should tackle it. Kiss Outkhtoum—cunt, your sister's vagina, fuck your sister or mother's clitoris—underlines the hidden evils of our society and women's humiliations. This expression, when used in relation to the Palestinian resistance, is striking. It marks two groups as subordinate—the Palestinian people and women.
>
> La sexualité est un sujet tabou dans notre société. Mais pour aller à la racine des problèmes, il faudra bien que nous l'abordions. Kiss Oukhtoum—con, vagin de ta soeur, baise ta soeur ou mère du clitoris—souligne les maux cachés de notre société, les humiliations de la femme. Cette expression, utilisée par rapport à la résistance palestinienne, est frappante. Elle marque deux tutelles: le peuple palestinien et la femme. (152)

The use of the vulgar expression "Kiss Oukhtoum" in this passage is an interruption of speech genres on several levels, and the unnamed narrator's disquisition on it is itself a different, but parallel, kind of intervention. First of all, by inserting this interjection within dialogue in the text, but also dwelling on it and exploring its meanings, Accad's strategy of interrupting the French language of narration with a vulgar Arabic expression can be read as connected to the billingsgate of Bakhtin, particularly as it comments on a series of ideas about Lebanese society and the war. The Lebanese man throws a commonly used, but offensive, expression right into the middle of a discussion about politics. The Arabic word marks itself as different, and without the narrator's explanation the French reader would neither understand its meaning nor the impact that it would have on an Arabic-speaking reader. This double layering of meaning for different audiences, then, is tempered by the long lecture that the narrator gives, serving to both "explain" it to the French readership and offer her own definition and analysis to all of her readers—those who know Arabic and those who do not. The effect of reading the vulgar expression "Kiss

Oukhtoum" and then having it explained by a young, unmarried Lebanese woman in a public setting is extremely powerful. As a second shift in speech genre, this time from a manly and even "macho" dialogue about the war to a woman's lecturing voice, this intervention is highlighted within the text. Her tone mitigates the impact of the expression's use because of the clinical nature of her exposé of the expression. Nonetheless both are meant to undermine the reader's complacency in thinking about the issues broached in this scene.

The technique of using a transliterated Arabic expression, which is translated with added commentary, addresses multiple audiences at once, both the "insider" audience, those who know Arabic as well as French, and the "outsider" audience, those who only know French. A world literature framework allows us to see this as a way in which the text travels between locations and expectations, conveying several messages at once. To the outsider reader confronted with a transliterated Arabic expression, the words have no meaning—they are exotic or interestingly shaped and interrupt the French text, spoiling its linguistic "purity." For the French reader, therefore, the explanation and discussion of the word or expression is what gives this mixing meaning.

The significance of this textual moment for such a reader is the intervention itself—the flow of the text is broken by words that are strange. This conjures up the Bakhtinian notion of languages as the object of representation. As a technique it can also be read as inscribing difference in the way proposed by Ashcroft, Griffith, and Tiffin (1989). Arabic here operates as a metonym—a word stands in for a whole language system. In a context of the "empire writing back" to the colonial center, its challenge is in some ways as profound for an insider reader as an outsider reader. The reader who knows Arabic as well as French can detect its additional layers—the Arabic will still interrupt the flow of the French narration, but with the crucial difference that this reader can supply a meaning based on previous knowledge in addition to the meaning spelled out by the author. For this reader, for example, an expression like "Kiss Oukhtoum" calls attention to itself not just because it is linguistically "other" but also because it is not an expression often reproduced on the printed page. The insider reader then continues reading the definition and contextualization, matching the translation and information given to information she or he has already supplied through knowledge of the language. How the word or phrase is translated is even more important for this audience because the author is working with and at times perhaps against the expectations of the reader who knows Arabic.

How she addresses these multiple audiences is crucial in understanding the dynamics of Accad's strategies of crafting the language of *Coquelicot du massacre*. It at first seems that Accad is not directly engaged in exploring the politics of Arabic and French language use in Lebanon per se, as Vénus Khoury-Ghata does through her metacommentaries. I would posit, however, that she is well aware of the implications of writing a novel about the Lebanese civil war in standard literary French. Accad is familiar with the audiences she is addressing and how the book will be received and categorized within linguistic categories as well as others. The political stance of this novel is a direct challenge to the stereotypical positions of the French-language community in Lebanon. She emphasizes this through her largely left-leaning characters, in a book that betrays an Arab nationalist bent, though I will later discuss the Lebanese exceptionalism inscribed within it. Indeed the critique of the Left in the novel is done from "within," as the political actors who discuss these things are engaged in the struggle for the rights of Palestinians and other disenfranchised groups. This is particularly clear in the way in which "Kiss Oukhtoum" punctuates this text—almost as an exclamation point at the very end!

In the context of 1980s Lebanon, the comparison of Palestinians and Phalangists reflects a specific and easily understood political position. The intervention by the unnamed Lebanese woman in this conversation is where Accad's formal strategy takes on further significance, in its links to feminist politics. The way in which this woman draws an explicit parallel between Palestinians and women is both a feminist defense of Palestinians and a political move to advance the message of women's rights. Moreover, this comment challenges concretely the glorification of Lebanese particularism against outsiders, which is formally echoed in the technique of using a transliterated and translated Arabic expression. To draw on Arabic words and expressions in this setting makes her point powerfully, as it shows how the person who stands up for Palestinians and for women is deeply implicated in the Arab setting, knows Arabic, and is engaging the language and situation on its own terms. Had all of this conversation been in French, without the feminist punctuation of Arabic, it would have had a considerably different effect poetically and politically.

Much as *Coquelicot du massacre* contains a critique of the Lebanese Left from "within," therefore, this textual moment itself is a critique from within, demonstrating how a woman can engage Lebanese society in its own language—though the novel is written in standard French. I do not wish to exaggerate the use of words marked as Arabic in this novel, they are sprinkled judiciously throughout the text and their impact should not be overstated. But as a poetic device, I propose, this polyglossia shows how a Lebanese author from a Christian background maintains a politically engaged stance in defense of the Palestinian cause within a novel written in French. Accad uses *Coquelicot du massacre* to demonstrate that Francophone novels are neither all totally estranged from the realities of Lebanon nor do they embrace fascist/Phalangist positions. The feminist punctuation here thus reinforces the antifascist, antiwar feminist messages so crucial to its project.

Feminism in Dialogue with Lebanese Nationalism

As a feminist novel set in a war, *Coquelicot du massacre* is both optimistic and pessimistic. Advocating a feminist message about Lebanon's future, it holds out hope that something new can be forged, though the realities of this war foreclose so many options.[6] The death of one man named Hope (Raja) in the final chapter is counterbalanced, for example, by the survival of the feminist-raised boy called Hope (Raja). The final pages of the novel are similarly balanced. A song closes the novel and suggests the possibility of a happier, more ideal Lebanon, one built on the feminist principles suggested throughout the work, where love can overcome suffering. The feminism Accad shows as necessary throughout

6. To better articulate her vision, Accad develops a concept that she calls "femihumanism" in multiple locations.

the entire novel is explicitly presented as a solution to the problems of Lebanon. In a number of sections, this feminism is linked implicitly with a certain Lebanese nationalism that itself is less well defined. Feminism and nationalism thus coexist and support each other in ambiguous ways in the novel. Though Accad clearly makes a stand throughout the text against exclusive nationalisms and those that are being used to perpetrate the war, her message is in fact infused by many of the very same symbols that were used by parties participating in the war in order to further their specific nationalist visions.

One extremely important moment in relation to this intertwining of nationalist imagery and ideology and Accad's brand of feminism is found in the same section discussed above where the narrator comments on the men's vulgarity. She is preparing coffee for her assembled guests when the American man asks her about the future of Lebanon. After he declares that Lebanon was a "still-born" nation, she snaps back that she feels "very Lebanese." One of her compatriots then queries her as to what this means and she responds with the sentence that is the epigraph to this chapter, "Lebanon is pluralism, the acceptance of difference within tolerance. Lebanon is tomorrow's sun" (154).

This answer is instructive in a number of ways, particularly in terms of how feminism and Lebanese nationalism are intertwined in the novel. On the one hand, the comment is aspirational: the narrator is trying to show something positive about a Lebanon faced with the horror of war. By recalling these ideas about a different, pluralistic Lebanon from the "good old days," she is providing a model of what Lebanon can be. In the context of the discourses and debates swirling in the Lebanon of the 1980s, however, this kind of comment as an ending to the novel can be contextualized in specific ways. The suggestion here that this female narrative "feels very Lebanese," because a pluralism and acceptance of difference is a latent "Lebanese" value that will somehow emerge from the ashes of destruction, evokes many of the classic national myths about Lebanon. Indeed, contrary to many ethnic nationalisms, Lebanese national identity is built on a notion of pluralism and difference, particularly between different religious, sectarian, and confessional groups that themselves have even been defined as quasi-ethnic groups, as Aimé Azar does in her introduction to Amy Kher's *Salma et son village* when she speaks about confessional harmony in northern Lebanon.[7]

Assigning the Blame: Lebanese Nationalism and Outsiders

This kind of argument for a latent pluralism existing in a Lebanon besieged by more than a dozen years of war can be read not only as aspirational but also as exclusionary and essentialist. Though the thrust of the novel challenges this, the foregrounding of a "Lebanese spirit" was linked with certain kinds of nationalist ideologies and images by participants in the war. One way in which this is reinforced in the novel is the assertion that all people in Lebanon "really want peace" and that the violence and fighting is being done by non-Lebanese. No act of violence, killing, bombing, and so on is ever explicitly identified in the novel as being perpetrated by a Lebanese actor. Though she does call it a civil war and does point out many flaws in Lebanese society (violence of men against women and parents against children, militarism, patriarchy, and so on), the only mentions of killing and bombing that are identified specifically are attributed to the Israelis or the Syrians (35, 45, 51).

This nationalist idea recurs in numerous other plot elements. Najmeh's struggles with drug addiction, for example, are paralleled with Lebanon's struggles to free itself from the war. As she is weaning herself off heroin, the analogy becomes explicit. She feels the changes in her body in the same way that "she receives the fear and violence of her country submitted to external forces. She swallows oppression and dependence, like her country welcomes its decline. Like her country, she did not choose" [elle reçoit la peur, et la violence de son pays soumis aux forces extérieurs. Elle avale l'oppression et la dependence, comme son pays accueille sa déchéance. Comme son pays, elle n'a pas choisi] (126). The parallel is instructive here.

7. Michel Chiha was one of the proponents of this ideological strand in Lebanese nationalism, for example in a short essay titled "Lebanese Truths," where he claims, "It [Lebanon] is a collection of confessional communities each having its own personal status codes . . . a composite of races, religions, wisdom, unruliness, truths, and errors" (1952, 246–47).

Neither Najmeh nor her country chose their oppression and dependence. The reader does feel empathy for Najmeh as she tries to get off heroin, one of the most addictive of drugs. However much the reader wishes to see her heroin free and believes that she did not choose the life of an addict, we know that at some point she did choose to take heroin and indeed that she took it to escape the terror she was feeling living through a war. Much in the same way, Lebanon—and ordinary Lebanese people—did not choose to be thrust into a prolonged civil war. Certainly local, regional, and global powers did exploit the Lebanese war as a battleground for other struggles, including occupation, the drug trade, regional dominance, the cold war, and so on. But some people did choose to fight in the war, and not all of this war was fought for and by "outsiders" to Lebanon.

I am not making a moralistic argument here that we should lay blame either on Najmeh for her heroin addiction or on Lebanon and the Lebanese for the war. I also am not trying to point out a fatal flaw in Accad's logic about the war and its causes. I pose these problems here, rather, to tease out the ways in which *Coquelicot du massacre*—perhaps partly despite itself—participates in nationalist discourses about the war through its reliance on Enlightenment values. Though it proposes itself as a challenge to the power structure through its feminist argument, it is fundamentally based on many of the same ideas. Even the use of the woman as a metaphor for the nation, the drug-ravaged Najmeh reclaiming herself as a model for war-torn Lebanon, reuses some of the most well-worn imagery available (126–27).

The Diversity of Hamra Street as a Symbol of Lebanon

Other sections of the novel reinforce the ideas that the war is somehow external to Lebanese people (what it is to "be Lebanese") and that there is a latent Lebanese spirit that is somehow lying dormant during the war. These are not messages that Accad advocates directly but rather layers into her text, revealing ideas about how a certain feminism is linked to a certain nationalist vision of Lebanon. A conversation between Hayat and Adnan reveals another articulation of these ideas. After Hayat complains that she no longer feels comfortable around Hamra Street because the former cosmopolitanism of Beirut has been destroyed, Adnan begs to differ:

> As you can see, this street, like this country—at the crossroads of civilizations—is still a mix of East and West. I could very well have ordered arak and hommos. What is happening in the streets with the men you spoke of is separate from the will and deep desires of the Lebanese people. I am convinced of it. The spirit of democracy, tolerance of difference, mixing of cultures, still exists but in a latent form. One day soon all of these values will once again rise from the ashes.
>
> Comme tu vois, cette rue, à l'image de ce pays—croisée des cultures et civilisations—est encore un mélange d'Orient et d'Occident. J'aurais très bien pu commander de l'arak et du hoummos. Ce qui se passe dans la rue, avec ces hommes dont tu as parlé, est indépendent de la volonté et des désirs profonds des Libanais. J'en suis persuadé. L'esprit de la démocratie, de tolérance des différences, le mélange des cultures, existent toujours, mais sous une forme latente. Un jour proche, toutes ces valeurs ressurgiront des cendres. (83)

Here Adnan invokes a number of specific images to bolster his argument about the Lebanese spirit lying dormant and soon to rise again. The first one he uses is again linked to food. He invokes hommos and arak as complementary but opposing Lebanese foods that symbolize a nationalism that is a crossroads of civilizations, the mixing of East and West. Presumably he is referring to hommos as a popular dish and arak because it is alcoholic and would be frowned on by some Muslims for religious reasons. He believes that the intolerance being displayed on Hamra street is counter to what he identifies as a deep will and desire of Lebanese people—despite evidence to the contrary, the ongoing civil war.

Accad's message seems wrong to criticize. In the voice of Adnan, she is advocating an open and tolerant Lebanon. She is expressing what is surely true—most Lebanese people do not want war and want to live their ordinary lives in peace. But to dismiss the years of fighting justified through religious, sectarian, and confessional differences by saying that Lebanese people always have embraced the mixing of cultures seems almost disingenuous. Several key points link this passage to the one cited above in the nationalist vein. First, the idea that Hamra Street represents all of Beirut, or somehow all of Lebanon, is itself problematic. Adnan labels it a crossroads of civilization, activating one of the most potent national ideas about Lebanon propagated by the framers of its independence, both Lebanese and French. The happy marriage of East and West with Lebanon standing proudly as an exemplar of the mixing is clearly disproved by a fifteen-year civil war, no matter to what extent this war was fought from the "outside" or "inside." Moreover, "his" Hamra Street clearly is not one shared by all Lebanese people, as Hayat herself tries to point out.

Lebanon Rising from the Ashes: "Cèdres et Cendres"

The final image invoked by Adnan above—Lebanon rising like a phoenix from the ashes—is again familiar. It recalls the Phoenician ancestry that some nationalists used as a basis to argue for Lebanon's unique identity against its Arab neighbors during the mandate period and beyond.[8] Accad does not simply include it in this section alone but rather sprinkles mentions of the "ashes" (cendres) caused by the war throughout the text. She uses these ashes most importantly as a framing device in the introductory chapters and the epilogue, where they are paired with the "most national" of Lebanese national symbols—the cedar tree.

The mix of cendres (ashes) and cèdres (cedars) is potent imagery. Accad couples them in a number of locations, including the third sentence of the book: "Ashes, dust, and twigs scatter in the wind, in the cedar forest [Cendres, poussière et brindilles s'éparpillent au vent, dans la forêt de cèdres] (5). This coupling then recurs at the very end of *Coquelicot du massacre* in the epilogue, where they reinforce the narrator's sense of pain during the war.

8. See Charles Corm's *La montagne inspirée* (1934). For an analysis of how this ideology was expounded by Michel Chiha, see Michelle Hartman and Alessandro Olsaretti (2003, 35–65). On Christian nationalism and Phoenicianism more generally, though not without its own political agenda, see Asher Kaufman (2004). For a historical critique, see Fawaz Traboulsi (2007).

> Like a dagger, already plunged many times into her Lebanese heart of hearts, she knows only too well the pain of a repeated injury, for thirteen long years of war, a fatal wound of the cedars and ashes of her country, living out an intractable drama.
>
> Comme un poignard, plongé déjà plusiers fois, dans son coeur de Libanaise, elle connaît trop bien la douleur d'une blessure répétée, pendant treize longues années de guerre, déchirure mortelle de cèdres et de cendres de son pays vivant son drame insoluble. (149)

This second example reinforces the nationalist element of the cedar and ashes combination that is only alluded to with the reference to the cedar forest in the first example. The narrator feels the pain of the war and its intractable drama not just as a woman or as a person living in war, but as a Lebanese woman with a "Lebanese heart."

These examples at first glance again may seem rather innocuous and used simply to reinforce Lebanese imagery in a war in Lebanon. By the 1980s, the cedar tree was well established as a symbol of the Lebanese state through its inclusion on the flag. Ashes of course are an obvious metaphor during a war. But the combination of the alliterative pair cendres et cèdres (ashes and cedars) again draws on the kind of Phoenician imagery that was used very specifically by particular groups, especially rightwing and fascist groups that are so derided in *Coquelicot du massacre,* to bolster their own nationalist, separatist, and even Christian supremacist agendas. Once again, Accad is presenting a feminist version of the war and a way out of it, but one that slips very easily into the Phoenician imagery of separatist Lebanese nationalist agendas far removed from the kinds of political stands that this novel tries to make in other ways.

Lebanese Exceptionalism and Feminist Utopianism

Lebanon's Phoenician ancestry—and its attendant imagery of Lebanon as a crossroads of civilization, a phoenix rising from the ashes, and a model of pluralism—lies just beneath the surface of the nationalist messages inscribed in *Coquelicot du massacre.* It comes to the fore, though, in the epilogue in a specific comparison between the United States and

Lebanon as nations. This comparison is foreshadowed in the novel, for example, where Hayat states that she would not like to live in the States. She goes on to point out that if the United States had undergone in recent years what Lebanon had, it would have ceased to exist because it has neither Lebanon's history nor its fortitude (110). This is followed by a utopian feminist vision of a life she wants to create in Lebanon that is female centered, where women can cohabit with men without marriage and also maintain total financial independence (110–12).

The comparisons between Lebanon and the United States then recur in the end, when the American guest arrogantly makes all kinds of pronouncements about Lebanon, in particular that it has no historical reason to survive. The narrator is annoyed and believes that the American feels himself superior to the Lebanese in attendance. As he spouts off reasons that Lebanon should not exist as a nation, she does not intervene because she deems his argument so superficial. She thinks that she will say nothing because no country has a historical reason for survival, and then, "she thinks about the Phoenicians, ancestors of her native land, creators of the alphabet—so many examples to bring to bear . . . but what good is it?" [elle pense aux phéniciens, ancêtres de son sol natal, créateurs de l'alphabet—tant des preuves à advancer . . . mais à quoi bon?] (149–50; ellipses in the original).

This example of Accad's implicit nationalism once again shows the tendency to present a reversed counterargument to problematic ideas rather than rearticulate the terms of the debate or discussion. Thus rather than follow the idea that no country has a historical reason for survival and deconstruct the national idea further—which would seem in line with her political agenda—the narrator actually thinks about "her ancestors" the Phoenicians, inventors of the alphabet. The Phoenician myth of course is powerful and could theoretically unite a Lebanon divided on religious and sectarian lines by activating an "invented tradition" (à la Hobsbawm) about Lebanon that pre-dates the monotheistic religions.[9]

9. Hobsbawm discusses this famous formulation ("the invention of tradition") in his introduction to the edited volume of the same name and argues that hearkening back

But this nationalist vision is also imbued with the baggage of the mandate and independence periods when certain thinkers used it in conjunction with visions of Lebanon that later would serve specifically elite Christian interests. Though the notion of shared roots might be appealing when the country is falling apart, the alienating nature of this particular nationalist myth is rather glibly glossed over here.

Coquelicot du massacre: Conclusions

Coquelicot du massacre attempts to articulate a Lebanese nationalism that is infused with a utopian feminist vision in order to narrate against the war and present possibilities for a peaceful postwar Lebanon. But can Accad's feminist Lebanese nationalism (or Lebanese nationalist feminism) reappropriate these symbols in a way that subverts their exclusionary meanings? It is difficult to see how this could work within Lebanon because of the power behind these images. It does not seem that Accad is able to invest these well-worn ideas about Lebanon with enough new meaning to overcome the force of what they already represent. I am not focusing on this nationalist strain in order to condemn Accad's message or her vision for postwar Lebanon, but rather to point to some of the ways in which the novel is linked very strongly to other discourses so prevalent in its time. I also wish to underline the contradictions to the political agenda of this work, because it does advocate a particular position.

Evelyne Accad articulates a specific political point about the Lebanese civil war again and again in *Coquelicot du massacre*. She argues that Lebanon and Lebanese people do not wish to have a war, that they are peaceful people who have known how to coexist for centuries, and that a feminist consciousness and practice is a solution to its problems. One of

---

to an ancient past provides the possibility for more common ground than more recent and therefore recently contested images and symbols (Hobsbawm and Ranger 1992, 1–14). I have argued in the case of Arabic literature that the pre-Islamic poet al-Khansa' is a literary figure who operates in this way to provide a "noncontroversial" figure of an "Arab woman writer" within English-language criticism of Arabic literature (Hartman 2011b).

the specific ways in which she forwards this agenda is her commentary on words marked as Arabic—usually made explicitly—and always made through a visible interruption in speech genres, serving as feminist punctuation. The way in which she comments on the Arabic language and uses polyglossia mirrors the didactic nature of the novel overall. Even Accad's use of a vulgar, sexist curse is deconstructed from a feminist point of view.

The message of Accad's novel breaks down, however, where she builds her feminist argument on the bases of problematic national myths spread in order to prop up a deeply flawed patriarchal system, though she tries to make them serve a peaceful, harmonious, feminist society. The idealized nationalist imagery that she draws on was in fact primarily used by coalitions of elite men, mainly but not exclusively Christians, in order to promote their vision of a Lebanese nation-state that would keep a small group of powerful people enfranchised. The male power structure that created Lebanon at the time of the mandate and independence drew heavily on these same tropes to secure its position. As Alessandro Olsaretti and I have argued, privileged Lebanese patriarchal elites used these very images to help put in place a specific economic and political system that favored the free market and left many traditional patriarchal social structures in place (2003). Accad critiques this system but remains attached to its very potent symbols.

This attachment to a specific kind of Lebanese nationalism, albeit one infused with feminist ideology, does not allow for the emergence of polyphony in the Bakhtinian sense, despite the creative use of multiple genres, speech genres and languages. The Lebanese civil war occupies the entire text but somehow is absent from the discussion of the "true" Lebanon and Lebanese spirit that its characters embrace and are meant to embody. One reason for this may be the work's focus on only one very specific sector of society, educated middle-class professors and students in Beirut. Though it is concerned in an abstract political sense with the disenfranchised, specifically women and Palestinians, none of the work's main characters are among the worst-off of Lebanese society. For example, there are no characters who are obviously Shi'a, none of the women discussed are poor, Palestinians are defended as a concept but there are no Palestinian characters in the book. The people are all members of a certain urban elite and display little horizontal or vertical diversity. There is not even a balancing figure like Khoury-Ghata's Madame Zakié—the contrasting characters here are all negatively drawn American "outsiders." The focus is primarily on the access that these educated, urban Lebanese middle-class women have to participate in conversations about the structures of society. This is not something that I wish to critique in and of itself. Not every novel can or should deal with every sector of society. In chapter 4, I showed how *Le sommeil délivré*, for example, uses the village as a foil in order to focus on the elite. But in order to make a certain kind of argument for the disempowered in a broader social sense, perhaps Accad's argument might have been extended more broadly. The way in which Accad uses the language of the street and the mixing of speech genres in this context makes a good contrast to Dominique Eddé's similar—but more extensive—use of words marked as Arabic in her French-language narration. Eddé's *Lettre posthume* also employs certain vulgar words and expressions, including and in addition to a good number of explanations of transliterated Arabic expressions, in order to advance a polyphonic vision of a Lebanon conveyed to both an insider and outsider readership.

8

Can a French Novel Speak Arabic?

Dominique Eddé's Lettre posthume

> And so, in the end, I was missing our supposedly mother tongue. . . . History's last word is that people like us, cloaked in the dignity of the French language, mainly resorted to their first language to communicate in the kitchen and in neighborhood shops.
>
> Enfin, voilà, notre langue, prétendue maternelle, me manquait. . . . Le fin mot de l'histoire, c'est que des gens comme nous, drapés dans la dignité de la langue française, avaient surtout recours à leur langue d'origine pour communiquer dans les cuisines et chez les épiciers du quartier.
>
> —EDDÉ 1989, 27

Arabic is relegated to the kitchen and neighborhood shops in Dominique Eddé's poignant meditation on the languages of the Lebanese bourgeoisie, who are deprived of access to the depths of Arabic's rich poetic and spiritual literary tradition. This is how the unnamed priest who narrates the epistolary novel *Lettre posthume* [A posthumous letter] (1989) contextualizes his relationship with the French and Arabic languages within his upper-class Lebanese world. He both loves and despises French; he is aware of his lack of ability to use his "first language" (langue d'origine) but also enjoys many of the advantages that being a French speaker gives him. A thoughtful novel that probes the psyche of its narrator, a (male) Lebanese priest of an upper-class background during the Lebanese civil war, *Lettre posthume* offers a glimpse into some of the ways in which a French-language novel negotiates class and status extensively in its reflections on its own narration and its practice of mixing of languages within the text.

Though the beauty of the French language is captured by Dominique Eddé's narration itself, the alienation of people from their "own" language, culture, and literary traditions is expressed self-consciously as a critique of both colonial language policies and this class's willingness to set itself apart from others by thoroughly assimilating to French. This metacommentary on language use is not unique to Dominique Eddé—we saw something similar in Vénus Khoury-Ghata's *Le fils empaillé*. It is, however, a distinguishing feature of Eddé's work that, developed even further in her later novels, informs and deepens the plot, themes, and issues treated in her first novel, *Lettre posthume*.

Lettre posthume is a departure from the works treated thus far in other ways as well. This epistolary novel, written almost as a confession, is a long letter written in a first-person perspective from a Lebanese (male) priest to a French (female) friend. Neither character is named, but both maintain a strong implicit presence within a narration of civil-war Lebanon. Because the text is written by a secular Lebanese woman author of Christian background, but told through the voice of a male Lebanese Catholic priest, the usual attention paid to autobiographical similarities between narrator and author are missing from commentaries and criticism. Moreover, few if any novels by French-language women writers from Lebanon are told solely through a male voice.[1] Like Accad's *Coquelicot du massacre*, *Lettre posthume* talks about the events of the war, particularly the destruction of Beirut and the beauty of the country before the war began. Also like *Coquelicot*, it focuses on women's and men's experiences of war as gendered in particular ways. It is different, however, in that its violence is implicit. Its pages contain no death, no drug addiction, no complete breakdown of law and order; the social structure of Lebanon remains intact within its pages.

1. An exception is another epistolary novel to which it has been compared. Published in the same year, Jacqueline Massabki coauthored (with François Porel) *La mémoire des cèdres* [The memory of cedars] (1989), a historical novel spanning the twentieth century and ending in the period of the Lebanese civil war.

Published just a year before the main violence and fighting of the war would be over—albeit just before the so-called Christian War of Liberation in 1989, which saw some of the worst fighting in East Beirut, where much of this novel is set—Eddé's novel is a harbinger of postwar writing. In contrast to Accad's novel, published only one year earlier and which clearly engaged the problem of the war directly as an ongoing event, *Lettre posthume* feels more like a work that is beginning to look back and take stock. *Coquelicot du massacre* is full of fraught, hotly contested debates; *Lettre posthume* is a somewhat dispassionate commentary on how the civil war changed Lebanon.

This itself is linked to another key difference between Eddé's novel and others—its self-consciousness, not only about the war but also in its critique of different social-status groups and the class divides present in Lebanon. The epistolary genre in some sense demands this self-consciousness; the narrator is all but compelled to take up the role of "native informant" explicitly, as he is the insider charged with "explaining the war" to an outsider, his addressee. Unlike the earlier novels that engage and challenge ethnography as a genre, *Lettre posthume* asserts enough authority through its priest-narrator to explain the war but holds itself at just enough distance to discuss it "neutrally." The novelized language created by Eddé through polyglossia thus negotiates multiple speech genres that play with the notion of authority. The insider-outsider roles are shifted from the "scientific" to the "personal" even as the languages are used to shift again from the "home" to the "street."

Within the novel's metacommentary lies its mixing of language and feminist punctuation. In some ways this is very similar to Accad's metacommentary, particularly in the extensive explanation of expressions, some of which are vulgar "street" language—not surprising given the epigraph I use to open the chapter. Other examples of "kitchen Arabic" that are inscribed into the text, while almost always still cushioned and explained like Accad's, function differently. Eddé's commentary on Lebanon and the war is linked to how language, educational status, and prestige are intertwined among a certain bourgeoisie in Lebanon. Her class-conscious message is achieved by words marked as Arabic "speak" within the literary French language of her text.

Kitchen Arabic, Languages of the House/Marketplace, and Social Stratification

When the narrator points out that he and other members of his elite social group only speak Arabic with their grocers and in the kitchen, it is not a boast but a lament. The theme of the cultural alienation of the Gallicized, Francophile Lebanese bourgeoisie runs throughout the book, emphasizing the constraints placed on someone who does not know Arabic. In this passage, for example, he refers to his "supposedly mother tongue" [notre langue prétendue maternelle] and how he "suffered" [(je) souffrais] from not knowing it properly (26). Such a lament—when narrated from a particular position of privilege—can be read on many levels. The narrator bemoans the fact that he expresses himself better, more frequently, and more fluently in the language that holds more prestige economically and politically if not socially. The language that he does not master is less prestigious socially and culturally, though he recuperates some of its cultural potential by pointing out its contribution to poetry and mysticism.

Despite his claim of being cut off from the Arabic language and therefore its cultures, the narrator does still manage to occupy a full place in Lebanese society and express himself to people outside Lebanon; the book is framed as a letter to a French friend. Moreover, he even poses as a sort of native informant explaining the Lebanese civil war, at least to an outsider audience. His lament when read in this light underlines the distinction between languages, further reinforcing stereotypes about them: the colonial language, French, is the language of analysis and reason, and his native tongue, Arabic, is that of poetry and mysticism. This recalls Vénus Khoury-Ghata's critique of the school system that left the Arabic-speaking Muslim students full of enthusiasm for ancient poetry and its symbolism, whereas the French-speaking Christian children had "dead eyes." If the narrator is sad for his loss of Arabic for only this reason, it seems that the commentary on the politics of language use in *Lettre posthume* will merely reproduce familiar categories of French as the prestige language in most fields and classical Arabic as holding a "separate but equal" position, reserved for things deemed emotional (like poetry and mysticism). *Lettre posthume*, however, is not so simple, and because of its metacommentary on language, blended with an exploration of languages within the text, it performs a more complex analysis of class divides. This commentary, like others in the novel, reveals the sharp class-status distinctions connected to language in Lebanon.

There are numerous examples of how the bourgeois are alienated from Arabic and Arab culture through their assimilation to all things French. One striking example early on in the novel places the narrator's alienation once again squarely back in the kitchen, this time as the location where he develops his first crush. It is dismissed as a case of puppy love, but the narrator tells us the reasons for the gap between him and his object of desire when he hides behind the kitchen door at fifteen,

> on the lookout for my first love, who was called the "little Shiite maid" and who was actually named Maliha. She was barely thirteen and served us at meals, in a getup including a white lace headdress and apron. . . . She was singing the songs of Asmahan, I was humming the tunes of Tino Rossi.
>
> à l'affût de mon premier amour qu'on appelait "la petite bonne chiite" et qui en réalité s'appelait Maliha. Elle avait treize ans à peine et nous servait à table, affublée d'une coiffe et d'un tablier en dentelle blancs. . . . Elle chantait des chansons d'Asmahan, je fredonnais des airs de Tino Rossi. (28)

Popular culture divides the would-be lovers. The boy is immersed in music that is all the rage in Europe, whereas the maid, Maliha, sings the equally famous Arabic songs of the iconic Syrian diva Asmahan. It is striking that this is the first mention of a Shi'i character in any of the novels discussed thus far, aside from a fleeting mention of a "métoualli" musician in Amy Kher's *Salma et son village* (61) and an appearance by a peripheral man called Ali in Vénus Khoury-Ghata's novel who is never actually identified as Shi'i and soon disappears (41). In this case, Maliha the Shi'i maid serves to reinforce vertical distinctions of status through her different language and pop culture interests.[2] Particularly in the context of the religious-sectarian cast of so much of the Lebanese civil war, it is relevant that the most politically and economically disenfranchised group in Lebanon should only begin to make an appearance in a novel largely devoted to exposing the foibles of the Christian bourgeoisie and that they make a class- and status-conscious critique of this social group.[3]

"May You Bury Me" Redux

Social stratification is not only depicted between a Shi'i maid and upper-class Christian boy in the urban milieu of Beirut, but also as existing in the green mountain villages that are in other ways idealized. Eddé uses a different kind of commentary about language to illustrate, for example, the vertical social gaps between members of the same Christian religious/confessional group. When the narrator as a boy spends time in his ancestral Christian village, he and the other boys of the prominent families come into contact with local villagers of more modest backgrounds. We see that he is faced with gaps in linguistic ability, even as a boy, through Eddé's representation of relexified versions of spoken Arabic expressions.

A good example of this is shown in the anecdote about a Maronite village shopkeeper in the village of the narrator's childhood Bécharé (the same large village mentioned in *Salma et son village*, located near Hadchit). The narrator recalls fondly that Abou Toni would not take money one time in two from the boys who would frequent his shop to buy candies and other treats. The pages leading up to the story about Abou Toni are filled with an idyllic portrait of the northern Lebanese mountains, not unlike

2. I have not discussed the names of the characters, particularly as the central characters remain unnamed, but it seems relevant to note that "Maliha" means "beautiful" in the sense of being agreeable, sharp, or witty. This name recurs in a very different character—a child of the haute bourgeoisie—in Eddé's third novel, *Cerf-Volant* (2003).

3. In part 3, we see novels with a different orientation. For example, a Shi'i character becomes central to the plot of *Sous les vignes du pays Druze* when the Druze protagonist falls in love with a Shi'i boy.

that of Amy Kher's *Salma et son village* and set in the same region. Abou Toni's way of speaking to the children also recalls Eveline Bustros's *Sous la baguette du coudrier* in his use of the expression "may you bury me":

> Abou Toni used to pamper us like sons and mumbled while he was serving us, "May God grant that you bury me," which more or less meant that he wanted us to live after him and for as long as possible.
>
> Abou Toni nous choyait comme des fils et marmonnait en nous servant "Dieu veuille que vous m'enterriez," ce qui veut plus ou moins dire qu'il souhaitait que nous vivions après lui et le plus longtemps possible. (46)

There are several differences between how Eddé puts these words in the mouth of Abou Toni and the way in which Anissa speaks them in Bustros's text. The first is that the Arabic expression "taqburni" is rendered as "Dieu veuille que vous m'enterriez," using the full expression with the reference to God, but also the more common verb, "s'enterrer," used to mean "bury." This has the effect of making the expression less odd in one way, with a more common verb, but still stand out within a French language narration as a relexification by lengthening an affectionate expression idiomatically meaning something like "honey" or "darling" and including its reference to God.

The boys understand this affectionate expression, clearly marked to be "local dialect," but is different from Bustros's text in that the narrator gives a brief explanation of what the expression means in French rather than letting the reader figure it out. The narrator's explanation of the expression once again underlines his role as an insider-outsider, the native informant giving information to the French reader of his work. This also makes it clear that the narrator himself does not speak like this, further setting himself apart from the local villagers. Therefore, as in *Le sommeil délivré*, we see a certain romanticization of the poorer villagers of the lower classes who speak Arabic, in contrast to the elite characters whose dialogue is faced with a symbolic poverty of Arabic expressions. The peasant in the village speaks with a colorful "local" expression and the Shi'i maid listens to Asmahan, much in the same way that the village women in

Le sommeil délivré speak French "with an accent." The narrator of *Lettre posthume*, like Samya, is alienated from them and also from what should be his "own" culture.

A third way in which Eddé's use of this expression differs from Bustros's is that Anissa refers to her own children when she says "may you bury me," the most common addressees for such an expression, whereas Abou Toni uses it to refer to the village boys because he treats them "like sons." It is relevant to the interpretation of this passage that the affectionate relationship depicted exists outside of blood relations and that it underlines the kinship role between the older, village man and the wealthier sons of the local elite. I underline this because the use of the expression is contained within a section of the novel/letter that presents a somewhat potted history of Lebanon on the pages just preceding it, which emphasize the debates over the shape Lebanon would take upon gaining independence and how the shape it eventually took contributed to the civil war. The story presents claims that there were two camps pitted against each other—one that wanted Lebanon to be part of a larger Arab nation, the other that wanted to be a part of France. It talks about how the National Pact was formed and that in asking each side to renounce something it made both orphans. These underlying enmities are what caused the slide into civil war and this section of the work points out the ironies of how people only protect "their own."

This brings us back to the affection that Abou Toni has for the boys who come to his shop and whom he treats as sons, because as kindly as he is with them, he quickly turns around and murders a man who insulted the Virgin Mary in his presence "with no regrets" (46). The juxtaposition of kindness and vengeance embodied in the same character is typical of *Lettre posthume*. The entire work is a balance between the narrator's memories of the "good old days" of prewar Lebanon and his more cynical interpretations of the present when the country is drowning in a bloody, sectarian war.

The commentary in this section underlines the oppressive hypocrisy of a system that allows you to be close only to those of your own background. Abou Toni wants to be "buried" or outlived by those of his "own kind" and is quick to attack, and even murder in cold blood, someone different. The literal meaning [may you bury me] of an expression that idiomatically is like “sweetheart” in English not only highlights the concept of death underpinning it to an outsider reader, but also reminds the insider reader of the nuanced meaning. In this second case, Eddé is making a comment to the reader who knows Arabic about the meanings layered within expressions that we take for granted. In this case, the deepening of meaning directs an antiwar message—through the use of layered languages and interruption of speech genres—at both audiences. The absurdity of the civil war is contextualized amidst the niceties of village speech and the narrator’s romanticized memories of childhood in the mountains.

Ma bi sir: Gender, Social Conventions, and Language Hierarchies

What it means to belong to Lebanon and where and how you belong occupies much of the narration of *Lettre posthume,* through both language and cultural participation. While Accad’s unnamed narrator affirms proudly that she belongs to Lebanon in the epilogue, Eddé’s unnamed narrator probes what this means more deeply. As in *Coquelicot du massacre* and the other novels discussed in this book, the preparation and consumption of food is crucial to explaining the meaning of belonging and there are plenty of mentions of foods and drinks in the text. The most important of these, I would suggest, is how coffee is discussed by the narrator. Coffee is a ubiquitous trope in the artistic representation of Arab cultures and its depiction in literature is richly varied. Numerous novels by Arab authors dwell on the drinking of coffee as an important symbol—socially, politically, culturally, and otherwise. One need only think of Mahmoud Darwish’s darkly humorous and poignant rendition of the different “daily coffees,” in particular his hoarding of his mother’s coffee in prison, to understand the deep impact of the meanings that coffee can activate within Arab literary production (1986, 18–21; 1995, 19–23). Likewise, Leïla Barakat’s depiction of the ritualized drinking of maté by the women in her village in *Sous les vignes du pays Druze,* discussed in chapter 10, invokes a similar range of issues and meanings.

Eddé paints a detailed scene around the drinking of coffee in *Lettre posthume* in order to depict a class-based negotiation of social customs through mixing language. The narrator uses the discussion of the rituals around drinking coffee to propel his commentary about women's activities in Lebanon for his French interlocutor, paralleled by Eddé's message to the putative French-language readership of the novel. Class and gender are brought together and shown to be inextricably linked in *Lettre Posthume*'s exposition on how coffee drinking rituals in Lebanon exemplify a certain intangible quality of what it means to "be Lebanese" and find a sense of belonging in Lebanon.

The narrator's rather cynical take on what this belonging means—as when he compares Lebanese people to spoiled children—is tempered by an indulgence reserved for poking fun at your "own." In this section, the narrator playfully cites a number of Arabic expressions that are conveyed relexified into French and put between inverted commas in order to give a sense of this way of being Lebanese, what he calls "une manière d'être assis" [a way of sitting; in Arabic: uslub al-qa'ida]. After explaining the contradictions of being Lebanese, such as being calm and impatient at the same time, the narrator moves on to discuss exactly how the coffee is prepared and the importance of this sacred ritual. In his discussion of how one boils Arabic coffee in a small pot above a fire—complete with the different methods; some people boil it three times, others six—the narrator refers to the Arabic terminology for different preparations of the coffee using French words:

> a "bitter" coffee for one, a coffee "with more sugar than needed" for another, a coffee that is "correct" like the word of a wise person, which is also called the "middle" coffee, or even better, a coffee "with a scent," just barely sugared.
>
> un café "amer" pour l'un, un café "avec plus de sucre qu'il n'en faut" pour l'autre, un café "juste" comme la parole d'un sage qu'on appelle aussi le café "du milieu", ou bien encore un café "à l'odeur", à peine sucré. (81)

These labels for the coffee sound exotic in French and recall in some ways the "scientific" labeling of customs, traditions, and foods presented by Amy Kher in *Salma et son village*. To have so many types or "levels" of coffee no doubt seemed more unusual in the pre-Starbucks age when the novel was published, but these words are simply literal translations of the well-known Arabic descriptions for different amounts of sugar added to coffee while it is being boiled. Bitter coffee is "murra," sweet coffee is "ziyadeh," "mazbout" or "wasat" means a medium amount of sugar, and the final term "ariha" indicates just a hint of sugar. The translations of these expressions into French in quotation marks mark the labeling of coffee as exotic, giving the exposition of these common rituals an ethnographic flavor. How they are connected to the larger meanings of drinking coffee though reveals much more about the negotiation of class and status, particularly in relation to gender, in *Lettre posthume*.

The translation of these expressions is followed by a more extensive section of translation and relexification where the women's coffee hour is discussed. Though the narrator is a man, he recounts the way in which the women's coffee provides them with an autonomous space separate from men. The Arabic expressions that filter into the French narration here are exceedingly familiar and, like the descriptions of the coffee, are used in everyday, spoken Arabic. The way in which these expressions are presented, moreover, reinforces the difference encoded within them. After introducing the women's coffee hour as a special time and space, a series is produced: one after the other, all of them are enclosed in quotation marks and follow each other without necessarily making sense. For example, the end of the section reads:

> "On my children's lives," . . . "be patient," "the country has gone but we are still alive," "Your unhappiness will go away the same way it came," "Life will bring what it may," "As God wishes," "If God wishes," and on and on like this.
>
> "Sur la vie de mes enfants," . . . "Prends patience," "Le pays s'est envolé mais nous sommes en vie," "Ton malheur repartira comme il est venu," "Que vienne la vie comme elle vient," "Comme Dieu veut," "Si Dieu veut" et ainsi de suite. (82)

The way in which relexified expressions are listed in order and described as strange recalls Vénus Khoury-Ghata's similar list of "franbanismes."

Here, though, Eddé is not saying that this is "how people talk" but rather using French to refer to Arabic, as in earlier text. The metonymic function therefore is slightly different.

This passage is instructive in how Eddé uses language in *Lettre posthume* to negotiate social relationships. First, she shows women speaking a language that is neither purely French nor purely Arabic; clearly she is rendering common, spoken Arabic expressions into French through relexification. Nonetheless, the way in which sentences and expressions are simply listed, one after the other, makes the passage to some extent nonsensical. Unlike the similar recounting of phrases in Khoury-Ghata's work, she does not say why they are listed. The words are neither included as part of a dialogue, a conversation between specific women, nor represented as reported speech. In this case, rather, she is displaying the type of conversation women might have, but leaves out the narrative thread, simply piling up expressions in a list. This can serve several purposes. One is to show women as upholders of local culture, customs, and, most important, language, particularly in the metonymic representation of culture that was proposed by Ashcroft, Griffith, and Tiffin (1989). In a passage that reads almost as gossip, Eddé proposes the women's coffee hour as holding the key to understanding Lebanese culture.

Though the unnamed male narrator laments not knowing Arabic because he lacks access to poetry and mysticism, we see that the French language is used as a vehicle for a different part of Arab culture—the language of everyday life, particularly women's preservation of some of "the old ways." They are shown to have different interests and to use words differently than men. We do not see any of the men or boys in the novel use this type of language in the way women do. The relexified expression used by Abou Toni is different in that it is one isolated expression that reinforces vertical class-status differences and in how it is directly then used to contrast his kindly behavior toward the boys with his cold-blooded murder of someone of a different religious background.

The elaboration of this coffee-drinking scene also underlines not only the gendered nature of these moments but also their class-based meanings. The passage cited above does not make a distinction between women of different social groups; it refers only to the women's coffee hour.

If we assume that this is a memory from the narrator's family as a youth, it implies that bourgeois women are relexifying and translating Arabic expressions, but also that they are using them with each other. On the one hand this can simply be seen as a logical extension of the "kitchen Arabic" that the narrator all but dismisses. On the other hand, however, we can also see elite women participating in the preservation and transformation of local culture by using expressions relexified in the colonial language.

Building on this argument further as the scene develops, I would suggest that Eddé's message here is larger, that she probes the solidarity between women of different classes, as Chedid does in *Le sommeil délivré*, and also underlines the ways in which class distinctions are important but possible to challenge. In a later section, Eddé shows how coffee unifies people, not only women, across class and status divides. She draws on a classic Arab cultural trope: no matter how poor you are you will always invite a guest to share what you have in your house, especially coffee. Stating that the poorest of people buy and drink coffee because it is not a luxury, she affirms that you only need go into someone's house to hear "'the coffee is on the fire,' and if you decline the offer someone will quickly answer you that 'this is not possible,' 'there is no question about it!,' 'this will not do,' *ma bi sir*!" ["le café est sur le feu" et si vous déclinez l'offre, on vous répondra aussitôt que "c'est n'est pas possible," "qu'il n'en est pas question!," que "ça ne va pas comme ça," *ma bi sir*!] (86). Coffee in this cultural economy is not a luxury but a necessity. People use coffee not only as a way to build social relationships but also as a way to maintain pride in a system that denigrates them. This passage explains the role of coffee in establishing social credentials of generosity and also gives an idea of how the Arabic language offers clues to social relations between members of different status groups. Generosity in offering coffee thus takes place across class lines. The transliterated Arabic expression that represents this has a stronger impact on the French-language narration—poetically and politically—than the previous translated and relexified expressions.

Though *ma bi sir* clearly translates the words that come before it and because it is followed by an explanation that cushions it for the reader, it nonetheless inscribes a visibly and visually different language into the text. The use of transliteration rather than relexification, however, gives the author more control over its presentation and meaning. The author explains to the French reader what the colloquial expression *ma bi sir* means through context, explanation, and translation. The transliteration thus signifies linguistic difference in a more striking way, giving even more weight to the narrator's explanation, "And this last little phrase, they utter it with such insistence that it reveals much more than a rote courtesy, it contains all the pride of people who can only cope with their misery because they have something to offer" [Et cette dernière petite phrase, ils la prononcent avec une telle insistence qu'elle révèle bien plus qu'une formule de politesse, elle contient toute la fierté des gens qui ne supportent leur misère que parce qu'ils ont quelque chose à offrir] (86). Here *ma bi sir* is tagged not only as a polite expression, but also as a repository for the aspirations of poor Lebanese who have nothing to offer but a little hospitality. The use of transliteration codes it as a way for subaltern classes to show equality and dignity to the elite. Being generous is negotiated through language and the complex use of a number of translated, relexified, and then transliterated phrases, all of which center around the idea of the preparation and consumption of coffee.

The irony of this extended coffee scene is that at the same time *Lettre posthume* seems to be challenging gender segregation, women's oppression in society, and class hierarchies through language, it also naturalizes these very ideas. Though here we see how poor people can maintain their dignity by using their own language and being generous by serving coffee, is this really dignity? There is a danger in such representations that the lives of the dignified poor will be shown to be "authentic" and "noble," preventing real change that would give them better access to society. Therefore at the same time that language reflects and represents challenges to class and gender hierarchies, it also produces a cultural notion of these as unchanging and difficult to transcend.

The Languages of "Good Families"

Lettre posthume is its most successful in challenging class and gender hierarchies when it concentrates not so much on contrasts between rich and poor, or the idealized and romanticized lives of peasants, but rather on the intricacies of the lives of the bourgeoisie. The challenges presented to the values and mores of the Lebanese elite are particularly forcefully rendered through the narrator's tales about his family. If class consciousness is understood in relation to social status, and social status in Lebanon is closely tied to one's family affiliation, then the narrator's expose of his family's customs can be read as a challenge to a naturalization of class privilege in the Lebanese context.[4]

An example is the poignant story of how the narrator becomes a priest and the difficulties his bourgeois family background posed to him. Just as Samya loses her status as a "fille de famille'" [daughter of a family] by attacking her husband, the unnamed narrator of *Lettre posthume* also puts his status as a "fils de famille" [son of a family] in jeopardy by his choice to join the clergy. As he articulates it, he should have married a woman of a certain family background, worked for his father, and "above all, yes, above all [been] a son who would have inherited my father's name as I did twenty years earlier" [surtout, oui, surtout un fils qui eût hérité du nom de mon père, comme moi, vingt ans plus tôt] (56). How the narrator comes to terms with his father and the pressures of being a member of a bourgeois Lebanese are reflected throughout the narrative in different ways.

The narrator's relationship to his mother demonstrates how *Lettre posthume* negotiates some of the realities of class and status through language. In discussing his childhood relationship to his mother, the narrator at one point describes how she refers to him as "mom" [maman]:

> Like so many other mothers, mine called me "maman" and I found it only natural because for me it was enough to understand, once and for all, that "maman" was simply a word with a double use. . . . And moreover maman was surely a synonym for love.
>
> Comme tant d'autres mères, la mienne m'appelait "maman" et je n'y trouvais rien que de très naturel puisqu'il m'avait suffit de comprendre, une fois pour toutes, que "maman" était tout simplement un

4. Suad Joseph has worked extensively on these issues from a sociological point of view (1988, 25–48; and 2000, 3–32, 107–36).

> mot à double emploi. . . . Et puis maman était assurément synonyme d'amour. (33)

This is an example of a marked difference between spoken Arabic and a language like French or English. A mother calling her child "mom" is a linguistic phenomenon defined in technical terms as the "reverse role vocative." This means that a speaker addresses another person with an affectionate title that describes the reverse relationship.[5] In Arabic, a mother calls both her son and daughter "mama," as that is her relationship to both of them regardless of their gender; a father addresses both his daughter and son as "baba." This is not a common means of address in French, as the person addressed would be referred to by their own social gender, not that of the speaker. The narrator incorporates this Arabic-influenced expression into the narrative in a way that both naturalizes it and underlines its difference.

This particular example of incorporating vernacular Arabic into the literary French of *Lettre posthume* is interesting on several levels. First of all, the narrator draws attention to it. By pointing out that it was not strange to him that his mother addressed him in this way, he demonstrates that he knows that it is something that the French reader would think is strange. Second, this example reminds us that not only Shi'i maids and quaint mountain peasants use Arabic expressions. Arabic speech and culture is translated, relexified, and employed by members of the upper classes as well. This example underlines this fact more so than the previous examples, where one is left to guess the social group affiliation of the women who are speaking during the coffee hour. Indeed the mother in this text is meant to represent the ultimate in bourgeois perfection. Unlike the lustful, passionate Eastern woman of the stereotype, embodied by the prostitute who is discussed in the next section, his mother is very much the "fille de bonne famille" [daughter of a good family] who his father married to continue his lineage.

5. Such use is not limited to Lebanese Arabic or even Arabic; many languages make use of them. For a study of the phenomenon in Lebanon, see Verna Robertson Rieschild (1998, 617–41), which builds on the earlier studies of Braun (1988), Schmidt (1993), and Yassin (1978), who also use the terms "inverse address" and "bipolar kin."

His mother's role as the perfect bourgeois housewife is articulated explicitly in connection to his father's relationship to her that the narrator learns about through his extended family. Upon becoming celibate as a priest, a distant cousin jokes to him that he takes after his own father, who has written this cousin a letter about his wife—the priest's mother—stating that she "was more at ease in a Napoleon III chair than in bed" [était plus à l'aise sur une chaise Napoléan III que dans un lit] (40). The celibate priest and his chaste, bourgeois parents thus are Lebanese who fly in the face of the stereotype of passionate Easterners. Elsewhere, as we have seen, the narrator proposes Arabic as a language of emotion and French as a language of reason. The peasants and maids are shown to speak Arabic and the elite to speak French, distanced from their culture. With the use of the reverse-role address system to call her son "maman," we see the priest's mother negotiate these linguistic divides in a creative way. She uses Arabic here, albeit for an expression connected to emotion, but remains refined and proper. Though the narrator believes that the word "maman" means love, we know also that it means love as an Arabic expression translated into a French form.

Finally, this use of the phrase "maman" as a reverse-role address is so interesting because the narrator's mother does not call him "mama"—as an Arabic speaker normally would—but rather "maman." In this way the words and expressions that she uses stand as a negotiation between Arabic and French. On the one hand, it could be an example of the narrator showing how his mother mixes languages, using a French word within an Arabic structure of expression. It might reflect how a person like her would "actually speak," actively mixing languages, registers, and codes. On the other hand, it could be read as an example of how the author herself employs polyglossia to show different ways in which expressions can be used within a text written in French. Though the narrator reminds us that his mother addresses him like "so many other mothers" address their children, there is an implication that a speech genre is interrupted here through the use of language. The Arabic expression is marked as different from the standard French narration. But the reverse works as well in this particular case because it is not the typical Arabic expression either. Therefore, though it may seem a less challenging textual strategy to interrupt the flow of the French-language novel—particularly because an explanation of the phrase is given that lends the text a didactic feeling—it works as a double disruption.

The particular expression once again punctuates the French-language narration with a metonymic representation of Arabic, using a word perfectly acceptable in standard literary French to do so. Moreover, the interruption by a French word used with Arabic grammar and its subsequent explanation is highly mediated by the ethnographic interventions on the part of the narrator that inform this section and to some extent overcode the "lettre posthume." The narrator admits openly that he is distanced from most speakers of Arabic in the text, however he has a certain social mobility in Lebanon by virtue of his bourgeois background and the ability to move among men and women because he is a priest; these both contribute to his peculiar insider-outsider status. On the other hand, this textual intervention invoking Arabic, like the others discussed above (and many others not discussed here for lack of space), also challenges the reader to rethink notions about languages, power, and prestige that the narrator challenges but also reinforces at times.

Hot-Blooded Lebanon: "Our Own Brothel"

The narrator uses the example of motherly love to show the emotionality of the Arabic language through a gendered example. He uses another gendered example at the other end of the spectrum, a prostitute, to do the same thing in seemingly the opposite way. Right at the beginning of *Lettre posthume* the narrator explicates the differences between Arabic and French, contrasting them as the languages of religion and degeneracy. Drawing on these well-worn stereotypes, the narrator invokes and then subverts them in a way that could be said to "decline stereotypes."[6]

6. I follow Mireille Rosello's development of the concept "declining stereotypes" in *Declining the Stereotype: Ethnicity and Representation in French Cultures* (1998), in which she presents the two meanings of the verb "decline" in order to talk about the possible subversive use of stereotypes by authors even as they appropriate them.

Read in this way, stereotypes demonstrate something about Lebanon and should be read in the vein of postmandate irony. The narrator states that Arabic is better adapted and more open to expressing emotions in Lebanon, "our own brothel" [notre bordel à nous] (25). Though normally a priest referring to a country and its language as a "brothel" would seem to be a harsh condemnation, it is clearly meant to be ironic here, and buttresses Lebanon's description as a "little hot-blooded paradise, so dear to orientalists" [petit paradis au sang chaud, si cher aux orientalistes] (25).

The narrator's likening of Lebanon to a brothel reinscribes the orientalist portrayal and stereotype of it as a "hot-blooded paradise," and also thus retains the idea of its inherent emotionality that he further expands on in this section. His gesture to the orientalists conjures up the stereotype of Arabic as an emotional language that is also flexible and adaptable and therefore contrasted to the constraints of standard French and the inflexible rigidity of French syntax (24). Casting French once again as the analytical and logical language par excellence, a notion promoted by the Académie française from the nineteenth century until today and echoed by so many works including Vénus Khoury-Ghata's *Le fils empaillé*, is a problematic reading of Eddé's use of polyglossia. Her narrator seems to parrot the paternalistic French colonial opinion about language—even as Arabic is praised, we can see in it echoes of universalist sentiments about French, such as Rivarol's famous statement, "French syntax cannot be corrupted. This is how it achieves its admirable clarity, which is the eternal foundation of our language. *What is not clear is not French*" [La syntaxe française est incorruptible. C'est de là que résulte cette admirable clarté, base éternelle de notre langue. *Ce qui n'est pas clair n'est pas français*] (1966, 112; emphasis in the original).

The priest has backed himself into a paradox that he must narrate his way out of in order to make sense of the relationship between Arabic and French. He spends much of the book clarifying his position. If Arabic is emotional and French rational, what implications does this have for language use in Lebanon? If one takes prominence, what are the social costs and benefits? He quickly takes pains to clarify his position about the two languages and their relative value in this passage. He states clearly that he does not value one language more than the other, modifying this by saying, "but you should know right now that I have always passionately loved brothels and their atmospheres polluted with desires and degenerate hopes" [mais sachez, au passage, que j'ai toujours passionément aimé les bordels et leurs atmosphères polluées de désirs et d'espoirs dégénérés] (25). But the problem for the narrator remains; a specific value is attached to each language if one is good only for emotion and the other is universal and rational.

Lettre posthume grapples with the issue of hierarchies of language in relation to the relationship between Arabic and French in some detail precisely through the site of the brothel and the character of the prostitute. It is crucial to the discussion above that not only does the narrator compare Lebanon to a brothel, with Arabic as its language, but he also "loves brothels in all their degeneracy." The narrator himself, however, composes this complex letter to his French friend and is a French speaker, extremely well educated and "rational." Is his love of brothels, and by implication Lebanon and Arabic, simply a kind of nostalgia for his own country's local color? What do Arabic and French represent in *Lettre posthume,* a novel that contains extended contemplations on the rifts between Arabic in French by a French-speaking Lebanese man who uses Arabic only as a language of the street and claims to love the seedy locations to which it is best suited? And how do inscriptions of Arabic within the text confirm, challenge, or otherwise comment on this relationship?

My reading of Eddé's use of vulgar Arabic interprets it as a parallel to Accad's use of the Arabic billingsgate, "Kiss Oukhtoum." By symbolically desecrating the figure of the priest, because he loves the degeneracy of brothels and the Arabic language, which expresses vulgarity, Eddé also comments on the desecration of Lebanon by the war. This linguistic rupture further textures the metaphor of Lebanon as a brothel and Arabic as the language of the brothel, layering complexity in the feminist messages of *Lettre posthume.*

The brothel is not only an abstract concept or metaphor in *Lettre posthume* but also appears as the location of actual prostitutes in Beirut during the war. An analysis of the extended meditation on one identifiably Arabic vulgar word, "charmouta" (prostitute, or whore), can help to unpack the dynamics of *Lettre posthume*'s commentary on language and its feminist message. The narrator comments on the brothel in *Lettre posthume* not only metaphorically, as in "our very own brothel" [notre bordel à nous], but also as an actual location, thereby commenting directly on brothels and prostitutes as well as Arabic and French.

The brothel portrayed in *Lettre posthume* recalls the metaphorical one in the opening, as it is an idealized space in which men of all backgrounds in Lebanese society meet—across boundaries of religion, sect, confession, class, and political affiliation. This somewhat clichéd portrayal of the whorehouse as a place where men lay down their arms in the pursuit of the common conquest of women itself recalls numerous representations of wartime Lebanon, including the mass-marketed film *West Beirut*.[7] It also lends texture to the narrator's previous statement about loving polluted locations and their degenerate desires and hopes. The narrator states that the prostitutes keep order in Beirut by respecting the multiconfessionalism of men's fantasies (74), and indeed the image of the prostitute as a repository of multiconfessionalism seems a fantasy of the narrator. At the end of the next page, the narrator lists the symbols and icons contained in the prostitute's room in Beirut, which he characterizes as a complete world almost reverentially: "A Qur'anic verse, a crucifix, the Holy Virgin on one side, Abdel Nasser on the other, King Farouk or the King of Greece, Leyla Gamal as the Queen of Sheba, De Gaulle and the Nile at sunset, Jerusalem, Oum Kalsoum, Farid el Attrache" [Un verset du Coran, un crucifix, la Sainte Vierge d'un côté, Abdel Nasser de l'autre, le roi Farouk ou le roi de Grèce, Leyla Gamal en reine de Saba, De Gaulle et le Nil au coucher de soleil, Jérusalem, Oum Kalsoum, Farid el Attrache] (75–76). The meeting of Lebanese men of all different backgrounds in the body of a woman thus is displaced onto a description of symbols and icons coexisting in the room of this woman. The prostitute

7. In *West Beirut* (dir. Ziad Doueiri) the two teenage boys have their sexual awakening in the brothel, which is shown to represent a place where militiamen literally and figuratively put down their weapons as demanded by the overbearing madam. The sign that a customer should be able to pass through to the brothel is a bra on the car antenna. The image of Beirut itself as a prostitute is prevalent in much of the fiction about the war (Accad 1990; Amyuni 1999; Cooke 1996).

represents a Lebanon of which all of these men, objects, and symbols are a part despite the war being waged to prove the contrary. Her room demonstrates that such competing symbols and ideologies can peacefully coexist and serves as a symbolic microcosm of a Lebanon free of war and conflict.

The prostitute is shown in her person, and her room, to embody the idea of Lebanon: her room symbolically shows a resistance to static, fixed ideologies of religion, confession, and sect; her person demonstrates the hypocrisy of society's sexism.

> The whore, the *charmouta*, as we say here (ultimate insult that is also directed at the wide range of women guilty of being a little "free"), embodied all of the unacceptable proof of a country that was, without knowing it, about to be abducted and punished for having been too beautiful to be true.
>
> La putain, la *charmouta* comme on dit chez nous (insulte suprême, qui s'adresse aussi bien à la panoplie des femmes coupables d'être un peu 'libres'), incarnait toute l'inadmissible évidence d'un pays qui était, sans le savoir, en voie d'être enlevé et puni d'avoir été trop beau pour être vrai. (76)

The word "charmouta" is presented initially as a translation of "putain" (prostitute), but the passage goes on to define and nuance this word, implying that the French word does not fully capture the nuances of "charmouta." This is reinforced by the use of the words "comme on dit chez nous" [as we say here] that recall a similar locution, the narrator's reference to Lebanon as "notre bordel à nous" [our very own brothel]. Constantly evoking "we" and "us" in his speech reminds the reader of this French text that there is another language implied and the narrator trades on his insider status as one of the major tropes of the work—explaining Lebanon to the French outsider.

The strategy of defining and redefining an Arabic word within French has the effect in this passage of allowing a "charmouta" to be redefined quite dramatically. A French reader who does not know Arabic learns that this word means whore (putain) and also is privy to an additional explanation of its nuances. But this is not where the importance of Eddé's strategy ends. Irony continues to be important. The irony of saying that the many women who are considered a "little free" are referred to using this word is clear from the passage. But he does not explain—though he does call it the supreme insult—the extremely vulgar nature of this word, which is not fully captured by "putain," a word that can be used in a milder and more frequent way in French than "charmouta" can in Arabic.[8]

As a poetic strategy to inscribe a social, political, and feminist message, Eddé is able to make this Arabic word do double duty. Through the irony of such a harsh insult being used to characterize this large group of women who are simply a "little free," she reveals the hypocrisy of sexism. And though the text is ostensibly written for a French-speaking audience that does not necessarily know Arabic, there is a double message within her use of this expression as well, pointing out to readers who do know Arabic how ridiculous such an idea is. The second message that is carefully intertwined with the first is that the charmouta should be seen as symbolically representing Lebanon. The image is neither new nor creative, but Eddé uses it somewhat differently than other writers. Rather than Lebanon or Beirut being represented as a whore who turns away from her people and is exploited by many invaders for their purposes and discarded, *Lettre posthume* shows the prostitute being punished for being too beautiful and a little free, linking the country's fate to that of women who seek to live their own lives. Though both women and Lebanon are shown to be victims, they are also shown as beautiful and a little free, and as able to combat the rigid ideologies tearing the country apart. The Beiruti prostitute's ability to allow confessional coexistence on her walls and in men's fantasies is paralleled with women being able to be freer in society. The poetic strategy of including the vulgar Arabic word "charmouta" in the French text and

8. In French "putain" is used as an interjection that is understood in context as much less vulgar than the word "charmouta," which is a taboo word in Arabic and considered insulting. Though of course there are equivalences and the words share many layers of meaning that could be interesting to explore, here I focus on the differences between these words in order to underline the anticolonial politics and use of language by Eddé and mirror her own definition of the words as different.

defining it in detail in these ways punctuates a feminist message linked to a larger message about Lebanese society during the civil war.

Defining "charmouta" not only reveals a political message layered with feminist meanings, drawing a parallel between the situation of women and the country at war, but also comments more broadly on the relationship between Arabic and French in a postcolonial context. Moreover, read together with the idealization of the brothel as a location of multiconfessional harmony, the meditation on charmouta shows additional interpretations of the priest-narrator's original statement about his love of the pollution of brothels. If indeed the prostitute's room is a space of confessional coexistence and prostitutes are women punished for being too "free" or too beautiful, then his claim to love these takes on a distinctly different cast. Could the "pollution" he refers to be ironic? Perhaps he is implying that certain sexist, exclusivist ideologies want to claim some religions, ideas, and/or women as pure and others as not, but that he rejects this, claiming for himself the allegedly "polluted," but actually more palatable, locations and women that embrace a different vision of what Lebanon is and could be. This certainly allows the reading of the priest-narrator's idealized brothel and prostitutes to be less clichéd and to advance a more nuanced message about Lebanon's complex postcolonial realities.

This strategy draws on the power of the notion of desecration. Figures and locations typically represented as holy and pure—the priest, the woman, the mother tongue, the colonial language, and the nation—are no longer sacred. The pollution of sacred figures and spaces has a complex effect on the text. First, it undermines their assumed purity and the naturalization of the very idea of purity and sacredness, challenging our assumptions about priests, nations, and languages. Second, it also draws comparisons between these figures as ideas—the woman who is shown to be a prostitute is paralleled to the Arabic language, the priest himself is paralleled with French, though he loves Arabic and being in the less-than-savory space of the brothel. Finally, the attention drawn to these images through their desecration can also have the reverse effect of ironically underlining their purity. Bakhtin's exploration of billingsgate and the carnival in Rabelais shows how, for example, such reversals both undermine and preserve the sacred. In *Lettre posthume* reversal has the effect not only of redeeming the woman who is the prostitute, but also Lebanon as the pluralistic, multiconfessional nation that it once was, offering the possibility that it will be again. The use of the transliterated, and then translated, word "charmouta" shows the fault lines not only between Arabic and French, men and women, and the rigid ideological views that led Lebanon to civil war, but also offers the possibility of a less pessimistic final reading of *Lettre posthume*'s message.

Conclusions: *Lettre posthume*

The Arabic language continually pierces the French-language veneer of the narrative of *Lettre posthume*, particularly with vernacular—and at times vulgar—words and expressions. This operates on a double level, both challenging the colonial language with the local one and disrupting the literary register of a formally written text with colloquialisms. Like other texts discussed here, in particular Andrée Chedid's *Le sommeil délivré*, *Lettre posthume* comments on distinctions of social status through a certain class consciousness. Though I would not argue that the novel proposes a radical alternative to the hierarchies that dominate the society it represents, I would propose that polyglossia is used to negotiate and at times destabilize them. The language of the house and the street, the kitchen and the grocer, passion and reason, come together in *Lettre posthume* to work through ideas about class and social status.

The narrator's voice and his view of the interpretations of events hold sway over the text. *Lettre posthume* reinforces and naturalizes conventional notions about class and gender hierarchies, making it more, rather than less, difficult to imagine how they could be undermined for the good of society. Subaltern voices do not have the ability to destabilize the narration of this novel in the same way that elite voices do. Though women are privileged in being able to preserve culture—they help to preserve language in intimate spaces and serve as a bridge between different levels of society—they alone do not break down class barriers even through their solidarity. A peasant man like Abou Toni does not truly infiltrate standard French with his relexified expressions, even if his voice can be heard at times in the narrative. I propose that one reason for these voices cannot penetrate the narrative more effectively is that the voice of the omniscient narrator, though critical and self-reflective, never lets go of his control over the text. Though there are moments of polyphony in this novel, the narrator and author maintain close control over most of it. Though the entire novel demonstrates a keen class consciousness, it is unable fundamentally to challenge the underlying assumptions of the system.

Lettre posthume in these ways is very much a novel of its time that uses feminist punctuation to prefigure the postwar period, envisaging a new Lebanon that can emerge from the destruction. Written at the very end of the 1980s when the war was waning, this novelized work represents a new voice and a new generation of language. The later novels of Dominique Eddé broach many of the same topics and use many similar poetic techniques of language mixing—in addition to others not explored here. In these later works, Eddé's explicit discussion of class, hierarchy, and language are similarly pronounced, but her challenges to the underlying notions of class structures and hierarchies are more drastically reflected in the way in which her use of polyglossia negotiates them. In part 3 of *Native Tongue, Stranger Talk*, we will see how these ideas are reprised and deepened by her other two novels—*Pourquoi il fait si sombre?* and *Cerf-Volant*—read together with Leïla Barakat's "new ethnographic novel," *Sous les vignes du pays Druze.*

Part Three ◆ *Writing as Translation*

9

Writing as Translation

Women's Fictions of Postwar Lebanon

The diverse uses of Arabic as feminist punctuation in the novels analyzed in part 2—Khoury-Ghata's *Le fils empaillé*, Accad's *Coquelicot du massacre*, and Eddé's *Lettre posthume*—foreshadow the ever more experimental kinds of layering of languages in postwar novels. Many novels published after the war are just as self-conscious in their commentaries on the French language as *Le fils empaillé, Coquelicot du massacre*, and *Lettre posthume* are. Indeed many novels published from the mid-1990s until today include similar types of metacommentaries on the French language, the Arabic language, and/or the relationships between them; postwar fiction written in French presents an increasingly self-conscious depiction of languages. Novels use diverse strategies to mark languages as different and to incorporate multiple levels of languages and types of expressions throughout their pages. The more sparing use of Arabic words as punctuation—from the kinds of reflections offered by Khoury-Ghata, to Accad's and Eddé's "lessons"—in these novels expand. Though many of the same words and expressions are included, their frequency and the way they permeate the texts change. Language is the centerpiece of the French-language postwar novel in Lebanon.

Part 3 argues therefore that postwar Lebanese fiction takes a more holistic approach toward using polyglossia, integrating language marked as Arabic deeply within the languages of the texts. Not all novels of this period attempt or achieve this of course, but a number of works—in different ways—aim for such an effect. Novels in which language marked as Arabic infuses the text throughout, making it read as different or "alien,"

I identify as "writing *as* translation." The French language is maintained but the extent of polyglossia increases and becomes part and parcel of the textual fabric informing all levels of its literary language. Something about the language of these texts often jars the ear; at times it is reminiscent of gendered interference, at times feminist punctuation. The difference is that this dissonance is sustained throughout the text, which almost always also contains passages with self-conscious reflections on the relationship between Arabic and French. This more daring approach to language can even lead to a Bakhtinian polyphony of voices, undermining the hegemony of the narrator's or author's voice, allowing others to question the narrator's or author's sole authority over the text.

Native Tongue, Stranger Talk does not argue that the way in which Arabic and French engage each other in texts by Lebanese authors is a chronological process, a linear process of development that culminates in the most recent works. Using the world literature framework means that this study is more interested in how language travels and changes; it understands language use as a process and literary works as constantly in dialogue with one another. It is true, however, that by the late 1990s and early twenty-first century, the texts, contexts, techniques, and strategies that inform literary texts written in French in Lebanon are richer and more diverse than ever before. Since all language use is built on previous language use, these later novels draw on strategies, techniques, and languages used before them.

The period of the postwar is thus particularly interesting, in part because there are so many previous literary and linguistic experimentations on which to draw. Though there is still little scholarship on the literature of this period, there has been a boom in literary production in the twenty-first century in French as well as in Arabic, connected perhaps to the optimism and rebuilding of the turn of the century and also to the instability of the political situation, particularly from the time of the assassination of the former prime minister, Rafiq al-Hariri (February 14, 2005). Just as novelistic production has increased in Arabic, English, and French, so too has the translation of works between all of these languages. They have traveled in their first languages and in translation as part of the process of literary movement and exchange that marks the twenty-first century, and therefore the concept of world literature becomes all the more pressing and relevant as a way in which to frame them.

The three chapters below discuss how "writing *as* translation" works in three very different novels: Leïla Barakat's first novel, *Sous les vignes du pays Druze* (1993) [Under the vines in Druze country], which was published just after the war ended; Dominique Eddé's second novel, which came out six years later (and a full decade after her first), *Pourquoi il fait si sombre?* (1999) [Why is it so dark?]; and her third, which appeared four years after that, *Cerf-Volant* [Kite] (2003). These works could not be more different in setting, theme, approach, or style. The first is set in the "timeless," green Chouf mountains; the second in ruined, postwar Beirut; the third in an optimistic and cosmopolitan postwar that moves between locations. They all, however, implicitly deal with the most crucial issues facing postwar Lebanon, including sectarianism, interfaith/intercommunal relationships of different kinds, class divides, and women's roles in society. They also all make extensive use of a variety of techniques of polyglossia to achieve a disruption of the standard literary French that serves as their medium of expression to make the text read as though written *as* translation.

Language, Travel, and Exchange In Postwar Lebanon

The postwar context of the novels discussed in part 1 is as complex and contested as the civil war itself. The many postwar realities of Lebanon are linked to class-status hierarchies, ethno-religious/confessional identity, and gender; these all play out in relation to place. The almost twenty-year period between the end of the war and the publication of Dominique Eddé's *Cerf-Volant*, the most contemporary novel discussed in *Native Tongue, Stranger Talk*, has been filled with debates over the shape of Lebanon. They not only reflect many of the conflicts prominent during the war itself but also those that recall the issues being disputed during the early independence and French mandate periods, all the way back to the fall of the Ottoman Empire. How Lebanon will reconstitute itself as a nation in an era dominated by particular kinds of nationalism, continued Zionist control over historic Palestine, regional power struggles, economic domination by the United States and its ongoing military intervention in the region, is still an open question.

The optimism and energy in Lebanon that accompanied the period of postwar rebuilding has all but dissipated in a country that once again is divided along a number of lines. Recurring outbreaks of violence and an atmosphere of tension has characterized the country since the 2005 assassination of Hariri, followed by those of a number of other prominent members of government, and attacks and murders of journalists and television presenters, which left the country reeling. Since then the political landscape of Lebanon has been divided into two large alliances, which have shifted, but that largely define themselves as pro- and anti-Syria.[1] The role that Syria, and its ally Hezbollah, may or may not have played in Hariri's murder remains an open question under investigation by the United Nations.[2] Syria's relationship to Lebanese politics is an issue contested by these alliances that has been debated since the time of the mandate and continues on as a civil war increasingly envelops the country after the people's uprising against Bashar al-Asad.

1. I wrote a first draft of this chapter in Lebanon just before the contested election in 2009 in which these two somewhat unlikely alliances battled for prominence. That election demonstrated how much postwar politics are dominated by many of the same names that were so important in the war itself. The once bitterly anti-Syrian Christian militia leader General Aoun has returned to Lebanon after his French exile to ally with the Shi'i Hezbollah Party. Usually defined as "Syrian-backed," they form the 8th of March coalition together with Amal and a number of other smaller parties. They are locked in battle against the newly allied "anti-Syrian" parties in the 14th of March alliance—Saad Hariri's "Future" Party; the Lebanese Forces, led by Samir Geagea; and Amine Gemayel's Kata'ib (Phalangist) Party. Walid Jumblatt's Progressive Socialist Party has often held the balance of power and been a swing vote. The names of the leaders dominating the political scene in Lebanon alone show the connections to the war. It is perhaps therefore not surprising that the accords have not been fully implemented and the country continues to face political instability, such as the inability to form a government in 2011 and again in 2013.

2. A novel about the UN investigation into the assassination of Hariri that shows the mood of Beirut in this period and the impotence of the Lebanese to react against it and its impact is Rabi' Jabir's *Taqrir Mehlis* (2005).

Many of the fundamental issues causing divides between people have not been addressed, including any type of genuine economic and political reforms that would improve the lives of the poor.[3] Only a year and a half after Hariri's assassination, in the summer of 2006, Israel waged a devastating war on Lebanon. Allegedly targeting Hezbollah, whose military wing it engaged, the wide-scale attack on Lebanon left the civilian population of the entire country terrorized, decimated the south and southern suburbs, and destroyed so much of the infrastructure of the country—the airport, roads, and especially bridges—that many were still unrepaired seven years later. The global economic crisis of 2008–2009 only worsened the rising poverty and unemployment, particularly among the most disenfranchised groups. The south of the country and Beirut's southern suburbs are still underdeveloped, as are large sections of the largely Shi'i Biqa' Valley. Palestinians are still living in substandard conditions in refugee camps and unable to access better standards of living; there are laws that bar them from a large number of professions and jobs.

The literary scene in Lebanon today must be understood against this context but also against the optimism of the turn of the twenty-first century, when Lebanon was undertaking massive rebuilding projects. Though its economic situation was at that time also facing major challenges, many Lebanese people had returned after the war to reestablish their lives or start afresh in a newly rebuilding country. New businesses were opened, some in connection to the highly contested project, led by then Prime

3. The Ta'if Accords officially ended the war in 1990; they called for the disarmament of the militias, a reassignment of seats in Parliament to reflect better the demographic realities of Lebanon (a one-to-one Christian-to-Muslim ratio rather than six-to-five as had been previously), and a redistribution of major government roles to redress the imbalance between Christian power and the number of Christians in Lebanon, weakening that of the (traditionally Maronite) president and expanding those of the (Sunni) prime minister and (Shi'i) speaker of the house. It also set a schedule for Syrian withdrawal but effectively formalized its role as peacebroker/occupier, which remains controversial to this day, particularly as Syria did not withdraw according to the schedule set out in the accords but rather more than ten years later in 2005. A number of other provisions of the Ta'if Accords have also not yet been implemented, including a gradual phasing out and elimination of the sectarian system of government.

Minister Rafiq al-Hariri, to rebuild the downtown with his Solidère corporation.[4] One of the aims of this project was to remake Lebanon into a center for regional and international tourism, particularly to attract petrodollars from Gulf countries. The surge in tourism by Arab and Muslim visitors after September 2001, when many were discouraged from traveling to North America and Europe, contributed to the opportunities and optimism that prevailed in this period.

With the frenzy of postwar rebuilding, especially the focus on business, trade, and increased tourism, the idea that English would supersede French in importance in Lebanon was bolstered. Long held to be the language of business for the twentieth century, the rise of English in Lebanon is not new. The stage was set for it to become important in all fields, especially business and trade, long before the war started. As early as the 1950s, shortly after independence, the architects of the new state were already commenting on Lebanon's need to deal with the United States because of its increasing involvement in the region. Deeply committed to France, the French language, and Francophile in his orientation, Michel Chiha, for example, recognized the ascendancy of the United States in the region and globally, encouraging Lebanese people to learn English for this reason.[5] The power dynamics of the region and the way in which the United States began to dominate it not only economically but also culturally through mass media, television, and cinema contribute to the increasing importance of English (Shaaban and Ghaith 2002). The 1994 reversal of the constitutional decree that mandated Arabic as the only language of instruction in primary school, opening the door for all private and public schools to decide which language was the most appropriate medium of instruction, helped in the promotion of English (Shaaban and Ghaith 1999, 10). In 1993, Elias Khoury echoed the feeling of many Lebanese coming out of the war when he asserted, "I think the Francophone

4. Some scholarly work and criticism has been done about how space in downtown Beirut has been rebuilt under the aegis of Hariri's Solidère corporation after the end of the war (Dados 2009; Khalaf 2007; S. Makdisi 1997).

5. See, for example, "Le monde aujourd'hui" (1966), a speech given at the Cénacle libanais on November 6, 1950.

phenomenon in Lebanon is finished. . . . There is no longer the colonial influence to sustain it. Lebanon as a producer of Francophone culture is no more" (Khoury 1993, 139).

Khoury was referring to the fact that the most important literary production in Lebanon was happening in Arabic at the time and that this was the primary site of creative production. Despite this and the rise of English as a preferred foreign language, which has become a reality in Lebanon, the predicted demise of the French language has not yet come to pass. Even if French has waned in importance as the major second language after Arabic, it has certainly not disappeared. Despite their study showing the rise of English in prestige and importance in Lebanon, Shaaban and Ghaith claim, for example, that in the mid-1990s 73.50 percent of classes in Lebanese private schools were French medium, as opposed to 27.50 percent that were English medium (1999, 12).[6] Moreover, the output of French-language creative work by Lebanese authors, both poetry and prose, has continued and even increased. Some of the most interesting novels to be published in the French language by Lebanese authors were produced in the 1990s and early years of the 2000s.[7] The French-language literary and cultural scene in Beirut is still rich and vibrant, with poetry and novels by Lebanese authors published in Lebanon and abroad (particularly in France and Québec). The Lebanese national myth that claims different places for each language emphasizes that French is the language of culture. This sentiment is captured well in a statement about languages by the scholar of Lebanese francophonie Zahida Darwiche Jabbour: "Each has its own domain and plays a particular, irreplaceable role. In Lebanon where French—it must be said—plays an integral role in cultural intensity, where Arabic—it need not even be recalled—is the

6. They are referring to National Center for Educational Research and Development (NCERD) statistics: *New Framework for Education in Lebanon* (1995).

7. It should be noted that more and more creative works by Lebanese authors and authors of Lebanese descent living in the English-speaking world have been published in English. This includes writers like Rabih Alameddine (who wrote during the war as well), Nada Awar Jarrar, Patricia Sarrafian Ward, Naeem Murr, and Nabil Saleh. See Syrine Hout, *Post-War Lebanese Anglophone Fiction: Home Matters in the Diaspora* (2012).

language of national identity, we have opted for a trilingualism where English is the language for access to information" [Chacune possède un domaine propre et joue un rôle particulière et irremplaçable. Au Liban où le français—il faut le dire—fait partie intégrante de l'intensité culturelle, où l'arabe—il est inutile de le rappeler—est la langue de l'identité nationale, on a opté pour un trilinguisme où l'anglais tient la place de langue d'accès à l'information" (2002, 23).

Of course French does not continue on unabated as one of the living languages of Lebanon simply because it is somehow a "language of culture," as Jabbour puts it, or a "natural" language for Lebanese people to speak, as the early Francophile Lebanese nationalists would have it.[8] Nor is it even because of a deeply rooted Francophilia on the part of some Lebanese, though of course this does exist. France has continued its deeply entangled relationship with Lebanon throughout the postwar period, including an active engagement through its cultural center, its funding of festivals, and its support of the arts. Beirut was decked out in the bright colors of symbols especially designed for the Organisation internationale de la francophonie (OIF) summit in 2002, which was held there amidst a great deal of global insecurity and some question as to whether it could be pulled off successfully after being postponed for one year because of the events of September 11, 2001. Beirut's hosting of these meetings showed support for its postwar tourist economy; events throughout the city and country celebrated the French language in multiple ways. Francophonie has detractors as vocal as its supporters in Lebanon, but the OIF summit was held there without incident, shoring up the continued institutional relationships between the organization, France, and the Lebanese state. Holding the 2002 OIF summit in Beirut underlines its identification as

8. See the poetry by the group around the *Revue phénicienne*, including its leader, Charles Corm, as well as Michel Chiha, Héctor Klat, and Elie Tyane. Some of their more flowery prose and poetry dedicated to the French language betray the sentiment that it is an appropriate or "natural" language for the Lebanese. "Le libanisme phénicien" that they espouse is intimately linked to the French language. The journal has been reissued in 2004 by the same press, revived in Beirut by Corm's descendants. Nadia Tuéni also claims this, but with a slightly tongue-in-cheek tone in *La prose* (1986a, 65).

one of the global locations where France's colonial linguistic policies took hold and had a deep effect. It also shows the commitment of the French-speaking world to Lebanon, and the reverse.[9]

Moreover, as groups retrench their identities in the postwar period, a commitment to French as a language, as a second language, a language of education, or main language of expression has been asserted by some Lebanese people. The public school system, already weak before the war because of a system of government that preferred to put such infrastructure into the hands of religious groups, was further weakened by the war. Private schools and universities, however, have maintained their prestige and high standards, encouraging people of all backgrounds to aspire to them. This is as true of the French-language educational system as the English-language one, so enrollments at the Université St Joseph, La Sagesse, École supérieure des affaires (ESA), Notre Dame, and others with French-language instruction has neither noticeably declined nor has their importance within Lebanon subsided.

French-language education produces French speakers and, even more important for this discussion, French-language writers. The role of schools and universities in Lebanon for this creation is crucial, but with a fifteen-year war, so is the role of education abroad. The huge number of Lebanese who left or sent their children abroad during the war resulted in more and more French-educated Lebanese, both inside and outside Lebanon. As noted in chapter 5, many Lebanese emigrated or lived for a number of years in French-speaking countries, France and Québec among others.[10] Many Lebanese capitalized on Canada's favorable immigration

9. The Organisation internationale de la francophonie (OIF) expresses a concept developed and articulated in 1962 by well-known French-speaking Africans, including Léopold Sédar Senghor, Hamani Diori, and Habib Bourghiba. The formal institutionalization of francophonie took place in 1970 using the British Commonwealth as its institutional model (Jabbour 2002, 14; Traisnel 2004, 107). The organization then also began to hold summit meetings every two years; the first took place in 1986.

10. There are large Lebanese communities in other French-speaking parts of the world including West Africa. Mara Leichtman, for example, has looked at the transnational relationships between Lebanon and Senegal in particular (2005).

policies during the war; laws aimed at recruiting French-speaking immigrants to Québec, together with family reunification policies, led to a large number of people, both French speaking and not, coming to Montréal in particular.[11] Local laws, promoting the French language for the education of all new citizens and permanent residents, meant that these immigrants' children became Francophones even if their parents did not.[12] Many people moved back and forth between Lebanon and locations in the French-speaking world; many children born during the years of the war grew up abroad and write from there or have returned to postwar Lebanon.

Literary Production in Postwar Lebanon

The literary scene that has emerged and still is emerging after the Lebanese civil war is as diverse as the authors who contribute to it. Much of the writing by Lebanese authors in the 1990s and afterward deals with the war in one way or another and exorcises its demons. This is even truer now as we enter the second decade of the twenty-first century than it was in the period immediately after the war. Neither the war alone nor even issues directly tied to Lebanon is treated by Lebanese authors in this period. Fictional works are increasingly diverse, again reflecting the diversity of the authors and their interests. The globalization of literary markets in general means that Lebanese authors have a worldwide audience and often make use of this in their fiction. Of course, this is one way in which French-language and Arabic-language authors from Lebanon are in significantly

11. Statistics Canada information from 2001 shows that almost 50,000 Lebanese people reside in Montréal, and though many Lebanese Canadians speak English, there is a high proportion of them who are bilingual or speak only French. Moreover, this is a growing community that keeps its ties with Lebanon. See http://www.statcan.gc.ca/pub/89-621-x/89-621-x2007015-eng.htm.

12. La charte de la langue française or Charter of the French Language is commonly referred to as Loi 101 or Bill 101 and is a product of the "Révolution tranquille." It defines French as the only official language of Québec, one of the results of which is that all children of immigrant parents studying in public schools must be educated only in French.

different positions, despite what they share. The realities of circulation and the market for works in the two languages are not the same and this affects the literary production and trends of each.

One way in which this can be seen is in a greater internationalization of topics by French-language authors from Lebanon. The first novel by the Lebanese Brazilian French writer Yasmina Traboulsi is a good example. Set in the slums of Brazil and dealing in particular with questions of poverty, *Les enfants de la place* (2003) [translated as *Bahia Blues*] was met with widespread acclaim and won the French Prix du Premier Roman in 2003. Vénus Khoury-Ghata has set one of her postwar novels in Mexico. Dedicated to the Mexican poet Octavio Paz, *La maestra* [The teacher] tells the story of a foreign woman in Mexico who, after leaving her husband, travels to the countryside and opens a school to educate local children (1996).

The internationalization of issues and topics does not mean that the novels are not in many ways still implicated in issues and debates that are crucial in shaping a Lebanon still affected by an extended period of civil war. The kinds of regional and international issues that emerge in fiction include, among others, French-language novels dealing with regional locations like Yemen (L. Barakat 1994), Iraq (L. Barakat 1995), and in particular Palestine (Awad 2003; L. Barakat 1997; Nassib 2004; Zein 2005). Lebanese novels written in Arabic tend to share more the regional concerns than the international ones, if indeed they are set outside of Lebanon or deal primarily with non-Lebanese settings. This is most true in relation to historical novels.

The historical novel, dealing with Lebanon or not, is also a prominent feature of Lebanese literature of the postwar period; this period has seen a proliferation of both French-language and Arabic-language historical novels. Historical novels can indicate a move away from the transparent representation of immediate concerns and even a desire for reflection on the events of the past. Historical novels penned in this postwar period often explicitly take up Lebanon's past but comment on issues centrally relevant to the twentieth century as well.

In the French-language context, a writer like Alexandre Najjar, who began his career as a young author during the war, has become even more prolific after the war with his series of historical novels, mostly set outside

Lebanon but connected somehow to the region: *Les exilés du Caucase* (1995), *L'Astronome* (1997), *Athina* (2000). All of these develop a fictional love story overlaid on historical events that somehow "reveal the past" (2005, 134). These works were followed by *Roman de Beyrouth* (2005), which sets a fictional story of a family across a century of Lebanon's, and specifically Beirut's, history.[13]

Najjar's novel recalls the recent series of similarly historical novels by the prolific Arabic-language author of the same generation, Rabi' Jabir, whose *Beirut madinat al-'alam* [Beirut, world city] has now run to three volumes (2003, 2005, 2007). He has also penned another story of Beirut, *Berytus, madina taht al-ard* [Beirut: A city underground] (2005; French translation, 2009b). Also like Najjar, he has attempted historical novels outside of Lebanon—such as *Amrika* [America] (2009a), which features Lebanese émigrés to the United States as main characters.

Many other French- and Arabic-language novelists have written historical novels in the postwar period dealing with Lebanon and other locations. One of the best-known Arabic works to emerge in this period is Elias Khoury's historical novel chronicling 1948 Palestine, *Gate of the Sun* [*Bab al-Shams*] (1998), which was made into a film with the same name.[14] The novel takes on epic proportions over more than five hundred pages and tells and retells through different voices and perspectives some of the most important events of the *nakba* in Palestine and continues as some of its characters take up residence in the refugee camps of Lebanon. Comparable in stature to Khoury's role as an Arabic-language novelist, the acclaimed French-language author Amin Maalouf is best known for his historical novels. Many of Maalouf's works deal with Lebanon and

13. More recently Najjar has also written a historical novel about ancient Phoenicia, which clearly links his novelistic projects to larger questions of national imagery, following in the footsteps of his early French-language Lebanese predecessors (see *Phénicia*, 2008).

14. The book has been translated into English (2008) and French (2003) and widely reviewed. The film, *Bab al-Shams*, directed by Yousry Nasrallah, premiered at the Cannes film festival in 2004.

the region, for example his Prix Goncourt-winning novel, *Le rocher de Tanios* (1993; English translation, *The Rock of Tanios*, 1995) which tells the story of a boy named Tanios in the northern Lebanese mountains at the end of the nineteenth century. Among Vénus Khoury-Ghata's work are historical novels, for example *Le moine, L'Ottoman et la femme du grand argentier* (2003). *Les fiancés de cap Ténès* (1995) is set in prerevolution, early nineteenth-century Algeria. Carole Dagher's pair of works set in nineteenth-century Lebanon combine love stories with a historical saga of the development of the Lebanese nation: *L'anneau de l'émir: Couvent de la lune I* (2002) and *Le seigneur de la soie: Couvent de la lune II* (2004). Other new male writers, too, have written grand historical novels, such as Cherif Majdalani's acclaimed *Histoire de la grande maison* (2005), which tells the story of one man's quest to propagate a big and important family by cultivating oranges in Lebanon at the end of the nineteenth century.

Of course many postwar novels in Lebanon are about the war and deal with the period between the war and the time of the author's writing. Claire Gebeyli, mainly known as a poet, published her novel *Cantate pour l'oiseau mort* in the "écritures arabes" series with L'harmattan (1996). She is joined by other authors who began publishing in the 1990s, such as Elie-Pierre Sabbag, whose pair of works *L'ombre d'une ville* (1993) and *Nous reviendrons à Beyrouth* (1997) both focus on the war. Ghassan Fawwaz's haunting narratives *Les moi volatiles des guerres perdues* (1996) and *Sous le ciel d'Occident* (1998) are also powerful indictments of the violence that Lebanon and Lebanese people suffered.

Many of the trends in French-language fiction are not identical to, but neither are they entirely different from, the main trends emerging in postwar fiction from Lebanon. Well-published and respected authors active during the war continue to publish novels that have the war as a part of their subject. Elias Khoury's brutal tale of rape, murder, and torture, *Yalo* [Yalu] (2002), has received acclaim in Arabic as well as in translation (2008b). One of Rashid al-Da'if's most powerful works, Dear Mr. Kawabata [*'Azizi al-Sayyid Kawabata*] (1995), uses the same generic form as Dominique Eddé's *Lettre posthume* (1989) and offers us a Lebanese narrator who explores the civil war through letters written to the Japanese

Nobel Prize winner.[15] Some newer novelists began writing only after the war, like Iman Humaydan (Younes), who published her first novel about the war, *B as in Beirut* [*Ba' mithl bayt mithl Beirut*], in 1997 and in 2011 published her third novel, *Other Lives* [*Hayawat Ukhra*], which exorcises its ghosts through settings in Kenya, Australia, and Lebanon. It should be noted that all of these authors of Arabic have also in the last twenty years published works not directly commenting on the war.

A newer trend emerging in the twenty-first century is writings that treat the war from a postwar perspective. The young writer Yasmina Traboulsi's second novel, *Amers* (2007), takes up what it is like to live in postwar Beirut, with the war very much in mind. Graphic novels in French by Zeina Abirached, for example, *Mourir, partir, revenir: C'est le chant des hirondelles* (2007) and *Je me souviens: Beyrouth* (2008), are an interesting complement to this trend, as she narrates from a child's view of the war, but they are very much works of the postwar period.[16] Lena Merhej's Arabic-language graphic novel *Laban wa murraba* [Jam and yogurt] (2011) tells the story of how her "mother became Lebanese" (the work's subtitle) during the civil war. Children's remembrance of wartime is present in recent works published in the same years by younger writers like Renée al-Ha'ik, *Salat min ajl al-'a'ila* [A prayer for the family] (2007), and Rabi' Jabir, *'I'tirafat* [Confessions] (2008).

Though my focus is on the novel, it should be noted that poetry continues to flourish in French in Lebanon and a number of plays have also been published in French that have met with great acclaim, including those by Thérèse Aouad-Basbous: *La nonne et le téléphone* (1996) and *Dent d'amour* (1999), among others. The prolific, Lebanese-Québecois playwright Wajdi Mouawad has published and produced many plays in this period, including *Littoral* (1999) and *Incendies* (2003), which were both made into films, *Rêves* (2002) and *Forêts* (2006). Both Aouad-Basbous

15. French translation, 1999; English translation, 2000.

16. Mazen Kerbaje has also self-published very interesting graphic novels, including one in the form of his diaries, *Journal 1999*, and a recent work with Dar al-Adab (2011). Many of his drawings appear on his blog, *http://mazenkerblog.blogspot.com/.*

and Mouawed have also published novels: *Mon roman* (1995) and *Visage retrouvé* (2003).

Writing *as* Translation: "Écrire l'Arabe en Français"

Postwar Lebanon has witnessed increasing globalization and circulation of literary texts, greater awareness of diverse literary traditions, and the rising prominence of postcolonial literary works from many literary and linguistic contexts. All of these factors influence the production of literature in the postwar period. In this rich and fertile atmosphere, novels in French craft languages that are ever bolder and more experimental.

The discussions of the three novels below demonstrate how they create a textual language that reads *as* translation by employing the same techniques that I identified in parts 1 and 2 of *Native Tongue, Stranger Talk*, along with others. For example, they tend to combine the use of both translated and untranslated transliterated Arabic words and expressions and also relexified Arabic expressions with and without extensive cushioning. In most cases, they repeat the use of the same expressions so that you have to remember what came before and learn from the context of the text what they mean. These texts tend not to use footnotes except in very particular situations and do not take on a didactic tone even when they are "teaching" or making a commentary on Arabic and French. The few instances of footnotes, however, are themselves consistent with the use of similar kinds of footnotes in translated texts. In these works, there is a far more extensive engagement with such reflections, coupled in most cases with deep and prolonged metacommentaries on language use and the relationship between Arabic French.

My claim that these texts read *as* translations is linked to how the language of the text therefore in many situations seems different or "alien." Languages in these works are reflected and refracted through other languages. In the works discussed in part 1 of this book, gendered interference allows for a commentary that is always subtle and kept limited. The feminist punctuation that I identified in the works in part 2, Arabic announces itself in many different locations and occasions, usually directly and usually with explanation. In the works discussed in this final part, the technique is both more obvious and subtler. In some cases the language mixing techniques are used to make certain voices sound like they "have an accent in French" and/or to make the reader remember that the characters are not speaking French—they are speaking Arabic though you are reading French. G. J. V. Prasad makes an argument about how this works in the case of the Indian English novel, showing how several authors employ strategies to make their works read as translations and the criticism they face in doing so (1999, 41–57). He puts the works he studies in the context of Samia Mehrez's argument about Abdelkébir Khatibi's *L'amour bilingue* being a radically bilingual text that creates a space "in between languages" (Prasad 1999, 55). Prasad uses translation as a metaphor for the work Indian novelists writing in English do and also as a material description of how language functions in many of their works. This metaphor of translation is similarly reflected in Tymoczko's argument to read postcolonial writing as analogous to translation (1999).

The next three chapters therefore identify how language is manipulated in a variety of ways to make three novels read *as* translations. Though I would identify a radical element in the use of language in these texts, I do not take my analyses in the same direction as Mehrez's claim of Khatibi's bilingualism. Theorists who struggle with this question—Tymoczko, Prasad, Mehrez, and others—identify the textual languages created by authors in postcolonial contexts as both a "mix" of recognized and recognizable language and languages unique to certain textual worlds. How then are these textual languages crafted in ways similar to the languages of literary translations?

The readings below identify concrete strategies through which authors write novels *as* translations and understand them through the theoretical concept of the "resistant" translation, as proposed by Lawrence Venuti. Venuti has argued powerfully in favor of foreignizing translation as a way that literary texts moving from one language to another can challenge hegemonic mainstream discourses, literary and otherwise. This is particularly true in the case of less powerful languages (particularly those of the Third World) that are translated into powerful colonial languages (like French and English). One strategy of foreignization in translation is to make the text clearly read "as a translation," not to naturalize or "domesticate" its linguistic and other differences. By inscribing and maintaining difference in translated texts, he argues, resistant translations therefore can challenge structures of inequality (1995). Venuti's history of translation demonstrates different ways in which translators have and have not chosen to use such techniques and strategies. Many literary texts—including the French-language novels studied in this part—operate similarly to translations in their use of creative polyglossia in language to resist structures of hegemony, including linguistic dominance.

The first work discussed challenges standard literary French narration in ways that we have not seen thus far in the texts analyzed. Leïla Barakat's *Sous les vignes du pays Druze* makes frequent use of Arabic in many different ways and is so extensive as to be all pervasive. Written just after the end of the war, Barakat's novel is a tale of forbidden love and a reengagement with the genre of ethnography to paint a portrait of a "little-known community," the Druze. Like Kher and Bustros, she details the customs and traditions of isolated people in the Lebanese mountains from an insider-outsider perspective, but those of the Druze community, which are rarely represented in French-language fiction in Lebanon.

Two novels by the same author, Dominique Eddé, are explored in the final chapters of the book. Though no work makes as extensive use of Arabic as Barakat's novel does, Eddé's works both use techniques and strategies that arguably make her texts read in many instances as "odd" in French. A meditation on those Lebanese who left the country and then come back to "learn about the war," *Pourquoi il fait si sombre?* is largely an interior monologue interrupted by copious exchanges of dialogue, in which the narrator explicitly states that she hopes to write a French that is "alien" to herself. Both this novel and the more recent *Cerf-Volant* face the issue of class consciousness and the elite status held by the French language and its speakers in Lebanon. This later novel is a multivoiced narration that moves between locations and characters, presenting mildly ironic, amusing snapshots of the lives of elite Lebanese "citizens of the world." The kinds of commentaries that are made through the use of a novel written in French that reads *as* a translation are linked therefore to a strong message critiquing both traditional gender roles and also class-status hierarchies.

10

A Francophone Druze Novel?

Postwar Ethnography and (Anti)Sectarianism in Sous les vignes du pays Druze

A full sixty years after Amy Kher published her ethnographic examination of northern Lebanese village life, *Salma et son village* (1933), Leïla Barakat's *Sous les vignes du pays Druze* [Under the vines in Druze country] (1993) appears, making the somewhat dramatic claim on its back cover that it is the "first Francophone Druze novel" ("premier roman francophone Druze"), describing itself explicitly as a "novel that is a chronicle of the Ben Maarouf" ("Chronique, roman des Ben Maarouf"). Like both Kher's and Bustros's (and to some extent Eddé's) works before it, *Sous les vignes du pays Druze* establishes its "ethnographic pact" with the reader explicitly from the outset. Particularly in highlighting that she belongs to a different religious community than the majority of French-language writers from Lebanon, Barakat guides her reader into a complicit relationship with the text from the outset, establishing her credentials in multiple ways.

Barakat confirms her position in the brief preface, where she specifically identifies her project as delineating the contours of Druze society and telling its tales with the sensitivity and knowledge of an "insider" to a French-reading audience. *Sous les vignes du pays Druze* therefore shares a great deal with earlier novels from the mandate and early independence periods in claiming to play the role of guide to a little-known community. The narrator, Arij, is the insider-outsider par excellence, a village-born Druze girl raised in Beirut. Its main difference from earlier novels—and most other French-language fiction from Lebanon— is that it focuses on the Druze community from the perspective of a self-identified Druze author.[1]

A novel about the Druze written in French was still enough of a novelty in the 1990s that critics praised it for revealing the hidden and supposedly secret world of the Druze. In his comprehensive study of works by Francophone Lebanese writers, for example, Ramy Zein praises this work as an exposé of Druze life and its contribution to knowledge about the Druze.

> Though short, *Sous les vignes du pays Druze* is rich in ethnographic information about the Lebanese Druze. You learn a great deal from it about the Druze community's way of life, traditions, rites, and religious and superstitious beliefs.
>
> Malgré sa brièveté, *Sous les vignes du pays Druze* est riche en indications ethnographiques touchant au druzisme libanais. On y apprend beaucoup sur le mode de vie, les traditions, les rites, les croyances religieuses et superstitieuses propres à la communauté druze. (Zein 1998, 84)

Zein's focus on the details that the (implied non-Druze) reader will learn about the Druze community marginalizes other readings of the text, even other ethnographic readings. He sees it neither as a portrait of a traditional mountain society or one woman's struggles within this community nor as a more general feminist tale of liberation from patriarchal religious norms. It shares all of these elements with both Kher's *Salma et son village* and Bustros's *Sous la baguette du coudrier.* It also shares a critique of gender roles within Chedid's *Le sommeil délivré* and Accad's *Coquelicot du massacre* and the cynicism about family bonds of Khoury-Ghata's *Le fils empaillé* and Eddé's *Lettre posthume.* In his description of the book, therefore, Zein further reinforces the assumption that one would most likely read such a

1. There is another Francophone novel focused on the Druze community that appeared at a similar time (Awad, *Khamsin,* 1994). It is relevant that *Khamsin* is not written by an author of Druze background, who makes this clear at the outset and thanks her Druze friends for their insight. It is interesting to compare these very different takes on the Druze.

novel to find out more about the Druze rather than for any other reason. He also assumes that the readership, particularly the Lebanese readership, for a French-language novel would be just as Christian as most Francophone authors are assumed to be. A work not set among Christians in a literary field dominated by authors of Christian backgrounds who populate their texts with Christian characters does stand out.

To be fair, Barakat's framing of the work itself trades on this difference and encourages such a reception—she claims that it is the first work of its kind, implying that it will expose certain perhaps previously unknown details. Moreover, even identifying herself as a Druze writer, writing a novel about the Druze titled *Sous les vignes du pays Druze* does imply that this is the most important information one might take from the novel. Barakat says that she knows, however, that she should not write a novel that "reveals the community's secrets" (7–8) and pre-empts potential criticism by making it clear that she is not actually betraying her community. In this, she is directly responding to misconceptions and outright fabrications that have characterized so much previous writing about the Druze.[2] As Barakat points out, the one-time "secrets" of this religious community are no longer shrouded in mystery and its holy book, the Hikmé, is found in libraries around the world, so there is no need to think of the Druze as secretive. Barakat asserts explicitly that her mission is not to "expose the community" but rather to "give life to the shadow of a community. Show its nobility without leaving out its faults. Depict all the ravages of the little Druze island" [animer l'ombre d'une communauté. Dévoiler sa noblesse, ne pas omettre ses défauts. Peindre l'îlot Druze de tous ses ravages] (8).

2. See, for example, travel accounts that reported on the Druze. De Volney discussed the Druze (1959, orig. 1787), but others dedicate considerably more space to this endeavor, for example Colonel Charles Henry Churchill, British consul in Beirut beginning in 1840 (Churchill 1853, 1862). Other less well-known accounts provided much the same view of the Druze (Farley 1858; Kelly 1844; Urquhart 1860). Lebanese writers also participated in this discourse, for example, Maronite Bishop Nicolas Murad (1844). Recent popular works have taken a similarly exotic, orientalized view of the Druze (Betts 1988). Nejla M. Abu Izzeddin (1984), Firro (1992), and F. Khouri (2004) all seek to redress this to some extent in their "sympathetic" studies of the Druze.

Barakat draws on and at the same time refuses the exoticism of the Druze, grappling with this issue throughout the novel. The discussions below will uncover how as a Druze she uses and manipulates the novel's somewhat unique position in order to negotiate issues of religion and community identity in relation to class, gender, and antisectarianism through layering multiple languages in the text to read *as* a translation.

Barakat uses the Druze country invoked in her title to set her work up within and against the rich field of ethnographic writing that constructs this region and community. Indeed the Druze have been a particularly fetishized subject for the European imagination and have served as fodder for many ethnographic studies, novels, and travelogues. With so many misconceptions and outright fabrications propagated about the community, it may not be a surprise that so few novels have been written by Druze people or people of Druze backgrounds that deal with the community directly until recently.[3] By being one of the first authors of Druze background to take this on, Barakat is able to promote her novel as unique: as a challenge to the stereotype that a Druze novel cannot be French and vice versa, and also to claim a status as the exception that proves this rule.[4] Most important, Barakat uses this space of double alterity in order to construct a work that both draws on and exploits the genre of the ethnographic novel by making use of Arabic within the French-language narration of her novel. Indeed Barakat's use of language-mixing techniques

3. In this context it is relevant that Awad is not of Druze background and that Barakat is, facts that they mention explicitly in their prefaces and dedications. From 2001 on, a number of works by Druze authors dealing with the community have been published in Arabic and English (Alameddine 2001; Awar Jarrar 2003 and 2007; Humaydan (Yunis) 2001; Humaydan 2010/2014; Jabir 2011). On reading Alameddine's *I, the Divine* as a "Druze novel," see Hartman (2013).

4. Though certainly there are a great proportion of Lebanese French-language novels (and Arabic novels, particularly by women) written by Christian authors, particularly historically, this is by no means solely the case. Writers of French belong to and have their heritage in different communities. Whether or not Barakat's work is the first Francophone Druze novel (meaning written by a Druze in French) may be true, but it is certainly not written in a vacuum, as other prominent Druze writers, thinkers, and intellectuals write in French.

is considerably more far-reaching than those of any other novel discussed thus far—it uses the most Arabic words that are translated, relexified, transliterated but not translated, and so on, and does so in multiple and diverse situations.

Establishing a New Language of Ethnographic Narration: Postwar Negotiations

Barakat's new language of ethnography, building on but significantly different from predecessors like Amy Kher and Eveline Bustros, is developed through her protagonist-narrator who is an insider-outsider. Like other texts, *Sous les vignes du pays Druze* uses this character both to establish and undermine the genre of the ethnographic novel. The novel's tragic heroine Arij plays the role of the "native informant" who leads the reader through the putatively secret and secretive world of the Druze in the Lebanese Chouf Mountains. The reader is meant to identify with Arij's difficulties in blending into the extremely conservative atmosphere of her native village, Amatour, while relying on her at the same time to explain its customs and traditions. Arij continually negotiates and renegotiates her insider-outsider status throughout the novel. The layered language developed throughout the text both reinforces and negotiates the larger issues that the novel poses.

After a brief introduction in which the village scene is set by a dialogue between two olive trees, the main narration of the novel opens with the sunrise in Amatour. It is Arij's first morning in the village and she has no time to be melancholy for what she has left behind in Beirut. As soon as she stirs, Arij is already being summoned to sit with the women busily knitting, embroidering, and gossiping in the living room. The very first words of dialogue in the novel both set the scene and also establish how the Arabic language will be used consistently in the coming pages. As if in one voice, the women say to her, "Welcome, my dear, welcome among us" [Bienvenue, *ya habibti*, bienvenue entre nous] (12). By setting the scene with words of welcome and an obvious representation of how people might greet a long-lost niece, the novel immediately draws the reader into a particular environment, a warm world of women in which

Arij is meant to feel comfortable. Here, she is referred to affectionately with the words "ya habibti." The vocative marker "ya" indicates that she is being addressed as "habibti" in a warm way, as one refers to a loved one. She then uses the Arabic grammar and words within a sentence that is mostly in French. Though "bienvenue" (welcome) and "bienvenue entre nous" (welcome among us) are far from exotic expressions in French, to a reader who knows Arabic they clearly invoke the ubiquitous words of Arabic greeting, "Ahlan wa sahlan" (welcome).

Arij ruptures this cozy image immediately by quickly reminding the reader that the situation—particularly her insider status as a niece—is complicated. The scene unfolds as the women pass a bowl of maté, the hot green tea-leaf drink brought to the region from South America by returning emigrants, around their circle. Arij does not wish to drink the maté but is well aware of the consequences of declining.

> The bowl of maté is now offered to me. I shake my head, my aunt insists, *chokran Khalto,* she insists again. How could I have forgotten? Belonging to this morning gathering, *El Sobhiyé,* comes through drinking. I had to inhale three mouthfuls for them to open doors of the community to me, a dozen for them to open their hearts to me.
>
> La jatte de Maté s'offre maintenant à moi. Je hoche la tête, ma tante insiste, *chokran Khalto,* elle insiste davantage. Comment ai-je oublié? L'adhésion à cette réunion matinale, *El Sobhiyé,* passe par la boisson. Il fallait humer au moins trois gorgées pour m'ouvrir les portes de la communauté, une dizaine pour m'en ouvrir les cœurs. (13; italics in the original)

In the brief moment Arij has "forgotten" about the importance of this morning gathering of women, she is able not only to describe the ritual itself—how the bowl is passed around and everyone drinks from it—but also that it signifies belonging. If she does not drink from it, the women will be closed to her. This example also establishes Arij as a local native informant, an insider-outsider with ethnographic knowledge and access who will be able to unlock the "secret" world of the Druze, and especially Druze women, to the French-reading audience. In this way, Barakat establishes an ethnographic pact with her readers, sharing a French-language complicity with them in order to further her project. The character of Arij is used to convey this pact to the reader—not only by her attendance at the morning gathering and knowing the correct way to act, but also in the "scientific" accuracy with which she labels the exact number of mouthfuls she will need to swallow in order for the women to open their hearts to her. Gesturing to the genre of ethnographic travelogues here allows the book to intervene not only into conversations about the Druze and rewrite the way that they are portrayed but also to destabilize the lines between outsiders and insiders in different spaces in Lebanon in the period just after the war.

The way in which the two transliterated Arabic expressions work in this example reinforces the message and also layers others into it. The first words used, "chokran Khalto," are not translated directly, but are cushioned with context; the second, "El Sobhiyé," offers an Arabic expression as a translation of the French words "réunion matinale" (morning gathering), placing it directly after them. Like the opening welcome, in which an Arabic expression, "ya habibti," is used side by side with the French word "bienvenue" (welcome, or "ahlan wa sahlan"), this short reflection could be read at first glance merely as a representation of speech, albeit one of reported dialogue with an explanation. A great deal more, however, is layered into this short paragraph, infusing meanings about the plot of the novel more generally, establishing its ethnographic position and credentials, and emphasizing the complexities of the insider-outsider dynamics between Arij and the village women already at play in this very first scene.

The seemingly transparent translation of the words "réunion matinale" (morning gathering) by the expression El Sobhiyé, for example, betrays some of this complexity. Barakat leaves no doubt about what these words mean, explaining rather than complicating the non-Arabic-speaking reader's interaction with the text. After all, this is a translation simply providing more information about how to understand the words of the text. Or is it? The inversion of the order of the words is crucial. In a French-language narration, especially one in which speech is being represented, the reader expects to find the "strange" word, an Arabic word, listed first and then translated or explained. Why would a French reader who does not know Arabic need to have a perfectly understandable French expression translated into Arabic? The reverse order of the words is a linguistic strategy that subtly shifts the reader's relationship with the text from one of engaging with a young woman, an "insider" staying with her aunt in a family environment, to one about a young woman "outsider-insider" who can provide this reader with ethnographic information about the way in which Druze village women live.

This scene is a good example of the rich ethnographic detail that Zein points to in his evaluation of the novel. Arij describes a morning gathering of women drinking maté, giving it what sounds like a fancy, even scientific, Arabic name—El Sobhiyé—adding to this morning's allure and mystery. By translating an expression that is already clear to the reader, she implies that you can understand the basic meaning through the words "réunion matinale" but that there is something more esoteric that you might miss if you do not know that this is actually a "Sobhiyé," and not just any morning gathering. This more exotic event may indeed imply something different, and in using language in this way Arij implies that she will be the reader's guide in figuring it out.

The first Arabic words used in this brief paragraph, "chokran Khalto," operate in quite the opposite manner. Not directly translated, these transliterated Arabic words challenge the reader more directly by forcing her or him to understand what they mean from context. Unlike the previous word, and the examples of relexification discussed in the book thus far, this technique is more directly confrontational to the colonial language. To this point we have seen relatively few examples of this direct inscription of Arabic with no translation, indicative of the mediating use of languages by the earliest group of authors and the more didactic challenges of the second. This is the technique cited admiringly by both Ashcroft, Griffith, and Tiffin (1989) and also Zabus (2007) as one of the subversive ways in which local languages can undermine dominant colonial languages written in literary texts. Though the word that means "Khalto"—"tante" (or "Auntie" in English)—appears within this paragraph, it does not appear as a translation of "Khalto" and its meaning is not made plain until later in the narration. The word is capitalized and thus perhaps indicates directly that it is a form of address to a person, even though its equivalent "tante" (aunt) is not similarly capitalized in French. The reader must figure out that the answer Arij gives to her aunt's insistence on drinking the maté (chokran Khalto) means literally, "thank you, Auntie." This kind of challenge works to remind the reader that these women are speaking Arabic, a point to which I will return below.

The crucial complication in this example is that even if you know the literal meaning of these words, they actually mean something opposite within their context than the French reader would likely assume. In French, as in English, if someone offers you something and you say "merci" (thank you), this usually indicates that you accept it. Here, however, Arij is using the polite Arabic way of rejecting something by answering her aunt's offer of maté by saying "thank you" (chokran), to mean in context, "no, thank you." This example demonstrates how Barakat is able to challenge her French-reading audience by using words marked as Arabic in a seemingly simple and innocuous way. The reader who knows only French will be forced to work out from context that Arij is saying "no, thank you, Auntie" to her offer of the drink. But if this reader takes "no, thank you" as the meaning for "chokran" it could lead to trouble later on in reading; as the meaning changes in other locations in the narrative, it only implies the negative in context. The idea that an Arabic word can be introduced within the text one time and then followed the second time without a translation or contextualization is bolstered on this same page by a second use of the word "sobhiyé" in further extrapolating on its meaning to Arij. "The grandeur and banality of this *sobhiyé*: a trivial bowl manages to cement the villagers' conviviality" [Grandeur et banalité de cette *sobhiyé*: une jatte triviale arrive à renforcer la convivialité des villageois] (13).

But unlike the way in which sobhiyé continues to mean a morning gathering, the word "chokran" does not continue in all future cases to mean "no, thank you," as its idiomatic contextual meaning demands here, but rather means simply "thank you."[5] Thus the reader who picks up the word from context, similarly to the reader who only knows the

5. The transliterated Arabic word "chokran" is used six times in the text. In addition to this example, it appears on pages 16, 26, 45, 56, and 68. Half of the uses invoke the contextual idiomatic meaning "no, thank you" and the other half the more literal "thank you."

literal meaning of the expression, may be confused. Even if you know that "chokran" means "thank you," you are still forced to revise the meaning from the context. Thus, the use of the expression here has a didactic purpose above and beyond simply its signification of an actual expression aimed at the reader who knows no Arabic, or only the word's literal, rather than idiomatic, meaning. This example therefore challenges the reader of French who does not know Arabic well to understand and work with the meanings of transliterated Arabic words from the context.

The way in which Arabic works within French in these textual moments shows how language use itself mirrors the experience of readers, allowing them to share in Arij's journey. As an outsider reader, you are fascinated by the linguistic and cultural differences underlined in the text by these words. We recall again the metonymy of "divergence" pointed out by Ashcroft, Griffith, and Tiffin, wherein an Arabic word can be used to represent the Arabic language or even function metonymically to represent Arab culture as a whole. You learn about these customs and traditions along with the city-educated Arij, who has "forgotten" them. But at the same time, as an outsider reader who does not know Arabic, you do not understand the expressions and have to figure them out based on the context and meaning of the text, just as she has to discern what is happening in the village and the appropriate ways in which she is meant to act.

These linguistic moments are not only meant for the outsider reader though, they also underline the difference between this reader and the one who knows Arabic well and show that the insider reader, like Arij herself, also may need certain things explained. Any Arabic speaker immediately understands all of the phrases that are used, particularly as none are esoteric expressions or even those only used in written Standard Arabic (*fusha*). Indeed all of the words used in Arabic in Barakat's text are colloquial Arabic that you would understand, as an Arabic speaker certainly one from Lebanon—even if you do not know the formal language at all.[6] This demonstrates that Barakat is addressing an audience that does

6. The issue of using colloquial as opposed to standard formal Arabic specifically in relation to the way in which socioeconomic and class background is discussed in the

understand Arabic, just as much as one that does not. It further reinforces the text's ethnographic stance and potential commentary on the genre of the ethnographic novel, by reinforcing Arij's in-between insider-outsider status. Additionally, it shows ways in which the novelization process here draws on multiple speech genres, like the everyday speech of women and "low languages" and vulgarity (as in the case of Accad and Eddé), within a text that also invokes the higher standard of literary French, such as that used in ethnographies and travelogues.

The ethnographic tropes that Barakat seizes on in her narration are thus buttressed by her use of Arabic in the French novel. The outsider-insider who forgets things sets the tone from the very beginning of the text; the opening scenes prefigure the later conflicts that structure the plot and message of the entire book. Arij's ability to fit into her village after announcing her love for a boy of another sect is foreshadowed by this seemingly innocuous early scene where she is reluctant to drink the maté. Like falling in love outside of the religion and bucking the conventions appropriate for young Druze women, not drinking maté is identified as a way to remain an outsider and not be accepted. Just sitting and drinking with the women is considered appropriate female behavior in the village. Arij's commentary on Druze village customs and traditions begins here and intensifies through the narration. As she herself articulates this at the funeral of a distant relative, in a moment when she is exasperated but still only gently critical of her community, "To know Druze customs you are struck with admiration, to live them you are struck down by exhaustion!" [À connaître les coutumes druzes, on tombe d'admiration; à les vivre on tombe de fatigue!] (27).

These two examples of layering languages into the text to create a unique narrative voice imbued with Arabic and French exemplify on these first few pages of the novel the way in which the entire novel develops.

---

text is discussed in chapter 12 in relation to Dominique Eddé's *Cerf-Volant* (2003). I show there how the contrast between formal versus vernacular Arabic is drawn in texts written in French and how many of these interventions can be seen as a sort of double interruption of speech genres, as almost all interventions by Arabic in French texts draw upon spoken, colloquial Lebanese Arabic.

Barakat teaches her readers in the case of "sobhiyé," and challenges them in the case of "chokran Khalto." The effect of these words does not make the text read extremely awkwardly, but it does interrupt the flow of French and gives some indication that she means to represent speech—"how people really talk." Moreover, it layers messages into the text that inform the reader not only about Druze country but also about how Barakat chooses to depict it. By using these words and their layered meanings, she does not simply reflect local speech or expose the community's secrets, but rather challenges the reader in several additional ways. The novel takes numerous Arabic words and expressions that "sound like Arabic" and renders them somehow within French to suggest their own alterity or difference. Analyzing the multiple ways that this works allows us to see how this novel might read *as* a translation.

"The Druze Are Good People": Death for Honor

The example of drinking maté shows how Arij forgets and then remembers village customs, offering a space to explain them to the reader while also allowing her to express her uncertainty about how much she wants to fit in with her female relatives. This seemingly innocuous example foreshadows some of her more consciously direct challenges to village mores. Arij does not understand, for example, why she cannot continue her chaste relationship with her boyfriend Nabil, who is a Shi'i Muslim, when she is living in Amatour. She goes to great lengths to convince her aunts that seeing him should not be forbidden and that she should not be shunned from the Druze community if she does. Stress from this standoff chips away at her health, just as her aunts chip away at her unsuccessful arguments throughout the novel. After a dramatic deathbed scene, Arij succumbs to the fate of so many tragic heroines before her—she dies of a fever. The echoes of Amy Kher's *Salma et son village* are palpable in *Sous les vignes du pays Druze*. The reason for her death, though, is left even more oblique. Was her fever caused by her jealous male cousin poisoning her? Her pious, traditional aunt? Was it a suicide, or simply a broken heart?

Arij's death must be looked as falling somewhere on the continuum between Amy Kher's Salma, who dies of a "broken heart," and Eveline

Bustros's "honor killing" of Anissa at the hands of her brother. Arij is not necessarily murdered at the hands of a family member, but she may have been. It is clear that stifling village customs, in one way or another, contributed to her untimely demise. In *Sous les vignes du pays Druze,* as in *Salma et son village, Sous la baguette du coudrier,* and *Le sommeil delivré,* a woman's inability to fit into her community, because of her desire for an inappropriate man, is the cause of her misery. There is less of a consensus among both the family and the larger community about Arij's death than about Anissa's, however, which is more or less universally accepted and even embraced by the villagers. Moreover, Arij cuts a different figure of the tragic heroine than Anissa. A young, unmarried, presumed-to-be virgin woman, Arij engages in a "love affair" with Nabil, a young man of a different religious background, but this relationship is chaste. The Beirut-raised Arij knows that the people of Amatour, her natal village to which she returns after her parents emigrate to Venezuela, will not welcome this relationship. She is determined neither to abandon Nabil nor to estrange herself from her family, community, and roots; this means that she cannot abide the outdated conventions and customs that stifle her individuality as a person and a woman and force rigid sectarian and religious blinders on people living in a multiconfessional Lebanon. The questioning of Arij's insider-outsider status within the ethnographic exposé of Druze country is mirrored therefore by how the work negotiates the role of the individual Druze woman within her relationship to the Druze community through language in the meeting of the ethnographic novel and the love story gone wrong in Amatour.

This can be seen in the way in which Arij's brother, Imad, copes with the news of her death when he returns to the village from Venezuela to investigate what happened to her. In direct contrast to Anissa's brother Khalil's contentment after her murder at his own hands, Arij's brother falls on the ground sobbing at her grave, the dewy grass mixing with his tears as he ponders, "How did she die? A fever? Does one really die of a fever? Suicide? For what reason?" [Comment était-elle morte? Fièvre? Meurt-on de fièvre? Suicide? Pour quelles raisons?"] (92). Imad is deeply disturbed to learn the circumstances of her passing as he travels through the village, visiting different families and soliciting their versions of events and accounts of her untimely demise. He learns from cheikh Mokhtar's family, for example, that it was a fever and the will of God; cheikh Hafez's family on the other hand implies that her jealous male cousin poisoned her in retribution for her love for Nabil. Cheikh Youssef's family rejects this theory completely, cheikh Amin accuses her aunt, and cheikh Salim's family rejects all of this gossip that they deem fanciful, leading Imad back to the theory of the fever. Though the reader is never privy to Imad's thoughts about his sister's behavior while she was in the village, he curses the fact that Arij was attracted to the idea of returning to her village and roots when the rest of the family emigrated to Venezuela and firmly lays the blame for her death on Amatour.

The contrast between Khalil's murder of his sister Anissa for family honor and Imad's angry but sympathetic reaction to Arij's death is striking. The similarities in their situations are clear: both women violate community and religious norms, both are in love with "inappropriate men" by community standards, and both have stained their families' honor according to their traditional mountain villages' normative codes of behavior. A number of factors, however, mediate these similarities, underlining their differences and the contrasting reactions of these women's brothers. First, Arij is already dead and Imad is mourning a sister whom he has lost. He is not first faced with the question of honor and forced to decide how to handle the situation. More important, he does not live in the village where her alleged indiscretions took place, nor does he intend to do so. Imad is not affected, as Khalil is, by the stress of daily life under the community pressure and shame related to his compromised family honor. Moreover, Arij was not discovered actually having an affair outside of marriage, but merely expressed the desire to continue seeing a boy whom she liked and who happened to be of a different religious background. Finally, and perhaps crucially, Imad, like Arij, lived in Beirut for most of his life and at the time in which the book is set does not live in Lebanon at all. Upon his return from South America in the last six pages of the novel, Imad is merely an observer in the village, an insider-outsider himself who collects information from the locals, as Arij had done before her death. Just as Arij had "forgotten" about the customs and traditions of their village, so too may have Imad. His difference from the villagers is underlined textually, for example, when he meets a group of foxes and is unsure how to escape them because "he was never a son of the land" [Il n'avait jamais été fils de la terre] (91).

The contrast between the actions of Imad and Khalil and their reactions to their sisters' behaviors and deaths reveal some of the ways in which language functions within the ethnographic novel in order to negotiate the relationship between women's individual identities and their religious/sectarian communities. Both narratives relate the female protagonist's death to a question of honor that is in turn linked to religious and community identity. Though both novels open with women's stories, are told primarily in women's spaces and through women's points of view, both also end with dead heroines and the reactions of their male relatives. These male reactions represent how the communities deal with women who stray from the paths that religious and social norms dictate for them. Reading the ways in which language negotiates the complex relationships between gender, religious, and community identities in *Sous les vignes du pays Druze* demonstrates how the genre of the ethnographic novel is reinforced, questioned, and also undermined by this work. This manipulation of the genre is then linked to the novel's commentary about community solidarity and identity and the (im)possibility of women's belonging within it.

The way in which Imad reacts to Arij and other women in the village is part of *Sous les vignes du pays Druze*'s construction of a Druze identity. After being confused by the conflicting reports of different families regarding the circumstances of his sister's passing, Imad is surprised on the road by Farida, one of the village cheikhas. Her cryptic words to Imad about Arij's death are full of meaning about how Druze identity is perceived within the village, but also within the textual logic of *Sous les vignes du pays Druze* more generally. Imad's head is spinning and he feels that the truth is teasing him with "a thousand and one whims" [mille et un caprices] (89) when Farida appears from nowhere, pronouncing, "The Druze are good people. But they do not use much reason. She did not have a choice" [Les druzes sont bons. Mais ils raisonnent peu. Elle n'avait pas le choix] (89). Imad is shocked not only by Farida's words, but also by the fact that she appeared to him and addressed him out of the blue, without first greeting him. "A woman who does not respect the code!" [Une femme qui ne respecte pas le code!] (89). This short interaction alone reveals a great deal about the messages layered within the ending of Barakat's novel.

To begin with, the thousand and one whims that dance in Imad's head connect this scene to the Orient of the Western imagination by invoking *One Thousand and One Nights*, the best-known work of Arabic literature in the non-Arabic-speaking world. Moreover, the invocation of *One Thousand and One Nights* also conjures up the world of jinn and 'afreet, supernatural forces that control humans and have visionary powers that ordinary people do not, which gives Farida a special sort of power in the scene. This power is suggested by her nontraditional way of greeting Imad and his shock at her acting in a way that does not "respect the code."

Imad's use of the word "code" here and his angry reaction to Farida's lack of conformity to it layers irony into the scene. First, if we see Farida as an almost otherworldly figure in this passage then she would be unlikely to conform to a human code of behavior. This particular word also indicates that there are unwritten rules about social interactions, once again providing an ethnographic detail about the customs of this village community. It is not clear in this scene, however, whether or not this code of behavior is one pertaining to Druze villagers in general or simply Druze women. Because Imad underlines that this *woman* does not respect the code of behavior, it is left ambiguous if he is disturbed as a Druze person or a Druze *man* at the way in which this woman behaved toward him. Further, "code" is the same word used in *Sous la baguette du coudrier* in relation to an "Oriental honor code" that demands the stoning of adulterous women. It is no accident that works exploring social norms and conventions, through the guise of providing ethnographic details, would refer to women's behavior in relation to codes. These very details indeed buttress the claim of these works to hold the key to explaining their societies. Finally, Arij's death is in some way connected to the idea that she herself was unable and unwilling to conform to the conventions or codes of her society as a Druze and a woman. This slowly becomes clear to Imad as he makes his rounds of the village. Though Arij's break with her community is more dramatic—partly because of her gender—Imad himself does not always conform to his village's codes. He does not know how to act around foxes, does not stay for an extra day with his aunt and uncle as tradition demands, and simply does not fit into the village as a "son of the land" would.

It is not simply how Farida addresses him suddenly and out of the blue that shocks Imad, however. In this scene, he also ponders what she says. When he asks Farida what she meant by saying that Arij "no longer had a choice," she replies that Arij was no longer in control of her life. Imad asks Farida how this is connected to her having had a fever. In reply, she scoffs at him. Her reaction enrages Imad, but he controls himself: "Were it not for his Druze upbringing, he would have slapped her" [N'était son education Druze, il l'aurait giflée] (90). Though he refrains from slapping her, he does nonetheless press her further and asks his sister might have taken her own life. Farida's reply is unequivocal, "God preserve me! Suicide is haram. She had a decent funeral. Never repeat that, her memory would be cursed" [Dieu m'en garde! Le suicide est haram. Elle a eu des funérailles décentes. Ne répète jamais ça, on maudirait sa mémoire] (90).

Three specific ethnographic details given in this scene contribute to the construction of Druze identity. First, the scene opens with Farida's declaration that the Druze are "good people"—they simply are without the power of reason. Second, suicide is shown to be forbidden by the Druze religion and it is posited that a Druze suicide would not get a decent burial. Finally, a Druze upbringing prevents a man from slapping a woman, even if he thinks that she may have insulted the memory of his dead sister. All three of these comments have layered implications for the multiple audiences addressed by a French-language novel about the Druze, which will be read by both Arabs and non-Arabs, Druze and non-Druze, who know French.

That the Druze do not use reason, but are good and upstanding people nonetheless, is a stereotype they share with many religious groups. Someone identified by religion and thus connected to it in more ways that simply an affiliation by birth would perhaps be likely to value spirituality over reason and logic. This description means to show Arij as a passionate person who is guided by her heart. As a comment on the construction of identity, it helps to reconcile Arij's own conflict between being a Druze woman and member of her community and an autonomous individual. She struggles with how to reconcile her own autonomy within the narrow confines of the Druze identity that her village community allows her to have as a woman.

Farida therefore identifies the way in which Arij acted in her last days as identifiably "Druze," not in that she may have acted illogically, but because she was "good" rather than bad. This is a redefinition of what it means to be Druze by one of the very cheikhas who made Arij's life so difficult throughout the novel. As such, this seemingly stereotypical and orientalist comment is employed with a double sense. It gives "local color" and ethnographic detail to the text, and also undermines fixed ideas about what this Druze identity actually means in the case of a specific Druze woman struggling with her situation.

The notion of the Druze as good people is reinforced by the third example, when Imad refrains from slapping Farida even though he feels that she insulted his sister. It is not just his "good," strict, religious, or other kind of upbringing, but his Druze upbringing specifically, that conditions his restraint. Even more than the previous negative stereotype cited above, this attribution of positive qualities to the Druze may seem simply to be eulogistic. However, within larger narratives involving stereotypes of Druze violence, this notion is more complex. Particularly as Arij's death may be interpreted as an honor crime, Barakat takes pains to show that this may be a village custom, but it is not "Druze."

Unlike in *Sous la baguette du coudrier,* the death of the female protagonist is not sanctioned by the woman's brother or openly by a religious figure in *Sous les vignes du pays Druze.* Different shaykhs and shaykhas have different opinions about her demise, as Imad learns in his rounds of the village. This difference may partly be due to the work's resistance to mainstream conceptions and misconceptions about the Druze. It is also very much the product of a certain era. *Sous les vignes du pays Druze* was published toward the end of the Lebanese civil war and set in this same period. The violence that plagued Lebanon was common to most communities, but their portrayal differed considerably. The "legendary" violence and fierceness of the Druze are commonly repeated stereotypes, particularly in foreign media, a location from which readers of this novel likely might have received information about the Lebanese civil war. Stories about Druze warlords, and about proud and violent Druze villagers and their defence of their community in this period, would only reinforce images constructed in the previous century through ethnographies and travelogues. The use of positive stereotypes, such as chivalrous behavior attributed to Druze men, can be read in direct connection to this imagery. Barakat's strategy once again recalls Eddé's *Lettre posthume,* in which the declension of stereotypes works to break them down even as they are constructed. Here, Barakat draws on reversals using ethnographic details about the Druze community to reinforce her messages plainly.

The way in which Druze identity is formulated through ethnographic details in this scene and in the entire novel, however, is not limited to stereotypes alone. Farida's statements about the religious prohibition on suicide also underline Arij's Druze identity upon her death. Farida insists that Arij did not commit suicide, which would be in contravention of religious laws. Her ambiguous death by a "fever"—poison, illness, or a broken heart—means that she can be embraced by the community after her death. That Arij is more of a community member in her death than she was in her life is a pessimistic statement about the possibility of reconciling contradictory elements of one's identity.

The particular manner in which Farida's comments are articulated uses two expressions marked as Arabic in order to draw greater attention to two shifts of speech genres. These polyglossic techniques, moreover, layer a larger message about Druze identity into it. The transliterated untranslated word "haram" directly follows the idiomatic French translation of the Arabic expression used elsewhere and transliterated as "Astaghfirallah," "Dieu m'en garde" (God forbid). The standard expression "God forbid" would not necessarily be connected to religion when spoken by a pious older woman, but in this context and connected to the Arabic word "haram," it clearly is meant to invoke a religious idea. The untranslated word "haram" is not particularly difficult to understand, as the text offers adequate cushioning. Moreover, the word "haram" is used previously in the text where the meaning "forbidden" is made clear. Earlier in the text it is also used in connection with death and a funeral. Arij expresses dismay that they are unable to celebrate the major religious festival Eid al-Adha this year because the village is mourning (40). The last Arabic word used in the novel, "haram," is significant in its connection to death and what is religiously forbidden, but also in its powerful emotional significance. A word frequently used to talk about codes, norms, and conventions, "haram" reminds us that it is because so many things are forbidden to Arij that she eventually succumbs to her tragic end. The Arabic word "haram" thus overshadows and overcodes the entire text. The concept embedded in this untranslated Arabic word has the power to control the life and death of Arij and also shapes her identity as a Druze woman.

Reading a French Novel as a "Translation"

Sous les vignes du pays Druze stands out among all of the novels discussed in *Native Tongue, Stranger Talk* because it uses so many words and expressions that represent Arabic, inscribing them through a wide range of techniques encompassing all of those explored in the previous chapters. Barakat's novel is the most formally experimental and engages the most challenging use of language of all the works discussed thus far. Most particularly, its extensive polyglossia goes further than in the other works to negotiate crucial issues directly by interrupting speech genres in creative ways.

The language/s of *Sous les vignes du pays Druze,* words and expressions marked as Arabic written within an ostensibly French text, reflect an insider-outsider ethos embodied in Arij. Continually reinforcing its distance and difference from the French language, while producing a text that is written in what could only be identified as French, *Sous les vignes du pays Druze* mediates between French and Arabic. In particular, Barakat's text interrupts the French language through different uses of and references to Arabic, marking shifts in speech genres. This includes the use of recognizable, transliterated Arabic words and relexifications, both of which continually remind readers that the language spoken in "Druze country" is Arabic.

If we analyze the language of Barakat's text using the terms of translation studies, she has "foreignized" her French through a writing strategy that makes use of Arabic words. Foreignization is a strategy advocated by many translation theorists, including Lawrence Venuti, in order to address the global inequalities of language that arise in translation, especially the disparities between more and less powerful languages and literatures. Venuti advocates translating in a way that allows the translated text to still read as though it were different and "foreign" to counter dominant paradigms in English-language literature and its reception.[7]

The way in which Barakat's text continually returns to assert some kind of strangeness within the French, in multiple ways and constantly throughout its pages, evokes foreignized translations. Moreover, the kind of ethnographic novel that comments on a community with love and affection, pointing out its positive attributes as well as its foibles, is well suited to such a technique. Barakat manipulates this expertly. Through these moves, Barakat praises as well as critiques aspects of the community that harm Arij specifically and also women more generally. It should not be overstated, but the linguistic challenges that Barakat inscribes within *Sous les vignes du pays Druze* make a statement about Arabic beyond its exoticism to the French-language reading audience. This makes her linguistic negotiations of gender, religion, and community resonate with other writers in Lebanon and beyond.

Conclusions

Language is one of the ways that *Sous les vignes du pays Druze* lays a particular claim to difference within French-language literature from Lebanon. Because it is written by a Druze author, contains Druze characters, and offers details of the contours of life in Druze country, its alterity within a literary field dominated by authors of Christian backgrounds is assured. Not only does the novel set itself apart as different within French-language literature, but it also flaunts the convention that Druze people should not expose the community to the gaze of outsiders. While bucking tradition in these ways, however, in conclusion I propose that Barakat actually does also conform to certain conventions. As the analysis of her novel shows,

7. This is a compelling argument and others have picked up his call to action, particularly in studies of Arabic-English translation (Boullata 2003; Booth 2008; Hartman, 2012).

many descriptions of Druze life in the mountains reveal them to be not all that different from other communities in Lebanon. Despite Thursday evening gatherings in the *majliss*, a belief in reincarnation, and some of the other more esoteric elements of the religion and customs that Barakat points out, we understand through *Sous les vignes du pays Druze* that the most important bonds between the people of Amatour are restrictions about the mixing of insiders and outsiders, particularly mixing between unrelated people of opposite sexes. Barakat's insistence on the "Druzeness" of her novel in some ways reinforces how similarly we can read the Druze experience to others of mountain-dwelling people, in particular Christians.

Barakat's novel uses its difference and "Druzeness" in order to define and structure itself as oppositional within a predominately Christian literary field, perhaps leading Barakat to pay closer attention to issues of stereotyping by "outsiders" who in her case would be doubly construed, religiously and linguistically. Arguing vehemently against the closed nature of her village, Amatour, Arij tries to show that having friendly relationships with other communities, exemplified in her case by a Shi'i boyfriend, is positive rather than negative. In its rejection of sectarianism, then, I propose *Sous les vignes du pays Druze* is very much a novel of its time. This means that its status as a "Druze novel" is less important than reading it as a "post-civil-war novel" of the early 1990s. The resonance of Arij's proud statement to her aunt that "J'abhorre le sectarisme" [I abhor sectarianism] (30) and her declaration of atheism (72) rings with a clear message to the ears of Lebanese (and non-Lebanese) people after a long war fought partly on the lines of such competing worldviews.

In these ways, then, it is not the "Druzeness" of Barakat's novel that sets it apart from the others in the most crucial ways, but rather its message that draws on its time and place. This too is inscribed within the challenges posed by its use of a "foreignized" language that reads like a translation. *Sous les vignes du pays Druze* is most concerned with its challenge to sectarianism and the ways in which Lebanese people can live together despite their different religious, sectarian, and other backgrounds, including choices of lifestyle. Far from the more idealized, vaguely depicted Christian-Druze coexistence alluded to by Bustros, or the mixing of Muslims and Christians as neighbors in Chedid's *Le sommeil délivré* and Khoury-Ghata's *Le fils empaillé*, interfaith dating here is confronted head on with the more closed, traditionally minded people expressing their opposition and Arij resisting this opposition all the way. This is a powerful and important statement in the immediate aftermath of the war. It is all the more important in the context of Barakat's multiple audiences.

Unlike many of the earlier authors, certainly Kher and Bustros, who published long before the civil war, Leïla Barakat's audience is global. Like Evelyne Accad's *Coquelicot du massacre, Sous les vignes du pays Druze* is published in L'harmattan's "écritures arabes" [Arab writing] series. This is an important change in the ways in which novels by Lebanese authors are received and marketed by French publishers. This wider distribution begins during the war, but becomes increasingly important at the turn of the twenty-first century with the globalized market for literature, increased circulation, and the availability of books on the Internet. French-language novels by Lebanese authors gain greater and greater exposure with the war and the end of the war. Leïla Barakat's works have not yet become as mainstream as Andrée Chedid's, published by Flammarion, or Eddé's works that have appeared with Seuil. Certainly L'harmattan's "Arab writing" series will provide this work with a far more wide-reaching potential audience than that of the ethnographic novels penned by her colleagues writing during the French mandate over Lebanon.

This broader implied readership allows Barakat to operate in different ways than earlier writers, free of the more specific constraints of the genre of "ethnography" or the ethnographic novel. It also perhaps led her to make certain kinds of choices in using language to represent the Druze. For example, she might be more likely to want to leave the death of her protagonist ambiguous—was it a fever, murder, or simply a broken heart?—to avoid the sensationalism of "honor killing" and stereotyping by a French-reading audience. By the 1990s, identity politics in France had led to a larger questioning of the colonial project, with works about Algeria achieving best-seller status. Barakat's novel therefore treads a fine line between exposing and describing a community and defending it. Barakat's *Sous les vignes du pays Druze* is in some ways typical of post-civil-war fiction in dealing with Lebanon, alluding to the war, and presenting issues as an insider-outsider to a French-reading audience. It maintains its uniqueness in reclaiming ethnography as a genre, particularly in a Druze setting, where there are so few French-language authors (or Arabic-language authors, for that matter).

11

The Tightening Corset of French

Writing the Postwar in Pourquoi il fait si sombre?

Described by the literary critic Edward Said as a "*tour de force* of linguistic virtuosity and imaginative vision," *Pourquoi il fait si sombre?* (1999) is one of the most engagingly challenging novels by a Lebanese writer of French (Said 1999, 7). Said goes on to praise the novel in glowing terms as his choice of the best book of the last year of the millennium in the *Times Literary Supplement*:

> Eddé's *Pourquoi il fait si sombre?* (Seuil) is a searing, astonishingly brilliant and compressed first-person fictional account of feeling, illness and violence taking place in civil-war Beirut and Paris. Its freedom of vision, as well as its white-hot intensity of narrative, establish it as *the* account of Lebanon's travail, tense, tender, luminous: it has already won two major French literary awards. (7)

One of the reasons for the acclaim and awards, and such glowing praise from a critic like Said, may be how this novel manages to free itself from the more expected patterns and constraints of the genre of the novel as conventionally defined. The works discussed thus far all fit into a recognizable category or subgenre of the novel: the ethnographic exposé of "local customs and traditions" (Kher, Bustros, Barakat), the feminist coming-of-age novel (Chedid), the feminist novel told through several voices to critique patriarchy (Accad), the tale of a family facing difficult times (Khoury-Ghata), and the epistolary novel (Eddé 1989).

Pourquoi il fait si sombre? exemplifies how strict generic conventions can be challenged through a mixing of voices, languages, and genres through a process of what Bakhtin calls "novelization." Bakhtin meant that the genre of the novel was unfinished, it was always in progress and therefore could challenge literary conventions through its very indeterminacy. The generic conventions of literary texts that Bakhtin was concerned with were vastly different than those at the end of the twentieth century. The novel today of course has developed its own series of more rigid codes and rules—as the other works discussed in *Native Tongue, Stranger Talk* demonstrate. Moreover, genres tend to be conceived of in less rigid ways today; the novel is able to absorb many other genres, as Bakhtin argued, but is also able to exhibit characteristics of definable subgenres. All of this helps to contextualize how Eddé's novel is more experimental formally than most novels, linguistically as well as in its narrative voice. This is particularly true in relation to other French-language works by Lebanese women authors. Its flexibility of language and genre exemplifies the issues of the close of the twentieth century in Lebanon and the region, as a text that bridges between other works of fiction treating the civil war for "insider" Lebanese audiences in Lebanon and abroad as well as "outsiders" from metropolitan France and elsewhere.

This chapter proposes that it is precisely *Pourquoi il fait si sombre?*'s use of polyglossia that produces a novelization process distinguished from other novels of its time. This is one reason why it has garnered such praise. The creative use of multiple languages and registers, poetic turns of phrase and expressions, and surprising interruptions of speech genres propel a story with a nonlinear plot and nameless narrator. There are no nostalgic portraits of Arabic-speaking peasants or villagers to be found in *Pourquoi il fait si sombre?* The ethnography of a Kher, Bustros, or even a more challenging Barakat has been left behind. It even challenges the kinds of cynical portraits of the Lebanese bourgeoisie as narrated by the priest of Eddé's own earlier work, *Lettre posthume*. Any nostalgia for a prewar Lebanon is highly mediated through the stories of the people living in Beirut's postwar aftermath. Though the narrator hails from the same elite social strata as Eddé's other narrators, the novel itself focuses less on the foibles of the bourgeoisie of *Lettre posthume* or the very upper echelons of Lebanese society than her later work *Cerf-Volant* (2003). Similarly, more diverse voices permeate this text than either of these other two novels.

Like Chedid's *Le sommeil délivré* and even more so Eddé's other novels, *Pourquoi il fait si sombre?* establishes its commitment to exploring and probing class consciousness from its very opening. What sets this work apart from others, however, are the many different voices that truly enter into the formulation of the narrative itself, considerably displacing the narrative and authorial voices in the process. The French-language narrative is not simply interrupted by a postman or a peasant; instead, subaltern figures who have lived through the Lebanese civil war continually challenge the voice of the unnamed narrator who herself did not. The novel is a serious attempt at negotiating the question of voice and the connection of voice to power and privilege. Voice, power, and privilege come together through Eddé's use of multiple languages, which can be characterized as a polyphonic novel as Bakhtin defines it.

Pourquoi il fait si sombre? is able to challenge and question class and social position through language so effectively partly because the sanctity of the novelistic text itself, as well as the story it is telling, is constantly called into question. Much of the work consists of the stream of consciousness of an unnamed female narrator who, after many years living in France, has returned to her native Lebanon with a French friend and colleague, Antoine, to write a book in French about the civil war. In order to undertake this project, she must interview people who have experienced the war. Their unwillingness to cooperate with her, while being so kind, generous, and open about almost everything else, makes her doubt that she should pursue the project at all. Even knowing little of Eddé's own personal biography and trajectory as a novelist, because we are reading a novel about the civil war written in French by a Lebanese woman who lived in France for many years and then returned to Lebanon, the metanarrative implications are difficult to miss. Though other novels discussed here contain many self-reflective passages calling certain values and practices of the French-speaking Lebanese bourgeoisie into question— Chedid's *Le sommeil délivré*, Khoury-Ghata's *Le fils empaillé*, and Eddé's *Lettre posthume* come to mind once again—*Pourquoi il fait si sombre?* takes these challenges to another level, questioning its own existence explicitly and then implicitly deconstructing it through its own pages.

"An Alien French": Polyphony and Class Consciousness

The class consciousness of *Pourquoi il fait si sombre?* is thus clear—the narrator's ambivalence about representing the subaltern is mentioned in its opening pages and recurs throughout the text. She is uncomfortable with the idea that she is able to represent people and tell their stories; she claims from the very beginning, and all the way throughout the text, that she cannot. Indeed in the very first passage of the book, the narrator underlines that the main reason for this inability is that her work will be written in French. Being able to write "in an alien French" therefore is a priority for her. She underlines that this is not the only reason but emphasizes that language is bound up tightly with other important questions of representation, class difference, and privilege.

Pourquoi il fait si sombre opens with a stunning run-on sentence of more than two pages, which consists of a numbered list. Upon encountering the opening lines of the book, the reader does not know what this list refers to. The first thing in the list is that the narrator is sitting on a straw hat, the second is that she actually is the straw hat on which she is sitting (Eddé 1999, 11). Eventually you learn that everything in the list somehow refers to the book that the narrator is planning to write. Surely this section is one of the moments of linguistic virtuosity to which Said refers; it is stunning in its flexibility, wit, and ability to capture absurdity as well as treat specific issues. One fact captured in her countdown is her vision of this book's language, "six, I would like so much to write French in a way alien to me" [six, je voudrais tant écrire le français d'une manière qui me soit étrangère] (11). She continues the list up through the twenties and then starts to lose the thread of her own delirious numbering of ideas. Writing in a French that is "alien to her," ironically something she achieves in her seemingly confused opening pages, is a priority to which she returns both as an explicit statement and implicitly through her poetic manipulations of language throughout the work.

These opening pages also allow the narrator to expose her own elite background, laying herself open to criticism by the subaltern voices to which she is attempting to give a voice through her text. Like Nadia Tuéni,

Eddé in *Pourquoi il fait si sombre?* underlines constantly the bourgeois associations that the French language conjures up in Lebanon and the privilege attached to it. After so much protesting, however, the work is itself everything that it claims it is not. It does translate the Arabic stories of the subaltern voices into French, it does show the story of the Lebanese civil war through the pen of an exiled Lebanese woman who did not live through it, and it is after all a novel. The result, however, is not a neat, well-ordered novel, written in standard French, which progresses according to conventionally understood generic guidelines. This text is experimental, but not so much that it is unrecognizable either as a novel or even as written in French. The disjointed stream of consciousness is not out of place in a French-language novel published on the cusp of the twenty-first century, but *Pourquoi il fait si sombre?* does make challenging interventions into the way in which polyglossia operates in a work written in French.

As in Khoury-Ghata's *Le fils empaillé* and Eddé's other novels, including *Lettre posthume*, a metacommentary on the politics of language use by the characters accompanies the textual mixing of languages. This is where a strong class consciousness is first established in *Pourquoi il fait si sombre?* Not only does the narrator seek to write a French that is "alien to her," but she also is able to articulate more specifically how French has affected her in a passage that links language, class, and gender together as constraints to the narrator and her text. The narrator embeds her poignant reflections within another long stream-of-consciousness passage; just after recounting how she was not served in cafés in France despite her perfect French, she states, "my French did not have a choice, the more I flirted with her, the more she tightened her corset, it was up to me to wrestle with her unceremoniously, a smile would have been enough, a smile and tears, we would have climbed mountains, she and I" [ma langue française n'avait pas le choix, plus je la courtisais plus elle serrait son corset, il ne tenait qu'à moi d'aborder sans façon, un sourire eût suffi, un sourire et des larmes, nous aurions soulevé des montagnes elle et moi] (105). French is a language that she loves and hates, that has opened up her world and alienated her from her country. It both allows her to and prevents her from telling her stories. Only from this small excerpt that are the opening lines of a much longer narration about the French language it is clear how Eddé combines a reflection on language with symbols connecting it to gender and class.

This reflection on the French language is much more detailed and part of a long stream-of-consciousness passage in which she ranges freely over languages and literatures and her conflicted relationship with them. Another part of the passage establishes the narrator as an elite Lebanese woman who is living a bourgeois life in France, full of conflicts:

> God knows if I loved this language and God knows if I resented it, it opened new horizons for me, taking away my country, it was the fiefdom without the livestock and the sea without the shore, the blood that rose in my cheeks, making my sentences paler, more correct, more refined, Gustave would say, the people who populate my books without stepping outside them, those who were in the street smiled when I took pains to roll an "r," and Oum Kalsoum? My piano teacher would say, you are not going to make me believe that you like her as much as Bach, I would shyly shrug my shoulders and slip away, repeating Allah!
>
> Dieu sait si j'ai aimé cette langue et Dieu sait si je lui en ai voulu, elle m'ouvrait l'horizon en me prenant mon pays, c'était le fief sans le bétail et la mer sans le rivage, le sang qui me montait aux joues pâlissait dans mes phrases, plus juste plus fin disait Gustave, les gens peuplait mes livres sans mettre le pied dehors, ceux qui étaient dans la rue souriaient du mal que je me donnais pour rouler un r, et Oum Kalsoum? Disait mon professeur de piano, vous n'allez tout de même me faire croire que vous l'aimez autant que Bach, je haussais timidement les épaules et je filais à l'anglaise en répétant Allah! (106)

Her complaint in these two passages is how she is alienated from that society for being Lebanese, though she feels herself to be as French as other people, marked in particular by her absolute command of the language. Though in the sections that follow, the gendered nature of her speaking French is highlighted more explicitly, here she relies on subtle imagery to convey this idea. When she tries to be friendly and "flirt" with French, to play with the language and be amused by it, it does not merely thwart her in any random way, but specifically by "tightening a corset." An image laden with powerful gendered associations, which are class-based as well, the corset here is not merely a constraint, but rather a particular instrument of torture used for women. The associations with corsets used to bind elite women's bodies are linked to the social control of women and aesthetic norms that inhibit their movement—even breathing!—and functioning in mainstream society dominated by elite men. It is a piano teacher, bourgeois symbol par excellence, who is disbelieving that she could appreciate the music of Oum Kalsoum, the Egyptian diva and perhaps the greatest singer of Arabic music of all time, as much as she could Bach. She resorts to shoulder shrugs and a diffuse feeling of alienation from the milieu in which she lives and from the language that she masters, but with a feeling of unease. This kind of reflection on language sets the stage for the incorporation of Arabic words into the novel and the permeation of voices from below throughout the work. Such explicit commentaries help to locate and situate the polyglossia, highlighting the links in her poetic and political commentary between class and gender.

Subalterns Speak

Another example of explicit textual interventions by the narrator as a commentary on her own use of language sets the scene for how Arabic is represented in this French-language novel. Because the stream-of-consciousness narrative style combines scenes with dialogue, monologues, reflections, shifts in voice, and so on, the narrator's commentary on her own project—to be read as a metacommentary on the novel itself—is frequent. So when the unnamed narrator is standing with her French friend and colleague Antoine, who has traveled to Lebanon with her, and he asks her to tell him one of the stories of the local people while they are waiting, she says she can't, "they speak Arabic and it is untranslatable—I know one (story) where they hardly speak at all, they make love in the shelter under the bombs, they never saw each other in the light of day, she is a seamstress and he is a waiter in a café" [ils parlent en arabe et c'est intraduisible—j'en connais une où ils ne parlent presque pas, ils font l'amour dans l'abri sous les bombes, il ne se sont jamais vus à la lumière du jour, elle est couturière et il est serveur dans un café] (16).

This short, seemingly innocuous response to Antoine's putatively innocent request for a story to pass the time encodes many important ideas within it. First, the narrator underlines the idea—recurring throughout the text—that Arabic cannot be translated. The lives of the poor people of the neighborhood are thus completely inaccessible to you if you know only French. After saying that she cannot tell their stories, the narrator then does go on to present the outline of the story—there are two people who make love without ever speaking and have never seen each other in the light of day. The very few, brief details given here in French after she states the very impossibility of conveying them in that language echo the title of the work, Why is it so dark?

Light and darkness infuse the text in diverse ways and the question of why it is dark is answered differently in different passages. Here, "darkness" is a cover for love between people who cannot reach beyond their own closed world. They find some solace in each other through sex, but their silence in darkness overwhelms their story. The lack of light thus can be read as metaphorical, as the narrator herself, and even more so her friend Antoine, cannot penetrate the darkness or the war. Just as they do not understand Arabic, as "outsiders" they simply may not be able to understand this kind of darkness, nor the war that causes it.

Something is written that takes the shape of the novel, *Pourquoi il fait si sombre?* The narrator who knows Arabic but has lived for so long abroad searches throughout its pages for a way to understand and then represent, or translate, the "untranslatable." This is exactly what the narrator is trying to express when she says that she needs a French "alien to herself" through which to express the war. The examples here can thus be read as a metacommentary on language by the narrator of *Pourquoi il fait si sombre?* similar to that provided by the priest in Eddé's earlier work, *Lettre posthume*. In this later work, however, Eddé takes her critique further, pointing out how difficult it is for someone of her status and linguistic abilities simply to write a French novel that will capture a reality lived by ordinary people in Lebanon in Arabic. She has moved beyond representing an idyllic countryside and is using this to challenge the values that led to the war. This novel provides a deeper probing of the war, exploring it through the lived experiences of a range of people, while always keeping a sharp, critical focus on her own class, the bourgeois elite.

This is why subsequent passages that advance similar arguments, but in other voices, are crucial for understanding how *Pourquoi il fait si sombre?* makes a complex contribution to the negotiation of class issues through language use, linking this to other questions. The protagonist has shown how she is tortured by the "corset" of French, how she cannot convey Arabic realities in French, and how she seeks a new French—she constantly doubts her own project of writing a novel about the war. Where *Pourquoi il fait si sombre?* begins to achieve its most powerful critique is when the text's other voices articulate these ideas directly through their own speech, in their "own words." This is where Eddé's text best exemplifies writing *as* translation. Very different in style, technique, and approach to Leïla Barakat's *Sous les vignes du pays Druze, Pourquoi il fait si sombre?* nonetheless also achieves a foreignizing effect in the French language through the multiple strategies of polyglossia, including its representation of Arabic. Using a French permeated by Arabic words, words and expressions that appear to be Arabic, and those that are meant to represent Arabic, Eddé's work achieves a strangeness of language that is identified as one of its own goals. Like Barakat, Eddé also uses this putatively "translated language" in order to inscribe her messages about Lebanon, the war, and particularly class and gender issues.

The men and women who inhabit the Sanayeh district of Beirut, for example, demonstrate their own awareness of the linguistic dilemmas faced by the narrator. They directly tell her, in fact, that they do not need her to represent them. Two of these characters emerge as central to the text: Abou Ali, a pimp, and Alia, a prostitute who works for him. The brothel where they work is officially called La Rose, but it is noted that it is more commonly referred to as Chez Abou Ali. Both names are French, the first a more poetic euphemism for the location's purpose, the second referring directly to the name of its proprietor. This double naming of an important location in Arabic and French recalls other examples of naming that the narrator insists on in the novel. The most important example is the area in downtown Beirut often called in English "Martyr's Square," best known recently for the large protests in 2005 after the murder of the former Lebanese prime minister Rafiq al-Hariri, in the so-called Cedar Revolution. Just as rival groups fought in this area that was a no-man's land during the war, its Arabic and French names do battle in Eddé's text: "Place de Canons in French and Sahat al Bourj in Arabic, it's impossible to say anything further, French and Arabic quarreling over words" [Place de Canons en français et Sahat al Bourj en arabe, impossible d'en dire plus, l'arabe et le français se disputant la parole] (46).

I draw out this parallel between the double naming of the brothel and Martyr's Square to underline the way in which a whorehouse is shown to be as important as one of the most iconic, high-prestige areas of downtown Beirut. The scene of intense fighting during the war, demarcating the green line between the divided city, Martyr's Square/Sahat al-Bourj/Place de Canons—in all of its linguistic incarnations—holds an important symbolic place as the center of the city.[1] La Rose or Chez Abou Ali holds a similar place in *Pourquoi il fait si sombre?* as does the brothel in Eddé's earlier *Lettre posthume.*[2] Unlike the brothel in the earlier novel, however, *Pourquoi il fait si sombre?*'s La Rose/Chez Abou Ali is not as much a place of reconciliation and interconfessional harmony for different groups in Lebanon, but rather where the narrator learns some of her most important lessons about the class divides that separate her from Abou Ali and Alia.

Abou Ali and Alia are crucial to the narrator's project because they constantly remind her of their relative social positions in the class-status hierarchies of Lebanon. This in turn reminds her of what she is unable to understand. From the beginning, they try to convince the already doubt-filled narrator that her book will and can have nothing to do with them, "No no no Alia says to me, what you have just written has nothing to do with our lives, your Abou Ali is not mine" [Non non non me dit Alia, ce que tu viens d'écrire n'a rien à voir avec nos vies, ton Abou Ali n'est pas le mien] (73). In this section of the narration, Alia goes on to wax

1. For a few examples of scholarship on this, see Dados 2009; Khalaf 2007; and S. Makdisi 1997. See also Tuéni and Sassine 2000.

2. Many critics have pointed out the symbolic importance of prostitutes and brothels in Arabic literature, more specifically in relation to the Lebanese civil war (Accad 1992; Amyuni 1999; and Cooke 1996).

philosophical about identity. She also goes into a long discourse about some of the hardships both she and Abou Ali have endured.

Putting these passages in Alia's voice allows Eddé to write the war from an allegedly less mediated position by allowing subalterns to speak back to the narrator. This means that the passages do not convey an image of Alia as a prostitute with a heart of gold or Abou Ali as a man meaning to do good but fallen on hard times, simply an urban equivalent of the colorful peasant. Their reflections are multilayered and conflicted. Alia and Abou Ali exist as complex figures outside of their professions of prostitute and pimp. They are flawed human beings, but not without human dignity. They swear and treat each other and others badly at times, but they are also intelligent and highly aware of the politics of who they are and what they represent to a woman like the narrator. By placing some of the most meaningful and insightful passages in the novel into their mouths as direct and indirect speech, Eddé symbolically elevates their status novelistically, in a way that the narrator cannot do for their social status.

This particular example recalls an earlier passage involving other characters who populate this same neighborhood of Beirut, the area around Sanayeh Park, some of whom are more interested than others in participating in the narrator's project. With all the men of the area gathered around, one warns the other about participating, "Watch yourself Abou Roro, she is a 'fille de riche' who is writing a book about our kind of people" [fais attention à toi Abou Roro, cette femme est une fille de riche qui écrit un livre sur les gens de notre espèce] (28). This bit of dialogue shows how people of different social strata are well aware of the political and other implications of telling their own stories to each other. The idea that a "fille de riche" (recalling the "fille de famille" from Kher and Chedid) is different from "our kind of people" shows the awareness of class divides and the caution urged by people on the lower end of it. The response to this warning is also instructive. "Speak for yourself . . . you never knew the time when people would cross the square running to shake my hand, tell me ma'am, do I seem poor?" [Parle pour toi . . . tu n'as pas connu l'époque où les gens traversaient la place en courant pour me serrer la main, dites-moi madame, est-ce que j'ai l'air d'un pauvre?] (28). Rather than contradict the proposition that poor people should not speak to rich people who have entered their space, the bald man Abou Roro tries to present himself as of a similar class to the narrator. Therefore, unlike other subaltern characters who draw attention to class differences and show themselves equal to elite characters in other ways, this character accepts the distinctions but argues that he is simply categorized on the wrong side. Other members of the community of people living in Beirut at the time are not only less accommodating, but they are also less willing to share their experiences with the narrator for her to include in her book.

Another example of the unwillingness of ordinary Beirutis to speak to the narrator about their lives reinforces these ideas. A conversation between the narrator, Abou Ali, and Alia first leads to deeper and more interesting reflections on how language is used to negotiate class. "Neither Alia nor Abou Ali wanted to speak about it, she went back to filing her nails and he to repeating his mother's life stories, I was wrong to insist, are you done sticking your nose into our business yet?" [ni Alia, ni Abou Ali ne voulaient en parler, elle s'est remise à se limer les ongles et lui à râbacher les histoires de sa mère, j'ai eu tort d'insister, tu as fini de fourrer ton nez dans nos affaires?] (104–5). The narrator knows that she is wrong to continue probing and prodding people who do not wish to discuss certain things. We also know that she is concerned with issues of representation and her distance from the underclass as an elite woman. The recounting of events ("she went back to filing her nails") together with an almost confessional admission ("I was wrong to insist")—straight on with no marking to direct speech that is not attributed to a speaker but is clearly not the narrator, who asks, "are you done?"—shows a complex polyglossia: the constant mixing of speech genres, speakers, and levels of language. The use of such a complex writing style enables Eddé to show how Abou Ali and Alia are clear about their intention to abstain from participation in the narrator's project, whereas the man in the park tries to elevate his own status by invoking his life before the war.

When the rest of the people in the park insist that the narrator mind her own business, there follows another long stream-of-consciousness narration that makes a commentary on the French language. Not only does this passage advance the critique of French as a colonial language that is contrasted and opposed to Arabic, but it also once again uses a narrative style that represents speech without clear markers of who the speaker is. The narrator seems to speak, as do the people in the park, and once again it feels within the passage as though perhaps it is the text itself speaking without the influence of the characters:

> why the hell write Arabic in French? it makes no sense, eyes lowered, Alia suppressed a smile, he is right Abou Ali, he is right, it makes no sense . . . he needed no more than this to get all worked up again, it's not even a question of sense, it is a question of taste! It's like making a garlic dish without the garlic, have you ever heard of making a garlic dish without the garlic?!
>
> à quoi ça rime d'écrire l'arabe en français? ça n'a pas de sens, les yeux baissés, Alia a réprimé un sourire, il a raison Abou Ali, il a raison, ça n'a pas de sens . . . Il ne lui en fallait pas tant à celui-là pour s'exciter de plus belle, ce n'est même pas une question de sens c'est une question de goût! c'est comme si tu faisais un plat à l'ail sans l'ail, a-t-on idée de faire un plat à l'ail sans l'ail?! (105)

Abou Ali poses a series of questions to the narrator that underpin the main ideas of the entire novel: Can you write Arabic in French? Even if you can, what is the point? Why tell the story of the Lebanese civil war in French? The answer is predicted by Alia's earlier statement that they cannot know the same Abou Ali—this will not even be the same story! Alia and Abou Ali concur that whatever reality the narrator does manage to capture in her book will never be their reality. Arabic cannot be expressed in French. The sort of metonymic representation of Arabic based on the articulation of Ashcroft, Griffith, and Tiffin (1989) that I showed in the works of the other authors discussed in *Native Tongue, Stranger Talk* is rejected here. It is about both sense and taste, Abou Ali says. In this specific passage, Eddé invokes a food metaphor to talk about how useless it is to try to use a colonial language to convey lived realities in Lebanon; Abou Ali's commentary underlines how languages stand for and represent entire cultures.

This passage is thus not only an anticolonial commentary on language layering and representation but also an intellectualization of the possibility of finding a space between languages and class-status positions. Taking further the narrator's metacommentary on language that proposes the

French language as a corset, this critique voiced by the subaltern characters uses a colorful food metaphor to convey the message more powerfully. What Abou Ali and Alia say, as well as Alia's condescendingly suppressed smile at the narrator, exemplify how Eddé reverses the power dynamics between an elite writer and those whom she is meant to be representing. Moreover, the metaphor that Abou Ali uses—a garlic dish without the garlic—is one that is both exotic and universal and understandable to all readers and listeners. The food metaphor, in particular connecting the "spicy" food, garlic, to Arabic, within the presumably blander French text, links this novel to others discussed in previous chapters on the level of imagery and symbolism. Looking back at the other works that draw on food to stand in for Lebanon metonymically—Accad's symbolic use of tabboulé, koubbé, hommos, and arak in *Coquelicot du massacre* or Kher's Sunday taboulée in *Salma et son village*—Eddé's use of a "garlic dish" to symbolize language use in Lebanon is not without a context. Eddé's activation of the food-nation trope, however, works differently here. Rather than functioning as a symbol of Lebanon to the outside, Abou Ali presents his food metaphor within a critique of class hierarchies and language in Lebanon, which is closely tied to the work's main messages.

The gendered nature of the narrator's dilemma echoes those faced by the narrators and protagonists of the novels discussed in previous chapters. What sets *Pourquoi* apart from these works, including Eddé's other novels, is that a pimp and prostitute demonstrate the dilemmas of language and the failings of French. The elite French-speaking narrator ties to articulate this, but the other characters must help her, rather than the reverse. Alia and Abou Ali are the catalysts for her redefinition of her own relationship with French because they challenge her directly. The effect is different from the narration by the priest in *Lettre posthume*, for example, who feels guilty about his power and status relative to the "Shiite maid" on whom he had his first crush.

The naming of characters is another way that Eddé's explicit reversal of class-status issues in her use of language can be seen in *Pourquoi il fait si sombre?* The narrator, like Evelyne Accad's narrator in *Coquelicot du massacre* and Dominique Eddé's in *Lettre posthume*, is unnamed, but as in most of the other novels, the Arabic names of the characters are meaning filled. The names Abou Ali and Alia are derived from the same Arabic root [ʻ-L-Y] meaning "lofty" or "well placed," echoing the meaning of Samya's name in *Le sommeil délivré* (though it is derived a different root, S-M-Y). *Pourquoi il fait si sombre?* reverses the class-status position of these working-class characters through their names. Rather than reflect their social position within a hierarchy, as Samya's name does, Alia and Abou Alia's names function like those of the peasants in Chedid's novel (Zariffa and Om El Kher): the subaltern Arabic-speaking characters have names that reflect their true personalities and not only their class positions. Moreover, these layered meanings can only be understood by the reader who knows Arabic because they are not explained to the outsider reader in the way, for example, that Accad's characters' names are in *Coquelicot du massacre.*

The kinds of interventions that Alia and Abou Ali make in their conversations with the unnamed narrator can also be read as a postwar permutation of the genre of ethnography that I discussed in relation to Leïla Barakat's *Sous les vignes du pays Druze* in the previous chapter. Much like this work, as well as Amy Kher's *Salma et son village* and Eveline Bustros's *Sous la baguette du coudrier,* discussed in part 1, *Pourquoi il fait si sombre?* presents itself as an ethnography at times. Of course, in form as well as in content it must be read also as contrasting with many of ethnography's more common manifestations—particularly in its stream-of-consciousness style and depictions of the problematic power relationships between observers and observed.

Despite these contrasts, it also engages these ethnographies and thereby deepens its messages. The narrator travels around the city, for example, asking people questions about their lives in the war in order to record them in her novel. The way in which the narrator approaches her subject of study, including the self-reflexive discussions about the author's transparency, is a direct contrast to Arij's recounting of village life in *Sous les vignes du pays Druze.* Similarly, its stream-of-consciousness narration contrasts directly with Barakat's more conventional development of a linear plot complete with the death of the protagonist at the end, followed by an epilogue. Ethnographic studies today demand the ethnographer work through the same kinds of issues that Eddé grapples with throughout *Pourquoi il fait si sombre?* Eddé's work does not offer the reader easy answers about Lebanon, Beirut, any one community, or the postwar period. It does not expose how Lebanon "really is doing" after the war, nor does it propose certain people's experiences in the war as representative of all Lebanese people. Indeed insofar as it does offer glimpses into these issues, it undermines them at the same time by reminding the reader that the narrator's Abou Ali is not Alia's Abou Ali—meaning that any representation is as much a creation of the representer as it is the reality of the represented. The polyphony of voices in this text, which allow the narrator's voice to be presented as one among many that "explain" Lebanon, the war, and society, is partly what makes the work challenging to its readers. This is as true in the rubric of reading it as engaging the genre of ethnography as it is in relation to its status as a novel.

Why Is It So Dark?

Another location in which language is used as a method to probe the larger questions posed by the book are the stories involving the character Nour. An evocative name shared with the mother in *Coquelicot du massacre,* Nour means "light" in Arabic. As in Accad's novel, light and darkness are important symbols in *Pourquoi il fait si sombre?* and indeed—because of its title—overcode the entire novel. Once again, Eddé nods to the Arabic reader and challenges the French reader by using an Arabic name for her character that is infused with symbolism and meaning, without translating it. Once more, an identifiably Arabic name does not operate merely as local color in the novel but rather highlights other textual messages. In *Pourquoi il fait si sombre?* Nour's story is tragic. As a young girl she is the most-beloved daughter of a Lebanese family living in Egypt who summered near the narrator in Lebanon. She is hit by a car at the age of seventeen, losing her memory and the ability to speak. The narrator is haunted by the memory of this figure walking slowly around her garden, held up by her mother. She is used directly to symbolize light and dark, her name and childhood representing the former and her current life the latter. The narrator repeats that there were two Nours, one for day and one for night (88). Other symbolic elements reinforce this dualism, for example the black-and-white pictures of her that remain on her mother's mantelpiece after her premature death.

It is not only through her Arabic name that Nour's character is invested with layers of meaning. Eddé uses other techniques, such as polyglossia, through which Nour negotiates gender issues. For example, people discussed Nour before her accident; "in Arabic it was said that she was as beautiful as the moon and then it was added in French that she was 'a princess'" [on disait en arabe qu'elle était belle comme la lune et on ajoutait en français que c'était 'une princesse'] (86). The brief recounting of Nour's life also emphasizes that she was looked at differently before and after her accident and that people eventually stopped speaking about her. This is all couched within a discussion of how the young girl is praised differently in Arabic and French. Recalling the double naming in Arabic and French for Martyr's Square and for Alia and Abou Ali's brothel, the double nicknaming of Nour highlights different systems of thought in Arabic and French. In this example, it operates in both gendered and class-status-based terms.

Both descriptions of Nour emphasize her beauty in one way or another, showing that the value placed on young girls is connected to physical appearance. But this is where the similarities in description end. In Arabic, she is compared to the moon, a common metaphor used to describe feminine beauty that one finds across Arabic dialects ("al-'amar" in Beiruti Arabic, and in standard Arabic *fusha*, "al-qamar"). It is an image drawn from nature, reflecting the light that infuses her name, Nour. In contrast, the French description refers to her status in society. By calling her a "princess," even metaphorically, it is not natural traits that are emphasized but rather that she is aristocratic and should be considered of a "better" class than ordinary people. The Arabic expression resists the dynamics of class, focusing on nature; the French one draws them out, making status-based distinctions a matter of praise.

When this brief description is read together with the depiction of Nour as a character in the text, these issues are thrown into even sharper relief. As a character, Nour shines as brightly as her name might suggest in a context where darkness is pervasive. Being compared to a moon or a princess in this context is thus also laden with meaning. The Arabic name is clearly the more positive in the overall context of *Pourquoi il fait si sombre?*, though in her own family context both names are meant as praise. Once again a message about class and class consciousness is subtly inscribed within the novel; the issues navigated through the use of polyglossia help the reader better understand some of its messages. The use of the name Nour, one of the most widely known Arabic names outside the Arab world in part because of the popularity of the American-born Queen Noor of Jordan, and the description of moon and princess are far from esoteric linguistic points; the way in which language politics are exposed by using words with such meanings makes a powerful statement.

Unlike some of the more subtle inscriptions of Arabic expressions and words within a text written in standard French, this example demonstrates how a simple commentary on the "translation" of a phrase can challenge the status quo. As in other examples of the explanation of words and expressions, often connected with ethnographic details, *Pourquoi il fait si sombre?* employs these contrasting examples to buttress its powerful message about the politics of languages and their connection to class and gender. This French-language novel, more directly and forcefully than others discussed thus far, questions the possibility of representing people of different classes and genders using words marked as Arabic. Because Eddé challenges these ideas even as she is writing the novel, her metacommentary on Arabic and French as well as the messages inscribed through polyglossia are all the more potent. In *Pourquoi il fait si sombre?* different classes of people craft their own languages and discuss language use and politics. Peasants and working-class urban characters do not serve merely as a foil for elite people to mount a lamentation, heavily tinged with nostalgia, about how wonderful prewar Lebanon was. Even when this nostalgia is challenged, as in *Lettre posthume*, there is still the implication that privileged people are yearning for a more pristine prewar idyll. In order for the elite characters, including the narrator, to take stock of their own positions of power and question their ability to represent others, they must engage in a thorough investigation of their own ways of understanding and using language/s—especially Arabic and French—both poetically and politically.

Conclusions

Pourquoi il fait si sombre? challenges the ways in which languages are represented and experiments with different ways in which they can be used within a French-language novel. This is achieved in a more complex way than in Eddé's earlier novel, *Lettre posthume*, and indeed propels the discussion of these issues further than any of the novels discussed in the previous chapters. By not only writing a metacommentary on language use and literary production but also experimenting with narration and voice, Eddé's text is more experimental and more provocative. She succeeds in writing a text that makes her French "alien" and can be read, like Leïla Barakat's *Sous les vignes du pays Druze*, as a translation. She achieves this effect by infusing her narration with multiple voices, allowing the speech of characters like Abou Ali and Alia to seep into her narration and speak directly to the readers, thus undermining her own authorial and narrative voices. Eddé not only "gives voice" to these characters by representing their speech but also often inscribes it into her narration without any attribution such as quotation marks or other formal devices to signal a change of voice. Within the multilayered stream-of-consciousness style, the narration explicitly rejects the very possibility of translating Arabic into French. At the same time, the French text can be read as a symbolically "foreignized" translation of the sort advocated by Venuti, where the language of the text constantly challenges the reader with its very "strangeness" or "foreignness." Because of her insistence on the constant questioning of her own subject position and her critical view of orientalism, she manages also to undermine the exoticism potentially attached to this position.

Through its self-reflexivity and multiple voices, *Pourquoi il fait si sombre?* makes use of Bakhtinian polyphony; its challenges to generic conventions of the novel exemplify Bakhtin's process of novelization very well. One example of the latter is that, midway through the book, a series of possible first pages are presented.[3] The work's unwillingness to adhere

3. This recalls a similar technique used in Rabih Alameddine's *I, the Divine: A Novel in First Chapters*, which he claims was inspired by Italo Calvino's *Se una notte d'inverno un viaggatore* (2001).

to generic conventions can be seen explicitly. "What is this book that is neither a novel nor an essay nor a poem, neither this nor that" [Qu'est-ce que c'est que ce livre qui n'est ni un roman ni un essai ni un poème ni ceci ni cela] (91). The narrator is referring both to her own project and to the text of *Pourquoi il fait si sombre?* The self-questioning in this novel is unrelenting; here the narrator disavows knowledge of the text that she is self-consciously writing. Because the narrative constantly jumps from idea to idea, from inner monologue to dialogue and reported speech, however, such self-reflexivity never becomes overwhelming. Moreover, the narrator continually reminds the reader that she is aware of her faults. She begins one new section saying that a friend has criticized her for writing a disjointed [décossu] book, "open to whomever, whenever" [ouvert à n'importe qui n'importe quand] (102).

The whomever and wherever that *Pourquoi il fait si sombre?* is open to are crucial points for reflection. On the one hand, the novel is extremely open ended: multiple voices from different social strata penetrate the text, allowing for a polyphony of voices not only in the simple sense of mixing languages and voices but also in the Bakhtinian sense that the author-narrator's authority is undermined by an equal textual prestige and status accorded to the voices "from below." This contrasts with the more controlled narration of Eddé's earlier *Lettre posthume* or Barakat's *Sous les vignes du pays Druze*, both of which emphasize the struggles of nonelite groups, but through an elite perspective that keeps firm control over the text by way of a unified narrative voice, albeit with interruptions by dialogue. Arabic permeates the French of Barakat's text extensively and uses the "translation" of these languages to negotiate gender issues. However, the more subversive questioning of gender and class poetically and politically in *Pourquoi il fait si sombre?* allows for the nonelite voices to control and drive the narration of this work, setting its agenda.

Though the multiple voices, nonlinear narration, complex style of writing, and free flowing stream of consciousness challenge many conventions, does this not also make the work more difficult to read? A book that is extremely difficult of course will be less likely to appeal to a wide readership, particularly outside of elite literary circles. A book that critics praise for its politics and poetics is not necessarily the one that will make the biggest impact on real-life social implications of class-status dynamics or how subaltern people navigate their own language use. As Eddé's own characters would point out, the people being represented here are unlikely to be able to read this book. These and similar types of questions are often raised in relation to the debate about "authenticity" in relation to writings by Arab writers and others in colonial languages. If a writer is inscribing a challenging message about class hierarchies and their intersections with gender in the Lebanese context, should this not be written in Arabic? How can a novel like this matter if few people in Lebanon can read French? If the novel is so difficult to follow even for a French reader, will French-reading Lebanese people read, appreciate, or enjoy it? Is this then not a hypocritical exercise by the author?

This novel is one of the few to address directly and without apology the issue of the implied "false consciousness" of French-speaking people by virtue of their language of expression. By demonstrating her commitment to class consciousness within her narration through her continued reflections on her own elite class-status position, Eddé counters simplistic assumptions about Lebanese writers of French and their political positions. Eddé grapples with these questions throughout the novel, though she does not provide a simple answer and chooses to conflate and confuse issues in her complex narration of the post-civil-war Lebanon that her narrator claims to be unable to recount. The novel itself is the answer to these questions.

12

The Arabic Language Leaked into It

Dominque Eddé's Cerf-Volant

A stinging send-up of the Lebanese bourgeoisie, *Cerf-Volant* (2003) is perhaps the most humorous of Eddé's trinity of novels. Like *Pourquoi il fait si sombre?*, it manifests a keen awareness of social inequalities, class dynamics, and the politics of social status, but it is written with a light touch that rarely becomes didactic. Less alienated than the narrator of her 1999 novel, *Cerf-Volant* is told through the amused and amusing voice of Mali—a nickname for Maliha—a Lebanese woman hailing from the same elite circles as Eddé's other narrators, who moves with ease through multiple locations around the world of the twenty-first century. Indeed Eddé's playful approach in her novel softens its cynical mockery of Lebanon's elite upper echelons somewhat, allowing some affection for this community to peep through while at the same time criticizing its problems. One way in which Eddé achieves this effect poetically is by loosening the narrator's control over the text and allowing more voices to penetrate it than she does in *Lettre posthume*.

As in *Pourquoi il fait si sombre?*, these voices speak directly to the reader not simply through dialogue but also in the narration. The third-person narrative style differs from both of Eddé's earlier works and allows the protagonist, Mali, to be described as well as to describe; narrative passages are mixed with letters, dialogues, and interior monologues, allowing for more diverse textual expression. The class consciousness of Mali and a number of her friends is therefore revealed less in direct passages but indirectly through actions and opinions on different situations. Inscribing Arabic into the French-language text is one aspect of polyphony and a way in which further messages—poetic and political—are advanced and negotiated.

Questioning Bourgeois Values: Arabic in French

The way in which Eddé subtly mocks the bourgeoisie in *Cerf-Volant* does not announce itself directly at first. The lives of Mali and those in her milieu are portrayed at first glance to be a transparent description of spoiled, clever, French-speaking young women—the sort of people Nadia Tuéni referred to when she spoke of writing French as writing bourgeois, writing rich, writing privilege. This portrayal is undermined in a number of ways throughout the novel and builds throughout it. Mali, for example, explicitly discusses her Arab nationalist sentiments and pro-Nasserite political leanings against expectations about a woman of her background. After this, Eddé includes a scene depicting the family of Mali's good friend Huguette. This scene experiments with the kind of linguistic play that allows for multiple languages to be layered within French and simultaneously reveals the lives of people within this society and gently pokes fun at it.

In a somewhat daring move, and one unusual for a French-language author in Lebanon, a number of characters in *Cerf-Volant* are based on well-known, French-speaking historical figures in Lebanon. Thus Huguette is identified as the daughter of Bechara el-Khoury, Lebanon's first president. Her mother is the sister of Michel Chiha, a banker and political figure who was a major promoter of the Francophone community, and she therefore is his niece. In the scene, Huguette challenges her family for having given her a French name, and not any French name but one that is uncommon, difficult to spell and pronounce. Complaining that she must always correct people who are unable to understand her name in Lebanon, she claims at this family gathering that "our Arabness is undisputable" [Notre arabité est incontestable] (56). Bechara el-Khoury and Michel Chiha are two important figures in the French-speaking Lebanese community who held widely acknowledged political positions that run counter to one proposing Lebanon's Arabness as "indisputable." As discussed in chapter 1, Christian nationalist strands of thought denied and co-opted Arabism in various ways. Eddé's novel offers a direct intervention, less into the early debates over Lebanon's "Arabness" than it does into postwar identities and affiliations. Huguette's harsh critique of the political stance of her extended family members thus contradicts expectations of the political affiliation of the French-speaking elite. This intervention also echoes the political stances taken by a number of Lebanese women writers of French, many of whom also hail from similar family backgrounds.

The mood of this indictment of Francophone Lebanese nationalist exceptionalism that would propose Lebanon as not-Arab and set apart from the rest of the region is lightened by Huguette's amusing recounting of a scene she witnessed recently. The larger implications of the family dispute are put aside for a moment as she shares her anecdote: "the other day I heard a conversation between a little boy named de Gaulle and his young uncle named Pétain. '*Waynak ya di Goule*,' one said, '*Ana hawn'amou Pitine, ana hawn*,' the other one replied" [j'ai assisté l'autre jour à un dialogue entre un petit garçon nommé de Gaulle et son jeune oncle nommé Pétain. "*Waynak ya di Goule*," disait l'un, "*Ana hawn'amou Pitine, ana hawn*," répondait l'autre] (56). A footnote to the italicized text clarifies what the Arabic phrases mean: "Where are you di Goule? I am here, uncle Pitine, I am here" [Où es-tu di Goule? Je suis là, oncle Pitine, je suis là] (56). This brief exchange is meant to be humorous and ruptures the serious tone of confrontation preceding it. Huguette's reporting of this anecdote shifts the mood from a direct and didactic conversation with her family to one that layers multiple meanings through humor. It also introduces a more serious meditation on the French language that follows it, describing how French has been the subject of a deep internal divide for Mali for a long time.

The humor in the dialogue is derived from several overlapping sources, which comment on the politics of language use in Lebanon. It is not simply the French language or the custom of using names of French political leaders in a Lebanese context that is being ridiculed, but rather an extreme Francophilia coupled with a lack of knowledge about French naming habits. Few in France would name a child de Gaulle or Pétain, and the Lebanese habit of choosing prestigious figures as namesakes without taking into account their context is mocked. Of course to a French audience this would be amusing and is a classic example of the kind of passage that might open the author to the charge of "false consciousness" and showing Lebanese peasants to be uneducated. After all, why should she make Lebanon's naming habits seem silly and open them to the ridicule of the French? Moreover, the mispronunciation of the names might imply that Arabs or Lebanese are ignorant.

There is more to the humor of this scene, though, than just opening Lebanese people to ridicule, and reading this passage carefully unpeels many layers of the commentary Eddé is making. This passage also shows that the Francophile Lebanese who are choosing such "French" names for their children speak Arabic and with accents from the countryside. The hard diphthong of the Lebanese countryside is encoded within di Goule's response, "ana hawn," a simple Arabic colloquial expression meaning "I am here." Eddé represents the sounds of how people speak rather transliterates these words within a "more correct" or standard Arabic transliteration system. Though she shows this colloquial style of speech in her transcription of the conversation, Eddé makes use of a footnote here, which she does extremely infrequently in her texts. It is relevant that she uses the footnote in this particular scene, one that is meant to be amusing, and a dialogue between two characters who are not central to the plot. The footnote is not used in the same way as those we saw previously in the first and second parts of *Native Tongue, Stranger Talk*. It is not offering the same kind of "scientific" validity to the text for the purpose of establishing the author's credentials.

One purpose of the footnote here is to mark the colloquial Arabic language as different. It shows that this language may not be understood by insider or outsider readers and needs to be explained. This particular dialogue is reported differently: it is neither integrated into the text nor incorporated into a larger metacommentary, both of which are favored strategies of Eddé elsewhere. Indeed, as in the case of a text like Amy Kher's *Salma et son village* that makes more extensive use of footnotes, explaining Arabic words in this way not only marks them but also shows them to be concepts that should be translated in more depth. The juxtaposition of these scenes demonstrates how this more "academic" style of explaining words and concepts is a strategy that works in the text to question how and why language is used in different settings. Unlike *Salma et son village*, however, *Cerf-Volant* never establishes the same kind of ethnographic pact with its readers. Its metacommentary is so developed and its character is written as so familiar to a presumed French readership that its mediations of the borders of French and Arabic work differently.

Fils de Famille: Who Narrates What?

Class-status concerns remain on the surface of *Cerf-Volant* throughout the entire novel. The use of transliterated Arabic with a footnote in the example above is complemented, for example, by relexifications that are also used more subtly to negotiate how the French-language-speaking community engages issues of class and status. In this novel, for example, Dominique Eddé uses the now-familiar relexified expression "fille/fils de famille," which I discussed in both *Lettre posthume* and Andrée Chedid's *Le sommeil délivré*. Class-status concerns are the central organizing principle of the concept encoded in this expression and its use in *Cerf-Volant* is no exception.

Many characters are introduced in *Cerf-Volant* and often class-status divisions are transgressed. This happens in both expected and unexpected ways, leading the reader to understand some of the kinds of questions Eddé is posing about Lebanese society after the war. In one of the early scenes in the novel, Mali has a conversation with her local postman Nizar. In the third-person narration of this section, we learn that Nizar—in sharp contrast to the well-educated, multilingual Mali—left school at nine and is virtually illiterate. In order to deliver the letters he is charged with, he slowly and discretely sounds out the names written on the envelopes that he delivers, letter by letter, so that no one will notice that he cannot read properly. We learn through this section that he is most easily able to deliver letters to those designated as "les fils de famille" [sons of a family] because their addresses are the easiest to read. "For those who are called 'sons of a family' the address need only contain three lines. An example: Doctor Jamil Salam, Beirut, Lebanon" [Pour ceux qu'on appelait "les fils de famille," il arrivait que l'addresse tienne en trios mots. Exemple: Docteur Jamil Salam, Beyrouth, Liban] (50). The Salam family invoked here are a well-established Sunni Beiruti family, members of whom have held government posts over time including one who was named prime minister in 2013.

The distinction between this postal carrier and the people whose post he delivers, including Mali and Doctor Jamil Salam, is thus underlined in more than one way. In particular, the use of the Arabic expression "fils de famille," made prominent by the inverted commas surrounding it, once again underlines this expression and its importance. In this passage, Nizar is not only described as barely literate, but also as a sensitive man who knows the mail by the envelopes and who is likely to receive which letters. He pays attention to the lives of the people to whom he delivers letters and what their situations in life are like. Thus, it is not only because Doctor Jamil Salam is a "son of a family" that his letter will be delivered correctly, but also that the postal carrier in Beirut knows all of the people and families so well that he is able to deliver the mail to the right location. His expertise and care in his work are valued by Mali and by the narration. Class and family status, however, is still crucial here because Nizar the postman also pays close attention to the people whom he deems to be important, well known, and well respected enough to receive many letters.

In this example, parallel to the "fille de famille" or "daughter of a family" in Chedid's *Le sommeil délivré*, a person of a certain status is accorded societal privileges. The novels both point out how different assumptions are made about people based on this status, and they are tied in each case to gendered understandings of class backgrounds. A daughter of a family has hands "too delicate to fight," a son of a family—in this case a doctor—is able to receive his post without having a proper address spelled out on the envelope. In *Cerf-Volant*, even more so than in *Le sommeil délivré*, the term is defined in a roundabout way for the French reader. Once again, the reader who knows Arabic can immediately identify this expression and supply the additional connotations and meanings loaded into the Arabic expression. Though the expression makes perfect sense in context and is not unknown in standard (albeit old-fashioned) French, the reader who knows only French is faced with a more complex proposition. To grasp the layers of the passage suggested by Eddé, this reader must understand the connotations of the short gloss provided by Nizar on the expression that he introduces into the narration.

This example is important, moreover, because a worker advances an analysis about the intersecting connections between language and class, offering his insight into the lives of the upper classes. Through the translation of an expression invoking Arabic into French, Nizar is able to explain the class-status divides that separate him from the people of "important families" whose mail he delivers. This is a major shift in the location of class-status analyses in other French-language novels from Lebanon, particularly the eight discussed in previous chapters of *Native Tongue, Stranger Talk*. Though in previous examples, peasants and other subaltern characters provide commentary and analysis about class-status gaps, the language brokering here is somewhat different. No longer is it a bilingual member of the Lebanese elite who is somehow playing this role as intermediary between quaint, local peasant expressions marked as Arabic to a presumed French reader. Similarly to Abou Ali and Alia's critique of the narrator in *Pourquoi il fait si sombre?*, this presumably Arabic-speaking worker explains the expression to the French reader himself, without mediation. He is more aware of class-status distinctions than most of the more privileged characters are and thus is better able to articulate them.

Nizar's commentaries and control within the text are one of the locations of its polyglossia, which underlines and undermines the contrast between the postman and the elite Lebanese bourgeoisie whose mail he delivers. His knowledge is shown to be valuable; he can participate in the community and navigate through languages and writing despite his minimal schooling. This is shown in other passages in the text as well, and the ways in which they work together provide the kind of complexity that allows the novel to question authority and therefore class-status distinctions at the same time. Another passage in which the gap in class status between Nizar the postman and Mali and her family is bridged is in the shared drinking of coffee. Once again, the ritual of preparing and consuming coffee, like the drinking of maté in *Sous les vignes du pays Druze*, is marked as a special ritual imbued with meaning. Here, rather than serving the ethnographic purpose of establishing Arij's credentials as an insider-outsider in her Druze village, the coffee-drinking scene allows the postman and bourgeois family to come together in a shared space.

In a first-person narration by Mali integrated into this novel, which is mostly a third-person narrative, she reflects on how her relative Salma is always waiting for Nizar to pass by and deliver her post. Mali reflects on how Salma always manages to be about to serve coffee just as he approaches her house: "*she put the* rakwé *on the fire and waited, still, for the water to start boiling. When Nizar pushed on the swinging door she called out,* 'Soubhan Allah! *Is it you? I was just in the middle of making coffee*'" [*elle mettait la* rakwé *sur le feu et attendait immobile que l'eau se mettte à bouillir. Quand Nizar poussait la porte battante, elle s'écriait*: "Soubhan Allah! *c'est toi? j'étais justement en train de faire un café*"] (48). Though she prepares coffee for Nizar daily, it is a ritual that is not made explicit or ever discussed. Mali's observation of this in the text is a voyeuristic moment for the readers, allowing them to glimpse this complicity between two people of different social groups that are not supposed to mix. As in few other social spaces, the drinking of coffee allows friendships to form. It is relevant that Mali uses Arabic words to narrate this scene of negotiation between Salma's upper-class household and the entry into it by Nizar, a worker. For example, she prepares her coffee in a rakwé, or Arabic coffee pot, underlining that it is Arabic coffee being prepared and not just any kind of coffee. Moreover, she uses an Arabic interjection of surprise, "Soubhan Allah!" (Praise God!), when she hears Nizar approaching, as a way to invite him in for a visit.

In this scene, class-status roles are once again reinforced—after all a wealthy woman serving a postman coffee is not a breach of either social etiquette or class roles and can be interpreted as an act of noblesse oblige. It is possible to read the roles here as slightly shifted, however. Clearly a member of the French-speaking elite, Salma speaks Arabic in this scene, Nizar does not, and the Arabic she speaks is a simple, vernacular Arabic. She has the power socially, but she maintains a longstanding friendship with Nizar. The way the Arabic dialogue permeates this section of first-person narration and reflection contrasts with similar examples from *Lettre posthume* that reflect the more controlled narrative style of that novel. *Cerf-Volant*, in contrast to this earlier novel, continually shifts voices from first to third person, from narration to dialogue. The greatest contrast between the narrations of these two novels is that the narrator of *Lettre posthume* is all knowing and explains everything to the reader; its epistolary form demands this omniscience, as its very premise is that the priest is explaining the civil war to his French friend in a letter. Here instead, the subaltern characters explain words and expressions—as Nizar does with fils de famille—and Arabic words are seamlessly integrated into Mali's thoughts and Salma's dialogues.

Reading Writing *as* Translation: A Metacommentary

A further way in which *Cerf-Volant* deals with the politics of language use is in its probing of the issue of translation directly within its metacommentary on language. In another contrast between this work and *Lettre posthume*, the latter's narrator simply translates ideas and thoughts for the French friend and reader, at least outwardly, as in many cases the Arabic words are embedded deeply in the text. *Cerf-Volant* takes a different approach and explicitly proclaims the difficulty and even impossibility of translation, echoing Alia's ideas in *Pourquoi il fait si sombre?* How can certain Arabic words, ideas, and phrases be rendered in French when the direct translation often sounds silly at best:

> "Ahlan, ahlan, ahla wa sahla," *he repeated, chanting all of these little "welcome" words that, when translated from Arabic, seem ridiculous half the time. (Try to translate one after the other,* hamdelah'ala'l salamé, tawalto el ghaybè, weyn khtafayto ya'amé: *God's glory on your wellbeing, you have extended your absence, or, where have you disappeared, my uncle?*)
>
> "Ahlan, ahlan, ahla wa sahla" *répétait-il, entonnant toutes ces petites phrases de "bienvenue" qui traduites de l'arabe tournent une fois sur deux au ridicule. (Essayez de traduire à la file* hamdelah'ala'l salamé, tawalto el ghaybé, weyn khtafayto ya'amé: *la gloire de Dieu sur votre bien-être, vous avez prolongé l'absence, où avez-vous disparu mon oncle?)* (74)

Once again the Arabic words drawn on for commentary are everyday expressions from the colloquial language, reinforced by their phonetic rendition in Latin letters and emphasizing the Lebanese pronunciation. These phrases are transcribed and translated both to give them meaning within the context of a French-language literary narration and to show the difficulty of arriving at a meaning in this context. At the same time that the narration defines these expressions as sounding "silly" when translated, it also demonstrates the complexity and beauty of the Arabic language. The theme of Arabic's uniqueness and richness as a language recurs in the novel. This list of expressions does not function in the same way as some of Mali's other, more profound, meditations on the language, but contextualizes these by highlighting that expressions are not ridiculous but are rather difficult to understand in translation.

This passage occurs in a section narrated in the first person by Mali, as is the section about Nizar the postman, and through it she declaims her frustration with Arabic expressions and how they are used. Her particular exasperation seems to be less that the phrases are not easily translated into French and more related to the social meaning of so many polite formulations that one is supposed to use continuously in social situations. This passage allows Mali to define and redefine these common expressions, challenging on the one hand the authority of conventional translation tools, such as dictionaries, available to a highly educated person like herself, and on the other hand their commonly accepted, every day meanings in Lebanon. By pointing out the futility of translation, while translating both literally and for meaning—her gloss, "these little welcoming phrases" allows us to understand their social function—Mali takes charge of producing knowledge about Arabic as it is used in her Lebanese social context. In this case she shows the complexity of Arabic. Her metacommentary on both language use, particularly welcoming phrases, and translation can be read in relation to other, similar commentaries in the novels discussed above. Recall, for example, Arij's comment about how she admires Druze customs from a distance, but when she lives them fully they exhaust her. This commentary can therefore be read as an intervention into the kinds of ways in which French-language writing often uses and incorporates Arabic welcoming expressions as well. All of the texts discussed in *Native Tongue, Stranger Talk* use these kinds of expressions, marked as Arabic, in one way or another. Their very ubiquity underlines that this passage can be read as a commentary by Eddé. Rather than use the expressions to set up an "ethnographic pact" with the reader, show the contours of a community, or underline rituals, here Eddé's intervention is more related to the complexities of language use itself.

This way of discussing language and translation fits well within a reading of the novel in terms of Bakhtinian polyphony and how it incorporates the language of the marketplace. In this novel, as in the others discussed in this part, spoken Arabic is used polyglossically within the literary French-language narration of the novel. In *Cerf-Volant*, as in *Sous les vignes du pays Druze*, one character, fluent in both languages, mediates these linguistic moments. Mali narrates this section and we read these commentaries on language and translation through the lens of her experience, but we see continually the many other uses of polite expressions that permeate *Cerf-Volant*. In the passage cited above, for example, Salma shouts "Soubhan Allah!" when Nizar the postman enters. This is an expression of welcome, an expression, and an interjection, all of which are better expressed by not translating it, but rather by expressing it in transliteration to be understood from context. In this example, Mali points out how useless it can be to translate such expressions, while at the same time implying how central they are for Arabic speech. Thus she demonstrates that even as a sort of native informant who explains words to the reader, like Arij does in *Sous les vignes des pays druze*, it is useless to convey the deeper meaning of important everyday Arabic expressions. The focus on language identified as "everyday Arabic" is important within the larger messages about language in *Cerf-Volant*.

Again similarly to Barakat's novel and all of the novels discussed in this book, *Cerf-Volant*'s comments on language, particularly its representation of Arabic, seem to be directed as much at an "insider" audience that knows Arabic as it is at an audience that knows only French. This is particularly true, for example, of the comment that Mali makes in parentheses. It asks for the reader's complicity and understanding, implying that we all know how difficult it is to translate expressions that sound "ridiculous" when they travel from Arabic into other languages. The translations that

Mali provides allow the French reader back into the joke: everyone can see how literal translations sound awkward and silly.

This brief passage therefore does double duty in reaching out to multiple audiences through multiple language use. Eddé manages to comment on the difficulty of translating Arabic into French—both linguistically and culturally—and subtly comments on the roles of these expressions socially. She lets French readers know that they may not understand as much as they thinks when encountering certain expressions, while simultaneously pointing out some of the complexities of the difficulties Arabs may face in translating their culture to others. In this way, *Cerf-Volant* is able to do some of the same kinds of work as both *Lettre posthume* and *Sous les vignes du pays Druze*. It negotiates a series of issues, most important, class consciousness and relationships across class-status boundaries, through language use. The ways in which the novel, through the story of Mali, explains social relations through language in some ways echoes an almost ethnographic stance, like the other novels, but yet establishes a different kind of narrative voice. The postwar engagement with the Arabic language in *Cerf-Volant* instead establishes a more polyphonic voice, undermining the author's and narrator's control over the text. Eddé's use of words and expressions marked as Arabic are subtly challenging and deeply embedded within the French-language narration.

Translating the Languages of the Elite: Formal Arabic

Translation is not only activated either in isolated locations or as a metaphor in *Cerf-Volant*. More so than in any other work discussed thus far, the question of translation is brought out directly, forcefully, and as central to its development. This issue is taken to a different level of discussion and analysis in *Cerf-Volant* than it is in other French-language novels by Lebanese authors. The metacommentary on language, particularly the French language, that is prevalent in French-language fiction by Lebanese writers here is supplemented by a parallel metacommentary on the translation of Arabic. This provides a deeper reflection not only on the colonial heritage and legacy of French, like *Le fils empaillé*, or the ways in which French separates class-status communities, as in *Lettre Posthume* or *Pourquoi il fait si sombre?*, but also on the Arabic language and its engagements with French.

The novel develops its commentary on translation, first and foremost, through the character of Farid, Mali's love interest in the novel. Farid is an erudite intellectual who is interested in a wide variety of issues, including language, and is himself a professor of Arabic. To have a central character who is committed professionally—and as we learn, politically and socially—to the Arabic language provides the text with more scope to explore the language on a number of levels. The character of Farid therefore allows *Cerf-Volant* to delve into the richness of the classical or standard Arabic language (*fusha*) rather than the vernacular alone. As the analyses in the chapters above have demonstrated, most other French-language texts by Lebanese authors incorporate words marked as Arabic that are a part of the daily, lived vernacular language. Most of the inclusions of words marked as Arabic either reflect the way that people speak, bring out elements of their daily lives, or invoke peculiar or specific expressions from the colloquial language. Even the proverbs or formal, polite set-expressions, while derived from classical Arabic, are also common in daily speech.

Cerf-Volant makes use of these same techniques and strategies as the other works discussed in *Native Tongue, Stranger Talk*. Moreover, specifically like its postwar counterparts *Sous les vignes du pays Druze* and *Pourquoi il fait si sombre?*, it does also "speak Arabic." The ways in which Mali and other characters incorporate words and expressions marked as Arabic from speech echoes other works. This novel also stands out, however, because of its more developed metacommentary on the Arabic language, particularly the formal Arabic language of writing and scholarship. This commentary on language is possible not only because of a plot that includes a character who is an Arabic professor, but also because he is not shown in contrast with the other characters. Unlike Madame Zakié of *Le fils empaillé*, the Arabic-speaking character here is shown very much to be part of the same circles and world as Mali and her community of friends and family. Moreover, they share a political inclination. The direct association of elite, French-speaking characters with "Arabist" politics—Huguette telling her notoriously Francophile family that they are Arabs or

Mali and Farid's political commitment to Palestine—also makes it distinct from other French-language novels from Lebanon.

The love story between Mali and Farid occupies much of the narration, through her divorce from Pierre, her life as a single woman, and her travels around the world. Mali considers herself politically a pan-Arabist Nasserite and is ideologically in favor of speaking Arabic, though she was raised as a French speaker. We learn this through descriptions of her life and also the fact that *Cerf-Volant* is told partially through her narrative voice. Within the text, Farid is shown in contrast to Mali's French-language orientation. Not only is he a professor of Arabic, but he is also shown to use Arabic in the text throughout the scenes in which he is depicted. He is the first character we have encountered who himself is a member of the elite who uses Arabic regularly and fluently—its formal as well as its colloquial variety. Characters who mainly or even partly speak Arabic in the other texts are almost universally represented as subaltern figures—either peasants, working-class figures, older people, and so on. He is explicitly shown to know both the spoken Arabic of everyday speech and the intricacies of formal Arabic *fusha*. Moreover, as a linguist, he is familiar with more esoteric features of the language—as when he travels to Palestine to give a lecture at Bir Zeit University on the use of the word "I" in Arabic (121).

This short example exemplifies the function of Farid within the narrative of *Cerf-Volant* and the kind of symbolic function he has as a character. First, it emphasizes that he is a professor who is important enough to be invited around the world for lectures. It further underlines the importance of the Arabic language to scholarship in that professors travel to give lectures on this topic in different locations. The invitation is not just to any university, but to Bir Zeit in Palestine, further reinforcing Farid's political commitment and the way in which the question of Palestine is given symbolic importance and value in the novel. Finally, the topic of the lecture is the pronoun "I." The topic serves a double function. First, it sounds very specialized and "scientific" linguistically—bolstering the reader's confidence in Farid's knowledge of the intricacies of grammar and language. Second, the emphasis on the "I" underlines the importance of how language is connected to the self and Farid's confidence in himself as an Arab.

A Polyphonic Narration: Arabic and French, Vernacular and Formal, High and Low Languages

Through multiple polyglossic strategies drawing on Arabic and French, vernacular and formal Arabic, spoken and literary French, high and low languages, Eddé creates a polyphonic novel in Bakhtinian terms in *Cerf-Volant*. As in *Pourquoi il fait si sombre?*, voices from different social strata destabilize and question the authority of the author-narrator. Though its narrative style is significantly different from Eddé's earlier novel, like the narrator in *Pourquoi il fait si sombre?*, the sometimes narrator-protagonist Mali in *Cerf-Volant* is in a constant state of self-reflection. She is a confident woman, but one able to acknowledge her weaknesses and doubts about many things, including her own identity and how it relates to language use. As a writer, one of her major life issues is how she uses language in her writing, and her doubts about her own use of language are amplified in her meditations:

> And it was exactly at the moment when Claire was leaving France for Egypt that the novel developed a leak. The Arabic language leaked into it. I did not know it well enough to write it and I did know it too well to write without it. Farid used to say that "a language is an instrument of conquest. One only dominates it in giving it to the world." How else can I say it to you? I had torturous relations with the French language, I held something against it—its excessive coherence, perhaps? I did not succeed in giving it the Arab world.
>
> Et c'est précisément au moment où Claire quittait la France pour l'Égypte que le roman a pris l'eau. L'eau c'était la langue arabe. Je ne la savais pas assez pour l'écrire et je la savais trop pour écrire sans elle. Farid disait "une langue est un instrument de conquête. On ne la domine qu'en lui donnant le monde." Or, comment te dire? J'avais des rapports tordus avec la langue française je lui en voulais de quelque chose—son excès de coherence, peut-être? je n'arrivais pas à lui donner le monde arabe (159–60).

This example shows that Mali is hyperaware of how she uses language, and her relationship with the French language in particular. In this reflection she poignantly links her personal relationship with French and Arabic to the politics of language use in Lebanon, echoing so many of her colleagues. Her frustration with French and feeling that it dominates her rather than herself being able to "give it to the Arab world" in many ways recalls the way in which French is discussed by the characters in Khoury-Ghata's *Le fils empaillé*. She attributes her awareness of the power of language to Farid, who has alerted her to its use as an instrument of conquest. This kind of anticolonial analysis tied to language, however, does not empower her in her writing but enhances her feelings of inadequacy as a creator and artist. Like the unnamed narrator of *Pourquoi il fait si sombre?*, whose self-doubts take the form of a hallucinatory stream of consciousness, or even the unnamed priest of *Lettre posthume*, who himself wishes he was more comfortable in his "first language" (langue d'origine), Mali's tortured relationship (rapports tordus) with the French language in *Cerf-Volant* is crucial to understanding the novel. Also like Eddé's other two narrators, Mali expresses that she is aware of the power French holds in Lebanon, the power she wields socially as a native speaker of French. One of the strategies that Dominique Eddé uses to undermine the power of the French language in this novel that is written in standard French, therefore, is to insist on its polyphony. In ways parallel to but different from her earlier *Pourquoi il fait si sombre?* and Leïla Barakat's *Sous les vignes du pays Druze*, she calls her own authorial voice into question by making *Cerf-Volant* read *as* a translation.

Reading *Cerf-Volant as* a Translation

Like other Lebanese novels written in French, *Cerf-Volant* uses multiple techniques of polyglossia in its negotiations of language politics, class status, gender dynamics, and other social issues. In addition to the metacommentary on the use of Arabic language and/or its translation, *Cerf-Volant* also uses techniques that make the French language of the novel read at times like a "foreignized translation," similarly to other postwar novels (Venuti, 1995). This technique manipulates the standard French language used in most of the novel, distorting it and making it "alien" or "strange." Though they do not necessarily draw on relexified Arabic words and expressions or on literally or idiomatically translated Arabic phrases, both metonymical and metaphorical invocations of Arabic play a role in *Cerf-Volant*'s construction of a challenging creative language. This technique is activated in the novel in particular to expose class dynamics in a stratified Lebanon.

Similarly to *Sous la baguette du coudrier, Cerf-Volant* uses historical events affecting the Middle East, and Lebanon in particular, as a parallel to events in the lives of the characters and their relationships. Though by no means a historical novel, it draws its narration largely through the depiction of historical events; historical and political events are constantly detailed as the plot of the novel unfolds. In one passage, for example, Farid undergoes treatment for his glaucoma just as Sadat prepares to make peace with Israel in 1978, Mali's friend Loulwa narrowly escapes an attack in Beirut Martyr's Square, and René Chami tries to negotiate the release of a cousin who has been kidnapped. These events are "historical" and are distanced from the contemporary postwar setting of the novel, partly through a third-person omniscient narration. These kinds of scenes, which are invoked throughout the course of the work, are shown to be crucial to understanding the postwar setting of the novel and the ways in which characters moved through their lives in this later time.

The last of these three events, which details the release and exchange of prisoners during the Lebanese civil war, is one example that demonstrates how Arabic is represented in the French narration. Here, the novel intervenes into a moment in history through the character René Chami, who is trying to secure his kidnapped cousin's freedom.[1] When Chami declares that he wishes he were dead rather than negotiating with the militias active in the war, his gardener replies (with direct reported speech enclosed in quotation marks), "never regret being alive, Sir, your cousin

1. Stories of the kidnapped and disappeared during the war are one of the most difficult issues in the postwar period because of the large numbers of people still unaccounted for. Creative works have begun to explore this painful and traumatic issue; see Rabi' Jabir's novel *'I'tirafat* [Confessions](2008), Iman Humaydan's novel *Hayawat Ukhra* [*Other Lives*] (2010/2014), and the recent film directed by Bahij Hojeij, *Chatti ya Dini* [Let it rain] (2010).

will tell you that: life is a monkey that turns into a gazelle when it threatens to leave you" [ne regrettez jamais d'être en vie, Monsieur, votre cousin vous le dira: la vie est un singe qui se transforme en gazelle, quand elle menace de vous quitter] (182).

The common trope of the older, wiser workingman offering sage advice to his social superior is evident. The way in which this man speaks to Chami recalls Om El Kher's advice to Samya in Chedid's *Le sommeil délivré*. Wise words are once again placed in the mouth of a subaltern character who speaks in a colorful way and has greater life experience. Placing these words in the mouth of the gardener therefore is not necessarily subversive of class hierarchies, simply because there is a reversal of status roles in giving advice. As I pointed out in relation to Chedid's novel, this can be read as an exceptional moment or one that raises the impoverished peasant, postman, or in this case gardener to a position "above his station" temporarily. The women of the village help Samya in Chedid's novel but their position is in the end naturalized—there will be no major transformation in land ownership, management, and labor that will significantly change their lives. Just because these characters have more information, insight, and experience, their living conditions and place in social hierarchies does not change. As *Cerf-Volant* is concerned in reversing class-status roles, mocking the bourgeoisie, and inverting paradigms that reinforce class-status hierarchies, however, it is relevant to question: Does this novel break out of this pattern or merely reinforce it?

This example equivocates. The moral of the gardener's quaint saying to René Chami is clear and is expressed, like most of the rest of the novel, in standard French. In another parallel to Chedid's novel, the way in which it is expressed is similar to the village women who speak to Samya. The gardener's expression is different from the bourgeois characters in that he uses a simile invoking gazelles and monkeys, alluding to well-known imagery. The comparison of monkey and gazelle is an Arabic expression used to refer to a mother's love—it is equivalent to the English expression "a face only a mother could love." Here the gardener is speaking about loving life and appreciating what you have in proverbial-sounding terms.

Rather than relexify an expression into unidiomatic French, translate the way in which a subaltern character might speak in French, or translate his words into French from Arabic in a way that he would not himself speak, Eddé puts flowery speech into the mouth of the gardener. This strategy works as a symbolic representation that is meant to evoke Arabic but uses French. By alluding to the foreignness of his expression, Eddé makes the text read *as* a foreignized translation.

This passage draws on the tropes of naturalization of social stratification while also challenging them in some ways. Poetic language and language mixing here highlight the gaps in characters' social position—the gardener calls René Chami "Sir," he uses colorful language that the bourgeois characters do not, and so on. The representation of Arabic as "foreign" and wise words placed in the mouth of a gardener are less subversive as an idea when read in isolation. This one example shows a similar strategy to Chedid. The potential for challenging these ideas is more potent when read in conjunction with other, similar examples throughout the novel. If this gardener's words are read together with Nizar's explanation of who is a "fils de famille," for example, and with the scene of Nizar drinking coffee with Salma, a more detailed picture emerges of how Eddé creates a multivoiced novel.

These strategies work together, I propose, similarly to the multiple strategies used in Barakat's *Sous les vignes du pays Druze* and Eddé's *Pourquoi il fait si sombre?* Like these texts, *Cerf-Volant* uses multiple polyglossic techniques to achieve the overall effect of polyphony. In the case of this novel, because so many different characters do speak, whether using languages marked as Arabic, awkward French phrases or transliterations, or those that sound like "foreignized translations" of Arabic, the multivoiced nature of the text is pronounced. Even more important, perhaps, polyphony is achieved by the way in which this textual language helps to challenge the unity of the authorial voice, allowing subaltern characters to make textual interventions and comments on class and hierarchy themselves. It is this polyphony that distinguishes the project and effect of *Cerf-Volant* from other novels discussed, even as it uses similar and overlapping techniques.

Mali as Teacher of Language

To achieve textual polyphony as articulated by Bakhtin, multiple voices must dominate the novel, undermining strict authorial control of the text. The loosening of control of the narrator's and author's voices in *Cerf-Volant* are achieved in a number of ways that are central to the work's polyphony and navigate the treacherous waters of representing class and status hierarchies through elite "French-speaking" voices. Mali's voice remains central to the novel and is privileged above other voices in the sections that are devoted to her first-person narration. Moreover, she is the work's central character and its focus. Her words and opinions are thus automatically accorded extra weight. Though she herself is not an Arabic professor, as her lover Farid is, there are a number of passages in which Mali is able to demonstrate her familiarity with the complexities and beauty of the Arabic language. These rather long explanatory sections recall the scene about coffee in *Lettre posthume* in which the rituals of its consumption are detailed. These scenes, and parallel scenes in *Pourquoi il fait si sombre?*, showcase Eddé's linguistic virtuosity. Though they are meant to be didactic in their own novelistic contexts, they do not read as ideologically laden, perhaps because of the cushioning of the lighthearted humor that pervades *Cerf-Volant*. It is this combination that allows Eddé a certain flexibility in advancing messages without seeming heavy-handed.

In *Cerf-Volant*, Mali has the opportunity to share her knowledge of the Arabic language with her English teacher, Jane. As the latter knows very little about Arabic, Mali not only explains what various words mean but also connects them to each other by explaining the system of triliteral roots common to Semitic languages.

> Do you know, Jane, that the root of the word snake, *hayya*, is the verb to live and that it is also from this that the word *hayawân*, which means animal, comes from? Abdallah—because this was his name—asked Mali to translate what she said into Arabic. *Hayya, hayawân*, I never gave it a thought, he replied pensively.
>
> Savez-vous, Jane, que la racine du mot serpent, *hayya*, c'est le verbe vivre et que c'est aussi de là que vient le mot *hayawân*, qui veut dire

> animal? Abdallah—car c'est ainsi qu'il s'appelait—demanda à Mali de traduire en arabe. *Hayya, hayawân*, je n'y avais pas pensé' repliqua-t-il, songeur. (213)

This discussion carries on for quite a long time, with Mali further connecting the root word *hayya* to the word for face. Jane is surprised by the connections between Arabic words based on the root system and Abdallah, Mali's friend and a native speaker of Arabic, admits that he has never thought about these connections before. A knowledge of the Arabic language is professed by Mali, establishing her as a linguistic authority with a particular "insider" status in Lebanese/Arab society, though she is an elite French-speaking woman of the Lebanese privileged classes. Much like her translation of Arabic expressions, she manifests her knowledge through dissecting and explaining roots of words. This has the double effect of showing her intelligence and control of words and ideas and also exposing the complexity and beauty of the Arabic language and its connections to a French reader. Further, by connecting life, animals, and more specifically, snakes, Mali shows the links between things that are not normally recognized.

Mali takes her arguments even further toward the end of this passage when she follows up. "But this is not all, resumes Mali, growing more and more elated, *hayawân* is also a complement of *janna*, paradise, *hayawân* is the 'real life' after death" [Mais ce n'est pas tout, reprit Mali de plus en plus exaltée, *hayawân* est aussi un complement de *janna*, le paradis, *hayawân*, c'est "la vraie vie" après la mort] (214). By connecting animals to life and death, Mali is arguably also making a more complex comment on social life and class stratification. In this passage, and the others like it, the educated and worldly Mali explains the Arabic root system and words formed from it to Arabic speakers and non-Arabic speakers alike. Moreover, in this particular passage she explains the roots to an Arabic-speaking Lebanese man, Abdallah the zookeeper, and her governess, Jane, at the same time. An elite French-speaking Lebanese woman explains to an English woman, herself privileged by virtue of her nationality if not profession, and a subaltern Lebanese man quite complex linguistic ideas about Arabic, albeit in a straightforward and somewhat poetic way. Jane the governess rejoins with a comment about how the snake, animal, and face therefore are three branches off the same tree.

Abdallah the zookeeper has no such insights, saying that he does not understand what these women are going on about, but that human desire is like a snake and does not like to be cheated. Once again, therefore, the wise words of interpretation are put into the mouth of a nonelite character. Though it is Mali who uncovers the complexities of the words and their connections through the root system, Abdallah is the one with the pithy proverb that unlocks its secrets. If his intervention is read in conjunction with that of the gardener, Nizar the postman, and other characters throughout, it becomes clear that Eddé's creation of a creative textual language is complex. Not only does she reverse the roles of who "speaks Arabic" in the novel, but also of who interpret these moments of ploygلossic rupture and difference. While remaining true to a representation of languages that reflects lived social realities of people speaking languages marked as different, Eddé challenges her readers' expectations throughout the novel, allowing different characters to make different kinds of observations. Here, for example, Mali sets out the linguistic and grammatical examples and Abdallah interprets them, much as Nizar explains what the expression "fils de famille" means in context. This destabilizing of one, unified narrative voice that controls the narrative is crucial in allowing *Cerf-Volant* to operate as a polyphonic novel. Its questioning of class-status hierarchies is reflected in this polyphony and is inscribed by it, making Eddé's novels one of the most formally challenging of the study.

Conclusions

Cerf-Volant, like Dominique Eddé's earlier work *Pourquoi il fait si sombre?*, challenges class and status hierarchies in Lebanon and explores how they are related to gender though their negotiations of language. Both of these works, like Leïla Barakat's *Sous les vignes du pays Druze*, take greater risks with their creation of challenging textual languages than do earlier works. The kinds of subtle strategies used by the earliest works discussed in this study, which I called gendered interference, very much reflect a more cautious approach to critiquing and challenging social mores and norms. The novels written in the mandate and early independence periods reflect their era in how they use creative languages in measured ways. The novels of the war then challenge this use of language with feminist punctuation, exploring works marked as Arabic and using them to almost shout out messages about women's equality to the reader. What sets the works of the postwar period apart is their more concerted attempts to craft textual languages that challenge the hegemony of French as a colonial language in multiple ways. *Cerf-Volant* uses many of the same techniques as *Sous les vignes du pays Druze* and *Pourquoi il fait si sombre?* to create this complex, creative textual language that deeply embeds words, expressions, and ideas marked as Arabic within its narration in Standard French. The ways in which Arabic is invoked in all of these texts is so extensive that their language reads as though it is not straightforwardly French. The commitment to mark and outwardly display difference in these novels can be read as parallel to foreignizing translations.

The strategies used in *Cerf-Volant* are not identical either to her earlier text or to Barakat's novel, however, both of which I have identified as achieving a similar effect of writing *as* translation. *Cerf-Volant* in particular also makes extensive use of a metacommentary on language use, more like that of the novels of the war period—Khoury-Ghata's *Le fils empaillé* and Eddé's first novel, *Lettre posthume*—with its multivoiced narration that echoes *Pourquoi il fait si sombre?* Moreover, the metacommentary that distinguishes *Cerf-Volant* from other texts most distinctly is not only on French as a colonial language but also on the way in which formal Arabic works and the function of the Arabic language within Arab societies. Less formally experimental in its narrative style than *Pourquoi il fait si sombre?*, *Cerf-Volant* favors a more standard third-person linear narration. Though it does mix the narrative voice with reported speech and some sections of first-person narration, a discernable plot dominates over a stream-of-consciousness meditation.

In its challenge to colonial knowledge production, as a French-language novel that invokes and manipulates Arabic, *Cerf-Volant* is unique. It is the only novel in this study that consciously and directly embraces an openly leftist, Arabist, Nasserite political position through its main character, her friends, and her beloved. Other works operate from a multiplicity of political positions—both explicit and implicit. Other characters are avowed leftists, feminists, and Arabists, including in Accad's *Coquelicot du massacre.* But *Cerf-Volant* takes the challenge to the Lebanese haute bourgeoisie and its Francophilia the furthest, particularly in its continual, multiple strategies of undermining class-status hierarchies. The linguistic techniques used to effect this subversion are multiple, and when read together are able to produce a genuinely polyphonic novel in the Bakhtinian sense that brings multiple voices to the fore. This destabilization of the voice that advances the novel itself is the key to understanding the anticolonial challenge of Eddé's language use in *Cerf-Volant.*

Conclusion

Like a Garlic Dish without the Garlic?

When Abou Ali and Alia challenge the narrator of Dominique Eddé's *Pourquoi il fait si sombre?* for writing her novel about the Lebanese civil war in French, they wonder aloud, "why the hell write Arabic in French?" (à quoi ça rime, écrire l'arabe en français?). To underline this point more forcefully, they emphasize that it is both a matter of not making sense and leaving behind a bad taste: "[it's] like you made a garlic dish without the garlic" ([c'est] comme si tu faisais un plat à l'ail sans l'ail) (Eddé 1999, 105). Abou Ali and Alia's voices work with others to create the polyphony that permeates *Pourquoi il fait si sombre?* They interrupt the narrator's stream of consciousness and call both the narrative and authorial voices into question. The garlic dish without the garlic, like so many other metaphors that Eddé invokes in her works, demonstrates her doubt that French is an adequate language of expression for certain of her characters' realities in Lebanon—it tightens its corset, it leaks into the text, it's bland and cannot convey the sharp taste of life in the war. Reflections on, insecurities about, and challenges to French language use in Lebanon comingle in Eddé's works with harsh critiques of it. Informed by anticolonial politics, characters of different social classes and milieus point out again and again how writing French is "writing bourgeois," as Nadia Tuéni so aptly phrased it (Tuéni 1986, 63).

But Eddé's toppling of the metaphor of writing Arabic into the French language as "local spice and flavor" contrasts with how Nadia Tuéni reclaimed the notion of writing Arabic in French as a compliment rather than a critique. I opened the preface to *Native Tongue, Stranger Talk* with Tuéni's claim that in her French sentences you can recognize "the rhythm and musicality of Arabic." In this pronouncement, she makes a statement about language, literature, identity, and belonging that is both poetic and political. Tuéni is proud to do what Abou Ali says is impossible. Vénus Khoury-Ghata echoes Tuéni's sense of pride and affiliation with the Arabic language when she directly announces her use of franbanais in French-language texts. Ideologically explicitly anticolonial, Khoury-Ghata redresses some of the violence the French language has wrought on Lebanon through her creative novelistic language. Eddé holds a similar political stance but her narrations accomplish this differently.

These and all of the writers whose works are discussed in *Native Tongue, Stranger Talk* in one way or another articulate political and ideological stances toward and relationships with the Arabic and French languages. This means that French-language fiction by Lebanese women writers is not just an expression of elite society, disconnected from Arab and/or Lebanese realities. It means that these novels are not merely exotic ethnographic exposés that train a European-influenced gaze on the Orient. These are outmoded ways of approaching a vibrant literary tradition that questions and challenges the colonial language imposed on Lebanon through experimentation with textual languages. All of the novels mount some form of resistance to the colonial language, French, through the crafting of creatively layered languages. They deal with political and ideological questions through language explicitly and implicitly, with less and more sympathy toward the French-language, but all of the writers create textual languages and worldviews that negotiate the borders and overlaps between the Arabic and French languages. They do this in their texts ostensibly written in French as insiders and outsiders to two languages identified as different and separate—Arabic and French. Because French is always a colonial language, despite the different ways in which the authors discussed in this study navigate their relationships to it, there is always a tension in how Arabic rubs up against French in their works.

What I have tried to draw out in *Native Tongue, Stranger Talk* is not only what Arabic and French represent within texts but also how they operate more concretely in relation to each other on the textual level. How languages that are identifiable as Arabic and French interanimate each other in producing creative novelistic discourse is crucial to the readings. Conventional wisdom about languages and language "mixing" is thus questioned. The language/s created in all of these texts resist dichotomies that would see them as separate and competing. My readings of the creative literary languages of the texts discussed here argue against the idea that languages can mix, it calls into question the borders between languages in the first place. It also asks if and how we can identify whole, unified languages that are meant to be only French or only Arabic.

It is in this sense of questioning the dividing lines between languages that the argument in *Native Tongue, Stranger Talk* intervenes in reworking Hegelian paradigms based on dichotomies between East and West. The difference between Arabic and French, Europe and the Arab/Islamic world, break down in conceptual spaces that are opened up by languages that challenge easy, neat linguistic and/or cultural categorizations. The ways in which these novels are positioned and position themselves between languages usually identified as French or Arabic therefore offers us the opportunity to think more deeply through unified subject positions, which are seen as somehow essentially different from each other. By reading the languages produced in these works not as "mixed" but rather as whole languages, unified within each text, this study undermines implied linguistic, cultural, and "civilizational" dichotomies. Such dichotomies, for example, proposal that the Arabic language represents some kind of "Arabic-Islamic" tradition bifurcated from modern, "Western" thought, represented by French. Infusing a language marked as French with words identified as Arabic therefore allows authors to craft textual languages and worlds. It is the interanimation of languages within these unique textual worlds that undermine such Euro-centered, Enlightenment worldviews and inscribe an anticolonial politics linguistically within texts written in colonial languages.

In the nine chapters devoted to reading the specific novels, I probed the wide variety of different techniques that the authors use to develop polyglossia in their novels. The three broad categories into which I grouped their strategies are linked to the times in which they were written and published. I identify the novels written in the mandate and early independence period that draw on words marked as Arabic within the French text as gendered interference; the works of the Lebanese civil war that utilize those words as feminist punctuation, and the texts of the postwar period that are written *as* translations. These categories are not distinct or discrete and certainly there are many examples of overlap and works fitting into more than one category. These three broad categories, however, are a useful shorthand to examine commonalities in the ways in which the Arabic and French languages interanimate each other, particularly in relation to the intersection of issues of class and status, ethnicity and religion, and gender. The novelized discourses that are created through polyglossia within all of the texts make different kinds of comments on these issues, particularly at areas of intersection between them.

What I have shown in these readings is how each of the novels in different ways comes to terms with the challenge of expressing its vision by creating a textual language. Far beyond using Arabic words as window dressing to spice up the texts, these novels create textual languages that question the boundaries between languages as we know them and use them on a daily basis. The metaphor of translation is once again a useful way to think through this issue. Writing a text, like translating, is not merely conveying information from one language or setting to another, or choosing the right word to express an idea. The ways in which ideas are expressed, the words, expressions and atmosphere used to convey the narrative, are as important as the story itself. The texts write a strangeness and alien-ness into their French language that can be compared with techniques of foreignizing or resistant translation. The very creation of novelistic discourse in all of these works shows how languages can dislocate meaning as much as they convey it. In the nine works here it is clear that appropriating language within the novel written in what appears on the surface to be French, using words and expressions marked as Arabic, means coming to terms with the foreignness—not only of these languages but of language itself.

The broader framework that holds these more specific readings of textual techniques and linguistic practices together is world literature. In this study, world literature has been used to propose that these novels exemplify exchange and travel, flows of information and capital, as well as language itself. The close readings of language in literary texts in *Native Tongue,*

Stranger Talk show how texts operate in different contexts of social reality and refract them through their use of multiple languages at the same time. Within the broader framework of world literature, then, these novels can be seen as participating in conversations beyond French-speaking Lebanon. A world literature framework gives a broader perspective on how Arabic and French engage and interanimate each other in all of these novels. Each of these languages is identifiable within the novels discussed here and each represents a constellation of things that shift and change. Moreover, while some uses of a given language are clearly marked and identifiable as such, others blend and slide between languages marked as different more easily. It is helpful to see these different and complementary writing strategies in establishing new textual languages of creative expression in the broader framework of exchange and travel that a world literature framework demands.

This larger framework is useful for thinking through connections between the kinds of work these texts perform with language. Languages are imbued with meaning. The world literature framework is one way in which to emphasize how these meanings work relationally. French and Arabic represent different things in novels: they are colonial and anticolonial, and they are invested with different amounts of status and prestige in different settings. But the languages of the texts that are investigated must be seen as much more dynamic than just representing these large concepts; the languages of the texts are also gendered languages, high and low registers of languages, the language of the home or "bayt," the billingsgate of the street and marketplace, the language of everyday speech and the language of literary writing. To understand the complexities of the novelistic discourses developed here, how class status and gender issues are explored through language, is a focus of the arguments.

Feminism, and in particular a critique of the roles of women and men in society, is another broad issue that the world literature framework can help to underline. Rather than see feminisms in a comparative perspective, however, I have limited my analyses to the ways in which these issues are tackled within the novels themselves. The feminisms that I am working with in these readings are not necessarily those familiar within the Western canon of feminist thought, writing, or literature. What I have done in each chapter is to argue how the particularities of language use in these works shape their feminist projects in different ways. In reading the various ways in which languages are gendered in texts, I show how words have different valences in different settings. The feminist project here, therefore, is not to see how women's use of language or linguistic strategies is similar or different across literatures or cultures, but rather to investigate from within texts what kinds of commentaries they are making about feminism, women's roles, and social attitudes toward women and their liberation. The feminisms embraced by the works are multiple and change and shift depending on their contexts.

The analysis of language in *Native Tongue, Stranger Talk* therefore is complex and multilayered. It focuses on class status and gender issues, it is feminist and it is anticolonial. All of these lenses work well together when read in relation to the concept of world literature, which opens these analyses of language to be interpreted through the multiple spaces that it inhabits. The context within which to read these works, therefore, is not merely Arab or Lebanese, or French or "Francophone," or Middle Eastern or women's writing, but rather all of these at once. It is crucial to pay careful attention to the way in which languages work in all of these spaces.

Within a world literature framework, the idea of the stranger and native also frames this study. The stranger talk used to address outsiders, the native tongue that is called into question, the complex position of the insider-outsider who is a stranger and a native at the same time, all deeply inform the readings. As the epigraph to the introduction reminds us, the poet Etel Adnan eloquently sums up her experience of the colonial legacy of French, which alienated her from the language and cultures of her birth and childhood, by saying she is both a "stranger and a native to the same mother tongue" (Adnan 1986–1987). French is her "native tongue," though she always remains a stranger to it as an Arab. Like other French-language authors from Lebanon, writing in French means estrangement and distance from an Arabic reading public and also from herself as an Arab. Arabic is Adnan's "native tongue" in a different way, but she cannot read or write it. In all of its detailed readings of texts and contexts, this book has questioned: Who is the stranger and who is the native? How one can be a stranger and native at the same time? Can one be a stranger to one's own native tongue?

When Adnan claims to be a stranger and a native to the same language and same mother tongue she lays bare the paradox with which the novels in this study all contend. In a sense all of the works discussed show how a person can sometimes not be only one or the other but must inhabit both spaces. Perhaps, then, part of the explanation for the seeming disconnect between Tuéni's and Khoury-Ghata's pride in writing Arabic in French and Eddé's claim that it cannot be done is because this process works on a continuum. On the one hand, the Arabic language "leaks into" French texts, as Eddé puts it. There is no way to avoid it—it is simply a fact. At the same time that the Arabic language can be a sign and symbol of pride, it also does not fit and clashes with French. French is a colonial language, feels imposed, and represents foreign domination of the region and bourgeois values; but French is a mother tongue too, to be used, challenged, and manipulated like any other language. This double challenge thus rejects both culturalist models of literary production and also colonialism and the colonial production of knowledge.

Bibliography

Index

Bibliography

Primary Sources

Accad, Evelyne. 1988. *Coquelicot du massacre* [A poppy from the massacre]. Paris: L'harmattan.

Barakat, Leïla. 1993. *Sous les vignes du pays Druze* [Under the vines in Druze country]. Paris: L'harmattan.

Bustros, Eveline. 1958. *Sous la baguette du coudrier* [Under the divining rod]. Beirut: Imprimerie Catholique. Reprint, 1988, in *Romans et écrits divers*, 153–337.

———. 1988. *Romans et écrits divers*. Beirut: Dar an-Nahar.

Chedid, Andrée. 1952. *Le sommeil délivré* [*From Sleep Unbound*]. Paris: Stock. Reprint, 1976, Paris: Flammarion.

Eddé, Dominique. 1989. *Lettre posthume* [A posthumous letter]. Paris: Arpenteur/Gallimard.

———. 1999. *Pourquoi il fait si sombre?* [Why is it so dark?] Paris: Seuil.

———. 2003. *Cerf-Volant* [Kite]. Paris: Arpenteur/Gallimard.

Kher, Amy. 1933. *Salma et son village* [Salma and her village]. Beirut: Mondiale. Reprint, 1972, *Salma et son village*. Introduction by Aimé Azar. Paris: Madeleine.

Khoury-Ghata, Vénus. 1980. *Le fils empaillé* [The son stuffed with straw]. Paris: Belfond.

Secondary Sources

Abbudi, Henriette. 1995. "Al-Kitaba bi-lugha ajnabiyya mazij min al-hurriyya ala-l'asar." *Al-Hayat*, 17 January, 16.

Abirached, Zeina. 2007. *Mourir, partir, revenir: C'est le chant des hirondelles*. Paris: Cambourakis.

———. 2008. *Je me souviens: Beyrouth*. Paris: Cambourakis.

Abisaab, Malek. 2009. *Militant Women of a Fragile Nation*. Syracuse: Syracuse University Press.

Abou, Selim. 1961. *Enquêtes sur les langues en usage au Liban*. Beirut: Imprimerie Catholique.

———. 1962. *Le bilinguisme Arabe-Français au Liban: Essai d'anthropologie culturelle*. Paris: Presses universitaires de France.

Abou, Selim, Choghig Kasparian, and Katia Haddad. 1996. *Anatomie de la francophonie libanaise*. Beirut: FMA/Saint-Joseph.

Aboul-Ela, Hosam. 2001. "Challenging the Embargo: Arabic Literature in the US Market." *MERIP: Middle East Report* 219: 42–44.

Abu Haidar, Farida. 2000. "Inscribing a Maghrebian Identity in French." In *Maghrebian Mosaic: A Literature in Transition*, edited by Mildred Mortimer, 1–11. Boulder CO: Lynne Reiner.

Abu Izzeddin, Nejla M. 1984. *The Druzes: A New Study of Their History, Faith, and Society*. Leiden: Brill.

Abu Jaber, Diana. 2003. *Crescent*. New York: Picador.

Abu Khalil, As'ad. 2001. "Didd Al-frankufuniyya: Batalan al-thiqafa al-lubnaniyya." *Al-Adab* 49, nos. 9–10: 22–43.

Abu Lughod, Lila. 1986. *Veiled Sentiments: Honor and Poetry in a Bedouin Society*. Berkeley and Los Angeles: University of California Press.

Accad, Evelyne. 1982. *L'Excisée*. Paris: L'harmattan.

———. 1989. *L'Excisée*. Translated by David Bruner. Washington, DC: Three Continents Press.

———. 1992. *Sexuality and War: Literary Masks of the Middle East*. New York: New York University Press.

———. 1993. *Blessures des mots*. Paris: côté femmes/Indigo.

———. 1996. *Wounding Words: A Tunisian Journal*. Translated by Cynthia Hahn. London: Heinemann.

———. 2000. *Voyages en cancer*. Paris: L'harmattan.

———. 2001. *The Wounded Breast: Intimate Journeys through Cancer*. Translated by Evelyne Accad. Melbourne: Spinifex.

Ackad, Tewfick. 1918. *Les martyres*. Cairo: np.

———. 1925. *Une nuit dans la vallée des rois*. Paris: France-Orient.

Adnan, Etel. 1977. *Sitt Marie Rose*. Paris: des femmes.

———. 1980. *Apocalypse arabe*. Paris: Papyrus.

———. 1982. *Sitt Marie Rose*. Translated by Georgina Kleege. Sausalito, CA: Post-Apollo Press.

———. 1983. "Tribal Mentality." *Off Our Backs* 7: 32.

———. 1986–1987. "To Write in a Foreign Language." *Connexions* 22: 13–17.

———. 1989. *Arab Apocalypse*. Translated by Etel Adnan. Sausalito, CA: Post-Apollo Press.

———. 1990. "Growing Up to Be a Woman Writer in Lebanon." In Badran and Cooke, *Opening the Gates*, 3–21.

Aghacy, Samira. 2009. *Masculine Identity in the Fiction of the Arab East since 1967.* Syracuse: Syracuse University Press.

Ahmad, Aijaz. 1992. *In Theory: Classes, Nations, Literatures*. London: Verso.

Alameddine, Rabih. 2001. *I, the Divine*. New York: W. W. Norton.

Alcalay, Ammiel. 1994. "Our Memory Has No Future." *The Nation*, 7 March, 311.

Allen, Roger. 1995. *The Arabic Novel: An Historical and Critical Introduction*. Syracuse: Syracuse University Press.

———. 2001. "Literary History and the Arabic Novel." *World Literature Today* 75, no. 2: 205–13.

———. 2003. "Translating Arabic Literature." *Translation Review* 65: 1–5.

Alshamma', Ghada. 1986. "A Sociolinguistic Study of Some Basic Characteristics of Expression of the Syrian Arab Personality." *Anthropological Linguistics* 28, no. 1: 106–14.

Amyuni, Mona Takieddine. 1999. "Literature and War, Beirut 1993–1995: Three Case Studies." *World Literature Today* 73: 37–42.

Antonellou-Achar, Natacha, Raya Boustani, and Dimitri Melki. 2002. *Nouvelle dramaturgie libanaise francophone*. Beirut: Dar an-Nahar.

Aouad-Basbous, Thérèse. 1989. *Dent d'amour.* Paris: l'harmattan.

———. 1995. *Mon roman*. Paris: L'harmattan.

———. 1996. *La nonne et le telephone*. Paris: l'harmattan.

Aoun-Anhoury, Najwa. 1987. *Panorama de la a poésie libanaise d'expression française*. New edition, 1996, Beirut: Dar al-Machrek.

Appiah, Kwame Anthony. 2004. "Thick Translation." In *Translation Studies Reader*, edited by Lawrence Venuti, 389–401. New York: Routledge.

Apter, Emily. 1999. *Continental Drift: From National Characters to Virtual Subjects*. Chicago: University of Chicago Press.

———. 2005. *The Translation Zone: A New Comparative Literature*. Princeton: Princeton University Press.

Ashcroft, Bill, Gareth Griffith, and Helen Tiffin. 1989. *The Empire Writes Back: Theory and Practice in Postcolonial Literatures*. New York: Routledge.

Attridge, Derek. 2004. *Peculiar Language: Literature as Difference from the Renaissance to James Joyce.* New York: Routledge.

Awad, Jocelyne. 1994. *Khamsin.* Paris: Albin Michel.

———. 2003. *Carrefour des prophètes.* Beirut: Antoine.

Awar Jarrar, Nada. 2003. *Somewhere, Home.* London: Heinemann.

———. 2007. *Dreams of Water.* New York: Harper.

———. 2009. *A Good Land.* New York: Harper Collins.

'Awwad, Tawfiq Yusuf. 1939. *Al-Raghif* [The loaf of bread] Beirut: Maktabat Lubnan.

Badawi, Mustapha M. 1993. *Cambridge History of Arabic Literature: Modern Arabic Literature.* Cambridge: Cambridge University Press.

Badran, Margot, and Miriam Cooke, eds. 1990. *Opening the Gates: A Century of Arab Feminist Writing.* Bloomington: Indiana University Press.

Bahri, Depeeka. 2003. *Native Intelligence.* Minneapolis: University of Minnesota Press.

Bakhtin, Mikhail. 1981. "The Epic and the Novel." In *The Dialogic Imagination: Four Essays,* edited by Michael Holquist, 1–40. Austin: University of Texas Press.

———. 1984. *Problems of Dostoyevsky's Poetics.* Minneapolis: University of Minnesota Press.

———. 1986. *Speech Genres and Other Late Essays.* Austin: University of Texas Press.

———. 1993. *Rabelais and His World.* Bloomington: Indiana University Press.

Barakat, Leïla. 1994. *Le chagrin de l'Arabie heureuse* [The sadness of Arabia Felix]. Paris: L'harmattan.

———. 1995. *Pourquoi pleure l'Euphrate?* Paris: L'harmattan.

———. 1997. *Les hommes damnés de la terre sainte.* Paris: L'harmattan.

Barakat, Najwa. 1986. *Al-Muhawwil* [The transformer]. Beirut: Mukhtarat.

———. 1995. *Hayat wa alam hamad ibn silana* [The passion of Hamad ibn Silana]. Beirut: al-Adab.

———. 1996. *Bus al-awadim* [The bus of good people]. Beirut: al-Adab.

———. 1997. *Le locataire du pot de fer.* Paris: L'harmattan.

———. 1999. *Ya Salaam.* Beirut: al-Adab.

———. 2004. *Lughat al-sirr* [The language of secrets]. Beirut: al-Adab.

Bardenstein, Carol. 2002. "Transmissions Interrupted: Reconfiguring Food, Memory, and Gender in the Cookbook—Memoirs of Middle Eastern Exiles." *Signs* 28, no. 1: 353–87.

Baritaud, Bernard, ed. 1995. *Regards sur l'oeuvre narrative et poétique de Ezza Agha Malak.* Paris: Écrivains.

Bashshur, Munir. 1978. *The Structure of the Lebanese Educational System* (in Arabic). Beirut: CERD.

Bassnett, Susan. 1980. *Translation Studies.* New York: Routledge.

Bassnett, Susan, and Harish Trivedi, eds. 1999. *Post-Colonial Translation: Theory and Practice.* New York: Routledge.

Bayumi, Nuha, and Nazik Saba Yared. 2000. *Al-Katibat al-lubnaniyat: Bibliografia, 1850–1950.* London: Saqi.

Bensmaïa, Réda. 2003. *Experimental Nations: Or, the Invention of the Maghreb.* Princeton: Princeton University Press.

Betts, Robert Benton. 1988. *The Druze.* New Haven: Yale University Press.

Beydoun, Ahmad. 1984. *Le Liban, une histoire disputée: Identité et temps dans l'historiographie libanaise contemporaine.* Beirut: Publications de l'Universite Libanaise.

———. 1993. *Le Liban: Itinéraires dans une guerre incivile.* Paris: Karthala; Beirut: CERMOC.

Bhabha, Homi. 1994. *The Location of Culture.* New York: Routledge.

Bocquet, Jérôme. 2004. "Francophonie et langue arabe dans la Syrie sous mandat: L'exemple de l'enseignement missionnaire à Damas." In Méouchy and Sluglett, *British and French Mandates in Comparative Perspectives,* 303–20.

Booth, Marilyn. 2001. "Beneath Lies the Rock: Contemporary Egyptian Poetry and the Common Tongue." *World Literature Today* 75, no. 2: 257–61.

———. 2003. "On Translation and Madness." *Translation Review* 65: 47–53.

———. 2008. "Translator v. Author: The *Girls of Riyadh* Go to New York." *Translation Studies* 1, no. 2: 197–211.

Boullata, Issa. 2003. "The Case for Resistant Translation from Arabic to English." *Translation Review* 65: 29–34.

Bouron, Narcisse. 1930. *Les Druzes: Histoire du Liban et de la Montagne Haouranais.* Paris: Berger-Levrault.

Boustani, Carmen, ed. 2003. *Aux frontières des deux genres: En hommage à Andrée Chedid.* Paris: Karthala.

Braun, Friederike. 1988. *Terms of Address: Problems of Patterns of Usage in Various Languages and Cultures.* Berlin: Mouton de Gruyter.

Brennan, Timothy. 2004. "Edward Said and Comparative Literature." *Journal of Palestine Studies* 33, no. 3: 23–37.

Burckhardt, John Lewis. 1822. *Travels in Syria and the Holy Land*. London: J. Murray.

Bushrui, Suheil, and Joe Jenkins. 1998. *Kahlil Gibran: Man and Poet*. Oxford: Oneworld.

Caiani, Fabio. 2004. "Polyphony and Narrative Voice in Fu'ad Al-Takarli Al-Raj' Al-Ba'id." *Journal of Arabic Literature* 35, no. 1: 45–70.

Carollo, Kevin. 2006. "Impossible Returns: The State of Contemporary Francophone Literary Production." *Journal of the Midwest Modern Language Association* 39, no. 2: 114–32.

Casanova, Pascale. 1999. *La république mondiale des lettres*. Paris: Seuil.

———. 2004. *The World Republic of Letters*. Translated by M. B. DeBevoise. Cambridge: Harvard University Press.

Chasseaud, George Washington. 1955. *The Druses of Lebanon: Their Manners, Customs, and History, with a Translation of Their Religious Code*. London: Richard Bentley.

Chedid, Andrée. 1983. *From Sleep Unbound*. Translated by Sharon Spencer. London: Swallow Press.

———. 1985. *La maison sans racines*. Paris: Flammarion.

———. 1989. *L'enfant multiple*. Paris: Flammarion.

———. 1990. *Return to Beirut*. Translated by Roz Schwartz. London: Serpent's Tail.

———. 1995. *The Multiple Child*. Translated by Judith Radke. San Francisco: Mercury House.

———. 1996. *Les saisons de passage: Récit*. Paris: Flammarion.

Chiha, Michel. 1952. *Politique intérieure*. Beirut: Trident.

———. 1966. "Le monde aujourd'hui." In *Visage et presence du Liban*, 58–108. Beirut: Trident.

Churchill, Charles Henry. 1853. *Mount Lebanon, a Ten Years' Residence from 1842 to 1852: Describing the Manners, Customs, and Religion of Its Inhabitants with a Full and Correct Account of the Druse Religion and Containing Historical Records of the Mountain Tribes from Personal Intercourse with Their Chiefs and Other Authentic Sources*. London: Saunders and Oatley.

———. 1862. *The Druzes and the Maronites under the Turkish Rule: From 1840 to 1860*. London: np.

Clark, Katerina. 2002. "M. M. Bakhtin and 'World Literature.'" *Journal of Narrative Theory* 32, no. 3: 266–92.

Clifford, James. 1988. *The Predicament of Culture: Twentieth-Century Ethnography, Literature, and Art*. Cambridge: Harvard University Press.

———. 1989. "Notes on Travel and Theory." *Inscription* 5: 177–88.

———. 1991. "Travelling Cultures." In *Cultural Studies*, edited by Lawrence Grossberg, Cary Nelson, and Paula Treichler, 96–112. New York: Routledge.

Cohen, David, ed. 1985. *Atlas linguistique du monde arabe*. Paris: Geuthner.

Cooke, Miriam. 1996. *War's Other Voices: Women Writers on the Lebanese Civil War*. Syracuse: Syracuse University Press.

Cooppan, Vilashini. 2001. "World Literature and Global Theory: Comparative Literature for the New Millennium." *Symploke* 9, nos. 1–2: 15–46.

———. 2004. "Ghosts in the Disciplinary Machine: The Uncanny Life of World Literature." *Comparative Literature Studies* 42, no. 1: 10–36.

———. 2009. *World Within: National Narratives and Global Connections in Postcolonial Writing*. Stanford: Stanford University Press.

Corm, Charles. 1934. *La montagne inspirée: Trois etapes de la vie du Liban*. Beirut: Revue Phénicienne.

———. 1948. *Les miracles de la Madonne aux sept douleurs*. Beirut: Revue Phénicienne.

———, ed. [1919] 1996. *La revue Phénicienne*. Beirut: Éditions la revue Phénicienne.

———. 2004. *The Sacred Mountain*. Translated by Carole-Ann Goff-Kfouri and Paul Jahshan. Notre Dame: Notre Dame University Press.

Corm, Georges. 1915. *Chez les humbles*. Beirut: Maison d'art.

Corm, Georges. 2003. *Le Liban contemporain: Histoire et société*. Paris: Decouverte.

Cronin, Michael. 2003. *Translation and Globalization*. New York: Routledge.

Dados, Nour. 2009. "Revisiting Martyr's Square . . . Again: Absence and Presence in Cultural Memory." In *Monument to Monument: The Making and Unmaking of Cultural Significance*, edited by Ladina Bezzola Lambert and Andrea Ochsner, 169–81. Hannover: Transcript.

Dagher, Carole. 2002. *L'anneau de l'émir: Couvent de la lune I*. Paris: Plon.

———. 2004. *Le Seigneur de la soie: Couvent de la lune II*. Paris: Plon.

Dagher, Jean Bechara. 1903. *Souvenirs d'Orient*. Paris: Vanier.

al-Da'if, Rashid. 1991. *Ghuflat al-turab*. Beirut: Mukhtarat.

———. 1993. *Passage au crepuscule*. Translated by Luc Barbulesco and Phillippe Cardinal. Paris: Actes Sud.

———. 1995. *'Azizi al-Sayyid Kawabata*. Beirut: Mukhtarat, 1995.

———. 1999. *Cher Monsieur Kawabata*. Translated by Yves Gonzalez-Quijano. Paris: Actes Sud.

———. 2000. *Dear Mr. Kawabata*. Translated by Paul Starkey and Margaret Drabble. London: Quartet.

———. 2001. *Fusha mustahdafa bayna al-nu'as wa al-nawm*. Beirut: al-Rayyis.

———. 2001. *Passage to Dusk*. Translated by Nirvana Tanoukhi. Austin: University of Texas Press.

Damrosch, David. 2003. *What Is World Literature?* Princeton: Princeton University Press.

———. 2006. "Where Is World Literature?" In Lindberg-Wada, *Studying Transcultural Literary History*, 221–50.

Darwish, Mahmoud. 1986. *Dhakirat lil nisyan*. Nicosia: al-Karmel.

———. 1995. *Memory for Forgetfulness: August, Beirut, 1982*. Translated by Ibrahim Muhawi. Berkeley and Los Angeles: University of California Press.

Dimock, Wai-Chee. 2006a. *Through other Continents: American Literature across Deep Time*. Princeton: Princeton University Press.

———. 2006b. "Genre and World System: Epic and Novel on Four Continents." *Narrative* 14, no. 1: 85–101.

Djebar, Assia. 1999. *Ces voix qui m'asssiègent: En marge de ma francophonie*. Paris: Albin Michel.

Donadey, Anne. 2000. "The Multilingual Strategies of Postcolonial Literature: Assia Djebar's Algerian Palimpsest." *World Literature Today* 74, no. 1: 27–36.

Dyson, Ketari Ketaki. 1993. "Forging a Bilingual Identity: A Writer's Testimony." In *Bilingual Women: Anthropological Approaches to Second Language Use*, edited by P. Burton, K. K. Dyson, and S. Ardener, 170–85. Oxford: Berg, 1993.

Eagleton, Terry. 1983. *Literary Theory: An Introduction*. Oxford: Blackwell.

———. 1991. *Ideology: An Introduction*. London: Verso.

———. 2003. *After Theory*. London: Penguin.

Eakin, Emily. 2004. "Studying Literature by the Numbers." *New York Times*, 10 January.

Eckermann, Johann Peter. 1827. *Conversations with Goethe*. London: Dent.

Elia, Nada. 2002. "The Fourth Language: Subaltern Expression in Djebar's *Fantasia*." In *Intersections: Gender, Nation, and Community in Arab Women's Novels*, edited by Lisa Suhair Majaj, Paula Sunderman, and Therese Saliba, 183–99. Syracuse: Syracuse University Press.

Eysteinsson, Ástrádur. 2006. "Notes on World Literature and Translation." In *Angles on the English-Speaking World, Literary Translation: World Literature or "Worlding" Literature?*, edited by Ida Kiltgard, 11–24. Copenhagen: Museum Tusculanam Press 6.

Fadil, Jihad. 1995. *Al-Adab al-hadith fi lubnan*. Beirut: al-Rayyis.

Farley, J. Lewis. 1858. *Two Years in Syria*. London: Saunders and Oatley.

Fawaz, Leila Tarazi. 1983. *Merchants and Migrants in Nineteenth-Century Beirut*. Cambridge: Harvard University Press.

———. 1994. *An Occasion for War: Civil Conflict in Lebanon and Damascus in 1860*. London: I. B. Tauris.

Fawwaz, Ghassan. 1996. *Les moi volatiles des guerres perdues*. Paris: Seuil.

———. 1998. *Sous le ciel d'Occident*. Paris: Seuil.

Firro, Kais M. 1992. *A History of the Druzes*. Leiden: Brill.

———. 2003. *Inventing Lebanon: Nationalism and State under the Mandate*. London: Centre for Lebanese Studies/I. B. Tauris.

Fisk, Robert. 1990. *Pity the Nation*. Oxford: Oxford University Press.

Forsdick, Charles, and David Murphy, eds. 2003. *Francophone Postcolonial Studies: A Critical Introduction*. London: Arnold.

Gates, Carolyn. 1988. *The Merchant Republic of Lebanon*. London: Centre for Lebanese Studies/I. B. Tauris.

Gauvin, Lise. 1997. *L'écrivain francophone à croisée des langues: Entretiens*. Paris: Karthala.

Gebeyli, Claire. 1996. *Cantate pour l'oiseau mort*. Paris: L'harmattan.

Ghandour, Sabah. 1997. "Contesting Languages: Tawfiq Yusuf 'Awwad's *Tawahin Bayrut*." In *Tradition and Modernity in Arabic Literature*, edited by Issa Boullata and Terri DeYoung, 135–50. Fayetteville: University of Arkansas Press.

Ghanem, Chékri. 1908. *Da'ad*. Paris: Fasquelle. [Reprinted in *Écrits littéraires*. Beirut: an-Nahar, 1994.]

Gibran, Kahlil. 1948. *Nymphs of the Valley*. Translated by H. M. Nahmad. New York: Heinemann.

———. 1990. *Spirits Rebellious*. Translated by Anthony Rizcallah Ferris. New York: Carol.

———. 1993. *Spirit Brides*. Translated by Juan Cole. Ashland, OR: White Cloud.

———. 1998. *Broken Wings*. Translated by Juan Cole. London: Penguin.

Gilsenan, Michael. 1996. *Lords of the Lebanese Marches: Violence and Narrative in an Arab Society*. London: Tauris.

Goethe, Johann W. 1984. *Conversations with Eckermann (1823–1832)*. Translated by John Oxenford. San Francisco: North Point Press.

Granara, William. 2005. "Nostalgia, Arab Nationalism, and the Andalusian Chronotope in the Evolution of the Modern Arabic Novel." *Journal of Arabic Literature* 36, no. 1: 57–73.

Gualtieri, Sarah. 2009. *Between Arab and White: Race and Ethnicity in the Early Syrian American Diaspora*. Berkeley and Los Angeles: University of California Press.

Gueunier, Nicole. [1993] 2004. *Le français au Liban: Cent portraits linguistiques*. Paris: L'harmattan.

Guys, Henri. 1979. *La nation Druse, son histoire, sa religion et ses moeurs*. Amsterdam: Philo. [orig. Paris, 1863]

Haddad, Katia. 2000. *La littérature francophone du Machrek*. Beirut: Presses Université St Joseph.

Hafez, Sabry. 1993. *The Genesis of the Arabic Narrative Discourse*. London: Saqi.

———. 1994. "Towards a Typology of Women's Narrative in Modern Arabic Literature." In *Love and Sexuality in Modern Arabic Literature*, edited by Roger Allen, Hilary Kilpatrick, and Ed de Moor, 135–55. London: Saqi.

Hahn, Cynthia, ed. 2010. *Ezza Agha Malak, à la croisée des regards: Littérature libanaise d'expression français*. Paris: L'harmattan.

al-Ha'ik, Renée. 2007. *Salat min ajl al-'a'ila* [Prayer for the family]. Beirut: Adab.

Hallaq, Boutros. 2008. *Gibran et la refondation littéraire arabe*. Paris: Actes Sud.

Harb, Sirène. 2005. "Translation, Resistance, and Revision in Evelyne Accad's *Coquelicot du massacre*." In *Discursive Geographies: Writing Space and Place in French/Géographies discursives: L'écriture de l'espace et du lieu en français*, edited by Jeanne Garane, 69–90. Amsterdam: Rodopi.

Hartman, Michelle. 2000. "Multiple Identities, Multiple Voices: Reading Andrée Chedid's *La maison sans racines*." *French Studies* 54: 54–66.

———. 2002. *Jesus, Joseph, and Job: Reading Rescriptings of Religious Figures in Lebanese Women's Fiction*. Wiesbaden: Reichert.

———. 2004. "Besotted with the Bright Lights of Imperialism? Arab Subjectivity Constructed against New York's Many Faces." *Journal of Arabic Literature* 35, no. 3: 270–328.

———. 2005. "Writings Arabs and Africa(ns) in America: Adonis and Radwa Ashour from Harlem to Lady Liberty." *International Journal of Middle East Studies* 37, no. 3: 397–420.

———. 2007. "Grandmothers, Grape Leaves, and Kahlil Gibran: Writing Race in Anthologies of Arab American Literature." In *Race and Arab Americans Before and After 9/11: From Invisible Citizens to Visible Subjects*, edited by Nadine Naber and Amaney Jamal, 170–203. Syracuse: Syracuse University Press.

———. 2011a. "Teaching Naguib Mahfouz as World Literature." In *Approaches to Teaching Naguib Mahfouz*, edited by Susan Muaddi Darraj and Wail Hassan, 41–52. New York: MLA.

———. 2011b. "An Arab Woman Poet as Crossover Artist: The Ambivalent Legacy of al-Khansa'." *Tulsa Studies in Women's Literature* 30, no. 1: 15–36.

———. 2012. "Gender, Genre, and the (Missing) Gazelle: Arab Women Writers and the Politics of Translation." *Feminist Studies* 38, no. 1: 17–49.

———. 2013. "Rabih Alameddine's *I, the Divine*: A 'Druze Novel' as World Literature?" In *The Rise of the Arab Novel in English: The Politics of Anglo-Arab and Arab American Literature and Culture*, edited by Nouri Gana, 339–59. Edinburgh: Edinburgh University Press.

Hartman, Michelle, and Maher Barakat. 2002. "Translator's Afterword." In Muhammad Kamil al-Khatib, *Just Like a River*, 111–18. Northampton: Interlink.

Hartman, Michelle, and Alessandro Olsaretti. 2003. "The First Boat and the First Oar: Inventions of Lebanon in the Writings of Michel Chiha." *Radical History Review* 86: 37–65.

Hassan, Waïl 2002. "Postcolonial Theory and Modern Arabic Literature: Horizons of Application." *Journal of Arabic Literature* 33, no. 1: 45–64.

———. 2006. "Agency and Translational Literature: Ahdaf Soueif's *The Map of Love*." *PMLA* 121, no. 3: 753–68.

Hatem, Jad. 1987. *La quête poétique de Nadia Tuéni*. Beirut: Dar an-Nahar.

———. 1988. "Reflexions sur les romans d'Éveline Bustros." In Bustros, *Romans et écrits divers*, liii–lxv.

Hirschkop, Ken. 1990. "Heteroglossia and Civil Society: Bakhtin's Public Square and the Politics of Modernity." *Studies in the Literary Imagination* 23, no. 1: 65–75.

Hobsbawm, Eric, and Terrance Ranger, eds. 1992. *The Invention of Tradition*. Cambridge: Cambridge University Press.

Holquist, Michael. 1990. *Dialogism: Bakhtin and His World*. New York: Routledge.

Hout, Syrine. 2012. *Post-War Lebanese Anglophone Fiction: Home Matters in the Diaspora*. Edinburgh: Edinburgh University Press.

Humaydan, Iman [Yunis]. 1997. *Ba' mithl bayt mithl Bayrut*. Beirut: Massar.

———. 2001. *Tut barri*. Beirut: Massar.

———. 2010. *Hayawat Ukhra*. Beirut: Rawi.

———. 2014. *Other Lives*. Translated by Michelle Hartman. Northampton: Interlink.

Ibnlfassi, Laila, and Nicki Hitchcott, eds. 1996. *African Francophone Writing: A Critical Introduction*. Oxford: Berg.

Ippolito, Christopher. 2009. "La collection 'Patrimoine' de Dar an-Nahar: Une bibliothèque de la Pléiade libano-francophone." *Contemporary French and Francophone Studies* 13, no. 3: 331–38.

Jabbour, Zahida Darwiche. 1992. *Poésie et initation dans l'oeuvre de Nadia Tuéni*. Beirut: Dar an-Nahar.

———. 1997. *Etudes sur la poésie libanaise francophone: Abi Zeyd, Naffah, Schéhadé, Stétié, Hatem*. Beirut: Dar an-Nahar.

———. 2002. *Parcours en francophonie(s)*. Beirut: Dar an-Nahar.

Jabbra, Nancy W. 1980. "Sex Roles and Language in Lebanon." *Ethnology* 19, no. 4: 459–74.

Jabir, Rabi'. 2003. *Beirut: Madinat al-'alam I* [Beirut, world city]. Beirut: Al-Markaz al-thiqafi al-'arabi/Al-Adab.

———. 2005a. *Beirut: Madinat al-'alam II* [Beirut, world city]. Beirut: Al-Markaz al-thiqafi al-'arabi/Al-Adab.

———. 2005b. *Berytus, madinat taht al-ard [Berytus: A city underground]*. Beirut: Al-Markaz al-thiqafi al-'arabi/Al-Adab.

———. 2005c. *Taqrir Mehlis [The Mehlis decision]*. Beirut: al-Markaz al-thiqafi al-'arabi/Al-Adab.

———. 2007. *Beirut: Madinat al-'alam III* [Beirut, world city]. Beirut: Al-Markaz al-thiqafi al-'arabi/Al-Adab.

———. 2008. *'I'tirafat* [Confessions]. Beirut: Al-Adab.

———. 2009a. *Amrika* [America]. Beirut: Al-Markaz al-thiqafi al-'arabi/Al-Adab.

———. 2009b. *Berytus: Une ville sous terre*. Translated by Simon Corthay and Charlotte Woilletz. Paris: Gallimard.

———. 2011. *Druze Belgrade*. Beirut: Al-Adab.

Jack, Belinda. 1996. *Francophone Literatures: An Introductory Survey*. Oxford: Oxford University Press.

Jak, Sana'. 1994. "Frankufuniyah ijbariyah." *Al-Naqid* 77: 69–71.

Jameson, Frederic. 1981. *The Political Unconscious: Narrative as a Socially Symbolic Act.* New York: Routledge.

———. 1986. "Third World Literature in the Era of Multinational Capitalism." *Social Text* 15: 65–88.

Jibran, Khalil. 1906. *'Ara'is al-muruj.* New York: Al-Muhajir.

———. 1908. *Al-Arwah al-mutamarrida.* New York: Al-Muhajir.

———. 1912. *Al-Ajniha al-mutakassira.* New York: Mir'at al-gharb.

Joseph, Suad. 1993. "Connectivity and Patriarchy among Urban Working-Class Arab Families in Lebanon." *Ethos* 21, no. 4: 452–84.

———, ed. 1999. *Intimate Selving in Arab Families: Gender, Self, and Identity.* Syracuse: Syracuse University Press.

———. 1999a. "Brother-Sister Relationships: Connectivity, Love, and Power in the Reproduction of Patriarchy in Lebanon." In *Intimate Selving in Arab Families,* 113–40.

———. 1999b. "My Son/Myself, My Mother/Myself: Paradoxical Relationalities of Patriarchal Connectivity." In *Intimate Selving in Arab Families,* 174–90.

———, ed. 2000. *Gender and Citizenship in the Middle East.* Syracuse: Syracuse University Press.

———. 2000. "Civic Myths, Gender, and Citizenship in Lebanon." In *Gender and Citizenship in the Middle East,* 107—136.

———. 2000. "Gendering Citizenship in the Middle East." In *Gender and Citizenship in the Middle East,* 3–30.

Julien, Eileen. 2006. "Arguments and Further Conjectures on World Literature." In Lindberg-Wada, *Studying Transcultural Literary History,* 122–32.

Kadi, Joanna, ed. 1994. *Food for Our Grandmothers: An Anthology of Arab American and Arab Canadian Feminist Writing.* Boston: South End.

Kassab, Elizabeth Suzanne. 1992. "The Paramount Reality of the Beirutis: War Literature and the Lebanese Conflict." *The Beirut Review* 4: 63–83.

Kaufman, Asher. 2004. *Inventing Phoenicia: In Search of Identity in Lebanon.* London: Tauris.

Kelly, Walter Keating. 1844. *Syria and the Holy Land, Their Scenery and Their People.* London: Chapman and Hall.

Khalaf, Sahar. 1974. *Littérature libanaise de langue française.* Ottawa: Naaman.

Khalaf, Samir. 2002. *Civil and Uncivil Violence in Lebanon: A History of the Internationalization of Communal Conflict.* New York: Columbia University Press.

———. 2007. *Heart of Beirut: Reclaiming the Bourj.* London: Saqi.

Khater, Akram. 2001. *Inventing Home: Emigration, Gender, and the Middle Class in Lebanon, 1870–1920*. Berkeley and Los Angeles: University of California Press.

Khatibi, Abdelkébir. 1983a. *Du bilinguisme*. Paris: Denoël.

———. 1983b. *L'amour bilingue*. Montpellier: Fata Morgana.

———. 1990. *Love in Two Languages*. Minneapolis: University of Minnesota Press.

———. 2008. *Essais: Oeuvres de Abdelkébir Khatibi*. Paris: Différance.

al-Khazen, Farid. 1991. "The Pact of Communal Identities: The Making and Politics of the 1943 National Pact." *Papers on Lebanon* 12. Oxford: Centre for Lebanese Studies.

Khouri, Fu'ad. 2004. *Being a Druze*. London: Druze Heritage Society.

El-Khoury, Barbara. 2004. *L'image de la femme chez les romancières francophones libanaises*. Paris: L'harmattan.

Khoury, Elias. 1977. *Al-Jabal al-saghir*. Beirut: al-Adab.

———. 1981. *Al-Wujuh al-bayda'*. Beirut: Al-Adab.

———. 1989. *Little Mountain*. Translated by Maia Tabet. Introduction by Edward Said. Minneapolis: University of Minnesota Press.

———. 1990. "The Unfolding of Modern Fiction and Arab Memory." *Journal of the Midwest Modern Language Association* 23, no. 1: 1–8.

———. 1993. "Politics and Culture in Lebanon: Interview with Elias Khoury." *The Beirut Review* 5: 131–42.

———. 1998. *Bab al-Shams*. Beirut: Al-Adab.

———. 2002. *Yalu*. Beirut: Al-Adab.

———. 2003. *La porte du soleil*. Translated by Rania Samara. Paris: Actes Sud.

———. 2007. *Un parfum de paradis*. Translated by Luc Barbulesco. Paris: Actes Sud.

———. 2008a. *Gate of the Sun*. Translated by Humphrey Davies. New York: Picador.

———. 2008b. *Yalo*. Translated by Humphrey Davies. New York: Archipelago.

———. 2009. *La petite montagne*. Translated by Saadia Zaim and Christian de Montella. Paris: Actes Sud.

———. 2010. *White Masks*. Translated by Maia Tabet. New York: Archipelago.

Khoury-Ghata, Vénus. 1984. *Les morts n'ont pas d'ombre*. Paris: Flammarion.

———. 1986. *Mortemaison*. Paris: Flammarion.

———. 1988. *Bayarmine*. Paris: Flammarion; Beirut: FMA.

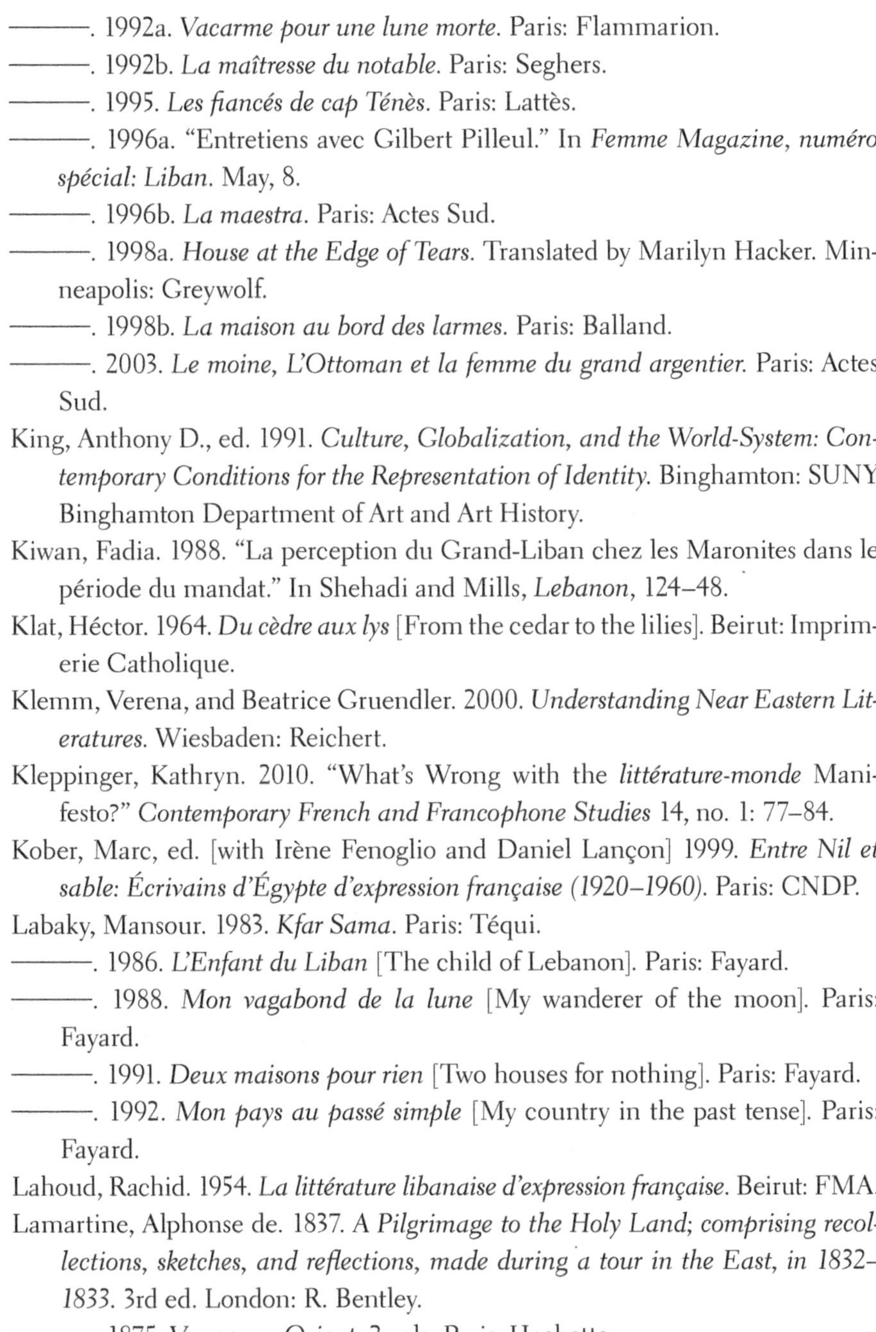

———. 1992a. *Vacarme pour une lune morte*. Paris: Flammarion.

———. 1992b. *La maîtresse du notable*. Paris: Seghers.

———. 1995. *Les fiancés de cap Ténès*. Paris: Lattès.

———. 1996a. "Entretiens avec Gilbert Pilleul." In *Femme Magazine, numéro spécial: Liban*. May, 8.

———. 1996b. *La maestra*. Paris: Actes Sud.

———. 1998a. *House at the Edge of Tears*. Translated by Marilyn Hacker. Minneapolis: Greywolf.

———. 1998b. *La maison au bord des larmes*. Paris: Balland.

———. 2003. *Le moine, L'Ottoman et la femme du grand argentier*. Paris: Actes Sud.

King, Anthony D., ed. 1991. *Culture, Globalization, and the World-System: Contemporary Conditions for the Representation of Identity*. Binghamton: SUNY Binghamton Department of Art and Art History.

Kiwan, Fadia. 1988. "La perception du Grand-Liban chez les Maronites dans le période du mandat." In Shehadi and Mills, *Lebanon*, 124–48.

Klat, Héctor. 1964. *Du cèdre aux lys* [From the cedar to the lilies]. Beirut: Imprimerie Catholique.

Klemm, Verena, and Beatrice Gruendler. 2000. *Understanding Near Eastern Literatures*. Wiesbaden: Reichert.

Kleppinger, Kathryn. 2010. "What's Wrong with the *littérature-monde* Manifesto?" *Contemporary French and Francophone Studies* 14, no. 1: 77–84.

Kober, Marc, ed. [with Irène Fenoglio and Daniel Lançon] 1999. *Entre Nil et sable: Écrivains d'Égypte d'expression française (1920–1960)*. Paris: CNDP.

Labaky, Mansour. 1983. *Kfar Sama*. Paris: Téqui.

———. 1986. *L'Enfant du Liban* [The child of Lebanon]. Paris: Fayard.

———. 1988. *Mon vagabond de la lune* [My wanderer of the moon]. Paris: Fayard.

———. 1991. *Deux maisons pour rien* [Two houses for nothing]. Paris: Fayard.

———. 1992. *Mon pays au passé simple* [My country in the past tense]. Paris: Fayard.

Lahoud, Rachid. 1954. *La littérature libanaise d'expression française*. Beirut: FMA.

Lamartine, Alphonse de. 1837. *A Pilgrimage to the Holy Land; comprising recollections, sketches, and reflections, made during a tour in the East, in 1832–1833*. 3rd ed. London: R. Bentley.

———. 1875. *Voyage en Orient*. 2 vols. Paris: Hachette.

Lane-Mercier, Gillian. 1998. "Travail sur la lettre: Politique de décentrement ou tactique de réappropriation?" *TTR: Translation Terminology Writing* 11, no. 1: 65–88.

Lawall, Sarah, ed. 1994. *Reading World Literature: Theory, History, and Practice.* Austin: University of Texas Press.

Layoun, Mary N. 1995. "Translation, Cultural Transgression and Tribute, and Leaden Feet." In *Between Languages and Cultures: Translation and Cross-Cultural Texts,* edited by Anuradha Dingwaney and Carol Maier, 267–89. Pittsburgh: University of Pittsburgh Press.

Leichtman, Mara. 2005. "The Legacy of Transnational Lives: Beyond the First Generation of Lebanese in Senegal." *Ethnic and Racial Studies* 28, no. 4: 663–86.

Lejeune, Philippe. 1975. *Le pacte autobiographique.* Paris: Seuil.

Leonard, Robert A., and Wendy J. Saliba. 1998. "Food and Ethnic Identity." In *The Asian Pacific American Heritage,* edited by George Leonard, 171–80. New York: Routledge.

Lindberg-Wada, Gunilla, ed. 2006. *Studying Transcultural Literary History.* Berlin: de Gruyter.

Lionnet, Françoise. 1995. *Postcolonial Representations: Women, Literature, Identity.* Ithaca: Cornell University Press.

Maalouf, Amin. 1993. *Le rocher de Tanios.* Paris: Grasset.

———. 1995. *The Rock of Tanios.* Translated by Dorothy Blair. London: Abacus.

Mackey, William Francis. 1975. *Langue, dialecte et diglossie littéraire.* Québec: CIRB/ICRB (Centre International de recherche sur le bilinguisme).

Majaj, Lisa Suhair, and Amal Amireh, eds. 2002. *Etel Adnan: Critical Essays on the Arab-American Writer and Artist.* Jefferson, NC: McFarland.

Majdalani, Cherif. 2005. *Histoire de la grande maison.* Paris: Seuil.

Makdisi, Saree. 1997. "Laying Claim to Beirut: Urban Narrative and Spatial Identity in the Age of Solidère." *Critical Inquiry* 23, no. 2: 661–705.

Makdisi, Ussama. 2000. *The Culture of Sectarianism: Community, History, and Violence in Nineteenth-Century Ottoman Lebanon.* Berkeley and Los Angeles: University of California Press.

Makward, Christiane, and Odile Cazenave. 1988. "The Others' Others: 'Francophone' Women and Writing." *Yale French Studies* 75: 90–207.

Marcus, George E. 1986. "Contemporary Problems of Ethnography in the Modern World System." In *Writing Culture: The Poetics and Politics of*

Ethnography, edited by James Clifford and George E. Marcuse, 165–93. Berkeley and Los Angeles: University of California Press.

———. 1995. "Ethnography in/of the World System: The Emergence of Multi-Sided Ethnography." *Annual Review of Anthropology* 24: 95–117.

Marcus, George E., and Dick Cushman. 1982. "Ethnographies as Texts." *Annual Review of Anthropology* 11: 25–69.

Mardam-Bey, Farouk, ed. 1999. *Liban: Figures contemporaines*. Paris: Institut du monde arabe circé.

Markels, Julian. 2003. *The Marxian Imagination: Representing Class in Literature*. New York: Monthly Review.

Marx, Karl, and Frederik Engels. 1978. "Manifesto of the Communist Party." In *The Marx-Engels Reader*, edited by Robert C. Tucker, 469–500. New York: Norton.

Massabki, Jacqueline. 1989. *La mémoire des cèdres*. Paris: Laffont.

Masters, Bruce. 2001. *Christian and Jews in the Ottoman Arab World: The Roots of Sectarianism*. Cambridge: Cambridge University Press.

Matthew, Roderic D., and Matta Akrawi, 1949. *Education in the Arab Countries of the Near East*. Washington, DC: American Council on Education.

Mehrez, Samia. 1991. "The Subversive Poetics of Radical Bilingualism: Postcolonial Francophone North African Literature." In *The Bounds of Race: Perspectives on Hegemony and Resistance*, edited by Dominick LaCapra, 255–77. Ithaca: Cornell University Press.

———. 1992. "Translation and the Postcolonial Experience: The Francophone North African Text." In *Rethinking Translation: Discourse, Subjectivity, Ideology*, edited by Lawrence Venuti, 120–38. New York: Routledge.

Méouchy, Nadine, and Peter Sluglett, eds. 2004. *The British and French Mandates in Comparative Perspectives Les mandats français et anglais dans une perspective comparative*. Leiden: Brill.

Métral, Jean. 2004. "Robert Montagne et les études ethnographiques." In Méouchy and Sluglett, *British and French Mandates in Comparative Perspectives*, 217–34.

Miller, Christopher. 1990. *Theories of Africans: Francophone Literature and Anthropology in Africa*. Chicago: University of Chicago Press.

Moretti, Franco. 1996. *The Modern Epic: The World-System from Goethe to García Márquez*. London: Verso.

———. 1998. *Atlas of the European Novel, 1800–1900*. London: Verso.

———. 2000. "Conjectures on World Literature." *New Left Review* 1: 54–68.
———. 2003a. "Graphs, Maps, and Trees: Abstract Models for Literary History I." *New Left Review* 24: 67–93.
———. 2003b. "More Conjectures." *New Left Review* 20: 73–81.
———. 2004a. "Graphs, Maps, and Trees: Abstract Models for Literary History II." *New Left Review* 26: 79–103.
———. 2004b. "Graphs, Maps, and Trees: Abstract Models for Literary History III." *New Left Review* 28: 43–63.
———. 2007. *Graphs, Maps, and Trees: Abstract Models for a Literary History.* London: Verso.
———. 2007. *The Novel*, vol. 2, *Forms and Themes*. Princeton: Princeton University Press.
Mouawad, Wajdi. 1999. *Littoral.* Montreal: Lemeac; Paris: Actes Sud.
———. 2002. *Rêves*. Montreal: Lemeac; Paris: Actes Sud.
———. 2003a. *Incendies*. Montreal: Lemeac; Paris: Actes Sud.
———. 2003b. *Visage retrouvé*. Montreal: Lemeac; Paris: Actes Sud.
———. 2006. *Forêts*. Montreal: Lemeac; Paris: Actes Sud.
Mufti, Aamir. 2010. "Orientalism and the Institution of World Literatures." *Critical Inquiry* 36: 458–93.
Murad, Nicolas. 1844. *Notice historique sur l'origine de la nation Maronite et sur ses rapports avec la France, sur la nation Druze et sur les diverses populations du Mont Liban*. Paris: A. Le Clere.
Murphy, David. 2010. "Literature after Empire: A Comparative Reading of Two Literary Manifestos." *Contemporary French and Francophone Studies* 14, no. 1: 67–75.
al-Musawi, Muhsin. 2003. *The Postcolonial Arabic Novel: Debating Ambivalence.* Leiden: Brill.
Naaman, Mara. 2008. "The Anti-Romance Antidote: Revisiting Allegories of the Nation." In *Transforming Loss into Beauty: Essays on Arabic Literature and Culture in Honor of Magda al-Nowaihi*, edited by Marlé Hammond and Dana Sajdi, 321–42. Cairo: American University Press.
Naïm-Sanbar, Samia. 1985. *Le parler arabe de Ras-Beyrouth*. Paris: Geuthner.
Najjar, Alexandre. 1989a. *La honte de survivant*. Québec: Naaman.
———. 1989b. *À quoi rêvent les statues?* Paris: Anthologie.
———. 1993. *Pérennité de la littérature libanaise d'expression française*. Paris: Anthologie.
———. 1995. *Les exilés du Caucase*. Paris: Grasset.

———. 1997. *L'Astronome*. Paris: Grasset.

———. 2000. *Athina*. Paris: Grasset.

———. 2005. *Le roman de Beyrouth*. Paris: Plon.

———. 2008. *Phénicia*. Paris: Plon.

Nasrallah, Emily. 1962. *Tuyur Aylul* [September birds]. Beirut: Nawful.

———. 1984. *Al-Iqla' 'aks al-zaman*. Beirut: Nawful.

Nassib, Sélim. 1992a. *Fou de Beyrouth* [Mad in Beirut]. Paris: Balland.

———. 1992b. *L'homme assis* [The sitting man]. Paris: Balland.

———. 2004. *Un amant en Palestine*. Paris: Laffont.

Ndiaye, Christiane. 2004. *Introduction aux littératures francophones: Afrique, Caraïbe, Maghreb*. Montréal: Presses de l'Université de Montréal.

Nerval, Gérard de. 1884. *Voyage en Orient*. 2 vols. Paris: Michel Lévy.

Nicolaides-Salloum, Sophie. 1997. "Le roman d'expression française: L'enracinement dans l'histoire." *Magazine littéraire* 359 (November): 110–12.

Nien-ming Ch'ien, Evelyn. 2004. *Weird English*. Cambridge: Harvard University Press.

al-Nowaihi, Magda M. 2000. "The 'Middle East'? Or . . . /Arabic Literature and the Postcolonial Predicament." In *Companion to Postcolonial Studies*, edited by Henry Schwartz and Sangeeta Roy, 282–303. Oxford: Blackwell.

Omri, Mohamed-Saleh. 2006. *Nationalism, Islam, and World Literature: Sites of Confluence in the Writings of Mahmud al-Mas'adi*. New York: Routledge.

———, ed. 2007. *Comparative Critical Studies* 4, no. 3.

Ostle, Robin. 1993 "The Romantic Poets." In Badawi, *Cambridge History of Arabic Literature*, 82–131.

Pettersson, Anders. 2008. "Transcultural Literary History: Beyond Constricting Notions of World Literature." *New Literary History* 39: 463–79.

Philipp, Thomas. 1985. *The Syrians in Egypt: 1725–1975*. Stuttgart: Steiner.

Philippe, Compte de Paris. 1860. *Damas et le Liban: Extraits du journal d'un voyage en Syrie au printemps de 1860*. London: W. Boyer.

Pizer, John D. 2006. *The Idea of World Literature: History and Pedagogical Practice*. Baton Rouge: Louisiana State University Press.

"Pour une 'littérature-monde' en français." 2007. *Le Monde*, 16 March.

Prasad, G. J. V. 1999. "Writing Translation: The Strange Case of the Indian English Novel." In Bassnett and Trivedi, *Post-Colonial Translation*, 41–57.

Prendergast, Christopher, ed. 2004. *Debating World Literature*. London: Verso.

Ragin, Charles, and Daniel Chirot. 1984. "The World System and Immanuel Wallerstein: Sociology and Politics as History." In *Vision and Method in*

Historical Sociology, edited by Theda Scokpol, 276–312. Cambridge: Harvard University Press.

Rakha, Youssef. 2000. "The Francophone Predicament." *Al-Ahram Weekly*, 22 July–2 August.

Rieschild, Verna Robertson. 1998. "Lebanese Arabic Reverse Role Vocatives." *Anthropological Linguistics* 40, no. 4: 617–41.

Rivarol. 1966. *Discours sur l'universalité de la langue française*. Paris: Belfond.

Rizk, Bahjat E. 2001. *L'identité pluriculturelle libanaise: Pour un véritable dialogue des cultures*. Beirut: iDLivre.

Roberts, John Michael. 2004. "The Stylistics of Component Speaking: A Bakhtinian Exploration of Some Habermasian Themes." *Theory, Culture, and Society* 21, no. 6: 91–114.

Rogan, Eugene L. 2004. "Sectarianism and Social Conflict in Damascus: The 1860 Events Reconsidered." *Arabica* 51, no. 4: 493–511.

Rosello, Mireille. 1998. *Declining the Stereotype: Ethnicity and Representation in French Cultures*. Hanover: Dartmouth University Press.

Rushdie, Salman. 1991. "Commonwealth Literature Does Not Exist." In *Imaginary Homelands: Essays and Criticism, 1981–1991*, 63–70. London: Granta.

Russ, Joanna. 1983. *How to Suppress Women's Writing*. Austin: University of Texas Press.

Sabbag, Elie-Pierre. 1993. *L'ombre d'une ville*. Paris: Buchet/Chastel.

———. 1997. *Nous reviendrons à Beyrouth*. Paris: Arléa.

Sacre, Maurice. 1948. *Anthologie des auteurs libanais de langue française*. Beirut: UNESCO.

Said, Edward. 1983. *The World, the Text, and the Critic*. Cambridge: Harvard University Press.

———. 1990. "Embargoed Literature." *The Nation* 251, September 17, 278–80.

———. 1999. "Books of the Millennium." *Times Literary Supplement*, 3 December.

———. 2007. "Foreword." *Little Mountain*, by Elias Khoury. New York: Picador.

Salem Manganaro, Elise. 1995. "Negotiating Feminist Ideologies within Lebanese Women's Writings." *Bahithat* 2: 163–73.

Salem, Elise. 2003. *Constructing Lebanon: A Century of Literary Narratives*. Gainesville: University Press of Florida.

Salibi, Kamal. 1990. *A House of Many Mansions: The History of Lebanon Reconsidered*. Berkeley and Los Angeles: University of California Press.

Samné, Georges. 1919. *Le Liban autonome.* Paris: Barnagaud.

Saussy, Haun, ed. 2006. *Comparative Literature in an Age of Globalization.* Baltimore: Johns Hopkins University Press.

Schilcher, Linda Schatkowski. 1985. *Families in Politics: Damascene Factions and Estates of the Eighteenth and Nineteenth Centuries.* Stuttgart: Steiner.

———. 1996. "The Famine of 1915–1918 in Greater Syria." In *Problems in the Modern Middle East in a Historical Perspective: Essays in Honour of Albert Hourani*, edited by John Spagnolo, 229–58. Reading: Garnet/Ithaca.

Schmidt, Richard. 1993. "Consciousness, Learning, and Interlanguage." In *Interlanguage Pragmatics*, edited by Gabriele Kasper and Shoshana Blum-Kulka, 21–42. Oxford: Oxford University Press.

Selim, Samah. 2004. *The Novel and the Rural Imaginary in Egypt, 1880–1985.* New York: Routledge.

Seyhan, Azade. 2001. *Writing outside the Nation.* Princeton: Princeton University Press.

Seymour-Jorn, Caroline. 2002. "A New Language: Salwa Bakr on Depicting Egyptian Women's Worlds." *Critique: Critical Middle Eastern Studies* 11, no. 2: 151–76.

———. 2004. "View from the Margin: Writer Ni'mat Al-Bihiri on Gender Issues in Egypt." *Critique: Critical Middle Eastern Studies* 13, no. 1: 77–95.

———. 2011. *Cultural Criticism in Egyptian Women's Writing.* Syracuse: Syracuse University Press.

Shaaban, Kassim, and Ghazi Ghaith. 1996. "Language in Education Policy and Planning: The Case of Lebanon." *Mediterranean Journal of Educational Studies* 1, no. 2: 95–105.

———. 1999. "Lebanon's Language in Education Policies: From Bilingualism to Trilingualism." *Language Problems and Language Planning* 23, no. 1: 1–16.

———. 2002. "University Students' Perceptions of the Ethnolinguistic Vitality of Arabic, French, and English in Lebanon." *Journal of Sociolinguistics* 6, no. 4: 557–74.

Sha'ban, Bouthaina. 1999. *Mi'at 'am min al-riwaya al-nisa'iyya al-'arabiyya, 1899–1999.* Beirut: Al-Adab.

El-Shamy, Hassan. 1979. "Brother and Sister Type 872: A Cognitive Behavioristic Analysis of a Middle Eastern Oikotype." *Folklore Monograph Series* 8. Bloomington, IN: Folklore Publications Group.

al-Shaykh, Hanan. 1980. *Hikayat Zahra.* Beirut: Al-Adab.

———. 1990. *Histoire de Zahra*. Translated by Yves Gonzalez-Quijano. Paris: Actes Sud.

———. 1992. *Barid Bayrut*. Cairo: Dar al-hilal.

———. 1994. *The Story of Zahra*. Translated by Peter Ford. New York: Anchor.

———. 1995a. *Beirut Blues*. Translated by Catherine Cobham. New York: Anchor.

———. 1995b. *Poste-restante Beyrouth*. Translated by Michel Burési and Jamal Chehayed. Paris: Actes Sud.

Sheehi, Stephan. 2004. *Foundations of Modern Arab Identity*. Gainesville: University Press of Florida.

Shehadeh, Lamia Rustum, ed. 1999. *Women and War in Lebanon*. Gainseville: University Press of Florida.

Shehadi, Nadim, and Dana Haffar Mills, eds. 1988. *Lebanon: A History of Conflict and Consensus*. London: Centre for Lebanese Studies/I. B. Tauris.

Sicard, Gilles, ed. 2005. *Ezza Agha Malak: Regards croisés francophones sur son oeuvre narrative et poétique*. Paris: L'harmattan.

Simon, Daniel, trans. 2010. "Toward a 'World Literature' in French." *Contemporary French and Francophone Studies* 14, no. 1: 113–17.

Spivak, Gayatri Chakravorty. 1986. "A Literary Representation of the Subaltern: Mahasweta Devi's 'Standayini.'" In *Subaltern Studies* 5: 91–134.

———. 1988. "Can the Subaltern Speak?" In *Marxism and the Interpretation of Culture*, edited by Cary Nelson and Lawrence Grossberg, 271–313. Urbana: University of Illinois Press.

———. 1993. "Woman in Difference." In *Outside in the Teaching Machine*, edited by Spivak, 77–96. New York: Routledge.

———. 2003. *Death of a Discipline*. New York: Columbia University Press.

Stanhope, Hester. 1885. *The Memoirs of Lady Hester Stanhope*. London: Henry Colburn.

Stone, Christopher. 2007. *Popular Culture and Nationalism in Lebanon: The Fairouz and Rahbani Nation*. New York: Routledge.

Suleiman, Yasir. 2003. *The Arabic Language and National Identity*. Washington: Georgetown University Press.

al-Sulh, Raghid. 1988. "The Attitude of the Arab Nationalists toward Greater Lebanon in the 1930s." In Shehadi and Mills, *Lebanon*, 149–65.

Tallman, Janet. 2002. "The Ethnographic Novel: Finding the Insider's Voice." In *Between Anthropology and Literature: Interdisciplinary Discourse*, edited by Rose De Angelis, 11–22. New York: Routledge.

Thompson, Elizabeth. 2000. *Colonial Citizens: Republican Rights, Paternal Privilege, and Gender in French Syria and Lebanon*. New York: Columbia University Press.

Toman, Cheryl, ed. 2007. *On Evelyne Accad: Essays in Literature, Feminism, and Cultural Studies*. Birmingham, AL: Summa.

Traboulsi, Fawaz. 1993. "Identités et solidarities croisées dans les conflits du Liban contemporain." PhD diss., Université de Paris VIII.

———. 1999. *Salat bila wasal Michel Chiha wa'l idiulujiyya al-lubnaniyya*. London: Riad El-Rayyes.

———. 2007. *A History of Modern Lebanon*. London: Pluto.

Traboulsi, Yasmina. 2003. *Les enfants de la place*. Paris: Mercure de France.

———. 2007. *Amers*. Paris: Mercure de France.

Traisnel, Christophe. 2004. *Le français en partage: Les 50 plus belles histoires*. Boulogne: Timée Éditions.

Trinh T. Minh-ha. 1989. *Woman Native Other: Writing Postcoloniality and Feminism*. Bloomington: Indiana University Press.

Tuéni, Ghassan, and Faris Sassine. 2000. *El Bourj: Place de la liberté et porte du Levant/Sahat al-huriyah wa bawabat al-mashriq*. Beirut: Dar an-Nahar.

Tuéni, Nadia. 1986a. *Les oeuvres poétiques complètes*. Beirut: Dar an-Nahar.

———. 1986b. *La prose: Oeuvres complètes*. Beirut: Dar an-Nahar.

Tymoczko, Maria. 1999. "Postcolonial Writing and Literary Translation." In Bassnett and Trivedi, *Postcolonial Translation*, 17–40.

Urquhart, David. 1860. *The Lebanon (Mount Souria): A History and a Diary*. London: Thomas Cautley Newby.

Valassopoulos, Anastasia. 2003. "The Legacy of *Orientalism* in Middle Eastern Feminism." *Thamyris/Intersecting* 10: 183–99.

Venuti, Lawrence. 1995. *The Translator's Invisibility: A History of Translation*. New York: Routledge.

Volney, Constantin-François de. 1787. *Voyage en Égypte et en Syrie*. Reprint, 1959, London: Robinson.

Wallerstien, Immanuel. 1974. *The Modern World-System: Capitalist Agriculture and the Origins of the European World-Economy in the Sixteenth Century*. New York: Academic Press.

Waterfield, Robin. 1998. *Prophet: The Life and Times of Kahlil Gibran*. New York: St. Martin's Press.

Woodhull, Winifred. 1993. *Transfigurations of the Maghreb: Feminism, Decolonization, and Literatures*. Minneapolis: University of Minnesota Press.

Yassin, M. Aziz F. 1978. "Personal Names of Address in Kuwaiti Arabic." *Anthropological Linguistics* 20, no. 2: 53–63.

Young, Robert J. C. 1994. *Colonial Desire: Hybridity in Theory, Culture, and Race*. New York: Routledge.

Zabus, Chantal. 2007. *The African Palimpsest: Indigenization of Language in the West African Europhone Novel*. Amsterdam: Rodopi.

Zamir, Meir. 2000. *Lebanon's Quest: The Road to Statehood, 1926–1939* London: Tauris.

Zeidan, Joseph T. 1995. *Arab Women Novelists: The Formative Years and Beyond*. Albany: State University of New York Press.

Zein, Ramy. 1986. *Le chant des ruines*. Paris: Arléa.

———. 1998. *Dictionnaire de la littérature libanaise de langue française*. Paris: L'harmattan.

———. 2005. *Le partage de l'infini*. Paris: Arlé.

Zeitlian Watenpaugh, Heghnar. 2004. "Museums and the Construction of National History in Syria and Lebanon." In Méouchy and Sluglett, *British and French Mandates in Comparative Perspectives*, 185–202.

Index